020 487 7449

Anglo-American Attitudes

Anglo-American Attitudes

From Revolution to Partnership

Edited by

FRED M. LEVENTHAL
and ROLAND QUINAULT

Ashgate

Aldershot • Burlington USA • Singapore • Sydney

Published by
Ashgate Publishing Limited
Gower House
Croft Road
Aldershot
Hants GU11 3HR
England

Ashgate Publishing Company
131 Main Street
Burlington
Vermont 05401–5600
USA

Ashgate website: http://www.ashgate.com

British Library Cataloguing in Publication Data

Anglo-American Attitudes: From Revolution to Partnership.
   1. Great Britain—Foreign public opinion, American.   2. United
States—Foreign public opinion, British.   3. Great Britain—
Relations—United States—History.   4. United States—
Relations—Great Britain—History.
   I. Leventhal, Fred M. (Fred Marc), 1938– . II. Quinault, Roland.
303.4'82'41'073

Library of Congress Cataloging-in-Publication Data

Anglo-American attitudes: from revolution to partnership/edited by
   Fred M. Leventhal and Roland Quinault.
     p. cm.
   Includes index.
   ISBN 0–7546–0030–0 (alk. paper)
   1. United States—Relations—Great Britain.   2. Great Britain—
Relations—United States.
   I. Leventhal, F. M., 1938– . II. Quinault, Roland E.
E183.8.G7A66   2000
327.41073'09—dc21   00–38982

ISBN 0 7546 0030 0

This book is printed on acid free paper

Typeset in Sabon by Manton Typesetters, Louth, Lincolnshire.
Printed and bound by Athenaeum Press, Ltd.,
Gateshead, Tyne & Wear.

Contents

List of Figures and Tables

Figures

Tables

Notes on Contributors

Walter L. Arnstein is Professor Emeritus of History at the University of Illinois at Urbana-Champaign. His books include *The Bradlaugh Case* (1965, 1984), *Protestant versus Catholic in Mid-Victorian England* (1982), and *Britain Yesterday and Today: 1830 to the Present* (8th edn, 2001), and among his publications are six articles about Queen Victoria. From 1995 to 1997 he served as President of the North American Conference on British Studies.

Christine Bolt is Professor of American History at the University of Kent at Canterbury. Her books include *American Indian Policy and American Reform* (1987), *The Women's Movements in the United States and Britain* (1993), and *Feminist Ferment* (1995).

Kathleen Burk is Professor of Modern and Contemporary History at University College London. She is the author of six book and the editor of two others, of which the most recent is a study of A. J. P. Taylor. She is the co-editor of the journal *Contemporary European History* and is Honorary Treasurer of the Royal Historical Society.

James Epstein is Professor of History at Vanderbilt University, Nashville, TN. His most recent book is *Radical Expression: Political Language, Ritual and Symbol in England, 1790–1850* (1994). He will become the co-editor of the *Journal of British Studies* in 2001.

Eliga H. Gould is Associate Professor of History at the University of New Hampshire, Durham, NH. He is the author of *The Persistence of Empire: British Political Culture in the Age of the American Revolution* (2000) and is currently writing a cultural history of international law in the eighteenth-century British Atlantic.

Peter L. Hahn is Associate Professor of History at Ohio State University, Columbus, OH, and associate editor of *Diplomatic History*. He is the author of *The United States, Great Britain, and Egypt, 1945–1956: Strategy and Diplomacy in the Early Cold War* (1991), and co-editor of *Empire and Revolution: The United States and the Third World since 1945* (2000). He is completing a monograph on US policy towards the Arab–Israeli conflict from 1945 to 1961.

David Hancock is Associate Professor of American History at the University of Michigan in Ann Arbor. He is the author of *Citizens of the World: London Merchants and the Integration of the British Atlantic Community, 1735–1785* (1995), and the editor of *The Letters of William*

Freeman, 1678–1685 (forthcoming). He is currently working on a study of the emergence of the Atlantic economy between 1651 and 1815.

Anthony Howe is Senior Lecturer in International History at the London School of Economics. He is the author of *The Cotton Masters, 1830–1860* (1984), and *Free Trade and Liberal England, 1846–1946* (1997).

Paul Langford is Professor of History at the University of Oxford and Chairman and Chief Executive of the Arts and Humanities Research Board. He has recently been appointed Rector of Lincoln College, Oxford. His numerous publications include *A Polite and Commercial People, 1727–83* (1989) and *Englishness Identified: Manners and Character, 1650–1850* (2000).

D. L. LeMahieu is Hotchkiss Presidential Professor of History at Lake Forest College, Lake Forest, IL. He is the author of *The Mind of William Paley* (1976), and *A Culture for Democracy* (1988).

Fred M. Leventhal is Professor of History at Boston University. He is the author of *Respectable Radical: George Howell and Victorian Working-Class Politics* (1971), *The Last Dissenter: H. N. Brailsford and his World* (1985), and *Arthur Henderson* (1989). He is the editor of *Twentieth-Century Britain: An Encyclopedia* (1995), and co-editor of *Singular Continuities: Tradition, Nostalgia and Identity in Modern British Culture* (2000). He is also a co-editor of the journal *Twentieth Century British History* and served as President of the North American Conference on British Studies from 1997 to 1999.

P. J. Marshall is Professor Emeritus as King's College, London and President of the Royal Historical Society. His extensive publications on British imperial history include two books on the British in Bengal in the eighteenth century, and he has recently edited *The Oxford History of the British Empire: vol. II: The Eighteenth Century* (1998).

Alan O'Day is Senior Lecturer in History at the University of North London. He is the author or editor of over twenty books, including *Irish Home Rule, 1867–1921* (1998), and *Charles Stewart Parnell* (1998).

Roland Quinault is Reader in History at the University of North London and was, until recently, the Honorary Secretary of the Royal Historical Society. He has published many studies on aspects of modern British political and social history, and is currently writing a book on prime ministers and democracy.

Reba N. Soffer is Professor of History at California State University, Northridge. Among her extensive publications on late nineteenth- and twentieth-century intellectual, social, and institutional history are *Ethics and Society in England: The Revolution in the Social Sciences* (1978), and *Discipline and Power: The University, History and the Making of an English Elite, 1870–1930* (1995). She has been a Guggenheim Fellow and served as President of the North American Conference on British Studies from 1993 to 1995.

Introduction

Fred M. Leventhal and Roland Quinault

There has been a serious lack of historical investigation of Anglo-American attitudes in the widest sense of the phrase. While many studies of 'Anglo-American relations' exist, they have focused primarily on diplomatic and government-to-government contacts rather than on social, economic, intellectual, or cultural connections. As a result there has been insufficient appreciation of the chronological depth and contextual breadth of Anglo-American connections. Historians have lavished attention on the problematic separation of the American colonies from England and on episodes of conflict or partnership between the two nations in the international arena, but their preoccupation with such topics has fostered a view of Anglo-American relations as discontinuous, rekindled only at moments of disagreement or co-operation.

Since the creation of the British colonies in North America in the seventeenth century, a constant exchange across the Atlantic of attitudes and artefacts, concepts and cash, ideas and images, policies and products has occurred. Neither wars nor bilateral conflict have seriously disrupted this traffic. Yet the national bias of each country's historiography and history curricula has ensured the neglect of Anglo-American connections after the United States became independent of Britain. Post-revolutionary Americans continued to look to Britain for ideas, but contemporary Britons were also strongly influenced by developments across the Atlantic, providing models either to be embraced or rejected. American constitutionalism was steeped in the traditions of Anglo-Saxon law and parliamentarianism, and evolving democratic aspirations in both countries can be ascribed to mutual parentage. Despite independence, Americans never sought a *total* separation from Britain. Their appetite for British products – and the British appetite for American goods – was only temporarily disrupted by the Revolution and the War of 1812. By the 1820s there was an unprecedented human, material and cultural traffic between the two countries that was to mushroom even further during the Victorian period. Britons debated the 'Americanization' of their country, while Americans experienced 'Victorianization' in the form of railroads, cotton and literature. Improvements in communications – like the packet boat, the steamship and the telegraph – dramatically improved transatlantic communications long before the twentieth century. These developments continually strengthened the material and mental links between Britain and America.

Studies of Anglo-American relations in the twentieth century have given disproportionate emphasis to diplomacy and economics. The theme of British imperial decline and expanding American dominance has long been familiar to students of economic development and global power. Politicians and publicists alike have either celebrated or discounted the 'special relationship' between Britain and the United States, a concept underscored by the Roosevelt–Churchill axis during the Second World War. That association may now be of diminishing significance, but it played a crucial role in determining the political and economic destiny of the world in the twentieth century. If that century has witnessed a transfer of hegemony from the British Empire to the United States, the process was a gradual one, achieved largely by mutual consent. At the start of the third millennium, Britain still remains the foremost ally of the United States and continues to exert a significant influence on its international policies.

During much of this century British critics on both the left and the right have decried the American cultural 'invasion', heralded by film and popular music, but extending to food and dress, as well as collo-quial speech. The wider context of Anglo-American relations has, however, been neglected. This is surprising because the introduction of air travel, radio, television and the Internet have vastly increased the speed, volume and range of Anglo-American cultural ties. In the media, for example, transatlantic connections have been so intimate that it has been difficult (and often impossible) to distinguish between 'British' and 'American' productions. If Britain and America remain, as Bernard Shaw suggested, 'two countries divided by a common language', their mutual misunderstandings are none the less revealing. They do not indicate the superficiality of Anglo-American relations, for close part-nerships are often accompanied by varying degrees of competition, suspicion and incomprehension.

Anglo-American attitudes have played a vital role in the evolution of the modern world. Their influence may indeed not yet have reached its zenith, for the growing ascendancy of English as *the* international lan-guage means that for more and more people throughout the world – regardless of national or ethnic identity – Anglo-American attitudes are becoming an unconscious part of their own heritage.

It is our contention, then, that the Anglo-American connection is a continuous, not an intermittent, process that warrants investigation over a longer historical period than the colonial period or the Second World War. The connection is, furthermore, multifaceted and symbi-otic. Without discounting the centrality of economics or diplomacy, we would argue for a variety of mutual influences that were enhanced by independence from and rivalry with the former mother country.

Perceptions and misconceptions of each country held by the other were central to popular imagination and to the attitudes which shaped the political culture of each nation.

Although the idea of a special relationship has been exaggerated in some respects, it would be difficult to deny an enduring sense of kinship and cultural synergy between Britain and the United States. Bonds forged through colonization, cultural heritage, language and religious ties have proved impervious to transitory disputes and mutual recriminations. While Britain and the United States have separate histories, they have a common one as well that transcends the geographical separation. Anglo-American history has a reality distinct from the histories of its component elements, and this is the particular focus of the contributors to this volume. Recent historians of the eighteenth century, inspired by Bernard Bailyn, Jack P. Greene, and J. G. A. Pocock, have adopted a wider Atlantic perspective to investigate the relations between colony and metropole, while commentators on slavery and the African diaspora, such as Paul Gilroy, have popularized the term 'Black Atlantic' to imply a broader and more diverse community. Following in their wake, we advocate not just a comparative approach, but a history informed by a blending of cultures and experiences. This collection is not intended to be comprehensive, but rather to suggest the rich diversity of Anglo-Americn attitudes and to encourage further research in this neglected field of historical inquiry.

The most obvious watershed in Anglo-American relations over the last three centuries was the creation of the United States. Both Peter Marshall, in his chapter on the British case for coercing the American colonies, and Eliga Gould, in his analysis of the American Revolution in Britain's imperial identity, stress that Britain's attitude during the crisis was much influenced by its concern with the disparate parts of the United Kingdom and the rest of the British Empire. Marshall notes that the British feared American insubordination primarily because it might lead to general imperial distintegration which could be exploited by the French. British insistence that the Americans were subject to the authority of the Westminster Parliament reflected both the idea of 'virtual' representation and a belief that Americans were an integral part of the British nation. Gould points out that this belief quickly distintegrated when hostilities broke out. Extreme measures on both sides fostered a sense of separate identity on the part not only of the Americans, but also of the British. The success of the Revolution served as a standing reminder to the British and their remaining colonists that imperial authority could be successfully resisted. Thus the American example profoundly influenced the evolution of British imperial policy and raised fundamental questions about political representation in Britain itself.

David Hancock examines the long-established trade in Madeira wine as a case study to determine what impact the Revolution had on transatlantic commerce. Before the Revolution, Anglo-American trade was part of a complex web of commercial relations which included many other parts of the Atlantic world including the colonies of Spain and Portugal, the British West Indies and parts of Africa. Hancock demonstrates that, despite economic disruption, increased globalization of the trade and greater participation by Americans, especially in overseas shipping, followed the Revolution. If the pattern of trade no longer conformed to old colonial norms, much of it continued to involve collaboration between Americans and British merchants, their relations becoming complementary as well as competitive as they sought new markets in Asia and elsewhere in the world. Thus in economics, as in politics, there was a global, not just a transatlantic, dimension to Anglo-American relations in the late eighteenth century.

Paul Langford seeks to determine the cultural roots of the stereotypes of British and American character that prevailed in the years after the Revolution. Descriptions of manners often presumed American provinciality and British gentility but, in fact, it was the resemblances rather than the differences in social usage that proved to be most striking. If rhetoric and travel literature suggest distinct American and British self-perceptions, practices indicate a commonality that independence had not substantively altered.

Walter Arnstein's chapter on Queen Victoria and the United States indicates the extent to which anti-monarchical sentiment in America had abated since the age of the maligned and misunderstood King George III. He shows that Victoria's interest in and sympathy toward America was warmly reciprocated by American politicians and travellers, who looked upon her as a model constitutional ruler. The depth of the mutual affection and admiration – which extended as well to Presidents Jackson and Lincoln – underscores the vitality of the post-revolutionary Anglo-American political community. Arnstein alleges further that the Queen played an emollient and not insignificant role in the sometimes thorny diplomatic relations between the two countries.

James Epstein probes Victorian literary perceptions of America as both a utopian space of naturalness and progress and a site of vulgarity and crass materialism. Such conflicting views coincided with a populist democratic narrative shaped by a vision of yeoman independence and republican virtue. The complexity of these multifaceted images of America suggests that British perceptions were based in part on preconceptions of observers, who tended to find what they were looking for and whose image may have had more to do with their own class and cultural perspective than with American reality. In the end the imaginative ordering of 'America' was fraught with ambivalence: who the Americans were seemed to depend on which Britons were asking the question.

As Roland Quinault points out in his chapter on Anglo-American attitudes to democracy, there has been little comparative study of political discourse in Britain and America. In the Victorian era, Americans regarded British politics as aristocratic, whereas Britons thought American politics were democratic. In fact, the populist rhetoric of Lincoln was less explicitly democratic than that of Gladstone, although Gladstone's views on democracy were influenced by the American Civil War. In the early twentieth century both Wilson and Lloyd George trumpeted their faith in democracy, yet they abandoned this rhetoric when faced by the realities of the post-war world. Churchill and Roosevelt also stressed the democratic aspect of Anglo-American opposition to Hitler, only to moderate their stance to avoid offending Stalin. From the 1850s to the 1950s, the tide of democratic discourse in Britain and America generally flowed at a similar rate, prompted as much by foreign as by domestic developments and often outstripping the pace of democratic practice.

Anthony Howe's discussion of the Anglo-American tradition of free trade initially suggests that the economic policies of the two nations evolved out of mutual antipathy. British protectionism helped foment the American revolt, while in the nineteenth century Britain's evangelical support for free trade encouraged Anglophobia and higher tariffs in the United States. When Britain adopted protection and imperial preference in the 1930s, Americans responded with a new commitment to freer international trade. American demands, in the 1940s, for an end to British imperial preference reflected not only a desire to subdue an old economic rival, but also the flattery implicit in imitation. As the United States succeeded Britain as the dominant economic power, it came to appreciate why Victorian Britain had regarded free trade as the economic basis of world order.

Alan O'Day's chapter on Irish nationalism and Anglo-American relations addresses an issue perceived as a major irritant in bilateral relations. He shows that the large Irish Catholic community in America was neither very cohesive, nor concentrated, and that its political influence was more often assumed than demonstrated. Irish-American financial support for nationalist movements fluctuated widely and amounted to less than the money sent back to relatives, charities and churches. Irish-Americans had little influence on American foreign policy, partly because they were seen to be foreign themselves and partly because the United States was determined to maintain good relations with Britain.

Christine Bolt demonstrates that, although there was an Anglo-American feminist movement before the First World War, involving mainly middle-class campaigners, shaped by a common liberal tradition, striving for political rights for women, the achievement of the suffrage did not engender greater unity. Instead the American and British movements pulled apart during the inter-war years as attention shifted to the international arena and as national loyalties became paramount. The accumulated goodwill between British and American campaigners was also undermined by the disparity between British support for protective legislation for women and American preference for equal rights. While feminists in both countries continued to co-operate, they were unable to find a common issue around which to rally in order to replace the unifying power of the vote.

Fred Leventhal's chapter studies the means by which Britain sought to project a favourable image in the United States before and immediately after the onset of the Second World War, at a time when the prohibition of official propaganda was stringently enforced by the Foreign Office and the British Ambassador in Washington. Events such as the 1939 visit of King George VI and Queen Elizabeth, the first by reigning British monarchs to the United States, the British Pavilion at the New York World's Fair, and the Museum of Modern Art exhibit of British war art were attempts to elicit American sympathies at a critical juncture while eschewing any overt political motives. These displays of the British public face attempted to highlight political and cultural affinities between the two nations while exploiting American nostalgia for a romanticized and largely mythical British past.

Reba Soffer's contrast of conservative historical writing in post-war Britain and America reveals some similarities, but perhaps stronger differences in the two traditions. While British and American conservative historians, often cultural outsiders in origin, shared a belief in the value of stability and continuity, the British clung to pessimistic presuppositions about the fallibility of human nature, whereas the Americans aimed to valorize notions of American exceptionalism and to proclaim the success of a democratic society based on equal opportunity. Soffer attributes these differences not only to distinct national histories, but to the homogeneous quality of academic life in Britain compared with the more disparate backgrounds of American historians, keen to impose a unified vision on a culture of diversity.

Kathleen Burk considers the growth of British dependence on American loans in her chapter on war and Anglo-American financial relations. What began as a mere convenience during the Boer War became a central strategy during the First World War and then a dire necessity during the Second World War, a process that accelerated the demise of Pax Britannica and the rise of Pax Americana. After the Second World War, old American fears of British economic rivalry yielded to new fears of Communist aggression, and Britain, now the stalwart partner of the United States, received Marshall Plan aid and military assistance. More recently, American financial assistance to Britain has dwindled, partly because of Britain's relative economic strength and partly because of America's growing public debt.

Dan LeMahieu contextualizes the reception of film and television depictions of British history and suggests that part of their popularity in America during the past 40 years can be attributed to particular contemporary' resonances. Rather than linking their success to a shared ideology of social or political conservatism, he concludes that these historical works had as much to do with the period in which they were made as with the period they were about. If they evoked class and social hierarchy, they also spoke to American values that subverted a traditional order. Equally, many of the programmes and films offered historical parallels from the British past to the upheavals of the 1960s and 1970s in the United States.

Peter Hahn contends that there has been a genuine 'special relationship' based on the dual bond of shared values and common national interests in world affairs since 1945. The closeness of this relationship has fluctuated over time and place, with tensions primarily linked to problems outside Europe. The American government was notably insensitive to British feelings about its loss of empire, while Britain's readiness to negotiate with Communist China and its refusal to participate in the Vietnam War irritated Americans. Despite disagreements over Palestine and Suez, the rift was soon repaired, and since the 1950s Britain has generally supported the United States in the Middle East, as it did during the 1991 Gulf War. Britain continues to serve as a reliable military ally of the United States, which looks to its transatlantic partner for effective support during an international crisis.

The contributions to this volume illustrate the continuity of Anglo-American relations over three centuries. North America played a crucial role in underpinning the British 'fiscal-military state' in the 1740s, as well as in the 1940s. Anglo-American disagreements over tariffs and trade have frequently generated intermittent tensions – most recently over bananas and genetically modified foods. Anglo-American relations have been strengthened as much by shared enemies as by shared values. Mutual threats – France before 1763, Germany in two World Wars, and the Soviet Union during the Cold War – have prompted a reaffirmation of Anglo-American ties. Many of the contributions to this volume illustrate that Anglo-American attitudes cannot be properly understood or assessed in isolation from the rest of the world. These attitudes have never originated exclusively in Britain and America, for both countries have been powerfully influenced by other parts of the world. For example, African and Caribbean music has been an important ingredient in modern Anglo-American popular music. Thus Anglo-American attitudes have been characterized by cultural complexity as well as historical continuities.

This volume has its origins in a conference jointly sponsored by the North American Conference on British Studies and the Royal Historical Society, held at the Minda de Gunzburg Center for European Studies at Harvard University in April 1997. Its primary aim was to establish closer organizational and scholarly links between these two professional bodies, but it was also concerned to use the occasion of a transatlantic conference to address Anglo-American history as a valid subject for exploration.

The editors would like to acknowledge the valued participation of Bernard Bailyn, James Cronin, Susan Pedersen and Harriet Ritvo as moderators of the conference sessions at which earlier versions of these chapters were originally presented. We would like to thank Charles S. Maier, Director of the Minda de Gunzburg Center for European Studies at Harvard, for providing congenial surroundings for our meeting, and David Evans, formerly of the British Council in Washington, for his encouragement. We wish to express our appreciation to the Executive Secretary of the Royal Historical Society for her assistance and to the Council of the Society for its support. Generous financial support for the project was provided by the British Council, but we are also grateful for contributions from the Department of History, Harvard University, the Department of History and the Humanities Foundation, Boston University, and from Richard M. Hunt and John Harris.

CHAPTER ONE

The Case for Coercing America before the Revolution

P. J. Marshall

In an essay first published over 20 years ago, Jack P. Greene posed some characteristically acute 'questions resolved and unresolved' about Britain's role in the coming of the Revolution. Why, he asked, did Britain launch restrictive policies directed at the colonies, why did successive governments persist in such policies, and why could the dominant strands in British opinion find no way to escape from an ultimate descent into violence, war and defeat?[1] These questions were, of course, old ones when Greene asked them and historians have continued to address them since then. The evolution of British policy and parliamentary responses to the revolutionary crisis have, for instance, been authoritatively elucidated in P. D. G. Thomas's trilogy.[2] Yet H. T. Dickinson, editor of a valuable collection of essays published in 1998, points out that, 'the motives and deeper justifications for the imperial policies that were pursued by successive British governments' have still not been explored to anything like the same depth as has been achieved in the vast corpus of writing on the American side of the Revolution.[3] His collection and the appearance of Eliga H. Gould's *The Persistence of Empire: British Political Culture in the Age of the American Revolution*[4] are evidence that exploration is continuing with vigour. This chapter is a limited foray into the still imperfectly known terrain of the preoccupations of Britain's rulers that underlay their imperial policies.

Greene has done much to establish the time-scale for understanding the British role in the revolutionary crisis. The traditional emphasis on 'new' British policies following the end of the Seven Years War in 1763 now looks unsatisfactory. In his essay '"A Posture of Hostility": A Reconsideration of Some Aspects of the Origins of the American Revolution', Greene assembled much evidence to show that British officials were deeply concerned about the state of the American colonies in the 1740s. 'The whole American empire from Barbados to Nova Scotia seemed to be on the verge of disintegration.'[5] The 1740s now seem also to have been crucial in two other aspects. In the first place, British opinion became increasingly aware of the vast potential of the North American market for the British economy and ultimately of its role in underpinning what has been called the British 'fiscal-military state'. Second, British concern about France, its commercial and maritime power and its supposedly hostile intentions towards Britain all over the world reached new heights at the end of the 1740s. In response to what they took to be 'le Projet de la Monarchie universale des Anglois', based on world-wide commercial hegemony, after the peace of 1748, the French became increasingly assertive outside Europe, and especially in North America.[6] Reports of French moves greatly alarmed British opinion. Ministers were determined that empire in America must be shored up to protect Britain's vital interests there and to keep France at bay.

The first attempts to restore British authority in North America were devised by the Earl of Halifax under the patronage of the Duke of Cumberland. What appeared to be overt French aggression and the failure of colonial self-defence from 1754 made reform a matter of urgency. Lord Loudoun, a commander-in-chief who developed strong ideas about the need to compel the colonies to act effectively under British leadership, was appointed in 1756. His relations with colonial governments were often abrasive. He was, for instance, close to taking winter quarters for his troops in Boston by force. But his military failures led to his dismissal in 1757 and to a shift under Pitt to a policy of conciliating colonial opinion. This policy included very large parlia mentary reimbursements for colonial expenditure.

As is notorious, conciliation did not survive the ending of the war. A slate of measures for regulating the colonies was enacted, most of them, the Proclamation of 1763, the Molasses Act, the Currency Act, the Quartering Act and the Stamp Act, during the ministry of George Grenville, but some, like the decision to maintain a large British garrison in America, pre-dating him. Current assessments would suggest that what was involved was less a planned programme of reform than a catching-up with old problems, such as the due enforcement of the Navigation Acts, and a response to urgent new ones, notably to the pressure of a huge debt incurred in wartime and to the need to provide for the government and defence of new conquests.[7] In nearly all these measures the authority of Parliament over the colonies was specifically invoked.

Over the next ten years the well-known story was to unfold of further limited measures of colonial reform, of partial retreats combined with tenacious adherence to the rights of Parliament and of the eventual attempt to coerce Massachusetts in response to what seemed to be its persistent disobedience. At that point compromise proved impossible.

On the British side there is no evidence of any systematic desire to subjugate America in these years. It is clear, however, that there was persistent anxiety on the part of certain colonial governors, Whitehall officials and politicians, such as Charles Townshend or Lord Hillsborough, who took a close interest in the colonies, about the state of British authority in America. They believed, as some of them had done since the 1740s, that the empire was not functioning effectively and that British authority was being seriously undermined. They feared a drift towards an effective separation. The scenario was rarely made explicit, but what was envisaged was not the emergence of a new independent United States, an inconceivable prospect even to nearly all Americans before the mid-1770s, but disintegration, with individual colonies becoming ungovernable and ceasing to obey the Navigation Acts, as Rhode Island and Connecticut were presumed to do already, the rise of internal disorder and outright conflict between colonies. As the North American empire fell apart, the French would pick off the colonies one by one.

It took at least until 1774 for the majority of Britain's political leadership to be brought to accept the gloomy prognostications of the self-confessed experts. Only when opinion became convinced that the survival of empire in America was at stake was there support for the deeply unpalatable course of armed coercion, although it was hoped that a limited application of force against what was taken to be a small minority of the irredeemably refractory would be all that was needed.

British national interests of the highest importance were believed to depend on the survival of empire. There is abundant evidence that at least from the 1740s ministers were convinced of the great importance of North America to British commerce and manufacturing, and therefore of its pre-eminent role in generating the revenue and the funds available for government borrowing on which British public finance depended. To quote one striking example, Thomas Robinson, a transient and not very effective Secretary of State, wrote of the perceived French threat in 1755:

> If the dispute turned upon a little more or less advantage in the trade in furs, or even upon whole regions of Deserts, France would not have pursued one fixed scheme of encroachments and usurpations for so many years ... The great object is still the same. Vizt the security of his Majesty's American dominions upon which the prosperity of these dominions so much depends. 'Full one third of the whole export of the produce and manufactures of the country is to our Colonies and in proportion as this diminishes or increases, the Estates of Landholders, and the business of the Merchant, the Manufacturer and the artificer must diminish or increase.'

In a supplementary paper, Robinson added that it was 'from the American colonies,' that

> the great part of the Revenues of these Kingdoms is derived; and it is from them the great part of the wealth we see, that Credit which

> Circulates, and those payments which are made at the Bank, and
> the bankers in London results; and they are so linked in with and
> dependent upon the American Revenues and remittances that if
> they are ruined and stopt, the whole system of public Credit in this
> country will receive a fatal Shock.[8]

The argument about Britain's economic dependence on America could,
of course, cut both ways. America could be portrayed, as it was by the
Rockingham administration in 1765–66, as so valuable that concession
must be preferred to any attempted coercion. For the Duke of Newcastle, who had been 'bred up to think that the Trade of this nation is the
sole Support of it', 'the very being of this country, as a trading nation'
depended on the repeal of the Stamp Act. The 'obstinate headstrong'
Americans could not be taxed and the consequences of their resistance
would be 'Riots, Mobbs, and Insurrections in all the great towns in the
Kingdom and Numbers of our Manufacturers turned to Starving'.[9]
Realistically, coercion of America could be seen as an invitation for
France and Spain to attack, a point made as early as 1766 by General
Conway, when he anticipated that 'a French and Spanish war ... connected with an American war would be the absolute ruin of this
country'.[10] Nevertheless for the majority in Parliament after 1774, the
consequences of imperial disintegration were so dire as to outweigh
almost any short-term economic price or any risk of international conflict. In the last resort, if effective control over the empire really was at
stake, there could be no alternative to coercion.

The survival of empire was deemed to depend on the acceptance by
the colonies of an ultimate metropolitan authority, even if in practice
this would only normally be exerted over certain limited if vital areas,
notably trade and defence. The degree of autonomy enjoyed by its
colonial populations was matter for pride and self-congratulation for
all shades of British opinion. Freedom produced commercial vitality. It
was what distinguished the British empire from those of other powers.
Nevertheless, Britain must retain reserve powers for emergencies that
overrode all local privileges, and her right to them could not be questioned. In the 1750s reformers were concerned with reinvigorating the
prerogative powers of the Crown. Anxious Americans like Franklin
believed that royal instructions to governors would be given the force of
law. British opinion was, however, turning towards a much more formi-
dable weapon, parliamentary statute. From the early 1760s obedience
to the will of a sovereign British Parliament was the British *sine qua non*
of empire.

American dissent from this proposition was unmistakable. During
the controversy over the stamp duties, limits were being set to the
sovereignty of Parliament, although, at least until the 1770s, the right

of Parliament to regulate the common concerns of the empire, such as trade, was generally conceded. Taxation was, however, definitely beyond parliamentary competence as, for most colonial opinion, was legislation affecting the internal 'police', that is, the domestic affairs, of the colonies. This was totally unacceptable in Britain. Even in 1764 the Massachusetts General Court was warned by its agent that he would 'only flatter and deceive' them if 'I led them to imagine, that any one Man of Consequence' in the Commons 'would stand up in his place and avow an opinion that ... Acts of Parliament ... were not obligatory upon all his Majesty's Subjects in all parts of his Dominion'.[11] Worse was to follow. By the 1770s the doctrine that Parliament had no rights over the colonies without their explicit consent and that the colonial assemblies were the equal under the Crown of the British Parliament was being clearly enunciated. The 'Intolerable Acts' were Parliament's response to such views.

In response to what was seen as an increasingly overt American challenge, British opinion took its stand on two fundamental issues: the nature of sovereignty and the basis of representation. These issues were closely linked. Sovereignty was to be exercised over the whole empire by a legislature consisting of the Crown and the two British Houses of Parliament, of which the lower, the House of Commons, represented the people of Britain, not because they directly chose it, but because they had in the past delegated their authority to it and because its members effectively represented the interests of the whole community and by extension of the whole empire. These were the rocks on which the British empire foundered.[12]

A sovereign Parliament exercising power over the whole empire in the interests of, but not at the behest of, the people as a whole was seen as the guarantee of both external and internal security. The rejection of metropolitan sovereignty over the empire would lead to disunity and the humbling of Britain as a significant power, while by subverting the doctrine of parliamentary sovereignty Americans were opening the way for an assertion either of untrammelled royal authority or of popular anarchy in Britain itself.

In George Grenville's view, were Parliament to give up 'its sovereignty in all cases over the colonies ... they are to be considered as independent communities in alliance with us'.[13] That was no basis for empire. For many British people the starkest example of political failure in the eighteenth century was that of the Dutch Republic. Britain's natural Protestant ally in holding back the tide of French aggression in the great wars of William III was thought by the 1750s to be declining into 'insignificancy'.[14] 'The days when Holland was a nation are passed', wrote a pamphleteer in 1778. 'It is nothing more than a disabled company of merchants'.[15] Explanations of decline were sought in the sapping of the Dutch martial spirit by the unbridled pursuit of wealth, but also in the lack of a strong central government. The lesson for Britain was clear. Americans must not be allowed to subvert the unity of the empire. 'Subdivision', Charles Yorke said, had 'brought Holland to destruction' but Britain was 'governed by one plan of uniform power'.[16] Lord Dartmouth insisted to General Gage in 1774 that

> the constitutional authority of this kingdom over its colonies must be vindicated, and its laws obeyed throughout the whole empire.
> It is not only its dignity and its reputation but its power, nay its very existence, depends upon the present moment; for should those ideas of independence ... once take root that relation between the kingdom and its colonies which is the bond of peace and power will soon cease to exist and destruction must follow disunion.[17]

In a statement of his political principles in 1767 George Grenville wrote that they included 'asserting and establishing the lawful authority of the King and Parliament of Great Britain over every part of our dominions in every part of the world'.[18] Concern for the acknowledgement of parliamentary sovereignty in the American colonies was indeed part of a wider preoccupation with maintaining metropolitan authority. Current scholarship about the Union of 1707 between England and Scotland emphasizes English insistence on an 'incorporating union', as contemporaries called it, that is, on a unitary sovereignty lodged in a single Parliament, not the confederation advocated by some Scots.[19] The Highlands were imperfectly included in the incorporating union in the first half of the eighteenth century, as the rebellion of 1745 made clear. This had been a dire threat to Britain during the war of the Austrian Succession. A very ambitious programme of legislation was introduced to eliminate any recurrence. The heritable jurisdictions of the clan chiefs must give way to the sovereign law. Lord Hardwicke, the architect of this legislation, explained in 1754 that his purpose was 'to proceed upon the uniform principles of extending the vigour and benefit of the laws over the whole country; of suppressing all private power that tends to obstruct the due course of those laws'.[20] To most informed British opinion the charters of Rhode Island and Connecticut, to go no further, were precisely such a species of 'private power'.

The British Parliament had proclaimed its sovereignty over Ireland in the 1720 Act that was the model for the 1766 Declaratory Act for the American colonies. Parliament did not use its power to tax Ireland, but within this constraint determined attempts were made to strengthen metropolitan authority. In a debate on America, Yorke emphasized similarities between Ireland and the colonies, and insisted that Ireland too was subject to an untrammelled parliamentary sovereignty. Ireland, for instance, had a military establishment authorized by a British not by an Irish Act of Parliament of 1698.[21] The augmentation of that establishment in 1768 may not have been a deliberate move against Irish autonomy, but it led to a sustained assault on the what was seen as the obstructiveness of the Irish political connections in the Dublin Parliament.[22] Lord Townshend, the Lord-Lieutenant, and Lord Rochford, the Secretary of State, agreed that they were aiming at 'a lasting superiority of the English government', or as Townshend put it: 'The grand principle of our constitution, I mean the general superintending and controlling power of the mother country over all its dependencies' required that 'the constitutional subordination of Ireland to Great Britain' could never be questioned.[23] This was giving force to a trend to greater English intervention in Ireland that historians perceive from the 1750s.[24] As with America, Pitt insisted on conciliation during the Seven Years War, to curb a 'contrary temper of national resentment and growing exasperation',[25] but that policy was abandoned after the war.

The developments in India that transformed Britain's role there also raised issues of sovereignty and metropolitan control. Similarities with America are not difficult to find. British interests in India were managed by a body claiming autonomies based on charters, that is, by the East India Company. While less was at stake than in North America or the West Indies, the value of the Company's trade and of the duties paid on its imports were of national importance. Claims were made that commercial credit would collapse if the Company were to be crippled.[26] From the 1750s the exclusion of Britain from India could also be depicted as one of the objectives in the French offensive all over the world. The forces of the Crown were deployed there, if on a much smaller scale than in the Americas. From the British government's point of view, the East India Company proved to be a rather more satisfactory partner in war than many American colonies. The Company raised large armies which won spectacular victories. The acquisition of territory was the consequence of these victories.

Territorial gains raised the issue of sovereignty. To whom did the new provinces belong? To eighteenth-century lawyers there was no doubt that conquests made by British subjects belonged to the Crown, but what of grants made by the Mughal emperor? When those grants were valued at some £3 million a year, a sum sufficient in Pitt's words 'to fix the ease and pre-eminence of England for ages',[27] much seemed to hang on the answer. The debates that ensued were protracted and confused. For various reasons it was deemed expedient to leave the management of British affairs in India in the hands of the Company and to continue to pay lip service to the allegiance owed to the Mughal emperor for Bengal. Nevertheless, by the 1770s the great mass of British opinion had come to see the East India Company's provinces as an integral part of the British empire. They were therefore presumed to be subject to the sovereignty of Parliament. The East India Company survived as the governing authority, but its affairs were regulated by a series of parliamentary enactments. Men in India, like Warren Hastings, were in no doubt that they were accountable for the government of Bengal not to any Indian authority, but to the Company and ultimately to the British Parliament. Hastings considered Bengal to be under 'the soveranty of the British nation'.[28] To the former governor of Massachusetts, Thomas Pownall, it was clear that 'the sovereignty of the native government of the country ... is abolished and annihilated'. In his view the Company exercised a *de facto* sovereignty in Bengal, but it could only do so legitimately because authority was delegated to it by the Crown, by which he clearly meant the Crown in Parliament.[29]

Any impression that the British empire in the second half of the eighteenth century was being hammered into some kind of centralized uniformity, subject to close bureaucratic regulation from Whitehall, would be entirely misleading. The Whitehall bureaucracy remained an unreformed sprawl and the empire was one of luxuriant diversity, which still included private colonies and territories subject to trading companies. Concrete reforms were limited in scope. The most that was ever aimed at was that the authority of the colonial executives in North America and the West Indies would be strengthened, and it was hoped that these colonies would pay something towards their defence. Some of the more objectionable chartered immunities might at some future date be curtailed. The Irish politicians must not be allowed to hamstring the working of the executive. The abuses in the way in which the East India Company conducted its affairs at home and in Asia must be corrected and its charter was to be regulated by statute. What was intended to be a more effective executive government was established in Calcutta. The very limited changes in imperial governance after 1783, in spite of the débâcle in America, indicates the relative poverty of the ambition of those who sought to reform the empire. They were, however, in no doubt that it was an empire and that what defined that empire was its subjection to the sovereign power of the British Parliament.[30] Limitations on sovereignty, however theoretical the exercise of most of its powers might be, could not be contemplated. An *imperium in imperio*, that is, a divided sovereignty, which Hillsborough called 'a polytheism in politics', was inadmissible.[31] It meant disunity. A disunited empire would mean that Britain was treading the path already trod by the Dutch.

American doctrines were seen as threatening not only to the essential unity of the empire but to the British constitution as it was being interpreted in the mid-eighteenth century. As Professor Pocock has put it, the Americans appeared to be expounding either a Tory or a Republican programme.[32] Neither was acceptable.

The Tory implications of American doctrine lay in its willingness to give the Crown a role in the colonies independent of parliamentary sanction. Such implications were spotted by Grenville and Yorke, among others, in the debates about the repeal of the Stamp Act.[33] For Grenville the idea that the colonies should refuse to pay parliamentary taxes but should grant money to the Crown on its requisition was particularly abhorrent.[34] Franklin's view that Americans should reject 'the usurped Authority of Parliament' while preserving 'a dutiful attachment to the King and his Family' was even more objectionable.[35]

Some of this indignation seems, however, more than a little forced. Parliament sought to enforce obedience to the prerogative instruments of the Crown, proclamations and instructions to governors, as well as to its own statutes. The raising of huge American armies on royal requisition during the Seven Years War had not been seen as a constitutional threat. George III showed not the slightest interest in a separate dominion in America and nobody seems to have supposed that he did.

What was certainly not forced was indignation at American theories of representation. They were said to embody principles that were Republican, a term which in common mid-eighteenth-century discourse was equated with little more than the subversion of a balanced constitution in favour of its popular elements. Governor Bernard warned in 1764 about 'republican forms of government' in New England, especially in Connecticut and Rhode Island.[36] By 1772 Gage was convinced that 'the Republican Spirit will appear upon every Opportunity' in Massachusetts.[37] The South Carolina Committee of Correspondence thought it worth instructing their agent in 1765 to refute such assertions. The 'word republican', they considered, 'conveys an insinuation so injurious and artful and at the same time so false with regard to Americans in general', who were 'true lovers of our happy limited monarchick constitution'.[38] The polemics over the Stamp Act seemed to many British people to show the falsity of such assurances. The House of Lords' dissentient to the repeal of the Stamp Act argued that American claims about what constituted representation may be 'extended to all Persons in this Island who do not actually vote for Members of Parliament' and thus would

> greatly promote the Contagion of a most dangerous Doctrine, destructive to all Government ... that the Obedience of the Subject is not due to the Laws and Legislature of the Realm, further than he, in his private Judgement, shall think it conformable to the ideas he has formed of a free Constitution.[39]

Underlying such reasoning was genuine apprehension about popular commotion. Such apprehensions were no doubt felt by the élite at many

points in the eighteenth century, but the 1760s seemed to be a particularly
threatening decade. In describing the cider riots in Devonshire and what
he called 'the Insurrections in Ireland of the *Hearts of Oak*', Lord
Hardwicke lamented to his friend the Duke of Newcastle, 'What a scene
of Confusion is here when mix'd with that which now exists in England'.[40] 'Ireland is not in more confusion, than to a degree, England is',
Newcastle agreed.[41] Speakers in the House of Lords in 1766 saw riots
in America and the disorder of the London weavers as part of the same
'contagion'.[42] In 1770 Franklin wrote:

> I have seen within a Year, Riots in the Country about Corn, Riots
> about Elections, Riots about Workhouses, Riots of Colliers, Riots
> of Weavers, Riots of Coal Heavers, Riots of Sawyers, Riots of
> Sailors, Riots of Wilksites, Riots of Government Chairmen, Riots
> of Smugglers in which Customs Officers and Excisemen have been
> murdered ... Here indeed one would think Riots part of the Mode
> of Government.[43]

Many British people feared that he was only too right. As the fighting
began in America, Lord Barrington, the Secretary at War, feared for the
security of London when the guards were sent abroad from the 'desperate and ill-affected people' there.[44] Subversive doctrines propagated
anywhere in the empire must be repressed. 'Law ... must either be
supported or we sink into a state of anarchy', was Hillsborough's
response to the Boston riots of 1768.[45]

The parliamentary speeches and the correspondence of the British
political élite in the decades leading to the Revolution show abundant
evidence of apprehension: anxiety about French designs in the 1750s
and then in the 1760s about French and Spanish naval building and
their desire for revenge, concern for the stability of the constitution and
fear of popular upheaval. But they also show an underlying confidence.
The willingness to coerce America grew out of confidence as well as
fear. British politicians were supremely confident in the ability of a
sovereign Parliament to manage the affairs of the empire with wisdom
and justice. Abuse of sovereignty was inconceivable to them.

By the mid-eighteenth century British and American political ideology diverged widely. If, in Professor Bailyn's now classic formulation,
Americans feared the incursions of power on liberty,[46] mainstream British opinion was far less fearful about power, so long as it was in the
right hands. Power, including a professional standing army and the
administration of complex public finances, could be safely lodged in the
hands of a political leadership accountable to Parliament. Britain's leaders saw themselves as the guardians of the 'common good' of the whole
empire.[47] This consisted in maintaining the constitution as they interpreted it, promoting commerce within the laws of trade, and beating off

the French. It was so self-evidently in the colonies' interest that they should submit to a proper degree of subordination to Britain that the proposition did not need arguing. Men who had actually been to America were aware of the huge range of peoples and interests now involved in the colonies as the result of spectacular growth of wealth and numbers. Loudoun pointed out how difficult it was to maintain authority in 'so extensive a country, inhabited by people from such a variety of nations and of such a variety of religions and so far removed from the centre of government in the mother country'.[48] But to most British politicians American interests and British interests were identical in essentials. Hillsborough told William Johnson

> that he was very sure his Majesty had equal affection for his American as for his other subjects and wished as far as possible to make us all happy; that I might be perfectly assured, that he and all his Majesty's Ministers had very great regard for that country, that they considered us all as Britons having one common interest with them.[49]

Where the colonies did have interests of their own which required consideration, the representative system of the British Parliament was deemed adequate for such consideration. Direct representation was unnecessary. The mid-eighteenth-century House of Commons prided itself on its capacity to respond to interests of all sorts, whether they were or were not directly represented. Recent historiography endorses this claim. As Paul Langford has put it, 'the most vigorous creators of wealth', in Britain, though not directly represented, were not usually advocates of parliamentary reform.[50] Yet he sees British arguments that the American colonies were 'virtually' represented in the Commons as 'at best imprudent, at worst cynical'.[51] People like Thomas Whately who used the concept of virtual representation were certainly ignorant and overconfident, but it seems doubtful whether they were being cynical. They genuinely believed that American voices could be heard in the Commons, through merchants dealing with the colonies or through the representations made by agents. It was common doctrine that legislation affecting the colonies should be delayed, as of course the Stamp Act was, for a session, until American opinion was heard. Jared Ingersoll relayed what he took to be the view of the Grenville ministry:

> ... we on our part find with pleasure that America is not destitute of persons who at the same time that they have the tenderest regard for their Interests are well able to Represent to us their Affairs and who if they do it with integrity and candor, will be sure to meet with our fullest confidence.[52]

For men who believed that they knew the best interests of America, which they thought in most respects were identical with those of Britain, and who considered that Parliament would respond to any genuine colonial grievance, American resistance could only be the result of the machinations of a disaffected minority, infected with the republican virus. If Britain stood firm against such people, the loyal majority would eventually rally to Britain's cause. Ministers persisted in this tragic delusion at least until 1775.

Complacency about Britain's institutions had been greatly boosted by success in the Seven Years War. In retrospect it seemed to Edmund Burke that success had been 'our ruin'. It had made us 'Proud and insolent to our dependencies'.[53] The historian of British foreign policy in this period has noted a 'new domineering attitude' in British dealings with other Europeans.[54] A domineering self-confidence was, however, built on underlying insecurities. Thus the British political élite saw no reason to change their underlying assumptions about empire and believed that it would be very dangerous to do so. They therefore faced an American crisis, whose depth and scale few could comprehend, with a deeply entrenched rigidity.

Notes

1. J. P. Greene, 'Explaining the American Revolution: Questions Resolved and Unresolved', in *idem, Understanding the Revolution: Issues and Actors* (Charlottesville, VA, 1995), pp. 1–9.
2. P. D. G. Thomas, *British Politics and the Stamp Act Crisis* (Oxford, 1975); *idem, The Townshend Duties Crisis* (Oxford, 1987); *idem, Tea Party to Independence* (Oxford, 1991).
3. H. T. Dickinson (ed.), *Britain and the American Revolution* (London, 1998).
4. E. H. Gould, *The Persistence of Empire: British Political Culture in the Age of the American Revolution* (Chapel Hill, NC, 2000).
5. J. P. Greene, '"A Posture of Hostility": A Reconsideration of Some Aspects of the Origins of the American Revolution', *Proceedings of the American Antiquarian Society*, 87 (1977), 43.
6. Daniel A. Baugh, 'Withdrawing from Europe: Anglo-French Maritime Geopolitics, 1750–1800', *International History Review*, 20 (1998), 13–16.
7. Thomas, *Stamp Act Crisis*, pp. 112–13. John L. Bullion, *A Great and Necessary Measure: George Grenville and the Genesis of the Stamp Act 1763–1765* (Columbia, MO, 1982), attributes a greater degree of overall coherence to the measures of the Grenville government.
8. T. Robinson, letter to Holderness, 29 August 1755, British Library (hereafter BL), Eg. Add. MS 3432, fos 292–3, 297–8.
9. To Archbishop of Canterbury, 2 February 1766, BL, Add. MS 32973, fo. 343.
10. R. C. Simmons and P. D. G. Thomas (eds), *Proceedings and Debates of the British Parliaments respecting North America*, 6 vols (Milwood, NY, 1982–87), vol. 2, p. 281.

11. Letter of J. Mauduit, 7 April 1764, 'Jasper Mauduit: Agent for the Province of Massachusetts Bay', *Massachusetts Historical Society Collections*, **74** (1918), 147 fn.

12. For a cogent statement of the British position, see H. T. Dickinson, 'Britain's Imperial Sovereignty: The Ideological Case against the American Colonists', in *idem* (ed.), *Britain and the American Revolution*, pp. 64–96.

13. Letter to T. Hood, 30 October 1768, Huntington Library, ST 7, vol. 2.

14. H. M. Scott, *British Foreign Policy in the Age of the American Revolution* (Oxford, 1990), p. 224.

15. Cited in Michael Duffy, *The English Satirical Print, 1660–1832: The Englishman and the Foreigner* (Cambridge, 1986), p. 31.

16. Simmons and Thomas, vol. 2, p. 137.

17. Letter of 3 June 1774, K. G. Davies (ed.), *Documents of the American Revolution c. 1770–1783*, 21 vols (Shannon, 1972–81), vol. 8, p. 124.

18. Letter to Bedford, 6 November 1767, Huntington Library, ST 7, vol. 2.

19. John Robertson (ed.), *A Union for Empire: Political Thought and the British Union of 1707* (Cambridge, 1995).

20. Letter to General Bland, 7 February 1754, BL, Add. MS 35448, fo. 63.

21. Simmons and Thomas, vol. 2, p. 137.

22. Thomas Bartlett, 'The Augmentation of the Army in Ireland 1767–1769', *English Historical Review*, **96** (1981), 540–59.

23. Rochford to Townshend, 25 May 1771, Townshend to Rochford, 22 December 1771, Public Record Office (hereafter PRO), SP 63/433, p. 332; 63/434, p. 290.

24. E.g Declan O'Donovan, 'The Money Bill Dispute of 1753', in T. Bartlett and D. W. Hayton (eds), *Penal Era and Golden Age: Essays in Irish History* (Belfast, 1978), pp. 55–87.

25. Pitt to Bedford, 2 February 1758, PRO, SP 63/415, pp. 203–5.

26. H. V. Bowen, *Revenue and Reform: The Indian Problem in British Politics, 1757–1773* (Cambridge, 1991), pp. 22–3.

27. Letter to C. Townshend, 2 January 1767, William L. Clements Library, Charles Townshend MSS, 296/3/35.

28. Cited in M. E. Monckton Jones, *Warren Hastings in Bengal 1772–74* (Oxford, 1918), p. 191.

29. T. Pownall, *The Right, Interest, and Duty, of Government as Concerned in the Affairs of the East India Company* (London, [1781]).

30. P. J. Marshall, 'Parliament and Property Rights in the Late Eighteenth-Century British Empire', in J. Brewer and S. Staves (eds), *Early Modern Conceptions of Property* (London, 1995), pp. 530–44.

31. W. S. Johnson to W. Pitkin, 3 January 1769, 'The Trumball Papers, I', *Massachusetts Historical Society Collections*, ser. 5, 9 (1885), 307.

32. J. G. A. Pocock, 'Political Thought in the English-Speaking Atlantic 1760–1790: Part I, The Imperial Crisis', in J. G. A. Pocock (ed.), *Varieties of British Political Thought, 1500–1800* (Cambridge, 1993), p. 275.

33. Simmons and Thomas, vol. 2, pp. 139, 145.

34. Letter to Knox, 15 July 1768, 'Knox MSS.', *Historical Manuscripts Commission: Various Collections*, 6 (1909), 97.

35. Letter to T. Cushing, 10 June 1771, L. W. Labaree et al. (eds), *Papers of Benjamin Franklin*, 34 vols to date (New Haven, CT, 1959–), vol. 18, p. 123.

36. Letter to Halifax, 9 November 1764, PRO, CO 5/755, pp. 135–40.
37. Letter to Hillsborough, 13 April 1772, C. E. Carter (ed.), *The Correspondence of General Thomas Gage with the Secretaries of State and the Treasury 1763–75*, 2 vols (New Haven, CT, 1931–33), vol. I, p. 321.
38. Letter to C. Garth, 16 December 1765, Library of Congress, Force Transcripts, 7E.
39. Simmons and Thomas, vol. 2, p. 334.
40. Letter of 1 August 1763, BL, Add. MS 32950, fos 1–2.
41. Letter of 2 August 1763, BL, Add. MS 35422, fo. 299.
42. Simmons and Thomas, vol. 2, p. 565.
43. Marginalia in L. W. Labaree et al. (eds), *Papers of Benjamin Franklin*, vol. 17, pp. 341–2.
44. Stephen Conway, *The War of American Independence* (London, 1995), p. 209.
45. D. De Berdt to T. Cushing, 26 August 1768, 'Letters of Dennys De Berdt, 1757–1770', *Publications of the Colonial Society of Massachusetts*, 13 (1910–11), 337.
46. B. Bailyn, *The Ideological Origins of the American Revolution* (Cambridge, MA, 1967), pp. 55–62.
47. Peter N. Miller, *Defining the Common Good: Empire, Religion and Philosophy in Eighteenth-Century Britain* (Cambridge, 1994).
48. To H. Sharpe, 3 November 1757, Huntington Library, LO 4747.
49. W. S. Johnson to W. Pitkin, 13 February 1768, 'Trumball Papers, I', *Massachusetts Historical Society Collections*, ser. 5, 9 (1885), 261.
50. P. Langford, *Public Life and the Propertied Englishman 1689–1798* (Oxford, 1991), p. 206.
51. Ibid., p. 199.
52. To T. Fitch, 6 March 1765, 'Fitch Papers, I', *Collections of the Connecticut Historical Society*, 18 (1920), 340.
53. Warren M. Elofson with John A. Woods (eds), *The Writings and Speeches of Edmund Burke*, vol. 3, *Party, Parliament, and the American War 1774–1780* (Oxford, 1996), p. 202.
54. Scott, *British Foreign Policy*, p. 51.

The American Revolution in Britain's Imperial Identity*

Eliga H. Gould

On 20 February 1775, Lord North laid his final proposal for peacefully resolving the imperial crisis in North America before the House of Commons. As North himself admitted, his Conciliatory Proposition, which promised to restore civil government to any colony that came forward with a regular subsidy for the common defence of the British Empire, was not likely to meet with approval from the radical patriots in America. None the less, the king's first minister claimed that the mere fact that the offer had been extended would not 'fail of doing Good in England'. According to the account that appeared in the *London Evening Post*, North insisted, first, that his proposal would demonstrate to the world 'the wisdom and clemency' and 'the humanity and justice, of [the] British Government's' actions against the rebellious colonists; second, that it would reassure England's 'traders and manufacturers' of Parliament's moderate intentions; and finally – and most importantly– that it would convince 'the officers and soldiers we send out to America' that they 'no longer fight for a phantom, and a vain, empty point of honour, but for a substantial benefit to their country, which is to relieve her in her greatest exigencies'.[1]

It is hardly surprising that the government sought to reassure the metropolitan public that the army would be serving their 'country' in the impending war in America. After all, by 1775, the British people had a long and distinguished history of making life miserable for any minister who used – or even appeared to use – the military and fiscal resources of the Crown for anything other than purely 'national' objectives.[2] At the same time, though, the patriotic language with which Lord North depicted the army's mission in the colonies raised the vexing question of exactly what 'country' the officers and enlisted men bound for ports like Boston, New York and Philadelphia were supposed to be serving. Presumably, most of the men and women who read the newspaper accounts of North's speech would have thought he was referring not just to England, but also to Scotland and Wales.[3] Some might also have assumed that he meant the subordinate kingdom of Ireland.[4] But was there any way to argue that the country that the army was supposed to be defending included the colonies of British North America? As I wish to suggest in the following pages, the American Revolution forced the metropolitan public to think about such matters far more deeply than they previously had. In the process, they discovered just how ill-defined Britain's internal frontiers were, and what sorts of difficulties were likely to arise when such elusive frontiers caused British patriots to clash with British patriots.

A transatlantic nation

For many Britons, of course, their country did include America. Not only were the British well aware of the domestic importance of transatlantic trade, but the metropolitan press at mid-century routinely described the colonies as 'national Property' much like 'any County in England,' and the Americans as 'our Brethren, *Englishmen* as we are, our own Flesh and Blood'.[5] Furthermore, Parliament explicitly recognized all white colonists except Catholics as natural-born English subjects, including Protestant and Jewish immigrants from the Continent who had been resident in North America for at least seven years.[6] Largely as a result of these commercial and political ties, matters relating to America came to enjoy an extraordinary interest among the eighteenth-century public.[7] Indeed, the Seven Years War (1756–63), during which the British succeeded in driving both France and Spain out of the eastern half of North America, played an especially important role in feeding these transatlantic sensibilities. As the London merchant and philanthropist, Jonas Hanway, confidently predicted in 1760, the 'stability' of an imperial connection based on a common sovereignty and a similarity of 'religion, politics, manners, language and laws' was certain to provide a far stronger system of defence than the 'fluctuating friendship' of the European alliances that had been central to Whig foreign policy since the Glorious Revolution.[8] There were likewise more than a few commentators who hoped that the sheer extent of Britain's triumph would consolidate the frontiers for a vast new empire of liberty, one where, in the words of the ageing Earl of Bath, 'Britons may now live in America adjoining to Britons, as secure from a foreign enemy as in an island'.[9]

While historians have not always given it the attention it deserves, this presumed national unity played a crucial part in shaping British attitudes to the American Revolution. For example, it helps explain why the decision at the end of the Seven Years War to leave a peacetime establishment of 10 000 regulars in North America and to finance it in part by raising a colonial revenue initially stimulated so little discussion in metropolitan England.[10] Although the few people with firsthand colonial experience insisted otherwise, most observers seem to have assumed that the Americans would consent to Parliament's dramatic extension of the State's military and fiscal powers because they considered themselves to be British subjects. This is certainly the line that George Grenville's secretary, Thomas Whately, took in the explanation of the Stamp Act that he published in 1765. According to Whately, Britain and America together comprised 'one Nation', whose colonial subjects were virtually represented in Parliament in the same manner as nine-tenths of the king's subjects at home, including most men and all women, regardless of the extent of their landed property: 'For every Member of Parliament,' wrote Whately, 'sits in the House, not as Representative of his own constituents, but as one of that august Assembly by which all the Commons of *Great-Britain* are represented.'[11] By taxing the colonists without their explicit consent, agreed the English Member of Parliament, Fletcher Norton, in 1766, 'we use North America as we use ourselves'.[12] Even after the Stamp Act's repeal, metropolitan commentators continued to maintain that the colonies in North America formed integral parts of the British nation, joined to the realm of England, according to the former Massachusetts governor Thomas Pownall, in the same manner as the 'counties palatine' of Durham and Chester had been before they were granted representation in the House of Commons during the later seventeenth century.[13]

The finer points of such theories may well have been beyond the comprehension of much of the British public. None the less, such arguments lent juridical rigour to the more generalized sentiment that the country for which the British government fought between 1775 and 1783 included the English-speaking provinces of North America. As the Scottish jurist, Sir John Dalrymple, observed in a recruiting pamphlet written in 1775, the conflict in America was 'a singular War' because it pitted 'English Subjects against English Subjects'.[14] The Archdeacon of Surrey, John Butler, made much the same point in a fast sermon from 1776: 'We cannot with Indifference, nor without many serious reflexions, behold a large number of Fellow-creatures, in Language and Blood our Countrymen, so self-condemned, and afflicted under the mighty Hand of God.'[15] The American Loyalists were especially important in this respect, for – in the words of the king's chaplain, Henry Stebbing – 'they are a part of us, a member of our political body, and *if one of our members suffer*, we feel to our sorrow that *the whole body suffers with it*'.[16] Indeed, one reason why peace with the United States proved to be such a bitter pill for many people to swallow involved the implicit abandonment of the substantial number of colonists who had suffered because of their desire to remain 'Denizens and Englishmen', as an anonymous pamphleteer wrote in 1783: British subjects 'descended from one common origin, and protected by [the] same Household Gods'.[17]

This unease over the Loyalists' ultimate fate is a reminder that the premise that Parliament might govern the colonists as if they represented so many members of a single British nation amounted to something more than empty rhetoric. Indeed, although it eventually foundered on the rocks of American independence, the notion of Britain's Atlantic empire as a vast, transoceanic nation proved so widespread that even Britons who opposed the policy of colonial coercion claimed to see 'no difference between an inhabitant of Boston in Lincolnshire, and of Boston in New England,' as John Wilkes put the issue during the early 1770s.[18] In the words of William Pitt – now Earl of Chatham – there was simply no reason why the Americans 'should not enjoy every fundamental right in their property, and every original substantial liberty, which Devonshire or Surrey, or the county I live in, or any other county in England, can claim'.[19] People might disagree over how best to respond to the difficulties posed by the American Revolution, but most assumed that the colonial crisis represented a 'civil war' that pitted Briton against Briton.

'A new class of men'

Yet the American Revolution just as surely demonstrated the limits of this transatlantic patriotism on Britain's imperial periphery. In the years before the Declaration of Independence, the colonists themselves took the lead in this process of imperial redefinition, eventually reaching the conclusion that Britain's Atlantic empire was best understood not as a unitary state uniformly subject to Parliament's unlimited authority, but as a confederation of independent states – much like the nineteenth-century British Commonwealth – bound together only by their mutual allegiance to the British Crown. With a few notable exceptions like Richard Price and John Cartwright, the British public initially greeted this proposed solution to the imperial crisis with unrelenting hostility. In their determination to show the pernicious effects of the Americans' rejection of Parliament's 'national' sovereignty, however, the British were effectively forced to adopt their own rhetoric of difference, first as a way to distinguish the government's cause from that of its provincial opponents, but ultimately as a more general critique of colonial society. The result was an imperial discourse that quickly undermined the transatlantic identity that had seemed so unshakeable only a decade before. Indeed, by the time of Britain's first great defeat at Saratoga (1777), these distinctions had already acquired enough clarity to introduce a kind of 'creeping federalism' into the way the British thought about their relationship with the colonies in America.

One of the earliest signs of this growing sense of difference involved the allegations of brutal atrocities and lawless acts of violence that appeared in the ministerial press during the early years of the war. In a widely read reply to the Declaration of Independence, for example, the English jurist and associate of the young Jeremy Bentham, John Lind, detailed numerous barbaric acts by the rebellious colonists, including the murder of a black river pilot at Charles Town, Massachusetts, the pillaging of a hospital that had provided wounded British regulars with shelter, and the destruction of the printing presses of the *New York Gazetteer* by Connecticut militia.[20] 'This is the land of liberty,' was how Hugh Finlay, the king's Surveyor of the Posts in North America, described his own hapless situation shortly after the Battle of Lexington. 'A man may say and do whatever he will, if he will execrate Lord North, call the Parliament a pack of corrupted rascals, every officer ... a pitiful tool, and speak contemptuously of all friends of Government.'[21] Some of the most affecting stories involved the suffering that the revolutionaries had inflicted on women, children and the elderly. As an American resident in Britain observed during the fall of 1775, 'the utmost industry of the Ministry is employ'd, to inflame mens minds here', while another cautioned a friend in Virginia about the importance of appearing 'respectable in the eyes of Europe' through a scrupulous regard for civilized customs like 'the treating prisoners with humanity – the shielding age & womanhood from the horrors of war – [and] the not being too hasty in making reprisals'.[22]

Not surprisingly, perhaps, the Church of England's clergy on both sides of the Atlantic took a leading role in spreading such accounts. Although most Anglicans were careful not to identify Parliament's imperial authority too closely with the Church's own particular interests, the enthusiasm evident in the American Revolution provided a vivid reminder of the overwhelming superiority that dissenters enjoyed in every colony except Maryland and Virginia. Throughout the war, for example, one of the recurring charges in the ministerial press involved the part played by the dissenting clergy in 'breathing the spirit of rebellion on the people', as one polemicist put it.[23] 'Every body knows that they have an inveterate hatred to our constitution both in church and state,' wrote another pamphleteer, 'The principles they suck in with milk naturally lead to rebellion.'[24] The fact that revolutionary crowds frequently singled out the Church's missionaries for particular retribution only enhanced this impression, leading one pastor, the Reverend Charles Inglis of New York City, to suggest that the story of his fellow divines 'would be no bad supplement to *Walker's sufferings of the clergy*'.[25] As Myles Cooper, President of New York's King's College, insisted in his controversial fast sermon at Oxford in December 1776, the dissenting clergy in America had made religion 'an handmaid to Faction and Sedition', with 'solemn Prayers, public Fastings, and pathetic Sermons' all being used 'to invigorate the Rebellion'.[26]

For all the obvious appeal among Anglicans, of course, such allegations carried dangers in terms of the Church's relations with dissenters in England, Scotland and Ireland. For this reason, British observers – including many among the higher Anglican clergy – often preferred to attribute the Americans' enthusiasm not to any one set of beliefs or religious practices, but to a more generalized anarchy born of the particular circumstances of the colonists' provincial situation.[27] Sometimes these anarchic tendencies appeared in racial terms, with polemicists suggesting that the colonists had degenerated into 'brutal savages' like their Indian neighbours.[28] On other occasions, commentators noted how the vastness of the Atlantic Ocean corrupted colonial patriotism by heightening the Americans' susceptibility to misrepresentations about 'public Persons, Measures and Events' in England.[29] Still other writers, echoing Samuel Johnson's famous question – 'how is it we hear the loudest yelps for liberty among the drivers of negroes?' – attributed the Americans' proclivity for violence to the colonial institution of slavery and the reckless arrogance that it encouraged in planters like Washington and Jefferson.[30] And more than a few Britons blamed the Revolution on a combination of all of these factors. 'It has been asserted,' remarked the Member of Parliament, William Innes, in November 1775,

> that the colonists are the offspring of Englishmen, and as such, entitled to the privileges of Britons. [But] I am bold to deny it, for it is well known that they not only consist of English, Scots, and Irish, but also of French, Dutch, Germans innumerable, Indians, Africans, and a multitude of felons from this country. Is it possible to tell which are the most turbulent amongst such a mixture of people?[31]

These religious, cultural and ethnic distinctions were enough to convince a growing number of observers of the futility of treating the colonists as integral parts of the British nation. From a metropolitan standpoint, though, the difference that mattered even more involved the Americans' apparent disregard for the English rule of law.[32] Early on in the imperial crisis, many Britons seem to have assumed that the regular army would enable local authorities in the settled regions of the North American seaboard to enforce the law in the same manner as it did in England or the Scottish Lowlands. As the Secretary at War, Lord Barrington, wrote to a friend in 1768, 'riotous Englishmen in New

England must be treated as their fellows in Old England, they must be compelled to obey the law & the civil magistrate must have troops to enforce that obedience'.[33] Even after the commencement of hostilities, some commentators affected to believe that the government was dealing with a kind of massive grain riot – an unpleasant business, to be sure, but hardly the sort of affair likely to endanger the liberties of most Americans, the vast majority of whom it was supposed still considered themselves to be loyal British subjects.[34] During the war's first three years, ministerial writers accordingly praised the 'humanity' and 'good conduct' of British officers.[35] After all, as long as the government continued to regard the colonists as English subjects, the law arguably required the king's troops to act with such restraint, because – as a pamphleteer noted in 1777 – even rebels were 'entitled to a regular trial by Jury' after they had been captured.[36]

The problem with this position, however, was that establishing the sort of civil authority under which the revolutionary leaders might be tried in an English court of law depended on achieving a complete military victory. In the absence of such an outcome, British observers were increasingly forced to discuss the war in terms that suggested the government was contending with a foreign power. Speaking of the controversial decision to use Indian auxiliaries in America, for example, one polemicist justified the government's actions on the grounds that 'the end of war is to destroy an enemy'.[37] Adam Ferguson, the Edinburgh Professor of Moral Philosophy who accompanied the Carlisle Commission to America in 1778, made much the same point when he observed that the rebellion would continue until the army began using 'every Species of War that is lawful against an ordinary Ennemy', including the punishment of civilian resistance in courts martial, the destruction of any materiel with military potential, and the imposition of contributions on occupied provinces.[38] Although the army generally refrained from employing such tactics, it was certainly no accident that one of the only occasions when the government attempted to silence the 'friends of America' in Britain involved the trial of Horne Tooke, who had accused the king's troops of 'inhumanly murder[ing]' their fellow subjects at Lexington and Concord on 19 April, 1775. As the Attorney General, Edward Thurlow, argued during the trial, murder was a civil offence, and thus constituted a seditious libel when applied to soldiers who had clearly crossed into 'an hostile country … from the moment they went out of Boston'.[39]

Given the vast size of the territory being contested, British officials obviously had no choice but to treat large stretches of North America as 'hostile country'. But such attitudes were not confined to those parts of the colonies under the effective control of Congress and its committees of public safety. Although the British claimed that their 'ultimate Purpose' involved 'enabling His Majesty's Faithfull subjects to resume their Civil governments', the government consistently refused to suspend martial law even in areas firmly under their control like the southern counties of New York.[40] The results were predictably demoralizing and chaotic. In Queens County on Long Island, for example, the reputedly loyal inhabitants not only had to contend with raids by rival freebooters like the Whig 'skinners' and loyalist 'cowboys', but they also found themselves subject to the arbitrary rule of an aristocratic officer corps who considered even those who took oaths of allegiance as 'a Levelling, underbred, Artfull, Race of people that we Cannot Associate with'.[41] It is little wonder that the British headquarters at New York was constantly besieged by complaints from Long Islanders ranging from charges of outright theft by regular officers to the forced sale of supplies at below-market prices. As the Reverend Leonard Cutting, rector of the Anglican church at Hempstead, observed in a letter to the secretary of the Society for the Propagation of the Gospel (SPG) in London, there were literally thousands of such instances 'that might be produced of the Tyranny we are under'; for 'where the Army is, Oppression, such as in England you can have no Conception of Universally prevails ... What a state must that people be in, who can find Relief from neither Law, Justice, or Humanity'.[42] In the terse words of another New Yorker, the upshot of such encounters was that 'we shall all soon, I believe, be Rebels'.[43]

Accounts like this were certainly troubling. From the standpoint of the metropolitan public, though, the most conclusive indication of the growing differences between Britain and the colonies involved the government's decision to grant its American opponents the same customary rights of war as if they belonged to a sovereign state. No event played a more important role in this respect than General John Burgoyne's defeat at the Battle of Saratoga in October of 1777. Even before news of the army's humiliation reached the British public, oppositionists like Edmund Burke had pointed out the apparent anomaly in the government's decision to conduct hostilities 'upon the usual footing of other wars'. 'Whenever a rebellion really and truly exists,' Burke explained in his *Letter to the Bristol Sheriffs*, 'government has not entered into ... military conventions; but has ever declined all intermediate treaty, which should put rebels in possession of the law of nations with regard to war.'[44] In the wake of Burgoyne's momentous capitulation, these concerns acquired considerably more weight. By agreeing to formal terms with the Americans, the British commander implicitly granted both Congress and the Continental Army many of the attributes of sovereignty so assiduously denied them by the government's apologists. 'The history of nations affords no instance of a convention or treaty, made with Rebels', insisted one of Burgoyne's many critics.[45] 'Their words and their actions are discordant', another observer wrote of the government's conduct. 'They call the *Americans* Rebels; yet in every instance they are treated like the Subjects of an Independent State.'[46]

The cumulative effect of such agreements was to introduce a quasi-federalism into the colonies' formal relationship with metropolitan Britain. As late as the fall of 1778, the peace commissioners whom the British government dispatched to negotiate with Congress still thought it worthwhile to use France's intervention as an occasion to call upon all Americans to join them 'in fighting the battles of the United British Empire against our late mutual and natural enemy'.[47] But the 'United British Empire' to which the commissioners referred had nothing to do with a common obligation to contribute to the national revenue; nor was it clear whether this transatlantic polity would retain a uniform citizenship. During the preceding spring, the North ministry had taken the fateful step of sponsoring legislation renouncing forever Parliament's right to tax the American colonists. As a result, the Carlisle Commission's instructions included the authority to negotiate directly with Congress, 'as if it were a legal body'.[48] As the Scottish painter, Allan Ramsay, remarked in 1777, the war was neither a dispute with a foreign enemy nor one with a domestic opponent. Instead, there had

> lately started up to view in America a new class of men, who will be found upon examination to belong to neither of those two classes; who for that reason, give great perplexity both to the Government and people of England, and [who] must ever continue to perplex them till their true nature, and their true relation to Great Britain is accurately known, and a suitable mode of proceeding with regard to them adopted.[49]

The limits of greater Britain

Historians have generally drawn one of the following conclusions from the situation that Ramsay so perceptively described. The first is that the appearance of this new class of people in America during the eighteenth century had already doomed Britain's grand experiment in imperial reform, even before George Grenville introduced his Stamp Bill in 1765.[50] The second conclusion is that the British government's belated recognition of this fact in 1783 eventually opened the way for a much more stable national identity to develop within the metropolitan confines of England, Scotland and Wales.[51] And finally, British historians have frequently remarked on the American Revolution's role in ushering in a period of authoritarian governance in order to check would-be imitators of the American example within the still substantial empire that the crown retained at the war's end in Canada, the Caribbean, West Africa, India and, of course, Ireland.[52]

There is no need to quarrel with any of these interpretations; however, the American Revolution arguably produced one further consequence, which was to convince the British as never before of the need for firm, clear boundaries not just between themselves and their European neighbours, but between their political centre, where a common sovereignty based on the ties of nationality and law could be assumed, and their imperial periphery, where it could not.[53] In this sense, the relief with which many Britons greeted the North ministry's decision in early 1778 to abandon the goal of colonial taxation was surely significant. Although the government remained committed to maintaining some sort of federal relationship with the colonists, many of North's own supporters welcomed his acknowledgement that Parliament's 'national' sovereignty could extend only so far. According to Henry Dundas, Scotland's 'slee' Lord Advocate, 'no miraculous illumination could ever persuade him that government should attempt impracticable things'.[54] Even North claimed – somewhat disingenuously – that he had never favoured taxing the colonists for revenue.[55] There was no question that the British were still fighting to preserve an imperial connection in North America. But the longest colonial war in modern British history ended up underscoring the vast differences between the breadth of Parliament's authority at home and the attenuated powers that it could reasonably hope to exercise abroad.

In this respect, moreover, the American Revolution cast a long shadow indeed. As the great imperial historian, Sir John Seeley, would write exactly a century after the war's end, the 'secession' of the North American colonies left 'in the English mind a doubt, a misgiving, which affects our whole forecast of the future of England'.[56] This uncertainty over Britain's imperial future was partly a natural outgrowth of the predominance within the Victorian empire of racially distinct dominions like India. Yet the problems that haunted imperialists like Seeley had at least as much to do with the way that the American Revolution stunted the development of a common nationality and a uniform system of government and law, even among colonies that were firmly under the control of white settlers. In a sense, the United States came to stand as an enduring testimonial to the limits of colonial patriotism throughout the British Empire, including the Protestant, English-speaking peoples who dominated regions like the West Indies, Upper Canada and Ireland.[57] By the time of George III's death in 1820, the British Empire included nearly a quarter of the world's total population. But it was not at all clear how many of these subject peoples belonged to the late monarch's native country.

Notes

*   Earlier versions of this chapter were presented to the North American Conference on British Studies (NACBS) and to the Conference on Anglo-American Attitudes, jointly sponsored by the NACBS and the Royal Historical Society at Harvard University. I wish to thank the participants for their helpful comments and suggestions, and to acknowledge the assistance of Bernard Bailyn, Linda Colley, Nicoletta Gullace, Fred Leventhal and Peter Marshall.

1.   *London Evening Post*, 25 February 1775, as quoted in R. C. Simmons and P. D. G. Thomas (eds), *Proceedings and Debates of the British Parliaments Respecting North America, 1754–1783*, 6 vols covering 1754–76 (White Plains, NY, 1982–86), vol. 5, pp. 435–6.

2.   In one of the more interesting inversions of the American Revolution, the Tory polemicist John Shebbeare, who had been prosecuted during the Seven Years War for criticizing George II's partiality to his native Hanover, published a defence of the North ministry in which he claimed that the coming war in America would be the first ever undertaken solely on behalf of the 'common people' of Britain: J. Shebbeare, *An Essay on the Origin, Progress and Establishment of National Society* (London, 1776).

3.   Linda Colley, *Britons: Forging the Nation, 1707–1837* (New Haven, CT, 1992), pp. 117–32; David Armitage, 'Making the Empire British: Scotland in the Atlantic World, 1542–1707', *Past and Present*, 155 (May 1997), 62–3.

4.   S. J. Connolly, 'Varieties of Britishness: Ireland, Scotland and Wales in the Hanoverian State', in A. Grant and K. J. Stringer (eds), *Uniting the Kingdom? The Making of British History* (London, 1995), pp. 193–207.

5.   *Reflections upon the Present State of Affairs, at Home and Abroad, Particularly with Regard to Subsidies, and the Differences between Great Britain and France. In a Letter from a Member of Parliament to a Constituent* (London, 1755), p. 29; *A Letter from Sir William **** Deputy Lieutenant of the County of **** to his Tenants and Neighbours. Seriously recommended at this Time to the Perusal of the People of England* (London, 1757), p. 10. The most thorough study of British involvement in trade with the colonies is David Hancock, *Citizens of the World: London Merchants and the Integration of the British Atlantic Community, 1735–1785* (Cambridge, 1995).

6.   The clearest statement of the rights of immigrants is in the Naturalization Act of 1740. For the status of both immigrants and native Britons in colonial America, see James H. Kettner, *The Development of American Citizenship, 1608–1870* (Chapel Hill, NC, 1978), esp. pp. 74–5.

7.   Kathleen Wilson, 'Empire, Trade and Popular Politics in Mid-Hanoverian Britain: The Case of Admiral Vernon,' *Past and Present*, 121 (1988), 74–109; Eliga H. Gould, *The Persistence of Empire: British Political Culture in the Age of the American Revolution* (Chapel Hill, NC, and London, 2000), ch. 2.

8. Jonas Hanway, *An Account of the Society for the Encouragement of the British Troops in Germany and North America* (London, 1760), pp. 52–3 n.

9. [William Pulteney, Earl of Bath], *Reflections on the Domestic Policy, Proper to be observed on the Conclusion of a Peace* (London, 1763), pp. 66, 68. According to Bath, 'Great Britain now forms one united state' (ibid., p. 65).

10. T. H. Breen, to cite but one example, has recently argued that metropolitan support for American taxation reflected the British conviction that the colonists were different and inferior and thus not deserving of the full 'rights of Englishmen': 'Ideology and Nationalism on the Eve of the American Revolution: Revisions *Once More* in Need of Revising', *Journal of American History*, 84 (1997), 13–39.

11. [Thomas Whately], *The Regulations Lately Made concerning the Colonies, and the Taxes Imposed upon Them, considered* (London, 1765), p. 109.

12. Simmons and Thomas, *Proceedings and Debates*, vol. 2, p. 169.

13. Thomas Pownall, *The Administration of the Colonies*, 4th edn (London, 1768), pp. 138–40.

14. [Sir John Dalrymple], *Considerations upon the Different Modes of Finding Recruits for the Army* (London, 1775), p. 14.

15. John Butler, *A Sermon Preached before the Honourable House of Commons, at the Church of St. Margaret's Westminster, on Friday, December 13, 1776; Being the Day appointed by His Majesty's Royal Proclamation, to be observed as a Day of solemn Fasting and Humiliation* (London, 1777), p. 10.

16. Henry Stebbing, *A Sermon on the Late General Fast, preached at Gray's Inn Chapel, on Friday the 13th Day of December, 1776, before the Worshipful the Master of the Bench, of the Honourable Society of Gray's Inn, and Published at their Request* (London, 1776), p. 4.

17. *A Letter to the Earl of Shelburne on the Peace* (London, 5 February 1783), pp. 13–14.

18. Wilkes to Junius, 6 November 1771, BL Add. MSS 30,881, fo. 27.

19. Speech of 20 December 1777, in William Stanhope Taylor and John Henry Pringle (eds), *Correspondence of William Pitt, Earl of Chatham*, 4 vols (London, 1838–40), vol. 4, pp. 454–5 n.

20. [J. Lind], *An Answer to the American Congress* (London, 1776), 98–9 n. See also Margaret Avery, 'Toryism in the Age of the American Revolution: John Lind and John Shebbeare', *Historical Studies*, 18 (1978), 24–36. Lind's pamphlet went through at least five editions during 1776 alone.

21. Letter dated 29 May 1775, in *Calendar of Home Office Papers of the Reign of George III, 1773–1775*, ed. R. A. Roberts (London, 1899), p. 366.

22. Anon. to Robert Carter Nicholas, 22 September 1775, PRO, CO 5/40/1, fo. 22; anon., 22 September 1775, PRO CO 5/40/1, fo. 17.

23. *A Letter from an Officer at New York to a Friend in London* (London, 1777), p. 3.

24. *Reflections on the Present Combination of the American Colonies against the Supreme Authority of the British Legislature, and their Claim to Independency. By a real Friend to Legal Liberty and the Constitution* (London, 1777), p. 7.

25. Letter from the Revd Mr [Charles] Inglis, New York, 31 October 1776, in *The Proceedings of the Society for the Propagation of the Gospel in Foreign Parts, from the 16th Day of February, 1776, to the 21st Day of February, 1777* (London, 1777), p. 7.

26. Myles Cooper, *National Humiliation and Repentance recommended, and the Causes of the Present Rebellion in America assigned, in a Sermon Preached before the University of Oxford, on Friday, December 13, 1776* (Oxford, 1777), p. 15.

27. For the higher clergy's reluctance to use explicitly Tory language or to turn the contest into a struggle over Anglican principles, see Eliga H. Gould, 'American Independence and Britain's Counter-Revolution', *Past and Present*, **154** (February 1997), 123–8; Paul Langford, 'The English Clergy and the American Revolution', in E. Hellmuth (ed.), *The Transformation of Political Culture: England and Germany in the Late Eighteenth Century* (Oxford, 1990), pp. 125–6.

28. *The History of the Civil War in America*, 2 vols (London, 1780), vol. 1, p. 87.

29. Butler, *A Sermon Preached ... on Friday, December 13, 1776*, pp. 17–18.

30. [Samuel Johnson], *Taxation No Tyranny; An Answer to the Resolutions and Address of the American Congress* (London, 1775), in D. J. Greene (ed.), *Political Writings*, vol. 10 of *The Yale Edition of the Words of Samuel Johnson* (New Haven, CT, 1977), p. 454.

31. Simmons and Thomas, *Proceedings and Debates*, vol. 6, p. 203.

32. For the larger problem of law and Britain's empire, see J. G. A. Pocock, 'The Limits and Divisions of British History: In Search of the Unknown Subject,' *American Historical Review*, **87** (1982), 320–31; Jack P. Greene, *Peripheries and Center: Constitutional Development in the Extended Polities of the British Empire and the United States, 1607–1788* (Athens, GA, 1986).

33. Barrington to General Thomas Gage, 1 August 1768, Suffolk Record Office, HA174/1026/107, fos 107–8.

34. See [Thomas Bradbury Chandler], *A Friendly Address to all Reasonable Americans, on the Subject of our Political Confusions: In which the Necessary Consequences of Violently opposing the King's Troops, and of a General Non-Importation, are Fairly Stated* (London, 1774), p. 26; [John Dalrymple], *The Address of the People of Great Britain to the Inhabitants of America* (London, 1775), pp. 3–5; *Conciliatory Address to the People of Great Britain and of the Colonies, on the Present Important Crisis* (London, 1775), pp. 21–4; [John Lind], *An Answer to the Declaration of the American Congress* (London, 1776), p. 94.

35. [George Chalmers], *An Answer from the Electors of Bristol, to the Letter of Edmund Burke, Esq., on the Affairs of America* (London, 1777), pp. 23–4. See also *A Letter from an Officer at New York*, p. 7; Edward Topham, *An Address to Edmund Burke, Esq. on his late Letter Relative to the Affairs of America* (London, 1777), p. 4.

36. *A Letter to the Earl of Chatham, concerning his Speech and Motion in the House of Lords, on the memorable 30th of May* (London, 1777), p. 17.

37. *A Letter to Lord George Germaine, Giving an Account of the Origin of the Dispute between Great Britain and the Colonies* (London, 1778), p. 15.

38. A. Ferguson, 'Notes on House of Commons Inquiry into Sir William Howe' (n.d.), enclosed in Ferguson to Eden, 10 May 1779, BL Add. MSS 34,416, fo. 333.
39. *King v. John Horne*, 4 July 1777, PRO, TS 11/24/62, fos 19 and 112.
40. Carlisle, Clinton and Eden to Germaine, BL Add. MSS 34,416, fo. 60b. For the failure of civil government, see Joseph S. Tiedemann, 'Patriots by Default: Queens County, New York, and the British Army, 1776–1783', *William and Mary Quarterly*, 34d Ser., XLIII (1986), 49; John Shy, 'British Strategy for Pacifying the Southern Colonies, 1778–1781,' in J. J. Crow and L. E. Tise (eds), *The Southern Experience in the American Revolution* (Chapel Hill, NC, 1978), pp. 155–73; Ira D. Gruber, 'Britain's Southern Strategy,' in W. R. Higgins (ed.), *The Revolutionary War in the South: Power, Conflict, and Leadership* (Durham, NC, 1979), pp. 205–38.
41. Letter from Capt. John Bowater, 4 April 1777, in Tiedemann, 'Patriots by Default', p. 49. See also Catherine S. Carry, 'Guerrilla Activities of James DeLancey's Cowboys in Westchester County: Conventional Warfare or Self-Interested Freebooting', in R. A. East and J. Judd (eds), *The Loyalist American: A Focus on Greater New York* (Tarrytown, NY, 1973), pp. 14–21.
42. Letter from Cutting to Secretary of the SPG, 9 December 1781, in Tiedemann, 'Patriots by Default', p. 48.
43. Anon. letter from New York, dated 7 February 1778, in *Historical Anecdotes, Civil and Military: In a Series of Letters, written from America, in the years 1777 and 1778* (London, 1779), p. 71.
44. *A Letter from Edmund Burke, Esq., One of the Representatives in Parliament for the City of Bristol, to John Farr and John Harris, Esqrs. Sheriffs of that City, on the Affairs of America*, 2nd edn (London, 1777), pp. 11–12. For more on the British policy on the rules of war in America, see Piers Mackesy, *The War for America, 1775–1783* (Cambridge, MA, 1964), pp. 32–7.
45. *A Letter to Lieut. Gen. Burgoyne, on his Letter to his Constituents* (London, 1779), p. 19.
46. Anon. letter from New York, dated 7 February 1778, in *Historical Anecdotes Civil and Military: In a Series of Letters, written from America in the years 1777 and 1778*, (London, 1779), p. 65.
47. 'Manifesto and Proclamation to the Members of the Congress, the Members of the General Assemblies or Conventions of the Several Colonies, Plantations and Provinces ... by the Earl of Carlisle, Sir Henry Clinton, and William Eden' (New York, printed broadsheet, 3 October 1778), in BL Add. MSS 34,416, fo. 38.
48. William Cobbett (ed.), *The Parliamentary History of England from the Norman Conquest to the Year 1803*, 36 vols (London, 1806–20), vol. 19, p. 764.
49. [Allan Ramsay], *Letters on the Present Disturbances in Great Britain and her American Provinces* (London, 1777), p. 20.
50. The literature on this subject is vast, but see Bernard Bailyn, *The Ideological Origins of the American Revolution* (Cambridge, MA, 1967); Jack P. Greene, *Pursuits of Happiness: The Social Development of Early Modern British Colonies and the Formation of American Culture* (Chapel Hill, NC, 1988), esp. ch. 8.

51. Colley, *Britons*, 143–5.
52. C. A. Bayly, *Imperial Meridian: The First British Empire and the World, 1780–1830* (New York, 1989), pp. 8–15 and *passim*.
53. Gould, *Persistence of Empire*, ch. 6.
54. Cobbett, *Parliamentary History*, vol. 19, p. 803.
55. Ibid., 762–3.
56. J. R. Seeley, *The Expansion of England: Two Courses of Lectures* (Boston, 1900; first published, London, 1883), p. 17.
57. Eliga H. Gould, 'A Virtual Nation: Greater Britain and the Imperial Legacy of the American Revolution', *American Historical Review*, **104** (1999), 476–89. See also the special issue of the *International History Review*, **12**, 1 (1990) dealing with the colonial societies of the British empire following the American Revolution – esp. Carl Bridges, P. J. Marshall, Glyndwr Williams, 'Introduction: A "British" Empire', 2–10; Thomas Bartlett, '"A People Made Rather for Copies than Originals": The Anglo-Irish, 1760–1800', 11–25; and David Milobar, 'Conservative Ideology, Metropolitan Government, and the Reform of Quebec, 1782–1791', 45–64.

CHAPTER THREE

Transatlantic Trade in the
Era of the American Revolution

David Hancock

'A more intricate and complicated Subject never came into any Man's thoughts, than the Trade of America,' admitted John Adams in October 1775. 'The Questions that arise when one thinks of it, are very numerous.' 'If the Thirteen united Colonies, Should immediately Surcease all Trade with every Part of the World, what would be the Consequence?' Or if they induced foreign courts to offer them assistance 'and ask for our Trade or any Part of it,' what would be the result? Ultimately, Adams was equivocal: 'It is not easy for any Man precisely and certainly to answer this Question. We must then say all this is uncertain.'[1]

I

Adams's subject is no less uncertain today. For unwittingly or not, a disagreement (a paradox) has been written into the commercial history of his American Revolution and its economic aftermath. Some historians have argued that the war was a hiatus, and that the peace ushered in a resurgence of imperial British commercial domination and a return to American subservience. Other historians have argued that the war created a discontinuity with the trading and shipping patterns that prevailed before the war. Which of these is true? Or in what sense is either of them true?

That the Revolution was costly, destructive and economically disruptive is in little doubt. Foreign trade was seriously damaged. Foreign exports and imports nearly ground to a halt. Wartime manoeuvres destroyed the New England fishery and Indian trade. The call for troops and troop movements hampered the production and transportation of agricultural crops, like corn and wheat. The financial support provided by metropolitan and colonial governments to fledgling agricultural commodities, like hemp and indigo, dried up. Military demands for ships and containers channelled resources away from merchant fleets and stocks.[2] Furthermore, congressional and parliamentary prohibitions on British-American trade, passed between 1774 and 1776, closed traditional markets and, in the colonies, halted European imports.

The First Continental Congress was the first to impose restraints on trade with the British. In September 1774, hoping to induce Parliament to repeal a dozen imperial laws it found objectionable, it banned the import of British and Irish goods, India tea, British–American coffee, sugar, molasses and rum, Madeira wine, slaves and foreign indigo, and prohibited the export of American goods to Britain, Ireland or the British Caribbean islands. One month later, it framed the comprehensive non-importation/non-exportation/non-consumption agreement known as the Continental Association detailing the manner of the enforcement of the boycott and embargo.[3] The pact effectively closed America's ports, 'cutting all Trade with every Part of the World', since the Americans had no other official, permanent trading partners. The obstruction to foreign trade was relaxed somewhat in succeeding months: Congress discussed opening the ports in late 1775 and early 1776; certain exceptions having to do with ammunition and stores were approved in November 1775; and the resumption of a trade to foreign, non-British lands was allowed in April 1776.[4] But the boycott of 'British goods, wares and merchandises' persisted, and successfully crippled British-American commerce.

In retaliation, Britain's Parliament slapped several restraints upon the rebels. At the end of 1775, its Prohibitory Act proclaimed the open resistance in America to be treason, and prohibited all traffic to and from the rebellious colonies; several months later, it authorized both navy-men and privateers to seize all ships ignoring the prohibition. The restraints were not repealed until 1783.[5] Moreover, Britain's blockade of northern ports kept foreign goods from flowing inward. Although the Americans got round the blockade for a time between 1778 and 1782, with the aid of the French, Dutch and Spanish who had entered the war as their allies, the British, by attacking the Americans' ships more frequently, vigorously and successfully, frustrated this assistance in the last year of the war. Over the course of the conflict, the quantities of imports into the former Thirteen Colonies fell dramatically from the levels that had prevailed before the war.[6]

There is general agreement on the effect of the war on transatlantic commerce *during the war*. The open questions relate to the effect of the conflict *after the war* in separating post-war patterns of trading and shipping from pre-war patterns. Some historians have argued that the War for America and political independence had only a temporary commercial impact on the economy of the states, and that the former Thirteen Colonies quickly returned to Britain as their principal trading partner, despite the hurdles that the British raised against the Americans who desired to trade with the empire. Some contemporaries, usually those unlucky in business, made this point. Brailsford and Morris of Charleston, for instance, wrote to Thomas Jefferson that to

> see the whole Wealth of our Country centering in the Hands of our decided Enemies; to see nine tenths of our Produce carried out of our Ports by British vessels; and in walking our Streets, whether convinced by the Dialect, or the names of those who supply our wants, that we should rather conceive ourselves in the Highlands of Scotland, than in an American State, is the source of painful reflection to every Citizen.

And historians have repeated the point: the principal share of American exports reverted to Great Britain. Likewise, most American imports once again came from Great Britain: starved of familiar manufactures, and drawn by liberal commercial credit from British merchants, the Americans rushed to buy British goods in voluminous quantities. While the immediate political and constitutional consequences of the war were significant, the economic and commercial results were not. 'Only very slowly did the U.S. advance out of its colonial economy', John McCusker and Russell Menard have suggested. 'The decade immediately following the end of the war looked economically much the same as the decade preceding it, in basic structure, if not in detail.'[7]

Other scholars, even some of the historians who argue for the absence of significant change, have viewed the American Revolution as a commercial turning-point. The dislocation wrought by the war sowed the seeds for economic revival; these sprouted during the war and flourished thereafter – they were not crowded out by the persistence of older forms. Colonial industries, no longer hamstrung by imperial regulations, and no longer forced to compete with more desirable, better produced European manufactures, came into their own. Iron and steel, pottery, leather, textiles, gunpowder: all were in great demand by the two principal armies during the war, and by a population no longer well-supplied with European goods.[8] Likewise, '[t]he Trade of America being now open to the World', colonial entrepreneurs, at least those with patriot sympathies or neutral stands, thrived in industry, finance and commerce during and after the war, forming new pursuits, arrangements and partners. This was a period of 'commercial innovation' and 'entrepreneurial efflorescence'.[9]

The peace firmly established American independence in British–American trading and shipping. Many long-standing transatlantic networks for exchanging commodities were damaged beyond repair.[10] Consider the case of tobacco. The war, Jacob Price tells us, 'destroyed old trading patterns, and these could not always be easily restored'. The amount of tobacco imported by Great Britain fell by more than half between the periods 1771–75 and 1783–91, as did the amount re-exported by Great Britain. The Americans now routed their tobacco directly to consuming countries like France. Many Scots tobacco factors and storekeepers had been expelled during the war and, while some returned to the port towns after the war, most did not, especially those who had worked the backcountry. Everywhere, local merchant-planters had replaced them, and the new aggressive entrepreneurs were hard to dislodge.[11] And what was true for tobacco was true for foodstuffs, textiles, hardware and medicines.

The pre-war markets for American staples in the British West Indies and Great Britain were closed during the war, and most of them were not reopened to Americans in its aftermath. Post-war Orders in Council allowed the import of some American agricultural commodities like tobacco into Great Britain, and in American ships. Britain also permitted American pitch, lumber and biscuit to be imported into the British West Indies, and approved the export of certain British West Indian goods to the States. But these were enumerated exceptions. Something similar occurred with shipping. Before 1776, a third of all ships built in America had been sold in Britain; after 1783, such ships could not be sold in Britain. Moreover, unless specifically exempted, ships built in America and owned by Americans could not be used in trading with the far-flung British empire. And, in the area of finance, many credit relations were never resumed. The drop in commerce with Britain was significant, but it was not unique. Spain, too, which had been America's ally during the war, closed its colonies to the ships of US captains, and to some or all US goods.[12] The mercantilistic restrictions on markets were chronic and widespread. Export statistics suggest the magnitude of the phenomenon: per capita exports from the US were roughly 25 per cent lower in the period 1791–92 than in 1768–72.[13]

Thus, the war closed or restricted old destinations and cut off recipients of American goods and services. At the same time, it opened doors to new ones: American entrepreneurs formed new customers in northern Europe, the Netherlands, France, Africa and Asia. The general China trade and the African slave trade were now open for the first time to the Americans, and they pursued them with vigour.[14] As Robert East has noted, the Revolution 'legalized' 'the development of a new world-wide commerce'. By 1789, the outlook was good: 'commodity exports were at levels at least as good and perhaps a bit better than they were before the beginning of the American Revolution'.[15]

So which explanation adequately describes the war's effect on subsequent American commercial affairs? Both explanations are correct, as far as they go, with the evidence they marshal. But neither explanation goes far enough, and so neither on its own is fully convincing. The

British did reappear, but their reappearance was not as uncontested and, more importantly, not as dominant as some historians have claimed. New American trading and shipping patterns appeared after the war, deviating from pre-war norms, but these deviations were not as radical as other historians have averred.

The truth of the matter is that the post-war commercial world has not been well described or well analysed in any detail. Evidentiary problems have plagued such study. The one exception is the work of James Shepherd and Gary Walton, who have surveyed the macro-statistical data for commodity exports in the 1780s; but reliable series are extremely rare for the 1780s and 1790s, as they readily admit. None of America's imports (except for slaves) has been studied, although they were arguably as central as her exports to the development of her economy. What of imported iron and hardware, cloth, fruit, wine, sugar, tea and salt? Furthermore, few of the new or enhanced trade regions have been thoroughly examined. What of northern Europe, southern Europe, India and Asia? Only the China and India trades have been described in any detail, but the narratives are largely out of date and in need of more intensive analysis.[16] The conduct of the commodity trades, as well as of post-war relations with America's new trading partners, must be assessed not only through a sifting of contemporary large-scale statistical compilations, such as those used by Shepherd and Walton or printed in *The American State Papers*, but also through a series of closely worked case studies.

Equally debilitating to an understanding of America's new commercial place in the expanding Atlantic world are the strong conceptual blinkers of its historians. Students of the period have folded the commercial transformation into the military struggle and political revolution. This is misguided. Although the American Revolution is undeniably one of the great events of world history, it was essentially a political, military and constitutional event. Subsuming commerce into it can cause one to miss the nature of Atlantic commercial life at the end of the eighteenth century. There was a revolution in trade, to be sure, a transformation witnessed, experienced and commented on by contemporaries between 1763 and 1812, but that commercial revolution was not the *American* Revolution. The American Revolution affected commercial and economic processes that were already under way – the fantastic elaboration of markets in the Atlantic world, within and across imperial boundaries, and the aggressive extension of these Atlantic markets into Asia and northern Europe. This revolution in trade started before the American Revolution, and ended after it. The two revolutions influenced one another, but they were distinct. The American Revolution in some ways accelerated the trade revolution; in other ways, it retarded it. The overlap between the two revolutions explains the confusion of previous historians – some claiming a hiatus, and others a discontinuity. Understanding the overlap demands a broader, subtler approach. New patterns of trade, with new commodities and players, emerged after the war, and old patterns persisted. These patterns have as much to do with the extension and intensification of trends first arising in the colonial Atlantic past as with the military and political events of the 1770s and 1780s.

II

This chapter attempts to connect these patterns. It does so from the perspective of Atlantic shipping, drawing upon the case of Madeira wine for its examples. Madeira's case, it happens, provides useful material. It was a transimperial commodity produced in a Portuguese territory and distributed around the Atlantic rim by British and American merchants and captains. Moreover, it was an import into the American colonies whose distribution developed and ramified over the course of the eighteenth century. How, if at all, was the importation and distribution of Madeira's wine affected by the War for America, colonial independence and the larger economic revolution in Atlantic commerce?

At the heart of the Madeira wine trade was a commodity that was produced on the Portuguese island of Madeira, 500 miles west of Morocco, in the middle of the Atlantic, and 'invented' between the signing of the Methuen Treaty in 1703 and the British occupation of the island in 1807. At the beginning of the eighteenth century, Madeira wine was a simple table wine, made from a base of white must to which the growers and exporters added varying amounts of red must in order to give it the colour, body, smoothness and flavour consumers desired; by the beginning of the nineteenth century, Madeira was a complex, highly processed drink, increasingly made from single varietals and fortified, agitated, aged, heated and packaged in custom-sized, custom-labelled and custom-decorated containers.[17]

The island's total must production did not rise much between 1703 and 1807. There was little change in normal output: in 1807, as in 1703, about 26 000 pipes (2.86 million gallons) of wine were produced. Nevertheless, as Table 3.1 and Figure 3.1 suggest, the traded volume rose. In the years from 1727 to 1807, the number of ships annually departing Funchal nearly doubled; and the quantity of wine they took with them more than doubled. Most of the expansion occurred in the last third of the period – after 1774 – a time when shipping prices of Madeira wine nearly doubled, ship departures almost tripled and wine

Table 3.1 Departures from the island of Madeira, 1727–1807

Year	Ships	Year	Ships
1727	57	1768	192
1728	202	1769	201
1729	154	1770	176
1730	140	1771	140
1731	152	1772	170
1732	140	1773	204
1733	146	1774	210
1734	149	1775	174
1735	180	1776	125
1736	161	1777	95
1737	152	1778	146
1738	156	1779	102
1739	96	1780	104
1740	118	1781	87
1741	114	1782	132
1742	145	1783	185
1743	143	1784	137
1744	116	1785	160
1745	109	1786	146
1746	105	1787	185
1747	98	1788	188
1748	133	1789	150
1749	157	1790	195
1750	150	1791	240
1751	136	1792	180
1752	135	1793	140
1753	133	1794	158
1754	142	1795	155
1755	115	1796	216
1756	9	1797	180
1757		1798	165
1758	91	1799	174
1759		1800	203
1760	64	1801	251
1761	79	1802	267
1762	37	1803	234
1763	154	1804	315
1764	186	1805	294
1765	181	1806	266
1766	159	1807	246
1767	197		

Source: Livros dos Entradas e Saidas, Provedoria e Junta da Real Fazenda, Arquivo Nacional da Torre do Tombo, Lisbon.

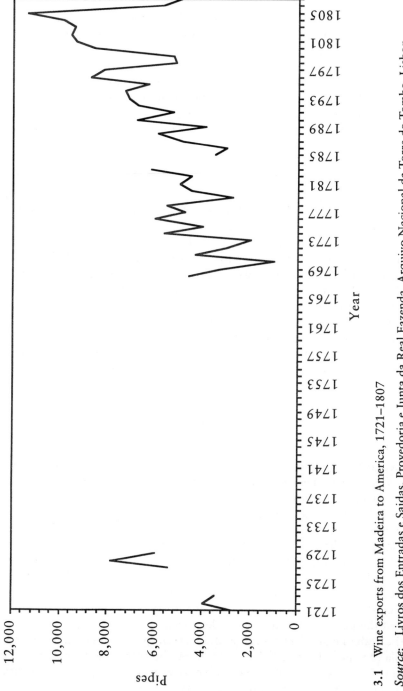

3.1 Wine exports from Madeira to America, 1721–1807

Source: Livros dos Entradas e Saidas, Provedoria e Junta da Real Fazenda, Arquivo Nacional da Torre do Tombo, Lisbon.

exports tripled. Wine that had previously been allocated for local consumption, manufactured into vinegar and brandy or marked for wastage was converted for export.

Chief among the destinations in the 1700s was British America. Exportation there began in the previous century, largely a function of geography and diplomacy. Transatlantic shipping surged overall during the seventeenth century, and British and American shipowners, cargo-owners and captains sought alternatives to spending one of the legs of the voyage in ballast. As Madeira was 'not much out of the way going down to the West Indies', it came to be regarded as 'generally worth a ship's while ... to touch' there, as it frequently 'met with some freight' that was of 'great service'. By taking on cargo in Madeira, British owners could recover some of their costs on two-thirds of an outbound voyage from Europe, and American owners could recoup all of their expenses on a return voyage to the colonies.[18] Moreover, British politicians and diplomats were keen to grant trade preferences to Portugal, as a means of checking the power of France. As early as 1663, Parliament exempted from import duties Madeira wines carried directly into British America. The exemption was unintentionally reinforced in 1703 by Paul Methuen's Commercial Treaty: by allowing Portuguese wines to pass into Britain at a third of the tariff charged on French wines, the treaty frustrated the desires of British re-exporters who wanted to develop a market in America for Madeira's greatest competitor in England, port.[19]

III

Geographic and economic logic, and mercantile law, as well as the presence of native substitutes in Spanish and Portuguese America, encouraged Madeira's distributors to concentrate on the market in British America.[20] Anecdotal mention of the ships leaving the island with wine suggests that the encouragement worked: according to one resident island merchant, more than two-thirds of all shipments in the years 1702–13 left for British America.[21] The more or less complete series of entrada books that begin in 1727 and list arrivals into and departures from the island confirms this dominance. The entrada records do not record outbound cargoes per se, but they do show ships' destinations and the pattern of Madeira's trade, which consisted almost entirely of the reshipment of European and American goods, and the export of island wine.[22] From 1727 to 1738, when the War of Jenkins' Ear broke out, 70 per cent of all departing ships went to the Americas. British settlements in the Caribbean were always the destination for the greatest share of the departing wine ships – never less than a third of them. British colonies to the north took a quarter, directly.[23]

War involving the Americas generally retarded the transatlantic wine trade. By the end of the Seven Years War, Madeira sent less than half its exports to British America. The British West Indies' share declined to 23 per cent during the period 1754–62, and Britain's North American colonies' share declined to 17 per cent in the same period. The struggles of the 1750s and 1760s were disruptive to Madeira shipping generally. Few vessels came to Madeira from Europe, on account of the high freights, high seamen's wages, and high insurance premiums induced by the threat of capture or destruction on the high seas.[24]

The Treaty of Paris (February 1763) ushered in a return to shipping patterns that had prevailed nearly 25 years before. The total share of Madeira ships going to British and European possessions in the Americas rose to 76 per cent, slightly more than had prevailed in the years before 1739; the share going to the British West Indies reached a new all-time high – 43 per cent – and the share going to British North America returned to its pre-war level – 24 per cent. Two new factors, in addition to the general resumption of trade following the peace, drove this renewal. The Treaty of Paris opened new lands to the British in the Caribbean and the parts of America wrung from the Indians in backcountry New York, west of the Appalachians, and in the Floridas. The resulting land rush introduced many new Madeira drinkers to the 'new' American world. In addition, to protect its expanded domain, the British stationed an occupation army in America; the expenditures it made to maintain the troops raised the ability of some Americans to purchase luxury and quasi-luxury imports.[25] Moreover, this increase occurred despite imperial reforms designed to tighten loopholes in the mercantile system. Parliament's 1764 Sugar Act imposed Crown duties on wines imported *directly* from Madeira and the Azores for the first time, setting them at £7 per ton, while it readjusted Crown duties on Portuguese and Spanish wines imported *indirectly* through Britain to £4 per ton. Petitions were presented and protests were staged in opposition to the new duty, but ultimately the colonists either acquiesced and paid or ignored the duty. Contrary to what Franklin testified to the House of Commons in 1766, the colonists could not either produce the goods themselves or forgo them altogether. Americans found themselves unwilling to do without their wine.[26] Some groups, like Virginia planters and Massachusetts firebrands, may have altered their habits; they certainly said they would. And prices were so high that other Americans may have refused to purchase, much less speculate in, the drink. But these threats seem to have had little effect on the level of imports.[27]

Subsequent duties, however, hardened American opposition and raised the rhetorical level. In response to Charles Townshend's duties on glass, paint, lead, tea and paper, first imposed in 1767, non-importation associations were formed in 1768 and 1769 in 12 of the 13 mainland colonies. While most groups simply banned goods from Britain or Europe (an area in which Madeira, which was generally described by geographers as lying in Africa, might not be grouped), the meetings in Maryland, Virginia, the Carolinas and Georgia specifically banned wines, and a few actually enumerated Madeira. In some places, the ban on Madeira was honoured, and 'a spirit of oeconomy' prevailed. In the end, however, the non-importers' resolve faltered and adherence to the ban was fitful. Everywhere, it was resented by the merchants who had distributed wine, even if they had voted for prohibiting its importation. In some places, it was ignored. Philadelphia wholesalers, for instance, continued to import the wine, arguing that the Madeira wine trade was a branch of the dry goods trade, an exception that had been recognized by the Pennsylvania non-importation association.[28] By 1770, after most colonies had repealed their bans, Madeira imports resumed as if nothing had happened. In the end, post-Townshend Acts attempts to use Madeira politically were more rhetorical than effective.

But something had happened: a precedent had been established. And so, when in autumn 1774 the First Continental Congress was looking for symbolic commodities to attack, it resolved to prohibit, among other things, the importation of all 'wines from Madeira, or the Western Islands [the Azores]' that came via Britain after November 1774, until the repeal of the duties considered most deleterious by the Americans to transatlantic trade. This time the ban stuck. In December 1774, Madeira distributors began to feel the pinch of the American independence movement.[29]

The years of the War for America witnessed a drastic decline in all wine exports from Madeira to British America, in large measure because of the interruptions in transatlantic communication and the hazards of transtlantic shipping. According to the *saidas* records, which begin in 1779, the British West Indies' share of Madeira's wine exports fell to 26 per cent during the war years (Table 3.2 and Figure 3.2). The Caribbean trade was decimated.[30] The 13 mainland colonies' share remained the same as before the war (roughly a quarter), but the pattern was different. All of 1779's shipments to the Thirteen Colonies, and two-thirds of 1780's and 1781's went to New York City, mostly for the use of the British Army and Navy stationed there during the conflict.[31] Most colonies imported nothing from Madeira during the war.[32]

As far as American importation and consumption are concerned, the world of wine was a very different place after 1783; the role of Madeira

Table 3.2 Wine exports from Madeira, 1779–1807 (pipes of 110 gallons)

	1779	1780	1781	1782	1783	1784	1785	1786	1787	1788	1789	1790	1791	1792	1793
British West Indies	2,239	1,399	2,051	2,606	3,205		2,373	2,249	2,971	3,726	2,285	4,154	4,883	5,001	4,335
13 Colonies/United States	369	3,073	2,915	1,903	2,973		1,118	568	1,695	1,961	1,402	2,647	386	1,564	2,550
Other British North America	125	0	0	0	0		0	174	187	252	228	0	0	164	218
European America	1,066	1,489	1,322	1,806	1,724		514	636	397	109	278	676	200	327	181
India, Asia and China	1,210	1,655	710	1,034	2,336		4,051	5,949	3,566	4,586	983	3,733	5,833	926	2,439
Other and None Listed	2,524	1,128	895	865	1,067		1,106	307	748	365	259	767	895	918	1,102

	1794	1795	1796	1797	1798	1799	1800	1801	1802	1803	1804	1805	1806	1807
British West Indies	3,659	3,283	5,468	5,149	3,301	4,883	6,076	6,624	6,890	6,303	5,838	8,651	3,288	3,635
13 Colonies/United States	3,419	3,035	2,913	2,588	1,485	386	2,307	2,231	2,369	2,927	3,549	2,468	2,342	1,301
Other British North America	195	0	341	448	374	0	165	481	291	122	449	273	49	0
European America	991	354	999	876	963	200	888	849	1,567	166	825	2,857	631	941
India, Asia and China	2,990	7,146	4,638	4,450	5,589	5,833	6,027	4,418	3,652	2,193	4,796	3,382	4,555	3,366
Other and None Listed	1,430	820	893	269	363	895	1,468	1,485	2,057	1,418	2,921	2,736	7,780	8,210

Source: Livros dos Entradas e Saídas, Provedoria e Junta da Real Fazenda, Arquivo Nacional da Torre do Tombo, Lisbon.

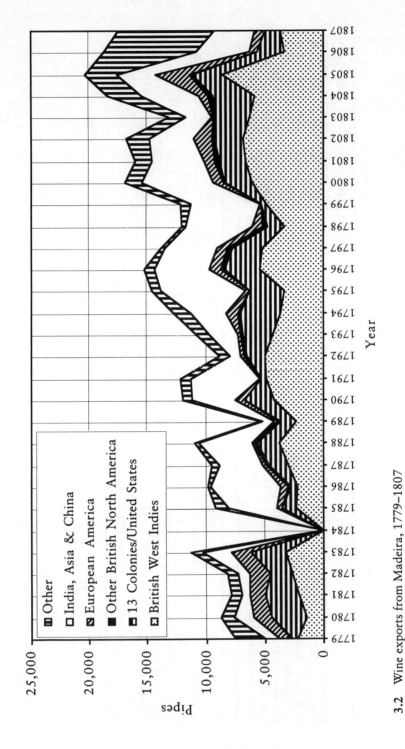

3.2 Wine exports from Madeira, 1779–1807

Source: Livros dos Entradas e Saidas, Provedoria e Junta da Real Fazenda, Arquivo Nacional da Torre do Tombo, Lisbon.

wine in the drinking life of the new nation fell from the almost unchallenged place it had held before 1775. Information on imports into America before the Revolution comes chiefly from the Naval Office Shipping Lists, quarterly accounts of all ships entering and exiting colonial ports that were kept by naval officers appointed by the Treasury and resident in the colonial ports.[33] Although not complete for all colonies for all years, their record of goods entered is quite full, and it is possible to use these data to construct a portfolio of wine imports, summarize the state of consumer preferences, and track changes in tastes between 1700 and 1775. Madeira dominates wine imports throughout the period (Table 3.3). Grouping all British North American port entries together, one finds that 64 per cent of all imported wine came from Madeira, 7 per cent from the Azores and 10 per cent from the Canaries. In contrast, wines from the Portuguese mainland, which dominated the market of England and Wales, comprised only 0.3 per cent of American wine imports, and wines from the Spanish mainland only slightly more – 1.3 per cent.[34]

In sum, some colonies imported well above the average percentage of Madeira: 84 per cent of New York's wines were Madeira, and this did not change much over the course of the century; similarly, 77 per cent of Virginia's wines were Madeira. But not all colonies preferred the wine to such an extent. Massachusetts, for instance, had a flourishing fish trade with southern Europe and the Wine Islands (not just Madeira but also the Azores and Canaries); over a third of Massachusetts' wines came from the Azores and another eighth came from the Canaries; only a fifth came from Madeira. However, overall and at least until the outbreak of the war, Madeira remained America's choice.

That dominance did not persist in the post-war period. Separation from Great Britain checked the trend, and connection with other countries weakened it further. Gradually, Madeira's hold on the American wine market slipped, as Table 3.4 suggests. In the years for which import data have survived – 1789–1806 – Madeira wine as a share of the quantity of all wines imported into the United States fell from 31 per cent in 1789–90 to 8 per cent in 1805–06. The volume of Madeira wine exported to the states rose in absolute terms – by one liberal estimate, roughly sixfold – between the 1750s and 1790s. But by the 1790s wines from other wine-producing countries, like Spain and France, were now regularly imported, and in large quantities, and they were taxed at lower rates and sold at lower prices. Sherry and St Lucar wines, to take just two cases, came into vogue; indeed, in half of the years between 1793 and 1807, the quantity of sherry imports actually exceeded that of Madeira. Nevertheless, despite the greater variety of wines and the stiff competition raised by the likes of sherry wine,

Table 3.3 Kinds of wines imported into the Thirteen Colonies, 1700–75

Year	Total pipes	Madeira pipes	Azorean pipes	Portuguese pipes	Canary pipes	Spanish pipes	Other Wines pipes
1700	14.0	5.0	3.0	0.0	0.0	0.0	6.0
1701	58.0	50.0	3.0	0.0	0.0	0.0	5.0
1702	2.0	1.0	4.6	0.0	0.0	0.0	0.0
1703	431.5	2.0	3.0	0.0	0.0	0.0	9.0
1704	598.1	0.0	0.0	0.0	0.0	0.0	5.0
1705	299.7	0.0	0.0	0.0	0.0	0.0	0.0
1706	179.5	0.0	0.0	0.0	0.0	0.0	0.0
1707	110.5	0.0	0.0	0.0	0.0	0.0	0.0
1708		0.0	0.0	0.0	0.0	0.0	0.0
1709		0.0	0.0	0.0	0.0	0.0	0.0
1710		0.0	0.0	0.0	0.0	0.0	0.0
1711		0.0	0.0	0.0	0.0	0.0	0.0
1712		0.0	0.0	0.0	0.0	0.0	0.0
1713	436.8	388.8	0.0	0.0	0.0	0.0	48.0
1714	355.8	245.5	0.0	0.0	0.0	0.0	110.3
1715	578.5	527.0	0.0	0.0	0.0	0.0	51.5
1716	682.5	646.5	35.0	0.0	0.0	0.0	1.0
1717	1,128.3	713.3	225.0	0.0	20.0	0.0	170.0
1718	977.6	605.5	336.5	0.0	1.0	0.0	34.6
1719	690.5	552.5	134.0	0.0	0.0	0.0	4.0
1720	516.5	515.5	0.0	0.0	0.0	0.0	1.0
1721	368.1	352.5	0.0	0.0	15.6	0.0	0.0
1722	498.0	422.5	0.0	0.0	75.5	0.0	0.0
1723	98.6	81.5	17.1	0.0	0.0	0.0	0.0
1724	952.1	919.0	0.1	0.0	22.0	0.0	11.0
1725	400.4	320.8	60.0	0.0	10.0	1.0	8.7
1726	931.3	598.8	0.0	0.0	287.0	33.0	12.5
1727	745.6	584.8	93.1	0.0	2.0	0.3	65.5
1728	1,103.3	1,058.3	0.0	0.0	1.0	12.0	32.0
1729	338.3	287.3	0.0	0.0	11.0	0.0	40.0
1730	466.5	399.0	0.0	0.0	20.3	0.0	47.3
1731	1,536.8	1,355.3	0.0	0.0	14.5	0.0	167.0
1732	765.0	420.5	0.0	0.0	0.0	0.0	344.5
1733	814.5	784.0	0.0	0.0	2.0	0.0	28.5
1734	873.3	744.3	0.0	0.0	5.0	0.0	124.0
1735	1,141.8	1,093.8	0.0	0.0	15.0	2.0	31.0
1736	633.0	331.5	0.0	0.0	103.0	0.0	198.5
1737	775.0	557.0	8.0	0.0	75.0	19.3	115.8
1738	1,425.2	968.8	0.0	0.0	423.3	9.0	24.2
1739	1,726.4	908.9	0.0	0.0	659.3	94.0	64.3
1740	1,126.1	1,071.2	1.0	5.0	2.0	3.0	43.9

Table 3.3   concluded

Year	Total pipes	Madeira pipes	Azorean pipes	Portuguese pipes	Canary pipes	Spanish pipes	Other Wines pipes
1741	1,135.4	1,076.3	0.0	8.0	1.0	0.0	50.1
1742	730.5	725.8	0.0	0.0	0.0	0.0	4.8
1743	767.3	717.0	0.0	5.0	0.0	0.0	45.3
1744	1,069.5	568.3	0.0	29.0	0.0	0.0	29.5
1745	699.7	147.8	0.0	0.0	1.1	1.0	109.3
1746	837.4	456.8	0.0	0.0	0.0	3.0	45.8
1747	836.0	354.5	0.0	0.0	0.0	5.0	0.0
1748	1,447.1	1,322.2	8.0	0.0	0.0	0.0	113.4
1749	2,102.9	1,064.3	11.0	0.0	0.0	0.0	39.6
1750	1,061.6	717.7	0.0	0.0	101.5	0.0	167.3
1751	1,822.3	707.9	64.0	1.0	0.0	0.0	318.7
1752	554.7	296.7	0.0	0.0	0.0	0.0	258.0
1753	718.9	395.0	308.5	0.0	0.0	0.0	15.4
1754	1,269.5	498.3	641.8	0.0	80.0	0.0	49.5
1755	815.9	308.5	130.3	7.2	61.5	0.0	308.4
1756	547.6	226.5	104.0	0.0	10.0	0.0	207.1
1757	274.0	110.9	100.0	0.0	0.0	0.0	62.9
1758	1,708.0	995.0	130.0	0.0	486.0	0.0	97.1
1759	901.5	211.5	62.0	0.0	613.8	0.0	14.3
1760	992.8	444.0	104.8	0.0	201.0	0.0	243.0
1761	683.5	88.5	113.8	0.0	262.5	0.0	218.8
1762	776.0	200.5	222.5	0.0	5.0	124.0	236.3
1763	4,192.0	1,243.9	271.8	30.0	1,460.0	357.5	808.8
1764	2,641.2	1,770.9	454.6	60.0	82.4	0.0	277.3
1765	874.9	65.8	177.8	1.0	8.3	39.8	537.4
1766	699.1	280.3	76.8	9.3	115.3	76.8	176.1
1767	100.3	43.5		0.1	33.5	3.0	2.1
1768	1,827.7	633.4					541.8
1769	1,109.9	40.8			0.2		523.5
1770	619.9						364.0
1771	1,005.5						572.0
1772	964.8						580.0
1773							
1774							
1775							
Total	59,565.8	33,224.1	3,904.8	155.6	5,287.3	783.5	8,821.2
% of Total		58.6	6.9	0.3	9.3	1.4	15.6

Source: Naval Office Shipping Lists, Public Record Office, London, as detailed in note 34.

Table 3.4   Wine imports into the United States, 1789–1806

Year	Madeira Wine pipes	Other Wine pipes	Spirits pipes	Beer, Ale and Porter pipes
1789–90	2,464	5,607	34,949	826
1790–91	2,815	6,987	36,070	1,109
1791–92				
1792–93				
1793–94				
1794–95	4,770	22,879	51,087	3,690
1795–96	3,246	20,578	50,968	3,005
1796–97	3,490	18,148	54,813	2,592
1797–98	1,780	9,298	48,073	1,125
1798–99	851	17,539	72,623	3,380
1799–1800	1,862	20,718	43,369	2,650
1800–01	2,548	22,164	72,118	1,964
1801–02	2,102	25,577	76,334	1,512
1802–03	3,024	16,946	80,222	2,058
1803–04	3,829	35,354	107,226	1,142
1804–05	2,897	54,028	53,786	1,791
1805–06	3,318	40,551	99,929	3,535
1806–07				

Source: *American State Papers: Documents, Legislative and Executive, of the Congress of the United States*, vol. 7 (Class IV): *Commerce and Navigation*, vol. 1 (Washington, DC, 1832), as detailed in note 35.

Madeira remained the single largest wine import – 'the demand for our wines in America' and especially 'the taste for fine old wines', one exporter observed, 'increases daily & must continue to increase with the opulence of the country'. Given its high market price ('fine old wines' commanded the highest price and 'the premium of bill'), Madeira's share of the value of all wines was still unmatched.[35]

IV

It appears, therefore, that there is evidence to suggest a hiatus in the trade. But is this all? A consideration of Madeira's trade must necessarily begin with its trade to North America: the Madeirans would have understood it that way. Thus construed, Madeira's trade is a particularly good example of the growth of 'the Atlantic world' economy, a topic which has received increasing amounts of attention in recent years. But the story of Madeira is broader still, for from it two critical, transformative trends emerge. First, to refer to 'Atlanticization' is somewhat misleading, for what is really at work is globalization. This chapter focuses on the Madeira wine trade, but to portray the developments in that trade accurately, one cannot examine the American trade unless one situates it alongside the India trade. Second, in addition to globalization there is Americanization. Americans were of course taking an increasingly creative and vigorous role in this expansion of world trade, and certainly the American Revolution made a difference in how American entrepreneurialism was channelled. But, and this is critical, the entrepreneurialism was on the rise throughout the century.

British India had been a destination for Madeira's wine for decades, and in the 1760s its consumption had grown dramatically. The first record of an official East India Company purchase of a cargo occurs in 1716, when Joseph Hayward consigned Madeira wine to Fort William (Calcutta) on board the *King William*. Unlike previous cargoes of claret, Florence and mountain wines, Madeira pleased. Acting on favourable reports two years later, the Court of Directors of the East India Company ordered 100 pipes of Madeira to be shipped each year to Fort St George (Madras) and her other factories.[36] Thereafter, a taste for Madeira spread rapidly. One cellar held up as model in the 1740s contained 4 bottles of beer, 12 bottles of Claret, and 100 bottles of Madeira.[37] In response to rising demand, a more elaborate system of procurement was introduced by the 1740s. The Forts ordered wine from the Directors, who in turn directed one or two of their ships to stop at the island for Madeira.[38]

After Clive's victory at the Battle of Plassey (1757) and the assumption of territorial rule, the India market increased significantly. The Company began directing three to six 'Company' ships per year to stop at Madeira on their voyage to the subcontinent; it also began allowing other 'extra' India-bound ships to venture on their own. Whereas India had been a destination for only 0.6 per cent of all ships departing Funchal in the period 1727–39, it had become a stop for 2.4 per cent in the aftermath of the Seven Years War.[39] 'The want of a Madeira ship,' which the Directors occasionally thought dispensable, laid a Presidency 'under a very great Inconvenience, which is particularly felt by the gentlemen of the Army whose fatigues required that they should be indulged with every refreshment that can be afforded for their relief'. While 'other Wines, as Lisbon & c.' might have been had 'in lieu thereof', the foreigners who imported these wines raised their prices 'in proportion to the Necessity'. 'Immoderate rates' and the fact that

Madeira was regarded as 'necessary to health' ensured a stop at the island.[40] During the 1760s and 1770s, 'unexpected demand' from the subcontinent was the order of the day and seriously disrupted traditional ways of doing business on Madeira. Superior wines were depleted, for instance, and inferior wines called into service. The London partners of Madeira wine firms jockeyed for the much coveted annual contracts, even if the right to supply was usually granted to those with partners previously or presently on the Court of Directors.[41]

To compensate for the loss of Caribbean markets and the disruptions in the North American trade during the American Revolution, some distributors turned to Great Britain or northern Europe; almost all looked eastward.[42] Island traders cultivated markets in India (mainly Fort William, Fort St George and Bombay, but also Combroon, Bussora and Fort Marlboro) and China ('that important branch of our Commerce'), especially Canton, Macao and Limpao. Conservative British and British-American firms that had previously been reluctant to enter eastern markets now accepted India contracts and developed consumer bases in that part of the world. Portuguese merchants were particularly adept at exploiting the new India trade: 'the natives,' Joseph Gillis informed his partner Henry Hill in Philadelphia, had 'got much into the spirit of trading' with the subcontinent by 1783 – 'no less than 4,000 pipes having been sent annually to India, for these four years past, and all in Portuguese ships & shipped by Portuguese'. Overall, India, China and other settlements in Asia absorbed roughly 16 per cent of Madeira's exports during the war.[43]

India, China and Asia markets allowed the Madeirans to weather overseas storms towards the end of the century. In the eight years between the close of the American Revolutionary conflict in 1783 and the outbreak of the French Revolutionary wars in 1792, the share taken by the India, China and Asia settlements (40 per cent of Madeira's exports) rose, as did the share taken by the British West Indies (33 per cent).[44]

V

As previously noted, the trade in Madeira's wine must be viewed in the context of two long-term transformative changes. First, the trade was globalized. As the decades passed, India, China and Asia became increasingly important to its conduct, and the evolution of America's relations with the island must always be viewed with the East as a backdrop. Second, there occurred another transformation – to wit, how the trade was Americanized. This is the story of the rise of the

Americans, and it is one that falls on both sides of the discontinuity/ hiatus bedevilling historians.

Turning first to the trading realm, the size of Madeira's merchant group tripled over the century and, as it did so, the roles played by the different national groups changed. The Portuguese always dominated the trade – in terms of the numbers of merchants and, early on, before 1703, in terms of the share of the wine they distributed. But by the 1750s and 1760s the most important traders were the British. In 1721, the earliest year for which there are reliable records, there were 63 exporters, of whom nine were British; all but one of the rest were Portuguese. Six years later, at least 160 exporters lived and worked on the island, and among these were 25 British (including four Irish and two Americans). By 1768, when the merchant group had grown to 216, the Portuguese still formed the overwhelming majority of the merchants (80 per cent), and the Britons still shipped the bulk of the trade. Among the latter, Scots had assumed a fairly strong position, forming more than a third of British residents. Six Americans had joined the ranks.[45] Nine of the ten largest shippers were British, including two of the Americans. By 1807, the number of British and American merchants increased to 67, and the British firms had shut the American distributors out of the top ten.

American colonists first came to the island to reside there and trade in significant numbers during and after the Seven Years War. They arrived in greater numbers during and after the Revolution, hoping to assume the North American clientele that the British could no longer claim by imperial fiat. This post-war American community on the island was relatively small – never greater than a dozen or so on the island at any one time – and its composition fluctuated greatly. Some houses failed. The small partnerships headed by Henry, Valentine and Robert Cock of Maryland, George and Thomas Patten of Maryland, and James Jenkins of Philadelphia, which had mushroomed in the euphoric speculation of the 1760s and early 1770s, were folded into British firms. Other firms unravelled slowly in the natural course of the evolution of family business, as did the three-generation house of Lamar, Hill, Bisset and Co., when the senior partners of the third generation decided to diversify their activities and establish residence in Philadelphia. Still other firms collapsed from fiscal imprudence; such was the case with the business managed by John Searle III and John Colpoys, who escaped their creditors in 1798 by fleeing – Searle to the Cape of Good Hope and Colpoys to Ireland – and Searle's cousin the American Consul John Marsden Pintard, whose imprudent financial and commercial speculations forced him to close up shop and return to Philadelphia and New York in 1799. Yet, their places were taken by new arrivals. In

1807, six or seven American merchants were counted among the island's leading merchants. Although they had fallen off the list of the ten largest exporters, the Americans had wrested the North American customers away from the British who had previously supplied them.[46]

Some British firms, not surprisingly, made attempts to return to the old familiar track, and some of these remained optimistic. William Johnston, for instance, tried thwarting attempts by his firm to move into the Bombay trade with a call to return to the Americans. 'In consequence of the peace', he wrote his partners in London, 'we look forward to America as a principal mart of our produce, and a country whence we may bring commodities to this market with more success than our importation has of late years been attended with.'[47] But Johnston was in the minority. Most firms were extremely wary of doing much business in America. The post-war depression was slow to lift, the pre-war debts of many Americans remained on their books, and the lack of transportation in North America and the destruction of what had existed dampened hopes for making great inroads into frontier markets. In addition, official American attitudes about European luxuries shifted between 1783 and 1793 – away from direct boycott and embargo as mechanisms for expressing disapproval and towards indirect discouragement though the imposition of high duties to finance the state.[48]

When British firms did attempt to renew commercial relations, the response was not positive. In writing to the Bostonian John Rowe, with whom his firm had done business for two decades, John Leacock suggested that 'the long unhappy contention of late years in America', which deprived Madeirans of 'all communication with the Continent', was the reason his firm had not written in eight years. Writing 'now these obstacles are removed & peace again restored', Leacock hoped to resume his shipments 'on the same footing ... as formerly'. Ominously, Rowe did not bother to reply to even one of his seven letters. He had already arranged for an annual supply of wine from the American firm John Searle and Co.[49]

Yet when external circumstances or prospects improved, and most houses returned to former correspondence with gusto, the British fared no better, perhaps worse because they had waited so long to return. The American houses, on the other hand, had wasted no time. By 1789, most people cognizant of the trade acknowledged that, even if the share of all wine taken by Madeira wine had shrunk since pre-war times, the bulk of the supply that continued was engrossed by two firms: Lamar, Hill, Bisset and Co. which supplied a preponderance of the customers from Philadelphia southward, and Searle and Co. which supplied those to the north. Time and again the story was the same: the Americans in

Madeira succeeded in winning and keeping American customers that the British in Madeira had educated and served for decades.[50]

In contrast to the *trading* realm, where gains were sometimes halting and imperceptible and where, after a revolution that reorganized national and imperial boundaries, Americans were squeezed into accepting a smaller role than the one they appeared to be enjoying in the third quarter of the century, in the *shipping* realm, Americans advanced to parity with the British in shipping Madeira wine after the Revolution. In 1727, 52 per cent of the ships whose *entradas* and *saidas* included listings of their nationality were British ships and 40 per cent were Portuguese. By 1768, some 87 per cent were British and only 5 per cent were Portuguese. But by 1807, however, their fortunes had reversed: the Portuguese had regained their footing, and their ships constituted 31 per cent of the fleet. The British share had fallen to 32 per cent. Entrepreneurs in the United States, who in 1768 had been included among the British imperial owners, now assumed the lead, taking 33 per cent in their own ships.

The nationality of the captains of these ships mirrors this pattern. In 1727, 56 ships dropped anchor in Funchal harbor and reported the nationality of their masters: of these, some 22 had British captains, and another 14 had British American captains; only 9 had Portuguese captains. Forty years later, when the reporting of captains' nationalities is nearly full, some 98 out of 194 ships were steered by British masters, and another 67 by British American masters. At the end of the period, in 1807, in witness to the increasing strength of the Portuguese, Portuguese captains from the Azores, Madeira and mainland constituted 30 per cent of the group, whereas some 32 per cent of all captains hailed from Britain and another 32 per cent from the States.

This about-face was considerably hastened by the conflict. From the 1750s at least, America's fleet had been making inroads, not only in the coastwise wine trade (in which it had always figured prominently) but also in the transoceanic segment. During the war, after non-importation and non-exportation constraints were removed on foreign trade in April 1776, Congress flatly prohibited trade with any subject of Britain's king or trade to any part of his empire, effectively proscribing the use of British ships and British crews by the inhabitants of the 'Thirteen United Colonies,' except in one or two instances.[51] The vacuum this created was not filled immediately, for as one trader noted, the 'times' were 'bad in the shipping way'.[52] But after peace was declared, American trade gradually resumed and the ascendancy of American shippers in the trade continued apace.

VI

In trading on the island, because the British had such a headstart and because the trading community and its management were so politicized, completely subject to the whim and 'venality' of Portuguese officials with little recourse to legal process for the redress of grievances, the British were able severely to handicap the Americans in trading. In shipping to and from the island, however, the Americans were able not only to take over and nearly control the North America to Madeira route but also to achieve parity with the British in the distribution of the wine around the world. One sees both globalization and Americanization converge in the push of the Americans to extend the Madeira wine trade to the East – India, China and Asia.

In the years following the onset of peace in 1783, as the Americans pushed into the trade between the States and the island, they also advanced beyond it, using it as a springboard into the island's burgeoning global trade. Building on a strong commercial base – merchants and houses on the island, a consul resident there and firms in America taking greater responsibility for managing the distribution in North America – they became more involved in the world-wide distribution of Madeira wine. With increasing frequency, many American sea captains and shipowners carried the wine for non-American distributors. At the same time, some American traders, rather than merely shipping the wine for British principals and earning a commission fee for the service, experimented with a whole new range of entrepreneurial possibilities. In particular, they began to buy the wine for themselves, bear the risk, distribute the wine and then reap the profits. In doing so, they began to compete more seriously with the British for the same Madeira wine and for the same customers.

New wine customers overseas were most easily found in areas which had not already been overrun by British traders, and among such places India was the biggest commercial prize. Demand for the wine there appeared, to contemporaries, to be growing daily after the Seven Years War: the army and bureaucracy were both expanding, and the rising number of British immigrants, as well as the growing Indian population, the upper caste of which appears to have been developing a fondness for the drink, growing apace. But before the 1770s, the wine could be supplied only by contractors or agents approved by the East India Company and transported only on the company's own official and 'extra' ships: Americans were automatically cut out of the former, and by the fact that their firms seldom had partners residing in London were effectively cut out of the latter, not having any partners capable of daily lobbying the Directors and the individual ships' captains. During the 1770s, however, parliamentary and Company reforms made it increasingly difficult for Company officials (including the captains) to engage in private trade. In response, in India, a number of 'free merchants' and 'agency houses' were established to fill the vacuum – a trend which culminated in 1799 when Governor-General Lord Mornington allowed any trader 'to take up and load ships direct for London on their own account'. In particular, Americans were allowed to participate fully, inasmuch as they were deemed eligible to serve as one of the two approved agent-contractors. In Britain and Madeira, private traders seized the opportunity to provision the ships and supply the British on the subcontinent.[53]

In this more relaxed trading environment of the last three decades of the eighteenth century, conditions which had nothing to do with the Revolution in America, Americans on the island began to flourish. The erstwhile New Yorker John Searle II, for instance, was for the first time able to make 'a big push' in 'the India way' by disposing much of his very low wine to the East India captains calling at the island and requesting wine. Between 1775 and 1785, Searle was among the top four players in the supply of wine to East India on the Company's extra ships, as he also was on ships of the East India companies of other countries. After 1785, when the India Company Directors for the first time in its history set out the business of the annual wine supply up at public auction, his son John III competed successfully for one of the two annual contracts for the remainder of the decade, winning these more public competitions with lower prices and quicker deliveries, and further wresting the trade that had once been open only to the British.[54]

At the same time, some merchants in the States began to compete (quite successfully) for the supply of British India as well as parts of Asia and China – sending the wine on their own account and, more commonly, shipping the wine for the account of the British. Initial forays into the trade were made by Philadelphia entrepreneurs in 1784: the *Empress of China* left for China in February, and the *United States* departed for China but changed its course for India in March. New York, Providence and Salem traders quickly followed. But the attempts were easily frustrated. The market in China, for instance, proved difficult to control: 'The Chinese had never heard of us', observed the purser of the *Empress*, even though its traders bullishly introduced themselves 'as a new Nation, gave them our own history, with a description of our Country, the importance and necessity of a trade here to the advantage of both'.[55] In India, the reception was better, the Americans better known and more familiar with the market, and a market for their wares and wines already in existence.

With respect to the mechanics of the voyage, in the decade immediately succeeding the peace, these merchants sent out their own ships and carried their own cargoes at their own commercial risk to India and Asia. 'The outward cargo' from the United States was 'chiefly Dollars, iron, lead, Brandy, Madeira and other wines, a variety of European articles, tar, large and small spars' and formed the basis of the barter for cotton and silk goods in India. Thus, the Madeira they procured was just one of many commodities they shipped, although often the bulkiest. More often than not, the wine was purchased from American firms on the island, like Searle and Co., the Cocks, or Lamar, Hill, Bisset and Co., and carried back to the States before the reshipment to India.[56]

But in the supply of the subcontinent, the British always dominated and, if they felt it necessary, could squelch the business of American firms on the island. So it was that, after 1789, when their unease about the durability of the republic waned, and their concern at losing supply contracts to the Americans mounted, the British came to solicit with increasing frequency the American India suppliers and to draw upon and eventually collaborate with them. The Scots firm of Newton, Gordon and Murdoch was the first to broach the possibility of transatlantic collaboration. Writing separately to Mordecai Lewis of Philadelphia and James Sheafe of New Hampshire, they suggested that if Lewis or Sheafe were 'inclined to take any share in furnishing the India market in Madeira wine', they would be willing to supply them. Eventually, in the 1790s, this form of commercial co-operation evolved into the situation where the Americans in the States were supplying the ship and the British on the island were providing the wine; sometimes the wine was jointly owned, but more often than not as the years passed Americans found it in their interest to leave that risk to others. The deal Elias Hasket Derby struck with John Searle III in 1790 and 1791 was typical. From Salem, Derby proposed to launch one of his own ships, a 600-ton vessel he himself designed for the East India trade. His plan was to either send her directly to Bengal via Madeira or indirectly to India via northern Europe (where, in Sweden, it would load a cargo of iron) and Madeira; either way, he wanted 150 pipes of wine. Accordingly, Derby proposed to

> take the wine on your [Searle's] account & risk, out and home.
> There shall be no freight taken out of the amount out or home; &
> upon the arrival of the property either here or [in] any part of
> Europe, the ship shall have one-third of the neat amount for her
> freight or I will take it free of any freight to the ship. The property
> to be at your risk, out and home. & For my freight, I will have the
> use of the property 'til the arrival of the ship at America or Europe.
> The money to be paid agreeable to the neat sales in Calcutta within
> four months after the arrival of the ship in America or Europe.

In effect, Searle would have to pay the captain all commissions and duties that may arise on it; the captain would sell the wine in India for export goods to Salem; Derby would then pay Searle, deducting a third for the freight. Inasmuch as it was so 'difficult in this country to raise a capital for such a ship' and not always possible to command a cargo for the outbound voyage, Derby pursued this and numerous similar co-operatively financed, owned or supplied ventures.[57]

The British dominated on the island, but the Americans were so strong in the realm of shipping that they became the normal *modus operandi* for the non-Company trading voyage to India. However sent, while the quality of the wine might have been low – 'hardly fit for a Madeira bush house & better adapted to the cleansing of hospitals than the supply of a Gentleman's tables', quipped connoisseurs – the quantity was immense. In one typical year, over 5000 pipes of wine would go to British India alone, and three-quarters of this would go in American ships.[58]

Examples of the efflorescence of the traffic in Madeira wine and of the convergence of older patterns set by globalization and Americanization, and newer opportunities created by the completion of the Revolution, are found in Elias Hasket Derby's business. The founder of this firm, Richard Derby, was born in 1712 and began his career as a sea captain and an importer of British goods into Salem. After retiring from life at sea around 1756, he built up an extensive import-export business in Salem: between 1750 and 1775, he owned and managed more than 20 ships, which carried New England fish, grain, and timber for sugar, molasses, rum, coffee, cocoa and wine back and forth across the Atlantic. The wine he imported from Madeira and then traded it wholesale, scattering the wine deep into the interior, as far north as Quebec and as far west as Albany, and up and down the coast, consigning to merchants in other colonies as far south as Charleston. He retired at the outbreak of the war and died in 1783.[59]

The control of Richard Derby's far-flung business passed to his son Elias Hasket Derby.[60] Once the war was over, young Derby followed the track first blazed by his father. Yet wine imports and handling were seemingly not as important to him. Far fewer ships than in his father's day arrived in Salem direct from Madeira. Instead, he focused more of his energy on developing the coastal trade.[61] Simultaneously, he devoted a considerable amount of money and time on furthering a business in carrying wine to the Indies. In much the same way that a stop in Madeira had facilitated the development of the Caribbean sugar trade in the late seventeenth century, a stop in Madeira now spurred the growth of the India export trade in the late eighteenth century. What one discovers on looking into the work of the firm is that a trade in

Madeira wine, already established by Derby's father, only really flourished when it was pushed as an adjunct to 'oriental commerce', and that
became possible only after the British imperial restraints and monopoly
company commercial restraints had been removed.[62]

Elias Hasket Derby came close to monopolizing America's burgeoning
India trade in the 1780s and 1790s. The initial commercial successes of
the mid-1780s achieved by Philadelphia and Providence enterprisers were
uncertain and inconclusive. Derby, however, had a stronger sense of the
possibilities that inhered in the freedom from Great Britain's mercantile
laws. In 1783 and 1784, he had backed nearly 25 separate overseas
voyages in what his biographer has described as 'a frantic search for
profitable markets'.[63] One of these, the voyage of the *Grand Turk* in
1784, neatly realized a return of 43 per cent, and Derby proceeded to
back venture after venture to the eastern seas, especially to Bombay,
Rangoon and Calcutta, often sending as many as four vessels yearly (in
1788, he dispatched nine).[64] The third voyage of the *Grand Turk* was
typical of the initial India voyaging. His supplier was, as for many
American importers, John Searle and Co. of Madeira, who by 1788
transacted 'the greater part of the American business at this island'. To
Searle, Derby shipped boards, butter, cassia, china, chocolate, codfish,
hides, iron, molasses, oil and Spanish dollars, some of which Searle
accepted in barter for 400 pipes of wine and some of which Searle sold.
Derby's captain then loaded the wine and carried it to India. This system,
it was widely believed, 'always leaves handsome profit'.[65]

VII

So what do we make of all this? Limpao, Bengal, Funchal, London,
Salem; Derbys, Searles, Gordons, Hills; Madeira, sherry, champagne,
claret? Was the American Revolution a discontinuity of trade, or a brief
hiatus in a culmination of longer trends? As always, the answer is: some
of both, understood in the right way. But what is the right way?

In the foregoing pages, I have stressed the importance of two long-
term trends that affected the trade in Madeira wine (and I believe all
other transatlantic trades). First, there was an increase in the global
character of the trade. What started the century as a primarily Atlantic
phenomenon ended the century as a world-wide activity; the trade of
the Americas was inextricably linked to the trade with India and Asia.
Second, the trade was transformed by the increase in the participation
of the Americans, especially by the tightening of their grip on overseas
shipping. These trends first appeared long before, and continued well
after, the war.

Did the Revolution make any difference at all to commerce? What role did it play in the day-to-day functioning of the Atlantic world? In essence, I have tried to argue, the Revolution, by redrawing national and imperial boundaries, significantly and directly affected the trade in Madeira wine. This was especially true in an age when and a world where economic policy was still basically mercantile, rather than ruled according to principles of free trade. That world was significantly different after the war and because of it. Consumption patterns shifted. What Americans drank changed; liberation from the British mercantile laws allowed other cheaper wines in. It meant that Madeira was still important, but it was no longer dominant. And as the years passed American entrepreneurs were squeezed into performing a much smaller economic role: initial attempts at trading on their own account gave way to increases in the role they played as wine shippers; and, if they persisted at and succeeded in trading as principals, it was mainly in collaboration with the British. American activities in trading were curtailed because after 1783, instead of being members of a favoured nation, they were merely counted as foreigners and competitors. The outcome was nothing short of a critical rechannelling of entrepreneurial aggressiveness into world-wide carrying activity. Although the rise of shipping was not a major discontinuity as such, for Americans had been making inroads into oceanic shipping well before the 1770s, both effects were the result of American consumers and merchants alike being in a different policy regime. The Revolution gave that regime a boost.

What, then, does all this say to the historians of John Adams's 'intricate and complicated subject'? To those who argue discontinuity: there is a lot of reorganization as a result of the war, but the reorganizations happened in the context of much larger-scale phenomena – globalization, and Americanization, essentially the rise of entrepreneurialism in America. And to those who argue hiatus: Adams's trade was not just a product of larger, sometimes impersonal forces, but the result of the interaction of those forces with discrete events. Perhaps, with Adams, we will have to live with the uncertainty – by blending the two together as we try to appreciate the real revolution in trade.

Notes

1. John Adams to James Warren, 7 October 1775, in R. J. Taylor (ed.), *Papers of John Adams*, vol. 3 (Cambridge, MA, 1979), pp. 188–9.
2. A brief useful cost/benefit analysis is provided by Claudia D. Goldin, 'War', in G. Porter (ed.), *Encyclopedia of American Economic History*, vol. 3 (New York, 1980), pp. 935–57.
3. W. Ford and G. Hirt (eds), *The Journals of the Continental Congress*,

1774–1789, vol. 1 (Washington, DC, 1904), pp. 41, 43, 51–2, 75–81. The single best account of the resolutions of September and the subsequent Continental Association appears in Jack N. Rakove, *The Beginnings of National Politics: An Interpretive History of the Continental Congress* (Baltimore, 1979), pp. 49–52. See also Edmund C. Burnett, *The Continental Congress* (New York, 1964), pp. 46–59.

4. Ford and Hirt, *Journals of the Continental Congress*, vol. 2 (1905), pp. 184–5; vol. 3 (1905), pp. 314–15, vol. 4 (1906), pp. 257–9.

5. 16 Geo. III, c. 5; 17 Geo. III, c. 7. The statutes were repealed by 23 Geo. III, c. 26. Danby Pickering (ed.) *Statutes at Large*, vol. 31 (Cambridge, 1775), pp. 135–54.

6. John J. McCusker and Russell R. Menard, *The Economy of British America, 1607–1789* (Chapel Hill, NC, 1985), p. 362. McCusker and Menard argue that the imbalance created by the fall in exports was partially compensated by the proceeds of American privateering, European lending, and British and French spending on food and other war-related provisions. The level of European imports into the new United States varied from port to port.

7. 31 October 1787, in Julian P. Boyd (ed.) *The Papers of Thomas Jefferson*, vol. 12 (Princeton, NJ, 1955), p. 299; James Shepherd and Gary Walton, 'Economic Changes after the American Revolution: Pre- and Post-War Comparisons of Maritime Shipping and Trade', *Explorations in Economic History*, 13 (1976), pp. 397–422, esp. pp. 406–7; and McCusker and Menard, *Economy of British America*, p. 367. Shepherd and Walton hedge their bets, however, for they admit that 'pre-war levels were not reached by 1790–1792'. Whereas exports to Britain in 1768–72 constituted 58 per cent of the whole, they constituted only 31 per cent in 1790–92. See also Curtis P. Nettels, *The Emergence of a National Economy, 1775–1815* (White Plains, NY, 1962); Gordon Bjork, 'The Weaning of the American Economy: Independence, Market Changes and Economic Development', *Journal of Economic History*, 24 (1964), 541–66; Stuart Bruchey, *The Roots of American Economic Growth, 1607–1861: An Essay in Social Causation* (New York, 1965); Jim Potter, 'The Effects of the American Revolution in the Economic Relations between the Former Colonies and the Mother Country', in Claude Fohlen and Jacques Godechot (eds), *La Révolution Américaine et L'Europe* (Paris, 1979) pp. 265–77, esp. p. 271; and Daniel W. Howe, *American History in an Atlantic Context* (Oxford, 1993), p. 9. The proponents of British resurgence echo sentiments expressed at the beginning of the twentieth century by Guy Callendar, in his *Selections from the Economic History of the United States, 1765–1860* (Boston, MA, 1909), pp. 88, 125.

8. Victor Clark, *History of Manufactures in the United States*, vol. 1 (Washington, DC, 1916), pp. 215–32.

9. George Abbott Hall, Collector of the Customs in Charleston, to Thomas Jefferson, 31 December 1784, *The Papers of Thomas Jefferson*, vol. 8 (Princeton, NJ, 1953), p. 200. Robert East, *Business Enterprise in the American Revolutionary Era* (New York, 1938); James B. Hedges, *The Browns of Providence Plantations*, vol. 1 (Cambridge, 1952); Bernard Mason, 'Entrepreneurial Activity in New York during the American Revolution', *Business History Review*, 40 (1966), pp. 190–212; Thomas Doerflinger, *A Vigorous Spirit of Enterprise: Merchants and Economic*

Development in Revolutionary Philadelphia (Chapel Hill, NC, 1986); Clarence L. Ver Steeg, *Robert Morris: Revolutionary Financier* (Philadelphia, 1954).

10. Potter, 'The Effects of the American Revolution', pp. 265–77.

11. Jacob Price, 'Reflections on the Economy of Revolutionary America', in Ronald Hoffman, John J. McCusker, Jr, Russell R. Menard and Peter J. Albert (eds), *The Economy of Early America* (Charlottesville, VA, 1988), p. 319; *Historical Statistics of the United States: Colonial Times to 1970*, Part 2 (Washington, DC, 1975), p. 1,190; M. L. Robertson, 'Scottish Commerce and the American War of Independence', *Economic History Review*, 9 (1956), pp. 123–31; and Charles J. Farmer, 'Country Stores and Frontier Exchange Systems in Southside Virginia during the Eighteenth Century' (PhD thesis, University of Maryland, 1984), pp. 269–83.

12. Jacques Barbier and Allan Kuethe (eds) *The North American Role in the Spanish Imperial Economy, 1760–1819* (Manchester, 1984).

13. Shepherd and Walton, 'Economic Changes', p. 413.

14. James B. Hedges, *The Browns of Providence Plantations*, vol. 1 (Cambridge, MA, 1952); Franklin Coyle, 'Welcome Arnold (1745–1798), Providence Merchant: The Founding of an Enterprise' (PhD thesis, Brown University, RI, 1972); John F. Stover, 'French-American Trade during the Confederation, 1781–1789', *North Carolina Historical Review*, 35 (1958), pp. 399–414; Edward C. Papenfuse, 'An Uncertain Connection: Maryland's Trade with France during the American Revolution, 1778–1783', in Claude Fohlen and Jacques Godechot (eds), *La Révolution Américaine et L'Europe* (Paris, 1979), pp. 243–64; Foster Rhea Dulles, *The Old China Trade* (Boston, MA, 1930); Jonathan Goldstein, *Philadelphia and the China Trade, 1682–1846* (University Park, PA, 1978); and James Rawley, *The Transatlantic Slave Trade: A History* (New York, 1981).

15. East, *Business Enterprise*, ch. 11; McCusker and Menard, *Economy*, p. 371 (seemingly contradicting their previous statement on p. 367, as well as Shepherd and Walton – it may be that the population had increased enough to turn a slight increase into a substantial per capital decrease or it may be a distinction between commodity exports versus all exports, the authors do not clarify the matter).

16. The work of G. Bhagat adds little to the economic story of the American trade with India. See his *Americans in India* (New York, 1970); *idem*, 'America's First Contacts with India, 1784–1785', *American Neptune*, 31 (1971), 38–48; and *idem*, 'Americans and the American Trade in India, 1784–1814', *American Neptune*, 46 (1986), 6–17. Jonathan Goldenberg's *Philadelphia and the China Trade, 1682–1846: Commercial, Cultural and Attitudinal Effects* (Philadelphia, 1978) is an exception to the lack of analysis.

17. The transformation is detailed in David Hancock, 'Commerce and Conversation in the Eighteenth-Century Atlantic: The Invention of Madeira Wine,' *Journal of Interdisciplinary History*, 29 (Autumn 1998), 197–219.

18. Spence, Leacock and Spence to William Woodmass, 1762, Spence, Leacock and Spence Letterbook 1762–65, f. 23, Leacock Papers, Casa Branca, Funchal.

19. For the 1663 statute, see 15 Car. II, c. 7, v. Detailed discussion of the exception appears in Charles M. Andrews, *The Colonial Period of American History*, vol. 4, *England's Commercial and Colonial Policy* (New

Haven, CT, 1938), pp. 109–11; and Lawrence A. Harper, *The English Navigation Laws: A Seventeenth Century Experiment in Social Engineering* (New York, 1939), pp. 59–60. On the development of diplomatic and commercial relations, generally, see V. M. Shillington and A. B. Chapman, *The Commercial Relations of England and Portugal* (London, 1919); and H. E. S. Fisher, *The Portugal Trade: A Study of Anglo-Portuguese Commerce, 1700–1770* (London, 1971).

20. Harper, *English Navigation Laws*; George L. Beer, *The Old Colonial System, 1660–1754*, 2 vols (New York, 1912); and A. D. Francis, *The Methuens and Portugal, 1691–1708* (Cambridge, 1966).

21. Of the 545 departing ships, some 48 per cent left for the British West Indies, another 20 per cent left for British North America (New England), and 6 per cent for other parts of America such as Brazil and Curacao. For the 1702–13 statistics, see G. Blandy (ed.) *Bolton Letters* (Funchal, 1960), pp. 21–68. There are no letters for 1711, and only those for January 1714 have survived. The 1695–1700 shipping has been similarly analysed in detail by José Manuel Azevedo e Silva in 'A Navegação e o Comércio Vistos do Funchal nos Finais do Século XVII', in *ACTAS III – Colóquio Internacional de História da Madeira* (Funchal, 1993), pp. 353–82, esp. tables II and III, and figures 1 and 2, on pp. 363–4 and 381–2. Of the 292 ship departures Bolton noted, 44 per cent left for the British West Indies, another 10 per cent left for British North America (all New England), and 5 per cent for Pernambuco (although four-fifths of the Brazil ships moved on to the Cape of Good Hope, Madagascar and India.

22. The statistics in this and the paragraphs that follow are culled from the *Livros dos Entradas e Saidas, Provedoria e Junta da Real Fazenda*, kept at the Arquivo Nacional da Torre do Tombo, Lisbon. They have been previously analysed by João José Abreu De Sousa, *O Movimento do Porto do Funchal e a Conjuntura da Madeira de 1727 a 1810: Alguns Aspectos* (Funchal, 1989). Maria De Lourdes de Freitas Ferraz has calculated exports from these records from 1780 to 1800. *Dinamismo Sócio-Económico do Funchal na Segunda Metade do Século XVIII* (Lisbon, 1994). Their calculations, however, are marred by numerous computational errors. More significantly, they group regional areas together in such a way as to hide more than they reveal.

23. The actual imports into North America were probably greater than this, however. The *entradas* usually list only the initial stops of outbound vessels, and many of the pipes listed as destined for the Caribbean were never unloaded there but held on board and eventually sent to North America. In addition, the *entradas* generally omit the comings and goings of British naval vessels, which did not have to pay duties when entering the harbours of friendly nations, and which left with goods.

24. Thomas Newton to Adoniah Schuyler, 22 January 1756, Thomas Newton Letterbook, Madeira Wine Company Archives. That the number of ships declined did not necessarily mean that the amount of wine shipped and consumed dropped with it. Especially in the Seven Years War, 'the number of troops and also the many privateers ... fitted out from' New York and other large ports was seen to have increased the consumption of Madeira wine. This was especially true after Spain declared war against Britain, Britain prohibited Canary wines from being imported into America, and Portugal declared against war against France and Spain. Thomas

Newton to Malcolm Campbell, 14 October 1756, Thomas Newton Letterbook, Madeira Wine Company Archives; Newton and Gordon to John Provoost, 17 June 1762, to John Tweedy, 27 June 1762, Newton and Gordon Letterbooks, vol. 3, fos 2, 10; and Alexander Hamilton to George Spence, 13 December 1758, Letterbook of Assorted Leacock Letters, Casa Branca, Funchal.

25. Thomas Newton to Newton and Gordon, 27 November 1762, Box 3, Bundle 1764–65, Cossart and Gordon Papers, Liverpool University Archives, documents the efforts of one army officer who 'sold out' and joined several of the 'principal Gentlemen' in New York City in 'a grand scheme of trade up in the Back Settlements.' The officer intended 'to do a good deal in the Madeira way'.

26. In 1761, America was glutted with Spanish and Canary wine, but in 1762 that flow was stopped by Spain's entry into the war. A desire to impede the return of such importation at the end of the war led to royal orders to British men of war to seize and make prize of all Canary and Spanish, as well as Lisbon, wines. Newton and Gordon to Johnston and Jolly, 21 September 1763, vol. 2, fo. 206, to Robert Hooper, 1 February 1764, vol. 3, f. 262, Newton and Gordon Letterbooks, David Cossart Papers. On the 1764 imposition of duties, see vol. 3, fos 158, 305, 315, 330. The Sugar Act was to take effect on 29 September 1764. 4 Geo. III, cap. 15, s. 12. See also R. C. Simmons and P. D. G. Thomas (eds), *Proceedings and Debates of the British Parliaments Respecting North America*, vol. 1 (New York, 1982), pp. 489–92; and *Journals of the House of Commons*, vol. 29 (London), p. 934. Many importers and consumers had hoped that the Act would allow direct importation of all wines from mainland Portugal. In this they were disappointed, although the Act did significantly reduce the cost of re-exportation, inasmuch as Portuguese and Spanish wines charged £4 on coming into Britain could draw back 10 shillings on re-exportation to British America; these same re-exported wines would pay only an additional 10 shillings on importation into British America. Thus, Portuguese and Spanish wines coming from Britain were charged only £4, whereas Madeira and Azorean wines were assessed £7. On a push to relax the rule requiring Portugal's wines to be shipped first to England and its failure, see the 'Reply to "A Portugal Merchant"', April 1768, in *The Papers of Benjamin Franklin*, vol. 15 (New Haven, CT, 1972), pp. 107–10. The unwillingness to relax the restrictions was compounded by the tightening of import regulations and the enforcement of customs laws in 1763, aimed in part at keeping out Tenerife, Fayal and Lisbon wines. John Searle to Thomas Riche, 25–26 August 1763, Society Collection, Historical Society of Pennsylvania, Philadelphia.

27. On the effect of the Act and of resulting high prices on Virginia planters and others, see Newton and Gordon to George and John Riddell, 3 June 1765, Newton and Gordon Letterbooks, vol. 3, fo. 413. Richard Derby, for instance, stopped all orders in 1766; the inhabitants of Salem, he wrote his supplier, were 'adverse to Madeira', and were cutting their consumption, on account of the price. Richard Derby to Chambers, Hiccox and Chambers, 3 April, 1 June 1767, Derby Papers, Essex Institute, Salem.

28. On the non-importation movements, see *The Case of the* Good Intent (Annapolis, 1772), reprinted in *Maryland Historical Magazine*, 3 (1908),

141–57; *South Carolina and American General Gazette*, 13 July 1769, and *South Carolina Gazette*, 6 July, 13 July, 26 October 1769; *Georgia Gazette*, 20 September 1769; and Sparks MSS, vol. 62, *sub* 10 March 1769, Houghton Library, Harvard College, Cambridge, MA. For a general discussion, see Charles M. Andrews, 'The Boston Merchants and the Non-Importation Movement', *Publications of the Colonial Society of Massachusetts*, 19 (1918), pp. 159–259, esp. pp. 201–21. For the response of Philadelphia wine importers, see Francis and Tilghman to Newton and Gordon, 7 March 1770, Cossart Gordon Papers, Box 5, Liverpool University Archives. Opposition to the 1768–69 prohibitions can be found in *The Pennsylvania Gazette*, 26 July, 23 August, 20 September 1770.

29.   On the Continental Association, see Ford and Hirt, *Journals of the Continental Congress*, vol. 1, pp. 62, 75–81. Apart from the wines and goods coming via Britain or Ireland, Congress prohibited East India tea, foreign indigo, and British Caribbean brown unrefined sugar, coffee, and pimento.

30.   A comparison of *entradas* and *saidas* for the years 1779–82 reveals that the share of wine exports taken by British America was somewhat greater than the share of wine ships that went to it, a fact which is attributable to the large imports by the military. Of the 421 departures in these four years, 16 per cent went to the British West Indies and 13 per cent to mainland British North America.

31.   Newton and Gordon to Francis Newton, 25 April 1779, Newton and Gordon Letterbooks, vol. 6, fo. 459. Johnston in Madeira urged both Newton and Gordon in London to waste no time in enlarging 'our acquaintance' in the West India Squadron and getting 'good introductions to Navy Agents at seaports', such as those that William Murdoch of Fergusson and Murdoch was obtaining. On deals struck with the Scotsman Daniel Wier, the Commissary General, stationed in New York, who happened to be a close friend of Newton and Gordon's London correspondent Wilkinson and Gordon, see Newton and Gordon Letterbooks, vol. 6, fo. 200, 208; and Daniel Wier Letterbooks, *passim*, New York Historical Society, and Historical Society of Pennsylvania. On the supply of American troops, see Lewis Pintard's letters, in the Boudinot Papers, American Bible Society. See also Oscar T. Barck Jr, *New York City during the War for Independence* (New York, 1931), p. 187.

32.   The cessation of shipping to the Thirteen Colonies during the war is reflected in the Bills of Lading of Madeira firms. See, for example, the books of both the Nowlan & Leacock and the Newton & Gordon firms.

33.   The foundation is shaky in places; it is not as solid as that provided by Funchal's *entradas* and *saidas* or even by Britain's Inspector General Ledgers. The lists do not contain entries for all approved customs ports (there are no lists for Rhode Island, Connecticut or Maryland, for example), or for all years (there are no lists for 1705–12 for any colony, for instance), or for all quarters in those years when entries have been entered in some quarters (sometimes only two quarters have survived); the officer or his clerk, in some ports, sometimes neglected recording certain categories of information, such as the nationality of the ship or the port the ship had just come from.

34.   A final category of 'other' wines included French and Italian wines and those listed simply as 'wines' constituted 17 per cent; the greatest share of

'other wines' were the unspecified. Colonies in North America for which Naval Office Shipping Lists have survived include: New Hampshire (1724–25, 1727, 1742–43, 1745–49, 1751–55, 1757–64, 1766–69); Massachusetts (1716–19, 1752–65); New York (1713–43, 1748, 1751, 1753–55, 1763–64); New Jersey (1723–27, 1733, 1739–41, 1743–51, 1754–55, 1757–59, 1763–64); Virginia (1700–1704, 1726–59, 1768–69); and South Carolina (1717–18, 1724, 1731–32, 1734–38, 1758–60, 1762–63, 1766, 1768–72). The lists are housed at the Public Record Office, outside London: New Hampshire, Massachusetts, New York, New Jersey, Virginia (CO 5/1446–7), South Carolina (CO 5/510–11); Georgia (CO 5/710); and East Florida (CO 5/573). Analysis of the Naval Office Shipping Lists for the British West Indian ports provides similar percentages: Jamaica (CO 142/15–19); St Christopher (CO 243/1/15 and T 1/512); Antigua (T 1/152); and Grenada (CO 106/1).

35. *American State Papers: Documents, Legislative and Executive, of the Congress of the United States*, vol. 7 (Class IV): *Commerce and Navigation*, vol. 1 (Washington, DC, 1832), *passim*. Compared to other wines, re-exports of Madeira wine were high: in 1790–91 (70 per cent), 1791–92 (39 per cent) and 1792–93 (21 per cent). After 1793, re-exports of Madeira wine averaged 4 per cent of total wine exports. In the period 1793–1806, Madeira re-exports constituted 26 per cent of Madeira imports. There are some discrepancies between figures culled from the Madeira *saida* records and those extracted from the *American State Papers*. On average, the latter are 8 per cent higher. In 1790, for instance, the Funchal *saidas* record 2657 pipes leaving for the States, while the *State Papers* register 2922 pipes arriving. The whole intricate subject of import duties during the period needs re-evaluation. At the time, it was certainly felt that American duties affected the export. New duties in America imposed in 1792, one islander noted, 'check'd our connexion with that country & prevented our having as large a call for low wines' (Americans having taken many of Madeira's low wines) and 'operate[d] a very great revolution in the general system of our intercourse with America'. Newton, Gordon and Murdoch to Thomas Gordon and Francis Newton, 25 July, 26 July, 8 August, 1 September 1792, Newton and Gordon Letterbook, vol. 14, fos 276, 279, 306, 322.

36. Fort William to Court of Directors, 4 February 1750/51, in K. K. Datta (ed.), *Fort William–India House Correspondence*, vol. 1 (Delhi, 1958), p. 465. Henry Love, *Vestiges of Old Madras* (London, 1913), vol. 2, p. 135, nn. 2–3. Madeira was probably shipped to the British East Indies before 1716. William Bolton's numerous letters make passing reference to India ships anchoring before Funchal and loading wine. But 1716 marks the date when the Directors began making official requests.

37. *Madras Dialogues* (1740–45), in H. Love, *Vestiges of Old Madras* (London, 1913), vol. 2, p. 330.

38. Fort William to Court of Directors, 4 February 1750/51, in *Fort William–India House Correspondence*, vol. 1, pp. 2, 465.

39. Fort William to Court of Directors, 4 January 1754, in *Fort William–India House Correspondence*, vol. 1, p. 722.

40. Fort William to Court of Directors, 16 January, 12 November 1761, in R. R. Sethi (ed.), *Fort William–India House Correspondence*, vol. 3 (Delhi, 1968), pp. 289, 358.

41. Newton and Gordon to Robert and Alexander Maitland, 8 September 1762, to Francis Newton, 14 January, 14 May 1768, 25 January, 29 May 1775, 5 April, 25 August 1777, Newton and Gordon Letterbooks, vol. 3, fo. 34; vol. 4, fos. 164, 250; vol. 5, fos 436, 575; vol. 6, fos 208, 265; Newton and Gordon to Thomas Newton, 25 March 1764, Box 2, Bundle 7; Francis Newton to Newton and Gordon, 14 August 1770, Box 5, Bundle 1770–71, Cossart and Gordon Papers, Liverpool University Archives. In the 1780s, the Portuguese, especially Pedro Jorge Monteiro and Dona Guiomar, along with John Searle and James Ayres, won most of the contracts. In 1786, the Court of Directors began to set out these contracts at public auction.

42. The West of England, for example, became 'more deserving of the attention of a Madeira concern'; as a result of 'the extensive manufactories spreading everywhere along the west coast and interior part of that country, opulence' was making 'rapid strides, and of course drags luxury along attendant'. Newton and Gordon to Thomas Gordon, 12 February 1787, Newton and Gordon Letterbooks, vol. 9, fo. 340. See also John Leacock Sr to William Leacock, 16 August 1791. The Leacocks enjoyed 'no prospect of deriving any advantage from our friends or connections in America' and therefore directed their 'principal attention to cultivate those we have fixed in England and to render them permanent'. Accordingly, William Leacock paid visits to Liverpool, Bristol and Bath.

43. Joseph Gillis to Henry Hill, 4 April and 6 May, 2 August, 26 August, 20 September 1783, Letterbook vol. 9, fos 2, 14, 16, Smith Family Papers, HSP.

44. The shift was facilitated by a long-term change in the commercial policy of the East India Company: since the 1750s, the strict control of shipping and trading within and around India had been loosening, and free merchants and agency houses were slowly allowed greater play in the market. Peter J. Marshall, 'British Merchants in Eighteenth-Century Bengal', *Bengal Past and Present*, 95 (1976), 157–9, and *idem, Problems of Empire: Britain and India, 1757–1813* (London, 1968), pp. 95–6.

45. The Americans included: James Jenkins from Pennsylvania, Thomas Patten and Joseph Gillis from Maryland – all three of Lamar, Hill, Bisset and Co.; John Searle II and James Ayres from New York; Henry Cock from Maryland; and Robert Brush from Massachusetts. The representation of Quakers and Huguenots was high.

46. Some of the successful Americans included John Leander Cathcart, Richard Foster, Marien Lamar, Lewis Searle Pintard, William Shaw, William Steinson, and George Day Welsh.

47. William Johnston to Thomas Gordon, 10 March 1783, Newton and Gordon Letterbooks, vol. 8, fo. 13.

48. Newton and Gordon to Thomas Gordon, 24 February 1785, to Hugh Moore, 30 April 1785, 22 March 1786, to James Young, 23 March 1789, and to Francis Newton, 10 September 1789, Newton and Gordon Letterbooks, vol. 8, fo. 381; 447, vol. 9, fo. 179; vol. 12, fos 13, 133. This change hit Madeira wine particularly hard, inasmuch as it was more highly taxed than any other imported beverage. Johnston's partner Thomas Murdoch was more on the mark when he wrote:

> we have not entered into a serious consequence with any person on that continent, things there being so little settled

and moneys in your hands being so scarce. We have merely, to keep people in mind of our firm, dropt, at different times, a few words to those whose names only we are acquainted with at Philadelphia and Charleston. But our correspondence has been confined to hints, a sort of war of ports, and skirmishes, as was that much mismanaged one which lost Great Britain her colonies.

It was not until 'the establishment of a permanent government, and the return of prosperity & cultivation' as evidenced in the lowering of 'very high prices' in America 'which precluded all probability of gain' that the firms seriously reconsidered their decision.

49. John Leacock Sr, to John Rowe, 30 June 1783, Nowlan and Leacock Letterbook, 1781–84, Casa Branca, Funchal.
50. Examples of American houses succeeding. Examples of British houses failing.
51. Ford and Hirt, *Journals of the Continental Congress*, vol. 4, pp. 257–9.
52. David Henry Smith to James and Alexander Gordon, 29 May 1775, Gordon of Letterfourie Papers.
53. For the easing of restrictions on private trade during the 1770s, see Charles Hardy, *A Register of Ships* (London, 1813), pp. 58–61, 92–9; Marshall, 'British Merchants', pp. 152–4; and James G. Parker, 'Scottish Enterprise in India, 1750–1914', *The Scots Abroad* (London, 1985), pp. 190–98. See also Newton, Gordon and Murdoch to Robert Lenox, 16 September 1799, Newton and Gordon Letterbooks, vol. 19, fo. 414.
54. Newton and Gordon to Francis Newton, 25 January, 29 May 1775, to Thomas Gordon, 20 May 1784, to Thomas Newton, 22 January 1786, and to Francis Newton, 8 November 1788, vol. 5, fos 435, 515; vol. 8, fo. 247; vol. 9, fos 133, 287, Newton and Gordon Letterbooks. Through 1785, the Company had funnelled all purchases through two approved island agents-contractors (two British merchant houses) reappointed each year; India captains on official ships would strike individual deals for individual shipments with these agents. India captains on extra ships could strike individual deals with any merchant. On Company purchasing of Madeira wine under the new post-1785 system, see Raghubir Sinh (ed.), *Fort William–India House Correspondence*, vol. 10 (Delhi, 1972), pp. 165, 312. Messrs John Searle and Co., for instance, contracted to ship 536 pipes in 1787 at £20 per pipe and 736 pipes the following year at £17 5s. per pipe.
55. John Swift Jr to John Swift Sr, 3 December1784, *Pennsylvania Magazine of History and Biography*, 9 (1885), 485; Samuel W. Woodhouse Jr, 'The Voyage of the *Empress of China* [1784]', *Pennsylvania Magazine of History and Biography*, 63 (January 1939), 31; the log of the *United States*, 1784–85, Historical Society of Pennsylvania. On Providence, see Holden Furber, 'The Beginnings of the American Trade with India, 1784–1812', *New England Quarterly*, 11 (1938), 238; and Gertrude Kimball, 'The East India Trade of Providence, from 1787 to 1807', *Papers from Historical Seminary of Brown University* (Providence, RI, 1896), p. 17. A good contemporary account of the new China trade is provided by Thomas Randall in his letter to Alexander Hamilton, 14 August 1791, in Harold C. Syrett (ed.), *The Papers of Alexander Hamilton*, vol. 9 (New York, 1965), pp. 38–45.

56. John H. Reinoehl (ed.), 'Some Remarks on the American Trade: Jacob Crowninshield to James Madison, 1806', *William and Mary Quarterly*, 3rd series, **16** (1959), 110–11.

57. Elias Hasket Derby to John Searle and Co., 15 December 1790, 18 January 1791, Elias Hasket Derby Letterbook, 1788–96, vol. 11, fos 120, 126, Derby Papers. If the ship went to India directly, the captain would also purchase 30 pipes for Derby's own private account.

58. Newton and Gordon to Thomas Gordon, 19 November 1794, Newton and Gordon Letterbooks, vol. 16, fo. 160. The high level of American imports into India may not have been sustained in all years, however. According to William Milburn, only 17 per cent of the Madeira wine sent to India in 1805 was the property of Americans: W. Milburn, *Oriental Commerce*, vol. 1 (London, 1813), p. 5.

59. Derby's life and career are discussed in Robert E. Peabody, 'The Derbys of Salem, Massachusetts', *Historical Collections of the Essex Institute*, vol. 44 (1908), pp. 193–219; and James D. Phillips, *Salem in the Eighteenth Century* (Boston, MA, 1937). The family is discussed in passing in a more recent study of Salem's families *c.* 1800: Bernard Faber's *Guardians of Virtue* (New York, 1972). Derby's wine-importing business is discussed in David Hancock, 'Markets, Merchants and the Wider World of Boston Wine', in C. Wright and K. Viens (eds), *Entrepreneurs: The Boston Business Community, 1700–1850* (Boston, MA, 1997), pp. 62–95.

60. Richard H. McKey Jr, 'Elias Hasket Derby, Merchant of Salem, 1739–1799' (PhD thesis, Clark University, MA, 1961).

61. In the late 1780s, for instance, he carried and generally consigned or sometimes sold Madeira wine to Ludlow and Gould in New York, Hewes and Anthony of Philadelphia, Carey and Tilghman of Baltimore and Shreve and Lawrason of Alexandria. This wine consignment trade managed by Derby became especially intense after the establishment of federal government, when the ships of European merchants began 'tumbling in in plenty' into American ports in search of eastern luxuries at cheaper prices. Carey and Tilghman to Elias Hasket Derby, 11 December 1787, 7 May 1788, box 11, folder 2; Ludlow and Gould to Derby, 21 November 1787, box 11, folder 4; Hewes and Anthony to Derby, 19 August 1790, box 10, folder 7; Shreve and Lawrason to Derby, 1 July 1788, box 12, folder 6; Hewes and Anthony to Elias Hasket Derby, 28 September 1789, box 10, folder 7, Derby Papers, Phillips Library, Essex Institute, Salem. The same Baltimore firm that handled wine consignments for Derby also sold china for him. In 1790, for instance, it notified him that, 'a quantity of well assorted china would ... meet with a pretty ready sale, such as tea & coffee cups & saucers, small & low priced tea & table setts, something like the two setts you sent here some time ago'.

62. Wines, fruit, mutton and candles were acquired at the Cape; sheep and mares were obtained at the Isle de France. Elias Hasket Derby Jr, to Mr Van Den Burg, 1 May 1791, and Elias Hasket Derby to Sebastian Van Renan, 4 May 1791, box 9, folder 8, Derby Shipping Papers, Derby Papers. By 1796, Derby's ships, laden with Madeira wine, were going as far east as Manila. For the beginning of the Manila trade, see the 1796 voyage of the *Astrea*, on which Derby shipped 100 pipes of Madeira wine, 12.5 pipes Lisbon wine and 12.5 pipes Carcavelos wine. Elias

Hasket Derby to John Bulkeley and Sons, March 1796, Elias Hasket Derby Letterbook, vol. 11, fo. 423, Derby Papers.

63. Richard H. McKey, Jr, *Elias Hasket Derby Merchant of Salem, 1739–1799* (PhD thesis, Clark University, MA, 1961), pp. 149, 151.

64. Elias Hasket Derby to Theophilus Cazenove, 23 April 1791, Elias Hasket Derby Letterbook, vol. 11, fo. 168, Derby Papers.

65. John Searle III to Elias Hasket Derby, 23 February 1788, and John Marsden Pintard to Elias Hasket Derby, 24 February 1788, box 12, folder 6, Elias Hasket Derby Correspondence, Derby Papers.

CHAPTER FOUR

Manners and Character in Anglo-American Perceptions, 1750–1850

Paul Langford

During the three-quarters of a century that followed the Declaration of Independence, certain stereotypes of British and American life emerged on either side of the Atlantic. Many concerned the make-up of society, its codes of behaviour and its interactions. These may be crudely summarized. In American eyes British society was incorrigibly aristocratic, bound by rigid upper-class rules, preserved by cringing lower-class servility and served by institutional conservatism. In British eyes American society was dangerously egalitarian, conducted according to barbaric ideas, governed by unprincipled democrats and bereft of decorum and order. Put simply, America was too democratic to be genteel, and Britain was too genteel to be democratic. These were, of course, merely bass notes for continuo players. On them could be composed chords offering variations. And from time to time other tunes might be heard. But the basic pattern of perceptions in each direction is remarkably consistent and coherent. When Emerson praised English traits and Hawthorne damned them, they were often agreeing on impressions only to differ in their opinion of them.[1] And the same might be said when Frances Wright applauded American manners and Mrs Trollope denigrated them.[2]

Such sweeping characterizations were not uncommon in this period. It inherited from the eighteenth century an absorbing interest in social conduct, in manners as they reflected the peculiar conditions of diverse societies. This was intensified by a sense of the changes sweeping over both the Old and New World during a time of revolutions in ideas and politics, and transformations of the economic order. There were those who thought the very newness of the American state made it peculiarly prone to judge and be judged by the way people 'were personally treated'.[3] And not least it was sharpened by the growing fascination with national character and the ethnic imprints of peoples as opposed to the impact of governors and governments. Even so, in the shared though often mutually hostile world of Anglo-American perceptions there were some features of this characterizing that seem relatively uncommon.

The first is that they lacked any obvious pre-history. The ways that European nations described each other depended on traditions that could be traced back for centuries. This does not seem to work in the Anglo-American case. Before the 1780s, for Americans to attribute a specific character to the British or vice versa, was unusual. As parts of the same empire neither started from an assumption of distinctiveness. Americans, as we are often reminded, had a large investment in their English past; they blamed rulers not subjects, corruption not character. 'Many of our own people', wrote William Austin in 1803, 'are strongly prejudiced against the English. This originated in the American Revolution, but it was not the English character that was *detestable*, it was the *English system*.'[4] And the English seem to have had such a hazy idea of the people who inhabited their North American empire that attributing any positive qualities to it would have been extremely difficult. Even so the contrast with later models is quite striking. It did not, for example, require a War of Australian Independence or even the formal concession of Australian home rule to generate some colourful and contrasting stereotypes of British and Australian life during the colonial era.

The second feature is that they belonged in a relatively finished, even literary cultural context. The United States and the United Kingdom (partially excluding Ireland) were the two most literate societies in the civilized world and they shared the same literature. 'Above all books, have united to make us feel as if we were but children of the same great family, only divided by the Atlantic ocean' wrote Benjamin Waterhouse, the New England doctor and author.[5] Most of the books were British. The consequence is well known for the slow establishment of American literary independence, but it is equally important for the transmission of Anglo-American perceptions. In the resulting war of words, literary organs and talents were perhaps more to the fore than they previously had been in the generation of national stereotypes. One has only to recall that the prime culprit in poisoning Anglo-American perceptions was generally said to be the *Quarterly Review* and also that many of the most luminous stars of English literature on either side of the Atlantic found the temptation to dip their pen in this poison almost irresistible.

Where, then, did the poison originate? One possibility, not to be altogether discounted even in these postmodernist days of perceptions and voices, revealing not reality but only the evanescent representations of shifting discourses, is that they were based on genuine observation, as the tide of emigrants or travellers in both directions swelled. Perhaps American gentlemen really were uncouth in deportment and conversation, and perhaps English lords truly did 'cold shoulder' their guests. Perhaps American women were familiar of address and dominating in manner, and perhaps English ladies were prudish in conversation and forbidding to strangers. Perhaps the American workman was indeed boorishly inquisitive and presumptuous, and perhaps the English labourer was unduly deferential and subdued. But even if so, it is obvious from the determination to make these social 'facts' characteristic that a good deal more is involved.

Take for instance the most common offence against politeness in the United States. This was said to be the habit of tobacco chewing and spitting, a subject on which practically no British visitor failed to remark, and which no American tourist seems to have recorded in Britain. But the significance attributed to this single habit was surely out of all proportion. As the *Edinburgh Review*, not unsympathetic to the United States, sarcastically observed: 'We are terribly afraid that some of the Americans spit upon the floor, even when that floor is covered with good carpets. Now, all claims to civilization are suspended till this secretion is otherwise disposed of. No English gentleman has spit upon the floor since the Heptarchy.' The point had relevance to victims of English snobbery within the British Empire as well as beyond it.[6] In any case most of what what was written about manners was much in the eye of the beholder. It concerned impressions that were selective in all kinds of ways, and belonged in a picture that was rarely formed without previous preconceptions.

It would be easy to account for hostile preconceptions. One might assume a massive dose of sour grapes on the British side as the masters of a mighty empire came to terms with a rebel society that had not only humiliated its rulers in war, but showed every sign of establishing a powerful empire of its own. Equally there might be on the post-colonial side an uncomfortable mixture of triumphalism and insecurity, heightened by the growing realization that Britain's star, far from waning after the loss of the Thirteen Colonies, appeared still to be in the ascendant.

We might, too, wonder about the sources of adverse commentary, particularly in the early stages of separation. On the British side it does seem possible that the officer class of the royal forces might have permanently jaundiced their countrymen's view of America. These were frequently young men whose politics were aggressively loyalist, who started from the assumption that their opponents were unworthy of them, and who as younger sons or ambitious tyros on the fringes of aristocratic society were prone in social matters to be *plus royaliste que le roi*. On the other hand, in the memoirs that actually survive, it is surprising how little of this prejudice occurs. Moreover, when they met Americans in a civilian context it was often among loyalists whose social rules they did not find very different from those encountered in

Britain. The sexual anxieties of patriot American males suggest, indeed, that some colonial society was rather too compatible with the manners of the mother country.[7]

On the American side there was no single body of opinion that could be characterized so simply. What there was, of course, was an upsurge of Republican rhetoric that might well predispose Americans to a negative view of British mores. On the other hand early nineteenth-century Americans were often at pains to explain that the bitterness of their fathers and mothers had not been passed on. Moreover the leaders of the American Revolution were in many instances self-consciously gentlemen, and the language and aspirations of their wives might not look in the least odd in the pages of Jane Austen.[8] It took the French barely three years of revolution to replace the politesse of the ancien regime with the equality of the new. Whatever else the Thirteen Colonies achieved between the summoning of the second Continental Congress and the surrender at Saratoga it was hardly that. There is plainly a tale to be told about the decline of aristocratic manners in the United States but it is long, uneven and certainly not marked by a spectacular Declaration of Independence from the dominion of English gentility.

A more profitable mode of enquiry is to ask what contemporary needs characterizations of this kind met. It makes sense to start with Britain. There are, after all, empires of manners as of trade or territory. But such empires are not regulated by treaty and in 1783 all the advantages were on one side. In the Western code of civility British manners occupied an established and increasingly respected place. American manners had to be invented or rediscovered. And even then to deprive them of any relationship with the mother country would have required unusual ingenuity or boldness.

Predictably, from the standpoint of people who considered themselves gentlemen and gentlewomen in London, the manners of America were considered at best provincial. It is important to separate such judgements from those that were manifestly hostile. Mrs Trollope's diatribes, even in the eyes of many Britons, were less than fair, based on virtually no mixing with the higher classes of the United States,[9] and confined largely to its inferior towns.[10] To compare Cincinatti with London was ludicrous; a fairer comparison would have been with the new towns of England's industrial frontier, Huddersfield or Salford, and it might not have been to their advantage.

In fact there was recognition from open-minded observers that the larger cities did challenge comparison with England. Philadelphia, New York and Boston were all deemed to have much the same customs as London, with the same fashions, albeit one year out of date, and visiting rules only slightly less elaborate.[11] What was wanting in these places was said to be a certain sophistication and polish. How could it be otherwise? High society in London had evolved codes of conduct suited to a wealthy, snobbish and censorious class who numbered at most a few thousand and spent the greater part of their lives in the same square mile. America had nothing to match this, and its decision to establish a new capital ensured that for the foreseeable future it would have nothing to match it. Isolating the nation's legislators from the great centres of wealth creation divided élite resources and made the emergence of a genuine Western metropolis unlikely. Washington was for many years a society of limited pride even among its temporary residents. Other places might have better claims to set the tone, but none of them ever conceded the palm to another, as Harriet Martineau found when she was compelled to prefer the pretensions of the ladies of Philadelphia to those of Baltimore, in the matter of bonnets, and vice versa in the matter of hospitality.[12] Such rivalry was characteristic of provincial centres in Britain.

I emphasize the term provincialism because it does not necessarily imply anti-Americanism. Polite society in London thought much the same of Bristol or Norwich as it did of Boston or New York. Significantly, visitors to either country often compared the provincial centres of England with the cities of America, Boston and Birmingham, Philadelphia and Bristol, and so on. This Englishness of American society before the Civil War was too frequently felt to be the result of mere patronizing superiority. In old age Fanny Kemble recalled that on arrival she had found

> the whole country like some remote part of England that I had never seen before, the people like English provincial or colonial folk; in short, they were like *queer* English people. Now there is not a trace of their British origin, except their speech, about them, and they are becoming a real nation.[13]

Reading the impressions of Americans who came to London, I am struck by their resemblance to those of Britons who came there for the first time. There was the same anxiety on the subject of one's own accent, language, demeanour, posture, dress and so on; the same amazement at the intricacy and complexity of the social rules that governed the life of a self-consciously potent ruling class; the same awe before the self-assurance, composure and superiority that marked its manners.

But, of course, before 1783, an uncouth American was simply one kind of backward Englishmen among many; after it he was specifically an American, condemned to backwardness by virtue of his origins. Particularly in the 1790s and 1800s when many believed that American governments were ranged on the side of French republicanism and Bonapartism, there was evident prejudice at work when Americans were encountered in a social setting. Some observers plainly were on the lookout for evidence of vulgarity.[14] And for many visiting Americans it was galling to realize that the ultimate reward for social success was to be taken for an Englishman or woman, rather than a representative of the breed of civilized Americans.

Even so much of what passed for anti-Americanism was only incidentally that. Obvious examples might be found in the way that Americans who made their career in Britain were treated. Artists such as Benjamin West and Charles Leslie were subject to some derision behind their backs. But what they had to endure was no worse and indeed very similar to what the West-Country born John Opie endured. Or take the example of the lawyer Lord Lyndhurst, who rose to occupy the highest legal office in the land, as Lord Chancellor. He, too, had to put up with snide innuendo and occasionally direct insult on account of his origins.[15] But these were less than the Newcastle-born Eldon, or the ill-bred Thurlow, had to put up with on account of their manners.

'In conversing with Americans', wrote Mrs Trollope, 'I have constantly found that if I alluded to anything which they thought I considered as uncouth, they would assure me it was local, and not national.'[16] This would have been a reasonable riposte in Britain or France. Why should it have been objectionable in the Americans? Largely because the British were determined to believe that America was indeed a locality, not an authentic nation. 'We drove them into being a Nation when they are no more fit for it than the convicts of Botany Bay' wrote Vere Foster, British representatative in Washington during the Napoleonic Wars.[17] Judgements of this kind revealed the reluctance with which generations of Englishmen recognized the separate existence of North America in a social as opposed to a political sense. Mrs Trollope's son Anthony even observed that 'The United States are, in the most proper sense, a British colony' though he said it, perhaps wisely, in a book on Australia rather than on America.[18]

From an American standpoint, provincialism was not a very satisfactory fate. Significantly the very term 'province', though it had a respectable pedigree in transatlantic discourse, seems to have dropped out of usage, partly, no doubt, because the provinces were after all self-designated states from 1776, but also because 'province' arguably implied colonial status. But, however Americans chose to define their standing, they faced a dilemma if they wished to locate their society on the map of civility. Confronted with the reality of society in London few of them were prepared to deny its superior gloss, graces and gorgeousness, what the young Audubon called 'perfection of manners: such tone of voice I never heard in America'.[19] Yet one of the most powerful priorities of the first half of the nineteenth century was the quite consciously perceived need to mark out the superiority, either implicit or explicit, of the young republic in all kinds of endeavours, not excluding the ease and assurance of its social life. And because manners were so crucial in contemporary analyses of national character, the relationship between the mores of Americans and those of Europe could not simply be ignored. It had to be faced.

Facing it proved troublesome. One difficulty was that when Americans sought to identify their emerging character as a people, it proved remarkably hard to do so in a fashion that distanced them from the British. The commonly boasted virtues of the American included energy and enterprise, honesty and candour, courage and determination, common sense and practical-mindedness. These were precisely the virtues that John Bull customarily claimed for himself. Much the same could be said of the alleged vices of each. The accusations of commercialism, hypocrisy and reserve against which Americans had to defend themselves were also levelled at the English. In fact generally most of what was described as American looked very like a somewhat heightened colouring of an English feature. The prudery that English men complained of in American women was just what European travellers found irritating in English women.[20] Another common complaint was of the superficially unwelcoming coldness of American men and their concealment of emotion.[21] Yet this, too, was precisely the European complaint about the English.

It is true that propagandists for American superiority did attempt to separate their claims from those of Englishmen. Take for instance Charles Sealsfield's attempt to argue that American bravery was of a different kind from British. He depicted the courage of the Briton as a showy, pretentious quality that could not bear comparison with the inspired patriotism of an American, not 'the swaggering British bull-dog courage, but always the constant, composed, decided, calm, unshaken and unshakable courage of the Americans'.[22] But substitute French for British, cockerel for bulldog, and Englishmen for Americans, and this contrast would be precisely the one that the British themselves might have deployed. Americans themselves often admitted the point. 'There are no very strong traits of character, which mark the difference between the Englishman and the American', wrote Mordecai Noah in 1819.[23]

The difficulty of identifying distinctive qualities of character made it all the more necessary to find distinctiveness in the nature of society rather than the individual. But differences about manners might merely be seen as arguing over trifles, and the fact was that Americans arriving in Britain were often hard put to find major divergences. 'The manners of the gentlemen were substantially the same with those of similar American circles' wrote Benjamin Silliman, after attending his first dinner party on landing in England at Liverpool in 1805.[24] Interestingly, a matching remark was made by John Griscom on his first dinner at Liverpool in 1823.[25] One senses not only the relief felt by young Americans getting off the packet at Liverpool, but also the rather misleading impressions that they had been led to expect. Moreover, for numerous foreign visitors, it was the resemblances between Britain and America that were most striking at any rate in point of social usages. Chastellux found examples of telling similarity ranging from the absurdly dictatorial ways of masters of ceremonies, to a liking for toasts, treatment of children and the deportment of politicians.[26]

An alternative tactic was to claim equality not so much by marking out distinctiveness as by emphasizing parity. This was the method adopted by Fenimore Cooper in his *Notions of America*. Cooper believed that Englishmen had missed the true character of Americans by largely ignoring the seaboard. 'Volumes have been written concerning the half-tenanted districts of the west, while the manners and condition of the original states, where the true effects of the American system can alone be traced, are usually disposed of in a few hurried pages.'[27] Cooper reckoned that New England formed the ancestry of four-fifths of all American whites in his time. He also thought that theirs was a stock of peculiar purity and vigour, directly traceable to the Plymouth settlers of two centuries before. And above all he believed that the type had produced in numerous instances a species of gentility that was entirely comparable to the aristocratic version to be found in England.

There was some force in these arguments. It was true that the English neglected the extent to which America had a culture already mature in 1776. It was also true that English travellers often side-stepped New England, especially during the teens and twenties, when much of the published literature had to do with the prospects of emigration and settlement in the new territories. And it was a well-established argument from the time of the Revolution, that Americans were, so to speak, the sound branch of the British tree, spared the corruption of political life and social manners that marked the decadent time of George III and his successors.

Unfortunately there were also snags. Emphasizing New England meant emphasizing Englishness, albeit a somewhat older and purer form of it. It also meant emphasizing the provincial nature of New England's inheritance, making American a kind of perpetual Far West Country, an extension of England's own West Country, one step further on the line of railroads and steamships that were stretching out from London to the Ohio as Cooper wrote. This assumption that Britain was the dog and America the tail produced some extraordinary sentiments, such as the speech made in 1851 at Baltimore by the ballad writer Martin Tupper in which he referred, apparently without irony, to the union of what he called 'Insular America and Continental England'. Tupper was one of those who believed that the highest compliment to be paid an American was to treat him as British. 'I tell you, brother Jonathan, That you're a Briton too!'[28]

The linguistic consequences were not the least obvious. Americans, led by Webster himself,[29] boasted that so-called vulgar Americanisms were in fact the correct English usage of the seventeenth century and purer than contemporary English. But occupying the rugged high ground of history left the fertile valley of modernity to others. As the British civil servant Sir James Bland Burges observed, 'The mischief of it is, that in the Eastern States, whose inhabitants are almost entirely English, or descendants of Englishmen, they retain all the local idioms and barbarisms from the country from which they migrated. Thus a barbarous dialect becomes a national language, and its corruption is perpetuated.'[30] An ingenious rejoinder was to point out that some American usages actually perpetuated the approved language of a former ruling class in London, a contention that could be supported by English friends who recalled such usages.[31] But even then it remained the case that metropolitan society had moved on. Every American attempt to trace its hereditary character was liable to encounter the accusation that the resulting character was hopelessly outdated.

There were, perhaps, other cards to play from this suit, but they did not carry much conviction. One would have been that other New Englishness, the regeneration of the English nation within a nation boasted by Cotton Mather and a long line of religious reformers, but this would have required some finessing to set against modern English gentility and it would certainly not have suited the ostentatious shunning of religious politics that was correct in Cooper's day.[32] The trump card was the South, where the genteel ethic flourished and where social confidence founded on concentrated wealth was achieved on a European scale, but that was a card that could not be played except by unashamed defenders of slavery.

There was also the awkward matter of ethnicity, all the more awkward given the increasingly racial tone that governed English perceptions of Englishness. The rise of Saxonism was to do something to mitigate self-conscious hostility between many English people and many Americans and was to figure heavily in the folklore of the special relationship. But it hardly served the cause of American identity at a time when the perceived need for a separate character was powerfully felt. Nor was it reinforced by continued English emigration. The common assumption seems to have been, to quote A. P. Thornton, 'of all emigrants to the United States, they were the English who took with them the deepest feelings of personal grievance and the least durable folk-memory'.[33] In some ways it was to prove more appealing at the end of the century when mass immigration from southern and eastern Europe was threatening Anglo-Saxon identity, than in mid-century when the descendants of Anglo-Saxons, whatever that meant, actually were predominant.[34]

And so they were driven back to the persistent belief that it was indeed politics that constituted the basis of the divergence between American and English manners. This worked well in that the American Revolution could be interpreted as a denial of the principles of hierarchy and heredity supposedly to be found in Britain. It worked doubly well in that Britain's resistance to the French Revolution seemed to reinforce this identification. And it worked trebly well in that the history of Britain itself up to and beyond the failure of Chartist revolution in 1848 seemed to reveal the link between political conservatism and aristocratic society. In respect of America, it also fitted a train of analysis culminating in Tocqueville's classic but anticipated by whole schools of self-appointed Montesquieus who searched for the social impact of an egalitarian republic. And, finally, it seemed to derive additional plausibility from the political importance attaching to the manners of the new republic. The interest generated by George Washington's driving in a coach and six, or Thomas Jefferson's reception of State visitors in his slippers, or Mrs Monroe's difficulties with visiting rules and drawing rooms, or John Quincy Adams's billiard table, were not trivial, for they reflected a deeper debate about the nature of a republican polity. In that debate the underlying thrust was not, to say the least, on the side of self-conscious gentility. Jefferson's slippers were not only a useful tactical weapon in the White House's recurrent warfare with British diplomats, but also belonged in the rather sterner domestic strife that made every evidence of ceremony or superiority a fatal concession to Federalist politics and European mores. And so the stereotypes of England as the home of the aristocratic gentleman and America as that of the man of the people became ever more entrenched.

Playing this game of stereotypes or, to put it another way, fighting this war of manners, reinforced the vanity of two societies, both in some respects quite insecure, both undergoing rapid change and both struggling to make their traditions and aspirations fit the requirements of unprecedented growth. If there were losers as individuals they were, I think, likely to be Americans.

North America was not at any point during this period part of a European's Grand Tour and was not often visited by the cream of English society. Only later did the British aristocracy take a closer interest in American society, resulting in some interesting developments such as the efflorescence of blue-blooded ranching in the West,[35] and the sudden appearance of American brides on the London marriage

market. But before the Civil War most of the judgements were made by
men and women who were no more than middle class in English terms.
John Griscom thought that the most anti-American people he met in
England were those, like a Manchester businessman, who had visited
America in a commercial capacity.[36] Others, the best known, made their
living from their writing at a time when the non-acceptance of men of
letters in England was a favourite topic of debate. As Tocqueville pointed
out, 'these pitiless censors furnish, for the most part, an example of the
very thing they blame in the United States. They do not perceive that
they are deriding themselves, to the great amusement of the aristocracy
of their own country'.[37] Of course, the first instinct of a parvenu is to
distance himself from other parvenus. Encountering a whole society of
parvenus had a certain charm in this respect and the Fanny Trollopes
and the Basil Halls derived more satisfaction from their American tours
than they recognized themselves.

Less happily circumstanced were Americans who did not themselves
find it very difficult to survive in both societies, but who were expected
to be offended by one and proud of the other. There were many such in
this period and, interestingly, they feature quite disproportionately in
the generation of Anglo-American perceptions.

Some of these were men for whom even high society in London held
few terrors. But their very success laid them open to a charge of treachery.
'There are Americans', wrote Calvin Colton, 'who, while visiting England, allow themselves to be *dined* and *toasted* out of their character.'
Colton urged such a man not to 'become less of an American than he was
before'.[38] Loss of identity is difficult to assess. It was a common observation that Americans who made a name in London were loath to admit
that they had been born on the wrong side of the Atlantic.[39] Talleyrand
said he had seen many Americans who wished to pass for Englishmen but
never an Englishman who wished to pass for an American.[40]

There were others whose patriotism was unimpugned but who plainly
had no difficulty in England. It probably is true that most of them were
in politics conservative and intrinsically sympathetic to the British,
whatever their family's stance had been during the Revolution. Some
distinguished diplomats were obvious examples. One was Rufus King,
whose politics were Federalist, and whose personal bearing suggested a
certain 'pride and hauteur in his manner offensive to the delicacy of
republicanism, and inconsistent with the nature of equality'.[41] This was
said in 1818 but there is no suggestion that he had picked it up in
England. So far as I am aware the only concession King felt it necessary
to make to life among London's élite was to give up smoking.[42] Much
the same was true in some other professions where residence in England
was an advantage if not a requirement. The American artist Stuart

Newton was a hit in what Maria Edgeworth called 'the very best society both in London and in country houses of the first style' when she met him in 1831.[43]

As Scotsmen, Irishmen or Welshmen, or indeed as provincial Englishmen, these instances would have been not very startling, as further examples of the extraordinary pull exerted by polite metropolitan society and the social and professional advantages that it could confer. The point to which I return is that in respect of manners Americans were indeed no more distinctive or disadvantaged than provincial Britons. But individuals are often bound by their national rhetoric and in the years following the Declaration of Independence a veritable ocean of rhetoric was separating American and British self-perceptions, often encouraged by subversive spirits in Britain itself for whom America was Britain's missed opportunity of national regeneration. James Barry's Phoenix or American liberty 'a new people of manners simple and untainted' represented a vision of enormous power and one that could not readily be gainsaid.[44]

Did any Anglophile American square this circle, by conceding that Old World manners might have something to be said for them? Irving, perhaps, but Irving glamourized old English life more than contemporary English life, and even so got into trouble with his compatriots for his complaisance.[45] Emerson was another who praised without prejudicing his own standing or indeed affecting his own estimation of what it meant to be an American. Emerson had a degree of social standing and self-assurance which could genuinely match what was to be found in England but which was perhaps not common outside his native Boston.[46] Perhaps anyway, by the 1850s, it was easier for an Anglophile American to admit that he might in Henry James's words 'remount the stream of time to the head-waters of his own loyalties' without compromising his own or his country's identity.[47] The pain of knowing that one's father or grandfather had indeed been a subject of Queen Victoria's grandfather was passing away and England was becoming 'a country to be toured, described, and pictured' not without sentiment certainly, but without excessively agonizing self-searching on the subject of identity.[48]

The English gentleman represented a social ideal whose full potency reached its apogee in the nineteenth century. It is, of course, possible to be a democrat and a gentleman, but the association was not a natural one and the process of reconciliation needed some ingenuity. Some of the most celebrated of Americans sought to achieve it.[49] Be that as it may, even when achieved the contradictions and ambiguities remained perplexing. It was easy for opponents to exploit them, as the *Quarterly Review* itself did whenever it came across examples of American democrats who showed a weakness for titles or a liking for etiquette.[50] At the very least such tensions highlight the social instabilities of a period that was once rather confidently interpreted as one of steadily growing national confidence but which now seems rather more problematic.[51] It was a subject on which King George himself, that tyrant of 1776, had pronounced views, though not without a certain self-deprecating sense of irony, as an anecdote retailed by Rufus King reveals. On 13 July 1797 he remarked to the American minister that he had read Adams's first speech as President and found it far superior to that of Washington. He had noted, he said, that Adams had addressed his hearers not as fellow citizens but as gentlemen. He also enquired of King whether Adams and his audience had been properly dressed for such an occasion, a point on which King was able to reassure him. His Britannick Majesty, we are told, showed his pleasure. Attention to such matters was important, he observed, where the authority of the magistrate was concerned. And, so Rufus King's memorandum tells us, as he spoke, he perceptibly winked.[52]

Notes

1. Ralph Waldo Emerson, *English Traits* (Boston, 1856); Nathaniel Hawthorne, *Our Old Home*, 2 vols (London, 1863).
2. Frances Trollope, *Domestic Manners of the Americans*, 2 vols, 4th edn (London, 1832).
3. Henry Bradshaw Fearon, quoted by James Chandler, *England in 1819: The Politics of Literary Culture and the Case of Romantic Historicism*, (Chicago, 1998), p. 444.
4. William Austin, *Letters from London: Written during the Years 1802 and 1803* (Boston, MA, 1804), p. 281.
5. B. Waterhouse, *A Journal of a Young Man of Massachusetts* (Boston, 1816), repr. *The Magazine of History* (1911), p. 13.
6. *Sydney Monitor*, 16 April 1828.
7. 'Correspondence of Arthur Middleton', 1781–82, *South Carolina Historical and Genealogical Magazine*, 26 (1925), 187.
8. L. H. Butterfield, Marc Friedlander, Mary-Jo Kline (eds), *The Book of Abigail and John: Selected Letters of the Adams Family, 1762–1784*, (Cambridge, MA, 1975), and more fully *Letters of Mrs. Adams, the Wife of John Adams*, 2 vols (Boston, MA, 1890).
9. *A Great-Niece's Journals being Extracts from the Journals of Fanny Anne Burney (Mrs Wood) from 1830 to 1842*, ed. M. S. Rolt (London, 1926), p. 47.
10. *Correspondence of Mr. Joseph Jekyll with his Sister-in-Law, Lady Gertrude Sloane Stanley, 1818–1838*, ed. A. Bourke (London, 1894), p. 307.
11. *The Diary of Joseph Farington*, eds K. Garlick, A. Macintyre and K. Cave, 16 vols (New Haven, CT, 1978–84), vol. 11, p. 3889; Henry Wansey, *An Excursion to the United States of North America, in the*

Summer of 1794, 2nd edn (Salisbury, 1798), vol. 1, p. 174; Isaac Weld, *Travels through the States of North America, and the Provinces of Upper and Lower Canada, during the Years 1795, 1796, and 1797*, 2nd edn (London, 1799), vol. 1, p. 266; Jacques-Pierre Brissot, *New Travels in the United States of America. Performed in 1788* (London, 1792), p. 94.

12. Harriet Martineau, *Society in America*, 2nd edn, 3 vols (London, 1837), vol. 2, p. 3.

13. Frances Anne Kemble, *Further Records. 1848–1883*, 2 vols (London, 1890), vol. 2, p. 240.

14. Henry Swinburne, *The Courts of Europe at the Close of the Last Century by the late Henry Swinburne, Esq.*, ed. C. White, 2 vols (London, 1841), vol. 1, p. 393.

15. Carola Oman, *The Gascoyne Heiress: The Life and Diaries of Frances May Gascoyne-Cecil* (London, 1968), p. 198.

16. Trollope, *Domestic Manners of the Americans*, vol. 1, p. 20.

17. Vere Foster (ed.), *The Two Duchesses* (London, 1898), p. 253.

18. Anthony Trollope, *Australia*, eds P. D. Edwards and R. B. Joyce (St Lucia, Queensland, 1967), p. 48.

19. Maria R. Audubon, *Audubon and His Journals*, 2 vols (London, 1898), vol. 1, p. 111.

20. C. F. Henningsen, *Analogies and Contrasts; or, Comparative Sketches of France and England*, 2 vols (London, 1848), vol. 1, pp. 178–9.

21. Catherine Traill, *The Backwoods of Canada: being Letters from the Wife of an Emigrant Officer* (London, 1836), p. 83.

22. Paul C. Weber, *America in Imaginative German Literature in the First Half of the Nineteenth Century* (New York, 1926), p. 135.

23. Mordecai M. Noah, *Travels in England, France, Spain, and the Barbary States, In the Years 1813–14 and 15* (New York, 1819), p. 51.

24. Benjamin Silliman, *A Journal of Travels in England, Holland and Scotland, and of Two Passages over the Atlantic, in the Years 1805 and 1806*, 2 vols (New York, 1810), vol. 1, p. 56.

25. John Griscom, *A Year in Europe*, 2 vols (New York, 1823), vol. 1, p. 37.

26. François-Jean de Beauvoir [Marquis de Chastellux], *Travels in North-America, In the Years 1780, 1781, and 1782*, trans., 2 vols (London, 1787), vol. 2, p. 175.

27. J. Fenimore Cooper, *Notions of the Americans*, 2 vols (London, 1828), vol. 1, pp. 131–2.

28. Martin Farquhar Tupper, *My Life as an Author* (London, 1886), pp. 257, 262.

29. Sterling Andrus Leonard, *The Doctrine of Correctness in English Usage 1700–1800* (Madison, WI, 1929), ch. 10.

30. *Selections from the Letters and Correspondence of Sir James Bland Burges, Bart.*, ed. J. Hutton (London, 1885), pp. 224–5.

31. *Autobiographical Recollections by the late Charles Robert Leslie*, ed. T. Taylor, 2 vols (London, 1860), vol. 1, p. 251.

32. Philip S. Haffenden, *New England in the English Nation, 1689–1713* (Oxford, 1974), ch. 2.

33. A. P. Thornton, *The Habit of Authority: Paternalism in British History* (London, 1966), p. 157.

34. Stuart Anderson, *Race and Rapprochement: Anglo-Saxonism and Anglo-American Relations, 1895–1904* (East Brunswick, 1981).

35. Lawrence M. Wood, *British Gentlemen in the Wild West: The Era of the Intensely English Cowboy* (London, 1990).
36. Griscom, *A Year in Europe*, vol. 2, pp. 256–8.
37. Alexis de Tocqueville, *Democracy in America*, vol.2, ch. 14.
38. Calvin Colton, *Four Years in Great Britain*, new edn (New York, 1836), p. 15.
39. J. Fenimore Cooper, *England*, 3 vols (London, 1837), vol. 1, p. 169.
40. Cyrus Redding, *Fifty Years' Recollections, Literary and Personal, with Observations on Men and Things*, 3 vols (London, 1858), vol. 2, p. 28.
41. *The Life and Correspondence of Rufus King*, 6 vols (New York, 1894), vol. 6, p. 680.
42. Ibid., vol. 3, p. 5.
43. Maria Edgeworth, *Letters from England 1813–1844*, ed. C. Colvin (Oxford, 1971), p. 496.
44. Nicholas K. Robinson, *Edmund Burke: A Life in Caricature*, (New Haven, CT, 1996), p. 33.
45. Christopher Mulvey, *Transatlantic Manners: Social Patterns in Nineteenth-Century Anglo-American Travel Literature* (Cambridge, 1990), p. 4.
46. R. W. Emerson, *Four Years in Great Britain*, new edn (New York, 1836), p. 15.
47. H. James, *English Hours* (London, 1905), p. 166.
48. Robert E. Spiller, *The American in England during the first Half Century of Independence* (New York, 1926), p. 237.
49. Edwin Harrison Cady, *The Gentlemen in America: A Literary Study in American Culture* (New York, 1949, repr. 1969).
50. *Quarterly Review*, 59 (1837), 328.
51. Stephen Fender, 'Revolution, Succession and National Identity in American Literature', *Proceedings of the British Academy*, 82 (1992), 285–301.
52. *The Life and Correspondence of Rufus King*, vol. 3, p. 549.

CHAPTER FIVE

Queen Victoria and the United States

Walter L. Arnstein

In recent years I have been involved in drafting a number of topical essays involving neglected facets of both the public and the private worlds of Queen Victoria. When I first pondered the possibility of exploring the subject of Queen Victoria and the United States, I consulted the dauntingly comprehensive bibliography compiled more than a decade ago by David A. Lincove and Gary R. Treadway under the title, *The Anglo-American Relationship: An Annotated Bibliography of Scholarship, 1945–1985.*[1] The carefully prepared index did not even list Queen Victoria by name.

That omission notwithstanding, further research revealed a plenitude of both secondary works and primary sources – many of them printed, others hitherto unpublished – that suggests that, even if the United States did not play a vital role in the world of Queen Victoria, it did play an important role. The queen in turn came to assume so significant a place in the minds of many Americans that a number of their descendants have come to look back on the nineteenth-century United States as 'Victorian America'.

My purpose will be to touch on three distinct, though intermingled, strands in the relationship between Queen Victoria and the United States:

1. The public relationship, i.e. the references made by Victoria to the United States in her public pronouncements, such as her annual speeches from the throne to the assembled Parliament and in her meetings with a succession of American ministers to the Court of St James.
2. The private relationship, i.e. the behind the scenes influence that the Queen and Prince Albert exercised on the course of Anglo-American diplomacy and her private comments about the United States, its culture, and its representatives.
3. An examination of changing American attitudes towards the queen, attitudes that ranged all the way from open hostility to avowed adoration.

This chapter will touch on all three of these interconnections in a roughly chronological manner as it deals first with Victoria's early years (up to the death of Prince Albert in 1861), then with her years of widowhood and, finally, with the years of the Golden Jubilee of 1887, the Diamond Jubilee of 1897 and Victoria's death in 1901, years of apotheosis that may well have played a vital if neglected role in the Anglo-American diplomatic and cultural *rapprochement* that began in the 1890s and came to fruition during the Second World War.

For many nineteenth-century Americans, British monarchs remained the direct heirs of the monarchical tyrant they had condemned in their Declaration of Independence, and for many British radicals the United States remained a beacon: a land without a hereditary peerage or a hereditary monarchy or an established church. It was a land in which, in Jeremy Bentham's words, 'all is democracy; all is regularity, tranquillity, prosperity, security ... no aristocracy; no monarchy; all that dross evaporated'.[2] What was a monarch such as Queen Victoria, after all, asked one contributor to the New York based *Democratic Review*? She was no more than the descendant of the bastard son of the Duke of Normandy by the daughter of a tanner of Falaise. What reason did she therefore have to take pride in her 'immaculate blood royal'? 'If we look back on the so-called nobility of England, we shall find more wantonness among the women and more libertinism among the men' than among the people of any other land. By contrast, Americans could look 'with pride ... to our own high standards of morals in our public men and distinguished women'. Were Victoria or her fellow monarchs truly 'heaven descended'? 'Could any of them at an election by the people secure a majority of the suffrages? ... if not, whence their right to rule'?[3]

Although the Princess Victoria was brought up to respect rather than to condemn the institution of hereditary monarchy, she had not been taught to despise the United States. Less than two years after the end of the War of 1812, her father, the Duke of Kent, had gone out of his way to toast 'The United States of America, and perpetuity of the friendship between Great Britain and them'. He had done so in the presence of John Quincy Adams, the American minister to Britain and future President.[4] The prickly Adams had privately condemned the Prince Regent as a compound of obtuseness and 'frivolity ... a Falstaff without the wit and a Prince Henry without the compunctions',[5] but he responded warmly to the words of the Prince Regent's younger brother and expressed the hope that 'the harmony between Great Britain and the United States may be as lasting as the language and the principles common to both'.[6]

When the young princess did accede to the throne in June 1837, the American minister, Andrew Stevenson, reported that she and her mother 'are believed to be strong friends to reform and popular rights'.[7] One individual who took a particular interest in that event was the victor of the Battle of New Orleans of 1815, President Andrew Jackson. A few years earlier, Victoria's mother, the Duchess of Kent had gone out of her way to tell the American *chargé d'affaires* in London, of her interest in President Jackson's life and of her concern for his health and welfare. She had also conveyed her wishes 'for the prosperity of the United States, for which she entertains the most friendly feelings and great admiration'. Jackson reciprocated with a long and complimentary letter to the princess and to her mother (who was then still the prospective regent), and he accompanied the letter with an inscribed portrait, a gesture reciprocated by the princess. When Victoria became queen, the ex-President therefore looked on her as a personal protegée, his 'little good friend', and he perused with intense interest reports about her coronation, her marriage and her children. Victoria and Albert, in turn, read a full-length biography of 'Old Hickory'.[8]

Nor was ex-President Jackson the only American to catch in the late 1830s a contagion that the *Democratic Review* condemned as 'Victoria Fever'.[9] The article told of an innocent visitor in 1839 to the city of Philadelphia, where the most important museum featured a 'splendid painting of Her Majesty Queen Victoria', where shops sold Queen Victoria hairbrushes, Queen Victoria clocks, and 'Queen Victoria soap, composed expressly for the coronation'. Also for sale were Victoria riding hats, Victoria canes, Victoria lace and Victoria gloves, and even Victoria bean soup, not to forget Queen Victoria's Family Pills. At the local music store one could purchase copies of the 'Victoria Grand March' and the 'Victoria Quadrille'. The local Baltimore House Hotel, moreover, had changed its name to the Victoria Hotel. The irate republican visitor wondered aloud 'whether the days of old had not returned, and we were yet bowing beneath the sceptre of England' and whether the city of brotherly love ought not to be renamed 'Victoria-delphia'.[10]

A succession of American envoys was to find Victoria readily approachable and easy to talk to. Thus Edward Everett noted in 1841 that the 22-year-old monarch had approached him with unexpected 'ease and simplicity of manner ... without formality or stateliness'. At dinner she addressed Everett, seated to her left, in English, and Albert, seated to her right, in German. Everett found the youthful Albert to be 'an exceedingly modest, intelligent, well-educated person, greatly above the average, I should think, of those of his rank in Europe'.[11] Subsequent Americans ministers made similar reports, though they sometimes felt compelled to note the queen's lack of physical beauty. 'She has not many personal charms', reported James Buchanan in 1853, 'but [she] is gracious and dignified in her manners, and her character is without blemish.'[12] Analogously, George Mifflin Dallas, the former Vice-

President, observed in 1856 that 'she is not handsome, but her expression of face and her manner are engaging, and very soon [she] put her visitors at ease'.[13]

American travellers were equally complimentary about the queen as a public speaker; at a time when very few women ever spoke in public, the queen read her semi-annual speeches from the throne with melodious clarity. Charles Sumner, the future senator from Massachusetts, reported in 1839 that he had 'never heard anything better read ... than her speech'.[14] Eight years later George Bancroft observed that Victoria addressed Parliament with far greater skill than did King Louis Philippe when speaking to the French Chamber of Deputies.[15]

Although they enjoyed English society, American ministers reminded themselves at regular intervals that they were republicans both at heart and in appearance. In 1853, indeed, Secretary of State William L. Marcy issued a circular to all American envoys abroad in which he insisted that, whatever the local court custom, they appear 'in the simple dress of an American citizen'.[16] James Buchanan therefore informed Major-General Sir Edward Cust, Queen Victoria's Master of Ceremonies, that he intended to abide by Marcy's protocol 'unless the Queen herself would intimate her desire that I should appear in costume'. Cust responded that, although the queen would not publicly object, she might find it privately disagreeable if Buchanan failed to 'conform to the established usage'. He might therefore receive no future invitations to the state opening of Parliament or to Court dinners or Court balls.[17] Buchanan concluded that, inasmuch as Victoria was 'a lady' and inasmuch as 'the devotion of her subjects towards her partakes of a mingled feeling of loyalty and gallantry', it might be best for him to seek out a happy medium. He would appear in a black coat, a white waistcoat and cravat, black pantaloons and dress boots, and a 'very plain black-handled and black-hilted dress sword'. As a good democrat, Buchanan would, however, altogether eschew both embroidery and gold lace. Apparently, Queen Victoria was well satisfied with the American minister's compromise outfit because at the first leveé of the 1854 season she greeted him with 'an arch but benevolent smile'.[18]

Visiting London for the first time in 1853, Senator Stephen Douglas of Illinois fared less well. Well-known as an Anglophobe whose head would remain unturned 'by the glitter of a star or the sound of an empty title', Douglas visited the House of Commons and conferred amiably with British radicals such as Richard Cobden, John Bright and Joseph Hume. When he requested an audience with Queen Victoria, however, he was told that he would have to appear in 'court dress'. To the satisfaction of his friends back home, he refused point blank. Douglas was subsequently received in civilian dress by the emperors of Russia and of France. 'The Queen did not relent', concludes Douglas's biographer, but it remains quite possible that the request never went beyond the chief of protocol and that Douglas was secretly delighted thus to uphold 'the honor and the glory' of the United States in the midst of 'crowns and coronets'.[19]

Not only could Britons be upholders of outmoded ceremonial, but they remained untrustworthy diplomatic rivals. In Edward Everett's words, 'John Bull is very amiable in private life ... but in foreign politics he is selfish and grasping; and where he dares, insolent'.[20] George Bancroft concurred. In the eyes of Lord Palmerston, 'John Bull is everything, and ... international law, treaties, and interests of all sorts must yield to British pretensions',[21] but now that in 1848 the French had thrown off their king, 'there will not be a crown left in Europe in twenty years'.[22] A few years later, George Mifflin Dallas set forth similar sentiments: 'All this magnificence of ceremonial and pretension is being fast undermined, even among the proudest peers, by our republican principles, accompanied by our wonderful prosperity'. Before the end of century ended, predicted Dallas, 'it will have vanished, like the hues of a rainbow, for ever'.[23]

In the course of their negotiations with the Court of St James, it is true, American emissaries often had to deal with topics that fitted uncomfortably with their republican ideals. Thus back in the 1830s Andrew Stevenson had objected strongly to steep 'injurious and indefensible' British duties on American tobacco, duties that were not only opposed to 'the just and liberal principles' in commerce that both nations professed but that also prevented the mass of the British public from smoking, chewing or snuffing tobacco of even tolerably acceptable quality. Queen Victoria, whose detestation of tobacco anticipated that of the American surgeon-general and the Food and Drug Administration by well over 100 years, was presumably not amused.[24] Nor was she sympathetic to American demands for reimbursement for American slaves who had found refuge and freedom in British ports or to ships engaged in the illegal slave trade that hoisted an American flag in order to avoid a search by British naval vessels off Africa's western coast. Britain's foreign secretaries – not only the militant Lord Palmerston but also the equable Lord Aberdeen – insisted that it was 'impossible for her Majesty's Government to make the slightest compromise on the subject of slavery ... when slaves were found within the British jurisdiction, by whatever means or from whatever quarters, they were *ipso facto* free'.[25] American ministers such as Edward Everett privately conceded that such controversies placed them in a truly awkward position, 'for whatever else might or might not be true of England, she was honestly and actively trying to suppress a most shameful practice'.[26] It was a subject

in which both Albert and Victoria took a strong interest. Albert's very
first public speech in England had condemned the continuing illegal
trade in slaves.[27]

Although Buchanan's mission in London was also troubled by unresolved Anglo-American disputes over the future government of Central
America, Buchanan himself became a highly popular presence in London, especially from 1854 on, when he was joined by his niece Harriet
Lane – attractive, flirtatious, well-mannered and well-read, and a star in
London's social world. She dined with Queen Victoria and she even
danced with Prince Albert, and at Buchanan's final conference with the
queen in 1856, Victoria talked mostly about 'dear Miss Lane'.[28]

It was President Buchanan who in 1858 exchanged the first messages
with Queen Victoria across the initial (and abortive) transatlantic ca-
ble.[29] It was President Buchanan also who – learning in 1860 that the
18-year-old Prince of Wales was to visit Canada – invited him to cross
the border as well. He became the first member of Britain's royal family
to tour the independent United States as a guest. Prince Albert had long
been fascinated by the New World, and he skilfully drafted the speeches
that his son would deliver.[30] That son proved to be a charming and
engaging young visitor who adored the crowds that came to cheer him.
In Canada he opened a new railway bridge across the St Lawrence
River at Montreal. At Ottawa he laid the foundation stone for what
became the federal Parliament building. He crossed the border at Detroit, and in the course of the next four weeks, he was enthusiastically
received in Chicago, St Louis, Cincinnati, Pittsburgh, Boston and in
numerous other American cities.[31] In New York City he received his
most tumultous reception. Was that not remarkable, asked Albert, 'for
the most republican city in republican America'?[32] So many young
women sought to dance with the prince that the ballroom floor collapsed. In Washington, he was the guest of honour at a great State
dinner in the White House. After the entire royal party had been accom-
modated for the night, President Buchanan discovered that all the White
House beds were full and that the Lincoln bedroom was not yet available. The President therefore had to sleep on a sofa.[33]

Victoria reproved her eldest daughter for writing about 'those horrid
Yankees' just after they had given her brother so 'marvellous' and so
'unexpected' a reception, a reception that the queen modestly attributed
to 'the (to me incredible) liking they have for my unworthy self'.[34]
President Buchanan judged the visit 'a triumph from beginning to end',
and Queen Victoria in turn described it as an 'important link to cement
two nations of kindred origin and character'.[35]

That cement seemed likely to crack within the year, as the outbreak of
the American Civil War soon threatened to involve Great Britain. After a

Union vessel had kidnapped two Confederate envoys from a neutral British steamer, the *Trent*, Lord Palmerston was prepared to demand immediate redress in peremptory terms. It was the dying Prince Albert who redrafted the dispatch so as to give President Lincoln and Secretary of State Seward the opportunity to save diplomatic face. Queen Victoria became persuaded (as have many historians), that Albert thereby prevented an Anglo-American war. For that reason, the widowed Victoria felt more sympathetic to the cause of the Union than did most members of Palmerston's ministry.[36] The American minister, Edwards Pierrepont, observed a few years later that in the United States there was 'a universal belief that the Queen, in our late Civil War, was on the side of freedom ... and that she prevented a recognition of the rebel states ... and thereby saved the lives of many thousands of our countrymen'.[37]

Only in 1866, in her speech from the throne, was Queen Victoria able to observe

> with Satisfaction that the *United States*, after terminating successfully the severe Struggle in which they were so long engaged, are wisely repairing the Ravages of Civil War. The abolition of Slavery is an event calling forth the cordial Sympathies and Congratulations of this Country, which has always been foremost in showing its Abhorrence of an Institution repugnant to every feeling of Justice and Humanity.[38]

In the mean time, the queen had been deeply shocked by the 'dreadful and awful' news of the assassination of Abraham Lincoln. As she wrote to her Uncle Leopold, 'one never heard of *such* a thing! I only hope it will not be *catching elsewhere*'.[39] Two days later she had personally drafted the following lines to Mary Todd Lincoln:

> Dear Madam, Though a stranger to you, I cannot remain silent when so terrible a calamity has fallen upon you and your country, and must express personally my deep and heartfelt sympathy with you under the shocking circumstances of your present dreadful misfortune.
>
> No one can better appreciate than I can, who am myself utterly broken-hearted by the loss of my own beloved husband, who was the light of my life, my stay, my all, what your sufferings must be; and I earnestly pray that you may be supported by Him to Whom alone the sorely stricken can look for comfort, in this hour of heavy affliction!
>
> With the renewed expression of true sympathy, I remain, dear Madam, your sincere friend, VICTORIA R.[40]

'They say', wrote Walter Bagehot in *The English Constitution*, 'that the Americans were more pleased at the Queen's letter to Mrs Lincoln, than at any act of the English Government. It was a spontaneous act of intelligible feeling in the midst of confused and tiresome business.'[41]

Sixteen years later, the queen was to take a comparable interest in the fate of President James Garfield. The American minister in London reported that, after Garfield was shot early in July 1881, 'from the Queen to the artisan, the feeling has been universal and very striking in its manifestation. The first question in the morning and the last at night for the first ten days after the news came was always: "How is the President?"' At Victoria's special request, a copy of every telegram from Washington to the minister in London about Garfield's condition was immediately forwarded to Windsor.[42] On 22 September she lamented: 'How sad is the poor President's death at last after such long sufferings & such alternations of hope and fear!'[43] Victoria immediately sent a telegram of condolence to Mrs Garfield and set a precedent by ordering the British Court into mourning for one week.[44]

From the end of the Civil War until the arbitration settlement of 1872, Anglo-American relations had been bedevilled by the *Alabama* claims, the widespread American belief that the ultimate victory of the Union had been delayed for two years by the success of the *Alabama* and two other Confederate cruisers in destroying Union vessels. Although the ships had neither been armed nor manned in British waters, they had originally been built in British shipyards, and Americans such as Senator Charles Sumner, the head of the Senate Foreign Relations Committee, claimed indemnification not only for 'direct costs' (the value of the Union ships sunk and their cargo) but also for the 'indirect costs' (the total federal war budget from 1863 to 1865). Admittedly he expressed his willingness to have the British pay, not in money but in kind, by forthwith handing the dominion of Canada over to the United States.[45]

For successive British foreign secretaries and prime ministers, the Alabama claims negotiations proved extraordinarily complex and frustrating, and they tried the patience of even the pacifically inclined William Ewart Gladstone. Queen Victoria, who could prove militant in upholding British honour in the face of the Russian and of French pretentions, remained remarkably temperate *vis-à-vis* the United States, and she never criticized Gladstone for his policy of appeasement toward the United States. She thought initially, indeed, that 'the Federal Government certainly have just cause for complaint',[46] and on several occasions[47] she urged British ministries to return a soft answer to senatorial wrath. She also successfully encouraged leaders of the political opposition not to undermine the policy of Gladstone's government.[48] The *Alabama* claims were at last resolved at Geneva in 1872, when an international tribunal asked the British government to agree to pay 'direct claims' of more than £3 million. In the opinion of the queen's Private Secretary, 'the judgment seems on the whole to be fair'.[49]

Queen Victoria was somewhat less indulgent towards Irish-American Fenians who in 1866 used the United States as a base for their own private invasion of Canada and as a source of dynamite for bombs exploded in Glasgow and London in 1883.[50] She and her Liberal Home Secretary were even more disturbed by the manner in which the United States, 'a country professing friendship for Great Britain', permitted publications such as the *United Irishman* of New York City openly to call for the assassination of the Prince of Wales and of other members of the royal family.[51] Although the American government proved publicly unresponsive to British complaints, American ministers to Britain such as James Russell Lowell were privately horrified by the manner in which Irishmen naturalized in the United States returned to their native land with the deliberate intent of poisoning Anglo-American relations and, if possible, embroiling the two nations in all-out war.[52]

In the mean time, a succession of American ministers continued to receive a friendly reception from the queen. General R. C. Schenck reciprocated during the 1870s by introducing that prototypical American card game, poker, to London's high society.[53] He had to leave his post in disgrace when he was caught up in the financial collapse of a western gold mine,[54] but that event may only have piqued Queen Victoria's own interest in the American frontier. And so, when Buffalo Bill's Wild West Show performed at London's Earls Court in 1887, Victoria was an admiring attendant at what she called 'a very extraordinary' spectacle involving cowboys and Indians. A mock attack on a coach and a ranch involved an 'immense amount of firing' and 'was most exciting'. She found the Red Indians 'with their feathers, & wild dress (very little of it) rather alarming' and 'their war dance quite fearful'. Colonel Cody himself was, however, 'a splendid man, handsome & gentlemanlike in manner'. The queen was so impressed with the performance that, when the troupe returned to England five years later, she imported the entire company for a performance on the lawn adjoining Windsor Castle.[55] In the mean time, she had visited London's Olympia in order to revel in P. T. Barnum's spectacle, *Nero, or the Burning of Rome*, with its cast of more than 1200 performers and almost as many animals.[56] In the queen's eyes, Americans did remain a somewhat wild and woolly bunch. As she noted to her eldest daughter in 1877, in England, engaged couples had nowadays lost all sense of 'modesty – for ... they go about driving, walking and visiting – everywhere alone ... In short, young people are getting very American, I fear in their views and ways'.[57]

The Americans whom the queen encountered in person were not necessarily either fun-filled or frivolous, however. There was, for example, Dr Henry Benjamin Whipple, the Episcopalian Bishop of Minnesota, who had served, the queen reported, as 'a sort of father & guide to the Red Indian tribes ... He spoke with affection of ... their trials, their attachment & devotion'.[58] There were also the black minstrels who sang 'extremely well' for the queen one summer in Scotland,[59] and there was the aged Jonah Henson, the original Uncle Tom of Harriet Beecher Stowe's famous novel. He visited the queen at Windsor in 1877, and he proved to be 'such a strong, fine, good old man – who has gone through such untold hardships. [He] wished to thank me for all I had done for the poor, suffering slaves'.[60]

Often the queen took public cognizance of events in the United States. After the great Chicago fire of 1871, she headed the list of 12 000 Britons who sent books to initiate a free Chicago Public Library; her contribution was a personally inscribed biography of Prince Albert.[61] When Americans celebrated the centenary of their independence in 1876, the queen sent several of her best paintings to the Philadelphia Exposition.[62] When Charleston, South Carolina, was struck by an earthquake in 1886, the queen immediately cabled her sympathy.[63] To an increasing degree, Americans responded in kind. Thus in 1874 British associations in Virginia and elsewhere in the United States began the annual custom of celebrating the queen's birthday – with religious services and dances, with historical lectures and lavish dinners.[64]

The shadow of the Irish Question darkened late-Victorian Anglo-American diplomatic and cultural relations. Disputes over fishing rights also recurred often,[65] and in 1895 President Grover Cleveland became attracted by the romance of the South American jungle and appeared ready to take on all-comers in defence of an ill-defined boundary between Venezuela and British Guiana [now Guyana]. Like other disputes, it was in due course resolved peacefully, though, as Colonial Secretary Joseph Chamberlain reported to the queen, in American newspapers, 'the motives of the British government are invariably misrepresented and denounced ... As a consequence the people at large are very ignorant of our institutions and character'.[66]

Shortly thereafter, Victoria's niece, the Queen Regent of Spain, appealed vainly to Britain for support against the manner in which the American government was preventing the Spaniards from suppressing an insurgency in Cuba.[67] When the Spanish-American War broke out in 1898, the American ambassador in London, John C. Hay, found indeed that Britain was 'the only European country whose sympathies are not openly against us'.[68] Privately, it is true, the queen was highly dubious. As she wrote to her daughter, 'this Spanish war distresses me very much ... No doubt Cuba was dreadfully governed, but that does not excuse America and the principle is dreadful. They might as well say we governed Ireland badly and they ought to take possession of it & free it'.[69] During the Anglo-Boer War of 1899, in turn, there were numerous Americans who were willing to compare President Paul Kruger of the Transvaal and the Boer soldiers with the American patriots of 1776.[70]

In other respects, however, the pendulum of Anglo-American relations had by then begun to swing from hostility to concord, and not the least of the reasons for this change were Queen Victoria's Golden Jubilee of 1887, her Diamond Jubilee of 1897 and her death in January 1901. On the occasion of the Golden Jubilee, President Cleveland sent a letter of congratulations that began with the words: 'Great and good Friend ... It is justice and not adulation to acknowledge the debt of gratitude and respect due to your personal virtues, for their important influence on producing and conserving the prosperous and well-ordered condition of affairs now generally prevailing throughout your Dominions.'[71] On the occasion of the Diamond Jubilee of 1897, President William McKinley went so far as to appoint a special American Jubilee emissary, Whitelaw Reid, the long-time editor of the *New York Tribune* and an out-and-out Anglophile. He spoke to the queen often; he made numerous speeches on behalf of the cause of Anglo-American amity; and he rode proudly in the great Jubilee procession.[72] The American ironist, Mark Twain, proved to be a most unironical spectator of that same display. Indeed, he celebrated its climax, the queen herself, as 'a symbol, [as] an allegory of England's grandeur and the might of the British name ... The procession', he concluded, 'stood for sixty years of progress and accumulation, moral, material and political'.[73]

When Queen Victoria died on 22 January 1901, the news was immediately flashed to Washington by telegraph, and in the course of the next few days American newspapers paid almost as much attention to her passing as did those of the United Kingdom. In Washington, DC, the House of Representatives immediately adjourned – in her honour.[74] President McKinley at once ordered American flags to be lowered to half-mast above the White House and every other executive department building. No foreign monarch had been so honoured before. On the day of the funeral, the New York Stock Exchange remained closed, and in Washington President McKinley and his entire cabinet attended memorial services at St John's Episcopal Church.[75] Former Republican President Benjamin Harrison observed that 'No other death could have excited so general a sorrow', and Democratic presidential candidate William Jennings Bryan agreed that Victoria's 'personal virtues [had] won for her the love of her subjects and the respect of the world'.[76]

Americans disagreed as to the extent of Queen Victoria's political power but not about the significance of her influence. In the words of Senator Hernando De Soto Money of Mississippi, 'Victoria as a woman and as a mother presents one of the most beautiful lives in all history'.[77]

The theme of Victoria as model woman was to be often repeated. According to the Reverend Washington Gladden, the Congregational Minister from Ohio of 'Social Gospel' fame: 'It was her pure womanliness that drew to her the hearts of her people, with a strength of affection that no English monarch has ever called forth.'[78] For President Francis L. Patton of Princeton University 'the purity of her court and the high standard of social morality on which she insisted, entitled her to the title of "Victoria the Good"'.[79] The St Louis *Globe-Democrat* agreed that 'the family throughout Christendom has been strengthened by her example'.[80]

Other themes were voiced also. Representative John B. Corliss of Michigan observed that 'her reign demonstrated that it is possible to give a good government under the form of a monarchy'.[81] As American minister to Britain between 1889 and 1893, Robert Todd Lincoln, the son of Abraham Lincoln, had often met the queen, and for him Victoria was 'one of the wisest women – probably the wisest who ever lived. I do not mean to say that she [was] a genius, but her great gift of common-sense, reinforced by her vast store of knowledge ... enabled her to counsel men and women of all classes and conditions with a wisdom which could not be excelled'.[82]

Let me conclude with four reflections.

1. Queen Victoria did not convert the vast majority of Americans to the virtues of monarchical government, but she did come to be looked on as a model ruler. As American minister Edwards Pierrepont had phrased the matter back in 1877, 'There is not a bit of love for kingly government in the United States, but a deep hatred of it – and yet towards your Queen there is a deep honest and sincere admiration'. She was 'in every relation of life a *true and most exemplary woman*'.[83]

2. The manner in which the queen's life was celebrated during her later years in the United States and the manner in which her death was observed completed her transformation into the personal embodiment of the Victorian virtues of duty, domesticity, character and dignity that a majority of both Americans and Britons publicly professed. No wonder then that, according to the *New York Herald*, 'all over the world Columbia's sons wept with those of Britannia'.[84] '[F]rom the Brooklyn Bridge could be seen thousands of flags floating at half-mast in token of sympathy with the sorrow of the nation whose dominance we had once resented.'[85]

3. Like other nineteenth-century Britons, the queen could privately be critical of American brashness and vulgarity, but ultimately those Americans who considered her a friend were right. Her independent

political power may have been limited, but her influence was less so, and that influence was consistently on the side of preventing disputes with the United States from leading to war.

4. The formal process of diplomatic *rapprochement* involving the governments of Britain and the United States between the years 1895 and 1914 that Bradford Perkins has charted[86] was notably, if coincidentally, assisted by the Diamond Jubilee in 1897 and by Victoria's death in 1901. By then the early nineteenth-century spirit of cultural rivalry had given way (certainly among the upper middle classes of the eastern seaboard and elsewhere) to the sense that they and their British counterparts were part of the same English-speaking civilization. It would be foolish to discount that phenomenon when we seek to understand on which side the United States ultimately fought during the First World War and the Second World War.

In 1901, the then well-known American poet and reporter, Ella Wheeler Wilcox, was asked by her editor to report on Victoria's funeral. She responded with a lengthy poem entitled *The Queen's Last Ride*. This chapter may close appropriately with the final stanza:

> Though in regal splendor she drives through town,
> Her robes are simple – she wears no crown.
> And yet she wears one; for, widowed no more,
> She is crowned with the love that has gone before,
> And crowned with the love she has left behind
> In the hidden depths of each thinking mind.
>
> Uncover your heads, lift your hearts on high,
> The Queen in silence is driving by.[87]

Inasmuch as readers may be altogether unfamiliar with that poem, it seems appropriate to note that it was included in the 1936 edition of *The Best Loved Poems of the American People*.

Notes

1. D. A. Lincove and G. R. Treadway, *The Anglo-American Relationship: An Annotated Bibliography of Scholarship, 1945–1985* (New York, 1987).
2. *The Works of Jeremy Bentham*, ed. J. Bowring, 11 vols (London, 1838–43), vol. 3, p. 447 cited in David Paul Crook, *American Democracy in English Politics, 1815–1850* (Oxford, 1965), p. 16.
3. Colonel Eidolon, 'A Pertinent Question', *Democratic Review*, 35 (March 1855), 216–18.
4. Cited in Beckles Willson, *America's Ambassadors to England, 1785–1929* (New York, 1929), p. 128.
5. Ibid., p. 136.

6. Ibid., p. 128.
7. Ibid., p. 216.
8. Ibid., pp. 206–8.
9. Anon., 'The Victoria Fever', *Democratic Review*, 6 (July 1839), pp. 74–6.
10. Ibid., p. 76. I owe this reference to Dr Robert Sampson.
11. Cited in Paul Revere Frothingham, *Edward Everett, Orator and States-man* (Boston, MA, 1925), pp. 193–4.
12. Cited in Willson, *America's Ambassadors*, p. 277.
13. Ibid., p. 295.
14. Cited in Sidney Lee, *Queen Victoria: A Biography*, new edn (London, 1904), p. 92.
15. M. A. DeWolfe Howe, *The Life and Letters of George Bancroft*, 2 vols (New York, 1908), vol. 2, p. 76.
16. Ibid., p. 282.
17. Ibid.
18. Ibid., pp. 284–5. See also Philip Schreiner Klein, *President James Buchanan: A Biography* (University Park, PA, 1962), pp. 228–9.
19. Robert W. Johannsen, *Stephen A. Douglas* (Oxford, 1973), pp. 383, 386.
20. Cited in Willson, *America's Ambassadors*, p. 241.
21. Ibid., p. 253.
22. Ibid., pp. 253, 256.
23. Ibid., pp. 297–8.
24. Ibid., pp. 222–3.
25. Ibid., p. 237. See also p. 217.
26. Ibid., p. 236.
27. Cf. Daphne Bennett, *King Without a Crown* (Philadelphia, 1977), p. 85.
28. Klein, *Buchanan*, 246–7.
29. Ibid., p. 320.
30. Bennett, *King*, p. 328.
31. The best brief account may be found in Dana Bentley-Cranch, *Edward VII: Image of an Era, 1841–1910* (London, 1992), pp. 20–34.
32. Bennett, *King*, p. 328.
33. Klein, *Buchanan*, p. 350.
34. *Dearest Child: Private Correspondence of Queen Victoria and the Crown Princess of Prussia, 1858–1861*, ed. Roger Fulford (London, 1964), p. 279.
35. Cited in Bennett, *King*, p. 328 and in Klein, *Buchanan*, p. 350.
36. *The Letters of Queen Victoria*, ed. G. E. Buckle, 2nd series, 3 vols [1861–78] (London, 1926–28), vol. 1, pp. 9–10; Lee, *Victoria*, pp. 316–19; Norman B. Ferris, 'The Prince Consort, *The Times*, and the *Trent* Affair', *Civil War History*, 6 (1960), pp. 152–6.
37. Cited in Arthur Ponsonby, *Henry Ponsonby, Queen Victoria's Private Secretary: His Life from His Letters* (New York, 1944), p. 326.
38. *Parliamentary Debates*, 3rd series, vol. 181, col. 22.
39. *Letters of Queen Victoria* , 2nd series, vol. 1, p. 265.
40. Ibid., p. 266.
41. Walter Bagehot, *The English Constitution* (Ithaca, NY, 1966), p. 86. The book was first published in London in 1867.
42. Willson, *American Ambassadors*, pp. 381–2.
43. Philip Guedalla, *The Queen and Mr. Gladstone*, one-volume edn (Garden City, NY, 1934), pp. 520–21.
44. *The Times* (London), 21 September 1881, p. 5.; 22 September 1881, p. 7.

45. A helpful summary is provided in chs 8 and 9 of Charles S. Campbell, *From Revolution to Rapprochement: the United and Great Britain, 1783–1900* (New York, 1974).
46. *Letters of Queen Victoria*, 2nd series, vol. 1, p. 252.
47. Cf. ibid., vol. 2, pp. 210–11.
48. Ibid., pp. 220–21. See also ibid., pp. 212–13.
49. Ibid., pp. 228. The United States had asked £40 million in 'direct claims' and c. £400 million in 'indirect claims'. See Campbell, *Revolution to Rapprochement*, p. 114.
50. Cf. *Letters of Queen Victoria*, 2nd series, vol. 1, pp. 373–6; vol. 3, pp. 417–18.
51. Ibid., vol. 3, pp. 222, 481. See also vol. 3, pp. 299–300, 421.
52. Willson, *American Ambassadors*, p. 380.
53. Cf. ibid., p. 359.
54. Ibid., pp. 366–7.
55. Queen Victoria's journal for 11 May 1887 is cited in Frances Dimond and Roger Taylor, *Crown and Camera: The Royal Family and Photography, 1842–1910* (Harmondsworth, 1987), p. 180.
56. Stanley Weintraub, *Victoria: An Intimate Biography* (New York, 1987), pp. 493, 179–80.
57. Roger Fulford (ed.), *Darling Child: Correspondence of Queen Victoria and the German Crown Princess 1871–1878* (London, 1976), pp. 257–8.
58. Queen Victoria's journal for 7 December 1890 is cited in Frances Dimond and Roger Taylor, *Crown and Camera: The Royal Family and Photography, 1842–1910* (Harmondsworth, 1987), p. 158.
59. Royal Archives (Windsor), Queen Victoria's journal for 7 May 1873. This citation is quoted by the gracious permission of Queen Elizabeth II.
60. Fulford, *Darling Child*, pp. 243–4.
61. Benjamin D. Rhodes, 'Anglophobia in Chicago', *Illinois Quarterly*, 39 (Summer 1977), 10.
62. *New York Daily Tribune*, 24 May 1877.
63. *Washington Post*, 23 January 1901.
64. *New York Daily Tribune*, 24 May 1877.
65. See *Letters of Queen Victoria*, 3rd series, vol. 3, pp. 606–8.
66. Ibid., p. 75.
67. Ibid., pp. 44–5.
68. Cited in Willson, *American Ambassadors*, p. 14.
69. Agatha Ramm (ed.), *Beloved and Darling Child: Last Letters Between Queen Victoria and Her Eldest Daughter, 1886–1901* (Stroud, 1990), p. 213.
70. Cf. Byron Farwell, *The Great Anglo-Boer War* (New York, 1976), p. 145.
71. Cited in Willson, *American Ambassadors*, p. 391.
72. Royal Cortissoz, *The Life of Whitelaw Reid*, 2 vols (New York, 1921), vol. 2, pp. 216–18. From 1905 until his death in London in 1912 Reid was to serve as American Ambassador.
73. Mark Twain, *Queen Victoria's Jubilee* (London, 1897), p. 20.
74. *Washington Post*, 23 January 1901.
75. Jerome Packard, *Farewell in Splendor: The Passing of Queen Victoria and Her Age* (New York, 1995), pp. 168–9, 258.
76. *Washington Post*, 23 January 1901.
77. *Chicago Tribune*, 23 January 1901.

78. Cited in Adrienne Munich, *Queen Victoria's Secrets* (New York, 1995), p. 11.
79. *Chicago Tribune*, 23 January 1901.
80. Cited in ibid.
81. *Chicago Tribune*, 23 January 1901.
82. Cited in Packard, *Farewell*, p. 134.
83. Cited in A. Ponsonby, *Henry Ponsonby*, p. 326.
84. *New York Herald*, 23 January 1901, p. 3.
85. Ruth Putnam, 'Two English Queens', *The Critic*, 42 (June 1903), 538.
86. Bradford Perkins, *The Great Rapprochement: England and the United States, 1895–1914* (New York, 1968).
87. Hazel Felleman (ed.), *The Best Loved Poems of the American People* (Garden City, NY, 1936), pp. 557–8.

CHAPTER SIX

'America' in the Victorian Cultural Imagination

James Epstein

The subject of America as seen from Britain during the nineteenth century is, of course, vast and complex, not least because no settled image prevails. What I hope to do, however, is to touch briefly on how various tropes about America were worked and reworked, to suggest how 'America' was put into discourse, offering often elusive points for debate and anxiety about Britain's own future as a modern polity and society. At one level, Jean Baudrillard's portrayal of Europe as forever chasing the shadow of America's radical otherness makes good sense.[1] But America's 'otherness' is always in question; the anxiety is often expressed not that America is something else, a space against which Europe is defined, but rather that it is a privileged site where Europe's future, for better or worse, is constantly being previewed. Whether Britain and America are comparable sites of civilization is a matter for debate. Moreover, I use the term 'imagination' in my title not to imply a 'real' America over an imagined space, but rather to suggest that it is precisely how America is to be imagined that is most crucially in question: what does America represent and for whom? Certainly many travelled to America from Britain, not least importantly the hundreds of thousands of working people seeking a brighter future, and found their images radically at odds with their actual experience of the New World. But people, particularly writers, travelled to America to see and prepared to see certain things, to test certain imaginative constructions. And, as Malcolm Bradbury notes, it was hardly necessary to go to America in order to construct such an imagined space.[2] No less of a champion of all things American than John Bright never visited its republican shores. America was a place to be imagined, debated and theorized – a 'true fictional space'.[3]

Above all, perhaps, America represents the site of 'the modern'. But the terms 'modern', 'modernism' and 'modernity' are notoriously diffi-cult to pin down.[4] Certainly 'the modern' entails a desacralization of tradition, an assertion of openness and freedom unbounded by the past or history, a restless desire to move within the horizon of an always imminent present. This also implies a national and individual doctrine of self-referentiality. Thus Thomas Paine believed that Americans must be taught 'the manly doctrine of reverencing themselves'. In the first instance, radicals envisaged America as a modern space characterized by the positive virtues of youth, simplicity, rusticity and innocence.[5] For Major John Cartwright, America stood like 'naked Eve – "when unadorned, adorned the most" – the Americans, when stripped of political garb of civil rule, appeared with the greater lustre, enrobed in political wisdom and virtue'.[6] Nakedness here stands for the unconditioned self: the enlightenment desire to strip away the trappings of past civilization; full development is premised on its own conditions of existence. Such visions of America as 'natural' space subject to the pure designs of natural reason and thus available for new beginnings ran up against the development of this space, its realization as modern space.[7] America still offered a utopian space of naturalness; the back country was the perennial site of utopian experimentation, whether pantisocratic, Owenite or Icarian. America rarely failed the romantic quest for the natural sublime, although monumental landscape succumbed to development: Niagara Falls becoming a site of commercial tourism.[8] Throughout the nineteenth century, the shifting western frontier loomed as a space of Nature and of freedom, a receding place just beyond culture and social order, of homesteads and farms, but also of wildness, untamed meanings and loss.

Literary visions: Dickens and Arnold

The paradox of development stands at the heart of British Victorian imaginings of America. What sorts of political, cultural, spatial and self development were characteristic of modern society and compatible with civilized everyday life? Most particularly, during the nineteenth century America functioned as a vexed site of rapid change and 'progress'. Travel was itself an important yardstick of modern progress – the passage over by steam packet, the roads and stagecoaches, canals and railways opening up space for modern civilization. America was constantly being tested by the largely metropolitan codes of Britain. The literature of nineteenth-century British travellers to America obsessively retraces its own tracks, revisiting the same institutional sites to check-out and to compare American 'progress': prisons and houses of industry, asylums for the blind, insane and poor, reformatories and common schools, law courts, libraries and universities. As telling as were the differences between various observers, is the sameness of where they sought out meaning and measured development.[9] Reformation and order were the keynotes struck.

Dickens, for example, whose *American Notes for General Circulation* offended Americans when published in 1842, was generally favourably impressed by the order, the neatness and humanitarianism to be found among the institutions of eastern cities. The Boylston indigent boys and juvenile offenders answered questions correctly without books, such as 'where was England'; they were well fed, acted in 'an orderly manner', sang a song 'about a farmer sowing his seed'; they were treated with kindness and taught to respect the values of 'sober industry'. Visiting an American state prison or house of industry, Dickens remarks that he found it difficult 'to persuade myself that I was really in a jail'. He concludes that in Boston, 'the unfortunate or degenerate citizens of the State' are 'appealed to, as members of the great human family', and are well on their way to being reformed and returned to useful citizenship.[10] Order is established from the city's edges of delinquency.

Like many Victorian travellers, Dickens was struck by the informality of American manners, by the lack of decorum and hierarchy of an American court of law, by the un-uniformed conductor and boisterous familiarity of the railway carriage, by American table manners and the nearly universal habit of tobacco chewing and spitting. Manners are, of course, anything but incidental to assessments of American cultural development since they speak of the regimes of self-discipline, the personal denials and restraints necessary to the civilizing process.[11] However, Dickens's early chapters are reassuringly up-beat. Thus the mill town of Lowell presents 'well-ordered' factories, mill girls well-dressed 'but not ... above their condition', and boarding-houses, with pianos, circulating libraries and even a periodical written by the girls themselves. All this stands in marked contrast to Lancashire's mill towns, 'those great haunts of desperate misery'.[12] In certain respects, in *American Notes*, Dickens writes against the grain of British urban commentary, including much of his own future journalism and fiction. Moreover, Dickens returns home in summer 1842 to a Britain on the verge of civil war throughout its industrial heartland. Against this background, much of his first volume may be read as exhibiting qualified confidence in the development of American urban life; a confidence that is generated primarily from regulated sites of discipline, improvement and urban order.

Only when he turns West does Dickens's vision truly darken. Unable to bear 'the pain of living in the constant contemplation of slavery', Dickens cancels his planned journey south. The South does not disappoint liberal expectations for it holds no promise. The West is where Dickens is allowed 'to dream again of cities growing up like palaces in fairy tales, among the wilds and forests'; and it is the West that disappoints, giving up America's inner meaning: its dullness, crass materialism, fakery and absence of civilized order.[13] Cincinnati is a 'beautiful', 'thriving' city, Dickens tells readers, but he has lost interest in sites of urban progress. It is the 'class of society', particularly indeterminate beyond its roughness, travelling down the Ohio and Mississippi rivers aboard steamboats that symbolizes the thinness, crudity and essential sameness of American life. Rather than functioning as a metaphor for the West's freedom, offering prospects for the full development of the individual, the river brings us face to face with loss. The foul, 'hateful' Mississippi takes Dickens to 'dismal' Cairo, ironically renamed 'Eden' in *Martin Chuzzlewit*. Moreover, the new settlements along the banks of the Ohio, the log cabins and frame houses, no better than the lodging for the settlers' pigs, have destroyed Nature's landscape. In a typical passage, Dickens reports: 'The eye was pained to see the stumps of great trees thickly strewn in every field of wheat, and seldom to lose the eternal swamp and dull morass, with hundreds of rotten trunks and twisted branches steeped in its unwholesome water.'[14] Development produces nothing here but loss.

If the back country and cities of the West are places of neither true liberty nor interest, the urban wilderness of New York yields adventure and a counterpoint to the city's sites of improvement. Dickens is conducted through the narrow streets clustered around Five Points – New York's equivalent to London's notorious Seven Dials – where 'nearly every house is a low tavern' and all is shrouded in darkness and filth; 'sleeping negroes' crowd the upper stories of ruined tenements from which Dickens eventually 'descends' into Almack's, 'assembly room of the Five Point fashionables'. Here he is treated to the minstrelsy of Juba (William Henry Lane), 'the greatest dancer known' and 'hero' of the scene. Fiddle and tambourine pick up the pace as Juba takes the floor:

> Single shuffle, double shuffle, cut and cross-cut; snapping his fingers, rolling his eyes, turning in his knees, presenting the backs of his legs in front, spinning about on his toes and heels like nothing but the man's fingers on the tambourine; dancing with two left legs, two right legs, two wooden legs, two wire legs, two spring legs – all sorts of legs and no legs ... he finishes by leaping gloriously on the bar-counter, and calling for something to drink, with the chuckle of a million counterfeit Jim Crows, in one inimitable sound!

Dickens produces swirling images of energy brought under bodily control, including industrial metaphors: 'wire legs ... spring legs'. Moreover, Juba is the real thing, no 'counterfeit' white face corked up to look black. As Eric Lott comments, the image of the black, male body is one of dangerous, erotic power: it both attracts and repels, is both exciting and vulgar.[15] But by the same token it cannot offer the site of 'real' American culture.

Thus two margins produce contrasting sets of meaning and anxiety. Whereas Juba may represent a radical (racial) otherness, both exotic and low, the West is geographically on the margin, yet central to what modern America means. Moreover, Dickens's indictment of America as 'that vast counting-house' where 'the almighty dollar' is worshiped, is directed at the commercial middle class and its lack of cultural refinement. Commerce rather than being a prerequisite for culture, as it was, say, for David Hume, becomes what marks America out as the modern site of anti-culture.[16] But around the sharp dismissals of American civilization and its social middle circulate anxieties about modern British civilization; that which is being denied is what is feared – that urban Britain and its industrious middle class bear an uncanny resemblance to the footloose boors opening up America's interior, an unrestrained commercial force neither tempered by nor productive of politeness and culture. Perhaps this is why Dickens's description of the sameness of his steamboat companions and the dulling environment of the West so closely parallels his famous description of the built environment of Coketown in *Hard Times* (1854), 'a triumph of fact' and market logic.[17]

In contrast, the pleasure as well as the anxiety surrounding the body of the black male dancer is distanced, moved into the space of the exotic. Dickens may here speak to what Norbert Elias identifies as the limited places allowed for excitement, pointing to the 'cover of restraints' that spreads, more and more evenly, over action and affect in modern society.[18]

It remained only for Matthew Arnold to complete this particular cultural circuit, mapping the two societies on to one another in terms of social class and culture. In replying to the charge that he regarded the American people as 'vulgar', Arnold states that he considers 'the people of the United States just the same people as ourselves'. He reiterates his formulation from *Culture and Anarchy* (1869): 'whereas our society in England distributes itself into Barbarians, Philistines, and Populace, America is just ourselves, with the Barbarians quite left out, and the Populace nearly ... That which in England we call the middle class is in America virtually the nation'. But ultimately both countries are dominated by a middle class characterized by 'a defective type of religion, a narrow range of intellect and knowledge, a stunted sense of beauty, a low standard of manners'.[19]

The case against America (and British culture) is built resolutely against a cultural middle ground. The 'populace' is less important to this analysis of 'Culture' and its undoing. Significantly, John Bright, popular Liberalism's champion and a great admirer of American society, represents what is narrow and deficient in Liberal-Nonconformist lifestyle in both countries. Arnold mocks Bright's faith in the American newspaper reading public and the interest it takes in politics and practical affairs, for America falls so far short of the spiritualized goals of Culture. In this regard, Arnold claims Britain is better off than America for the troubling reason that it still has an aristocracy. Troubling because Arnold was an opponent of both aristocracy and class society. Indeed, Culture stands beyond or outside the divisions of class. The problem for both Dickens and Arnold is where to find or cultivate the purveyors of culture ('sweetness and light') after having rejected both the aristocracy and middle class for this role.

When he finally visited America in 1884, Arnold was surprised by 'how far his superior liveliness (to his British counterpart) and naturalness of condition ... would carry the American Philistine', and was favourably impressed by 'the homogeneous character' of American society. In what seems an odd reversal, and certainly one at odds with both Dickens's account and later nineteenth- and twentieth-century criticism of modern America as producing a culture of conformity, Arnold now sees the relative sameness of condition prevailing in America as a positive value. Despite variations in wealth, America has not, as predicted, become more like Britain because what commentators like Lord Macaulay forgot was that the United States 'are without what certainly fixes and accentuates the divisions between rich and poor – the distinction of classes'. The United States was born 'not amid the circumstances of a feudal age, but a modern age; not amid the circumstances of an epoch favourable to subordination, but under those of an epoch of expansion'. A modern expansionist nation, America is without class divisions. Deficient as judged by the standards of Culture, American society is homologous to Culture in being situated beyond class.

Certainly Arnold erased some rather important differences within America to arrive at this position; thus he argues that one reason class differences do not exist in America is because domestic service is done for 'them' (i.e. Americans) 'by Irish, Germans, Swedes, negroes'. A few sentences later, however, he tells readers that as soon as an immigrant to the United States arrives he or she is an 'American'.[20] Nothing stands against 'them' since everyone is put into motion as an American. The lack of fixed position and the movement of people into amorphous space is what is disturbing in Dickens's *Notes for General Circulation*, the word 'circulation' being key to title and text.

What accounts for Arnold's revision of his imaginative mapping of America? Perhaps his actual experience of America had something to do with it. But I would suggest that 'America' is subject to constant revision because it is a highly volatile signifier and because of intensified British concerns by the 1880s about such issues as class conflict, social violence and the fate of Liberalism, Irish home rule and schemes of federation for reworking imperial relations more generally – issues that appeared to make American experience directly relevant to late nineteenth-century Britain. What remains suppressed is the increased anxiety over what Robert Young has identified as the cultural politics of 'hybridity', the ways in which English culture was divided against itself in the later nineteenth century, faced with rapid colonial expansion and the subversion of the binary opposition between sameness and differ-ence.[21] Arguably this also gave force to the Anglo-Saxonism that figures so prominently in the writings of scholars such as James Bryce and E. A. Freeman who stressed the essential sameness and unity between the two great branches of the English people.[22]

Populist (re-)visions

Needless to say, the Dickens–Arnold circuit constitutes only one reac-tion to modern development. Against the negative views of democratic life expressed in literary works such as those of Dickens, Frances Trollope and Captain Frederick Marryat, one might cite Harriet Martineau's qualified enthusiasm or Isabella Bird's account of her travels in the far West.[23] One might also compare Dickens's and Arnold's responses to the radical-populist rendering of America, particularly to the vision of the Chartist press and its working-class readers.

In summer 1845, for example, the *Globe*, a whiggish newspaper, published a notice of Andrew Jackson's death in which Jackson was compared unfavourably to Earl Grey who had also recently died. Whereas Grey had preserved and purified the aristocratic element in England's institutions, Jackson had surrendered to the populace and their 'univer-sal thirst for an actual share in power'. Jacksonian America resembled ancient Athens in its public scramble for petty office, although the *Globe* condescendingly acquitted Jackson of actually knowing anything about ancient Greece.[24] Chartism's great journal, the *Northern Star*, responded to the *Globe* with a front page engraving of 'General Jackson', full accounts from the American press of tributes paid to him, and a lead editorial on Jackson and Grey, entitled 'The Republican and the Aristocrat Contrasted'. Jackson is presented as the perfect figure of the principled patriot: disinterested, independent, driven solely by republi-can virtue and duty to the nation. Jackson retired from office to his farm, like Cincinnatus, 'contenting himself with the results of his own skill in the cultivation of the soil', and receiving no further rewards for his services to the nation. In contrast, Grey, the self-serving aristocrat, 'had relations of every rank and degree stuck into office'. The *Star* predicted future generations would learn to lisp the name 'Old Hickory', while Grey would be cursed for having brought England the new Poor Law. As for the two countries, Britain and America, knowledge of Jackson's career would allow young men in England 'to contrast the character of this hero and legislator, sprung from the ranks of the people, with the generals and field-marshals, and hereditary and class-elected lawgivers of their own country', and thus convince themselves of the superiority of the American system 'which invests sovereignty in the people' as opposed to 'a few hundred land-robbers, and a few thousand profit-mongers, with the addition of a gilded, powerless, puppet, dubbed Queen!'[25] America's meaning derives from its classlessness, expressed here in political terms whereby 'the people' stands against Britain's privileged élite, both bourgeois and aristocrat.

It is worth lingering over the populist vision of America and its Jacksonian embodiment. During the nineteenth century, the populist impulse was pre-eminently political. The heroic vision of Jackson was part of a populist democratic narrative on both sides of the Atlantic that found expression, for instance, in the cheap, popular biographies of various American presidents. William Cobbett, whose views on America were at best ambivalent, published a *Life of Andrew Jackson*, heavily plagiarized from an American campaign biography.[26] Unlike Washington and Jefferson, however, Jackson and Lincoln were not just for the people but of the people, leaders who never forgot their humble origins. British opponents of democratic reform constantly pointed to the decline in the quality of America's political leaders, to their lowly origins and lack of education. For British popular radicals, however, Jackson represented the self-made man as democratic leader. The *Northern Star's* editorial makes much of Jackson's origins as the son of poor Irish immigrants; of his victory as a general leading a band of 'raw backwoods farmers' at New Orleans against a British army under aristocratic command; of his own success as a farmer. When he failed in business because of the misconduct of his partner, the *Star* relates, that 'rather than endure the vassalage of debt', Jackson sold off his own estate 'which his early enterprise had acquired ... with the fields which he himself had tamed to the ploughshare – with the forest whose trees were as familiar to him as his friends, and chose rather to dwell ... in a rude log cabin, in the pride of independence and integrity'. The *Northern Star* also published an engraving of the Hermitage, Jackson's Tennessee mansion, not as a symbol of unmerited wealth, but of individual achievement.[27] Rather than the back country as a site of cultural disappointment, barrenness and unbridled greed, it becomes the testing ground for the development of republican character, of manly independence and honour which is inextricably linked to the land.

This is not to forget what is missing from such visions. The *Northern Star* consistently opposed American slavery, but the dark side of the

American frontier is suppressed from populist view: the violence to both land and peoples, the genocide, lynchings, the materialism and greed remain unspoken.[28] Indeed, Jackson was famed not only for his defeat of the British at New Orleans but as an Indian fighter largely responsible for the removal of Native Americans west of the Mississippi. The moving frontier was never innocent. In terms, however, of constructions of British national identity the American back country was an affront to what Elizabeth Helsinger terms 'the rural scene' and its relationship to the contested construction of the 'national symbolic': the shared meanings that affirm a national subjectivity, 'the common language of a common space'.[29] The roughly hewn and cleared American landscape clashed with concepts of bounded spatial order indicative of land shaped either for viewing or civilized life and by extension for citizens. But for British radicals, the American back country was most obviously a space in which human labour is rewarded with its full, true value. 'Deep England' was thus challenged by a raw, unbounded space, free of hierarchy and ennobled by labour; the vision of a harmonious landscape of villages and ancient churchyards was met by a masculine vision of yeoman independence and republican virtue.

It has recently been argued that radicalism's idyllic vision of America – where republicanism engenders a rough equality of social as well as political condition – came under critical pressure from the late 1830s and that a strongly negative model of America emerged as popular radicalism took on more social as opposed to political emphasis: 'The logic of capitalism had defied republican virtue.'[30] While there is some truth to this assessment, more impressive than British radicalism's rejection of America was radicalism's resistance to this negative model in the face of considerable contemporary evidence to support it. America remained a place of dreams, of populist yearning. The vision of the western republic based on the free yeoman farmer – free from religious, economic and social controls – died hard. One need only survey the publications of G. W. M. Reynolds, the most successful radical publisher of the 1850s and 1860s, to appreciate the continued force of this image, of the counter-ideal of a space opposed to both modern industrial life and social hierarchy. Moreover, the American Civil War, as Eugenio Biagini argues, was to offer a crucial point of mediation between respectable (male) working-class radicalism and British Liberalism in support of the moral truth of the North and Lincoln's leadership, and the slogan 'free soil, free labour, free men'.[31]

The populist vision of America never really vanishes, although in the twentieth century it takes a distinctly cultural turn. Needless to say, the radical-populist view did not go unchallenged and was often contested in cultural terms. Thus Arnold tellingly refers to Mrs Lincoln as affording 'a spectacle to vulgarise a whole nation', something from which aristocracy at least saves Britain.[32] For Goldwin Smith, a Liberal intellectual generally sympathetic to America – to the point of leaving his position at Oxford to teach at Cornell – Jacksonian democracy had been a warning that had gone unheeded in Britain. 'A multitude', he wrote in 1888, 'can exercise power and trample down hated superiorities only by concentrating its force in a man, who thus becomes a demagogue despot.' Goldwin Smith thought that Jackson, 'a barbarian to the core ... not under the restraint of moral civilization', was a well chosen leader of '"the masses" against the "classes"'. Britain, having blindly extended the franchise, was now itself subject to a similar 'demagogic despotism' and rule by the 'masses'. Two decades earlier Smith had contributed an essay on America to the famous collection of *Essays on Reform* (1867) in which he defended America against Robert Lowe's anti-democratic attacks. Even in 1867, however, Smith identified America's greatest problem as its 'lack of culture' and a national past; Americans were a new, 'rough people'.[33] The anxiety, largely sublimated in his 1867 essay, is expressed in the fault lines between the key terms 'the people', 'classes' and 'masses'; only the restraining power of 'moral civilization' (i.e. Culture) can prevent a 'rough people' bred to equality turning into 'the masses' with all that is implied about a lack of civilized order and identity.

Culture: high/low

What Arnold termed 'vulgar' and Goldwin Smith 'rough' went to the heart of much Victorian criticism of America's democratic culture, its language and literature as well as manners and social conventions. Victorian travellers usually complained about the state of American language, its looseness and aggressive vulgarity. Linguistic order was inseparable from social and spatial order, the construction of cultural authority and definitions of both personal and national identity. Throughout the nineteenth century, in terms of both the spoken and written word, the American mixture of the crude and refined confounded distinctions; the 'stylistic bricolage made it maddeningly hard to divide the world into the few and the many'.[34] The same was true of American literature. The *Edinburgh Review* recognized Joel Barlow's *Columbiad* (1807) as the 'first great specimen ... of any considerable work composed in the American tongue', and went on to denounce its bold innovations and 'utter disregard of all distinctions between what we should call lofty and elegant, and low and vulgar expression'.[35]

America's perceived lack of social distinctions was inscribed in its literary language and cultural institutions, in the refusal to distinguish between polite and vulgar idioms. Again the fears expressed were those of the drift into an amorphous middle ground. Museums randomly mixed serious works of art and science with popular curiosities, particularly 'execrable' were the waxworks that most museums exhibited. Thus Captain Marryat commented on the 'want of taste and discrimination' that characterized even the best American museums:

> Side by side with the most interesting and valuable specimens, such as fossil mammoth, &c., you have the greatest puerilities and absurdities in the world ... In some, they have models of celebrated criminals ... or such trophies as the bonnet worn by Mrs., _____ when she was killed by her husband ... The most favourite subject, after sleeping beauty in the wax, is General Jackson, with battle of New Orleans in the distance.[36]

Similarly, during the first half of the nineteenth century, American theatres regularly mixed high and low works in the same evening's programme. And the raucous, casual behaviour of socially diverse audiences, including the prostitutes who roamed the upper tier, appalled English critics who called for a rationalization of cultural space. Midway through his American tour in 1844, the great Victorian actor William Charles Macready wrote despairingly in his diary: 'I am sick of American audiences, they are not fit to have the language in which Shakespeare wrote.' Macready concluded that the 'the state of society here and the condition of the fine arts are in themselves evidences of the improbability of an artist being formed by them'.[37]

America lacked, and would continue to lack Culture because of its failure to establish the crucial hierarchies separating high from low, polite from vulgar, art from mere entertainment, hierarchies on which cultural taste and judgement depend. Thus the reckless disregard for linguistic and social hierarchy found in the poetry of Walt Whitman could be seen as emblematic of this state of cultural anarchy. A great lover of New York theatre and stump oratory, admirer of the b'hoys of the Bowery, Whitman celebrated in his poetry the street and the urban crowd.[38] His views on language, following in the steps of Jefferson and Webster, were irrepressibly democratic. 'The Real Dictionary,' wrote Whitman, 'will give all the words in use, the bad words as well as any ... Many of the slang words among fighting men, gamblers, thieves, prostitutes, are powerful words.'[39] The self-appointed poet of democracy was relentlessly chastised by British (as well as American) literary critics for the looseness of his language, his use of words that were either not English or vulgar, his 'neglect of syntax' and his irregular line, his bombast and 'intense egoism'. As one critic put it, Whitman's poetry was an offence to 'civilized manners'.[40] In his key book *The Poetry of the Period* (1870), Alfred Austin devoted a chapter to Whitman as the poet of the future; taking his British champions at their word, Austin quoted William Michael Rossetti's judgement that the *Leaves of Grass* was '"*par excellence*, the modern poem"'. But Austin found nothing to admire about Whitman's 'poems' which 'swarm with pages upon pages of whose horrible and ineffable nastiness' readers can hardly judge. Austin echoes Carlyle's loathing for the '*Swarmery*' – 'the Gathering of Men in Swarms' – sharing Carlyle's fear of modern democracy and mass culture. Austin concedes that Whitman is indeed the poet of democracy, 'being, like it, ignorant, sanguine, noisy, coarse, and choatic! Democracy may be, and I fear is, our proximate future; and, as a matter of course, its poetry along with it'.[41] For commentators like Austin and Carlyle, the crisis in post-1867 British politics was inextricably bound to an aesthetic crisis, and 'America' presented an unsettling sign of Britain's future.

'America' moved under the sign of 'the modern'. If its frontier was opened up by steamboats and railways, its lack of literary culture was often put down to the nation's passion for mass-circulation newspapers. By the mid-nineteenth century, British liberal culture emphasized the civilizing effects of print. Among Gladstone's great triumphs as Chancellor of the Exchequer was to have lowered the price of newspapers; indeed, he cited the expanding circulation of cheap newspapers as among the improvements making working men fit for the vote. Moreover, although Gladstone was famous in the role of gentleman orator, introducing the American-style whistlestop campaign to British politics, the main audience for Gladstone's speeches was the newspaper-reading public.[42] Newspapers were seen as moulders of national and individual character. In the American context, however, newspaper reading, a particularly American habit, was often regarded as the antithesis to Culture. 'There is something very striking in the fact ... that the country which can boast of a greater expenditure of Paper and Print than any other in the world, is the country which can NOT boast of even an approach to National Literature', wrote a vitriolic mid-century critic. Towards the century's end, an essay published in *Nineteenth Century* made the same claim: 'One of the most noticeable features of the wilderness of printed matter which crops up daily throughout the country is the absence of anything like literary thought or writing.'[43]

British views of American newspapers are revealing in a number of regards. First, the phrase 'wilderness of print' reasserts the undifferentiated quality of American print culture, the difficulty in making distinctions. The American penny newspaper, unlike British papers of the 1840s and 1850s, lacked order. 'Its miserable whity-brown paper; its dingy, uncomfortable print; its perfectly ridiculous non-arrangement; its jumble in one hopeless mass ... ', were indicative of this disorder, as well as the popular status of the press.[44] Newspapers are themselves an extraordinarily open literary form; readers wander freely from column to column, taking bits and pieces, reading some articles, skipping some, moving forward and backward – in effect, shaping their own reading structure rather than the paper imposing narrative or temporal order on readers. There is something undisciplined about even the careful newspaper reader.

Second, the newspaper is a decidedly modern form, associated with the construction of the 'bourgeois public sphere', the urban metropolis and the imagining of the modern nation. It was a highly commercialized literary product, sold in huge quantities on a daily basis and increasingly financed by advertisements; the late nineteenth-century newspaper was thus closely tied to the rise of the department store which depended heavily on newspaper advertisements to move goods quickly.[45] James Gordon Bennett's entrepreneurial vision of the newspaper also introduced an industrialization of production and reporting. By the mid-nineteenth century, news was associated with speed and movement; news was carried over telegraph wires and in papers brought in by trains. Among the dubious virtues of the American newspaper reporter was his 'knack ... of "getting there"', the scramble for news was seen as distinctly American. Americans were in a hurry and so were their newspapers. The style of American journalism was described as 'racy', 'smart' and 'bright'. The fragmented format of the newspaper also gave the impression of a world in flux; the spectacle of the newspaper page, the bold headlines and leaders, was a spectacle of modern life. Above all, American newspapers thrived on 'sensation'; the word, as used in this new way, was regarded as a vulgar, American neologism. Britons had already been entertained by Barnum and his midget Tom Thumb, Catlin's troupe of Indians, visual travelogues down the Mississippi, and by the late nineteenth century Buffalo Bill and his Wild West show. The sensationalist press, however, was a contradictory phenomenon, low and popular, but also promising a heightened sense of the 'real' and the democratic, exposing corruption, observing no polite boundaries, putting the latest 'scoop' before the public for its judgement. And it was these sorts of contradictions that were to fuel debate over Britain's own 'new journalism', prompting questions about what sort of press, or mechanisms of communication and information, were compatible with mass, democratic culture and society.[46]

As Dickens complained, the American press lacked any sense of decorum, sensationalism and viciousness were merely part of a crude commercial culture. At the same time, however, America represented 'the popular', modernity, the future. Even the term 'vulgar', in its original sense of pertaining to the common masses and as meaning a lack of refinement, carried radical connotations. It is hardly surprising, there-fore, that 'America' should stir deep anxieties, possessed of the exciting and dangerous prospects of modern life. Or that 'America' should circulate so uncertainly across the spectrum of likeness and other, not merely at different periods and between different observers, but often during the same period, within the same text or in works by the same author. During the nineteenth century, ambivalence presides over the imaginative ordering of 'America'; an ambivalence not to be confused with indifference. The range and depth of emotion testify to the impor-tance of Victorian imaginings of 'America' as a space and culture at once disturbingly familiar and yet distant, stirring utopian longings and prophetic foreboding, as a 'real' place where one's imagined hopes, fears and desires could be tested but not resolved.

Notes

1. Jean Baudrillard, *America* (London, 1988); also see Barry Smart, 'Europe/America: Baudrillard's fatal comparison', in C. Rojek and B. S. Turner (eds.) *Forget Baudrillard?* (London, 1993), pp. 47–69.
2. Malcolm Bradbury, *Dangerous Pilgrimages: Transatlantic Mythologies and the Novel* (New York, 1996), p. 5.
3. Baudrillard, *America*, p. 95.
4. See, however, Lewis Perry, *Boats Against the Current: American Culture between Revolution and Modernity, 1820–1860* (New York, 1993), ch. 20; Marshall Berman, *All That is Solid Melts into Air: The Experience of Modernity* (New York, 1988), introduction; Raymond Williams, *The Politics of Modernism: Against the New Conformists* (London, 1989), ch. 1; James Vernon, 'The Mirage of modernity', *Social History*, 22 (1997), 208–15.
5. Jack P. Greene, 'Paine, America, and the "modernization" of political consciousness', *Political Science Quarterly*, 93 (1978), 74, 78–9.
6. John Cartwright, *The Commonwealth in Danger* ... (London, 1795), p. xci.
7. See Berman, *All That is Solid Melts into Air*, pp. 105–10.
8. See Elizabeth McKinsey, *Niagara Falls: Icon of the American Sublime* (Cambridge, 1965).
9. On British travellers to America, see Richard Rapson, *Britons View America: Travel Commentary* (Seattle, 1971); Max Berger, *The British Traveller in America, 1836–1860* (New York, 1943); Richard Mullen, *Birds of Passage: Five Englishwomen in Search of America* (New York, 1994).
10. Charles Dickens, *American Notes for General Circulation* (London, 1972, first published 1842), pp. 99–103.
11. See Norbert Elias's classic, *The Civilizing Process: The History of Man-ners and State Formation and Civilization* (London, 1982, first published 1939); John F. Kasson, *Rudeness and Civility: Manners in Nineteenth-Century Urban America* (New York, 1990).

12. Dickens, *Notes*, pp. 115–18.
13. Ibid., p. 174.
14. Ibid., pp. 194, 199, 206–07, 216; Bradbury, *Dangerous Pilgrimages*, ch. 3.
15. Dickens, *Notes*, pp. 136–9; Eric Lott, *Love and Theft: Blackface Minstrelsy and the American Working Class* (New York, 1993), pp. 112–17.
16. See J. G. A. Pocock, 'Hume and the American revolution: The dying thoughts of a North Briton', in his *Virtue, Commerce, and History* (Cambridge, 1985), particularly pp. 131–2.
17. Charles Dickens, *Hard Times* (Harmondsworth, 1969), p. 65. Moreover, the town, like the steamboat, is 'inhabited by people equally like one another'. Compare Dickens, *Notes*, p. 204: 'The people are all alike, too. There is no diversity of character.' Also see Alex Welsh, *The City of Dickens* (Oxford, 1971), pp. 33–41.
18. Norbert Elias and Eric Dunning, 'The Quest for excitement in leisure', *Society and Leisure: Bulletin of the European Centre for Leisure and Education*, 2 (1969), 50–85.
19. Matthew Arnold, *Culture and Anarchy* (Cambridge, 1969), pp. 19–20; idem, 'A Word about America', *Nineteenth Century*, 11 (May 1882), 681, 684, 687, 694–5 (reprinted in *Complete Prose Works of Matthew Arnold* (Ann Arbor, MI, 1974), vol. 10.
20. Matthew Arnold, 'A Word more about America', *Nineteenth Century*, 17 (February 1885), 219–36 (reprinted in *Complete Prose Works of Matthew Arnold* (Ann Arbor, MI, 1974), vol. 10, pp. 194–217).
21. Robert J. C. Young, *Colonial Desire: Hybridity in Theory, Culture and Race* (London, 1995) chs 1–3; see also Homi K. Bhabha, 'Signs taken as wonders', reprinted in his *The Location of Culture* (London, 1994), pp. 102–22.
22. James Bryce, *The American Commonwealth* (London, 1888); Edward A. Freeman, *Lectures to American Audiences* (Philadelphia, 1882); Hugh Tulloch, *James Bryce's American Commonwealth: The Anglo-American Background* (London, 1988).
23. Frances Trollope, *Domestic Manners of the Americans* (London, 1997, first published 1832); Captain Frederick Marryat, *Diary in America*, 3 vols (London, 1839); Harriet Martineau, *Society in America*, 3 vols (1837, London); Isabella L. Bird, *A Lady's Life in the Rocky Mountains* (London, 1879).
24. *Globe*, 21 July 1845, p. 2.
25. *Northern Star*, 2 August 1845, pp. 1, 4; also ibid., 19 July 1845, p. 4.
26. *Life of Andrew Jackson of the United States*, abridged and compiled by William Cobbett (London, 1834); also see *Republicanism v. Monarchy: The Farewell Legacy of General Jackson ...* (London, nd [1837]).
27. *Northern Star*, 2 August 1845, p. 4; 24 May 1845, p. 3; Patrick Joyce, *Democratic Subjects: The Self and the Social in Nineteenth-Century England* (Cambridge, 1994), p. 215.
28. *Northern Star*, 27 April, 1844, p. 4, 'What is democracy?': '*Democracy comprises all*; the negro as well as the white man.'
29. Elizabeth Helsinger, *Rural Scenes and National Representation: Britain, 1815–1850* (Princeton, NJ, 1997), pp. 11–12, 19, 28; also see David Lowenthal, 'British national identity and the English landscape', *Rural History*, 2 (1991), 205–30.

30. Gregory Claeys, 'The Example of America a warning to England? The transformation of America in British radicalism and socialism, 1790–1850', in M. Chase and I. Dyck (eds), *Living and Learning: Essays in Honour of J. F. C. Harrison* (London, 1996), pp. 66–80. Cf. Henry M. Pelling, *America and the British Left* (New York, 1957).
31. Eugenio F. Biagini, *Liberty, Retrenchment and Reform: Popular Liberalism in the Age of Gladstone, 1860–1880* (Cambridge, 1992), pp. 67–93; Leo Marx, *The Machine in the Garden: Technology and the Pastoral Ideal in America* (New York, 1964).
32. Arnold, *Culture and Anarchy*, p. 84.
33. Goldwin Smith, 'American Statesman', *Nineteenth Century*, 24 (August 1888), 269, 273; idem, 'The Experience of the American commonwealth', in *Essays on Reform* (London, 1867), p. 221.
34. Kenneth Cmiel, *Democratic Eloquence: The Fight over Popular Speech in Nineteenth-Century America* (Berkeley, CA, 1990), p. 15; also see Dennis E. Baron, *Grammar and Good Taste: Reforming the American Language* (New Haven, CT, 1982).
35. Quoted in David Simpson, *The Politics of American English, 1776–1850* (New York, 1986), pp. 100–101.
36. Marryat, *Diary in America*, pp. 174–5.
37. *The Diaries of William Charles Macready, 1833–1851*, ed. William Toynbee, 2 vols (London, 1912), vol. 2, pp. 229, 270; Lawrence W. Levine, *Highbrow and Lowbrow: The Emergence of Cultural Hierarchy in America* (Cambridge, MA, 1988), pt 1.
38. David S. Reynolds, *Walt Whitman's America: A Cultural Biography* (New York, 1995), ch. 6; also see Larzer Ziff, 'Whitman and the crowd', *Critical Inquiry*, 10 (1984), 579–91.
39. Walt Whitman, *An American Primer* (Boston, MA, 1901), p. 6. Not published at the time, this pamphlet was written in the early 1850s. As well as Simpson's book, for the politics of American English, including chapters on Whitman, see Thomas Gustafson, *Representative Words: Politics, Literature, and the American Language, 1776–1865* (Cambridge, 1992); Michael P. Kramer, *Imagining Language in America: from the Revolution to the Civil War* (Princeton, NJ, 1992).
40. G. C. Macaulay, 'Walt Whitman', *Nineteenth Century*, 12 (December 1882), 902–18; Peter Bayne, 'Walt Whitman's poetry', *Contemporary Review*, 27 (December–May 1876), 29–30, 47, 52, 61, 68.
41. Alfred Austin, *The Poetry of the Period* (London, 1870), pp. 197–8, 207, 218, 223; Thomas Carlye, *Shooting Niagara: And After?* (London, 1867).
42. See James Vernon, *Politics and the People: A Study in English Political Culture, c. 1815–1867* (Cambridge, 1993), ch. 3; John Belchem and James Epstein, 'The nineteenth-century gentleman leader revisited', *Social History*, 22 (1997), 187–9.
43. [John Forster], 'The Newspaper literature of America', *Foreign Quarterly Review*, 30 (1843), 197; Edward Delille, 'The American newspaper press', *Nineteenth Century*, 32 (July 1892), 13–28; also see, for example, Arnot Reid, 'The English and American press', *Nineteenth Century*, 22 (August 1887), 219–33.
44. [Forster], 'Newspaper literature of America', 200–201.
45. Jürgen Habermas, *The Structural Transformation of the Public Sphere* (Cambridge, MA, 1989); Benedict Anderson, *Imagined Communities:*

Reflections on the Origin and Spread of Nationalism (London, 1991 edn), pp. 33–5; Gerald J. Baldasty, *The Commercialization of News in the Nineteenth Century* (Madison, WI, 1992), pp. 46–8, 56–7.

46. R. A. Scott-James, *The Influence of the Press* (London, 1914), pp. 149–55; Judith Walkowitz, *City of Dreadful Delight: Narratives of Sexual Danger in Late-Victorian London* (Chicago, 1992), pp. 83–5, and ch. 3, *passim*; Joyce, *Democratic Subjects*, pp. 210–12; Richard Altick, *Deadly Encounters: Two Victorian Sensations* (Philadelphia, 1986), pp. 4–6.

CHAPTER SEVEN

Anglo-American Attitudes to Democracy from Lincoln to Churchill

Roland Quinault

It is widely assumed that Britons and Americans share a common commitment to democracy. Yet this assumption raises many questions: how long have the two nations believed in democracy and have they always meant the same thing by the term? These comparative questions have been little studied, but historians are now showing a new interest in transatlantic political discourse. J. C. D. Clark, in *The Language of Liberty*, has argued that 'liberty' was the key term in the conflicts which rent the English-speaking world in the early-modern period, but that after the creation of the American republic, 'democracy' came to be regarded as 'the essence of the American experiment'.[1] Andrew Robertson has claimed, in *The Language of Democracy*, that the nineteenth-century transition from government by government to government for the people evolved more quickly in the United States than it did in Britain.[2] Yet Robertson, despite his book's title, did not examine the use of the term 'democracy' and no one has made a comparative study of democratic discourse in twentieth-century Britain and America. Thus there is ample scope for further study of the evolution of Anglo-American attitudes to democracy.

In order to test the comparative development of British and American attitudes to democracy I will examine the use of the term by three contemporary 'pairs' of statesmen – one British and the other American – at important times in national development. I will also consider the attitude of these statesmen towards democratic reform and the extent to which their views were subject to influence from across the Atlantic.

William Gladstone and Abraham Lincoln were the two outstanding liberal statesmen of the Victorian era. They were also exact contemporaries: both were born in 1809. Yet they never met or crossed the Atlantic and neither showed any direct interest in the other. Even Lincoln's assassination did not prompt any public statement from Gladstone.

Their mutual disinterest reflected both the gulf created by the Atlantic before the advent of the transoceanic telegraph and steamer, and also personal differences. Gladstone, the son of a very wealthy merchant, had an élite education at Eton and Oxford, whereas Lincoln, the son of a humble pioneer, had only a year of formal schooling. Nevertheless the two men shared a common cultural heritage: both had a good knowledge of Shakespeare, the Bible and Blackstone – the standard legal textbook in Britain and America.

There were also some similarities in the political careers of Gladstone and Lincoln. They were first elected in their early twenties: Gladstone became a Member of Parliament (MP) in 1832 and Lincoln a member of the Illinois legislature in 1834. Both later became the leader of a new political party, yet they regarded themselves as reactive, rather than proactive politicians. Lincoln's admission: 'I claim not to have controlled events, but confess plainly that events have controlled me' provided the leitmotiv for David Donald's recent biography.[3] Gladstone similarly believed that the orator had no choice but 'to be what his age will have him, what it requires in order to be moved by him'. This led Walter Bagehot to describe Gladstone as 'a man who cannot impose his creed *on* his time, but must learn his creed *of* his time'.[4]

Both Gladstone and Lincoln justified their policies by reference to simple concepts, rather than an elaborate political philosophy.[5] Lincoln showed little interest in constitutional questions, but was a strong believer in liberty.[6] Gladstone likewise had a general belief in liberty which 'he appeared to think would of itself be the parent of all good'.[7] Gladstone's commitment to liberty at home and abroad was matched by Lincoln's support for 'liberty, not alone to the people of this country, but I hope to the world, for all future time'.[8]

Despite their common commitment to liberty, Gladstone and Lincoln held different views on slavery. Whereas Lincoln made his name as a critic of slavery, Gladstone began his career by endorsing it. In his maiden speech in Parliament, Gladstone defended his father's slave plantation in Demerara and opposed the immediate abolition of slavery on the grounds that it would harm the slaves themselves. After the abolition of slavery in the British Empire, Gladstone long retained a distaste for those he termed 'negrophilists'. His claim, in 1862, that the South had made a nation, led Bright to observe: 'He was born of a great slave-holding family and I suppose the taint is ineradicable.'[9] Yet Gladstone's admiration for the Confederacy was prompted, not by pro-slavery prejudice, but by the apparent military success of the South. When that success evaporated – only a year later – he concluded that the war would lead to the end of slavery and the re-establishment of the Union.[10] His pragmatism was shared by Lincoln, who wrote in 1862 that his paramount object was to save the Union, rather than to free the slaves.[11]

For most of the twentieth century, however, Lincoln has been presented – on both sides of the Atlantic – as a man of unbending democratic principle. Harold Laski, for example, described Lincoln as 'the supreme figure in the democratic tradition of the nineteenth century'.[12] Roy Basler claimed that 'Democracy was to Lincoln a religion, and he wanted it to be in a real sense the religion of his audience'.[13] Yet Basler's claim was not borne out by his own scholarship, for the word 'democracy' does not figure in Lincoln's writings and speeches – not even in the Gettysburg Address. That speech has been subjected to intense scrutiny by historians, but its democratic credentials have been assumed rather than demonstrated. Even Lincoln's famous phrase, 'Government of the people, by the people, for the people', left it unclear *who exactly* were the people and how they were to control the government. Lord Charnwood, Lincoln's English biographer, thought that Lincoln's faith in democracy was best enshrined in his comment: 'As I would not be a slave, so I would not be a master. This expresses my idea of democracy.'[14] This aphorism, however, was never publicly used by Lincoln and is of doubtful attribution and unknown date.[15]

Lincoln, unlike Gladstone, seldom referred to the electoral system or the suffrage. When Lincoln sought re-election in Illinois, in 1836, he favoured 'all sharing the privileges of the government, who assist in bearing its burthens' – which meant those who paid taxes or bore arms.[16] These criteria disenfranchised women, men without property and non-whites.[17] Lincoln's views on the suffrage were Whiggish, not just in the American, but also in the contemporary British sense of the term. The 1866 English reform bill, for example, proposed to enfranchise men who were military volunteers or paid taxes.[18]

Lincoln defined his own political position in 1855:

> I think I am a Whig; but others say there are no Whigs, and that I am an Abolitionist ... I now do nothing more than oppose the extension of slavery. I am not a Know-Nothing, that is certain. How could I be? How can any one who abhors the oppression of negroes be in favour of degrading classes of white people? Our progress in degeneracy appears to me pretty rapid. As a nation we began by declaring that 'all men are created equal,' we now practically read it, 'all men are created equal, except negroes'. When the Know-Nothings get control it will read, 'all men are created equal, except negroes, and foreigners and Catholics'.[19]

Lincoln's belief in equality reflected his admiration for the Declaration of Independence. He claimed that all his political feelings sprang from 'the sentiments embodied in the Declaration of Independence' and he regarded its chief author, Jefferson, as 'the most distinguished politician of our history'.[20] Jefferson, of course, was not a democrat in the modern sense of the word, since he accepted slavery and believed that political power should reside in the hands of rural freeholders. Neither the Declaration of Independence, nor the American Constitution, made any reference to 'democracy'. Lincoln also avoided the 'd' word because it had a superficial association with the Democratic party. Yet in the mid-nineteenth century Democrats were no more committed than their Whig or Republican opponents to modern notions of democracy.

Commentators – from Tocqueville in the nineteenth century to Laski and Robertson in the twentieth – have described mid-nineteenth century America as a political democracy.[21] Yet universal suffrage did not exist – even for white males. Although the property, religious and tax qualifications for the suffrage were reduced in most states from the 1820s to the 1850s, the process was piecemeal and incomplete – as Cobden noted when he visited the United States in 1859.[22] Moreover the growth of enfranchisement amongst male citizens was partly offset by the simultaneous increase in slaves and immigrants who did not possess the vote. At the 1860 presidential election, over a third of adult males did not vote and only 40 per cent of those who did, voted for Lincoln. His election eventually led to emancipation and the Fifteenth Amendment, but not to franchise reform. The continued exclusion of African Americans from southern electoral rolls reflected not only racial prejudice, but also the absence of constitutional guarantees of universal male suffrage. The political ideology of the post-Civil War era was illustrated at the rebuilt Capitol, in Washington, where a statue of Liberty crowned the dome, but Democracy was not represented.

In Britain, in the earlier nineteenth century, it was the extent of American democracy, rather than its limitations, which engaged public attention.[23] The breakdown of the American constitutional consensus in 1861 prompted British politicians to take a close interest in the American political system. Disraeli thought that the Civil War would 'tell immensely in favour of aristocracy'.[24] Gladstone initially took a similar view, but as the Civil War progressed, he noted that it had unleashed in America 'a kind of volcanic force not yet suspected to exist'.[25] After the war, he observed that the heroic resistance of 6 million to 20 millions and the courage and perseverance which finally overcame it, represented energies which 'surpassed our scale and measure'.[26]

Gladstone had exceptional energies of his own, which Bagehot attributed to the American character of his birthplace: Liverpool.[27] In a speech at Liverpool, in 1866, in defence of the Liberal government's modest reform bill, Gladstone declared that American institutions could no longer be held up as a bugbear to prevent franchise extension:

'Recent events which have taken place on the other side of the Atlantic have demonstrated to us how, by enlarging the franchise, augmented power can be marshalled on behalf of the government and increased energy given to the action of a nation.'[28] Gladstone exaggerated the extent of American enfranchisement and popular commitment to the war effort, but his comment was not just a passing debate point. He repeated the same American example, 18 years later, when he spoke in favour of another Liberal reform bill:

> The strength of the modern State lies in the representative system ... never has this great truth been so vividly illustrated as in the War of the American Republic. The convulsion of that country between 1861 and 1865 was, perhaps, the most frightful which ever assailed a national existence ... The exertions by which alone the movement was put down were ... only rendered possible by the fact that they proceeded from a nation where every capable citizen was enfranchised, and had a direct and an energetic interest in the well-being and the unity of the State.[29]

Gladstone thought that England stood between the feudal, class-based, society of Europe and the principles of equality which formed the basis of society in America. His analysis reflected the influence of Tocqueville's *Democracy in America* which he had read in 1840.[30] Many years later, he described Tocqueville as 'the Burke of our age'.[31] Gladstone combined elements of both Burke and Tocqueville in his speech at Liverpool in 1866:

> The word 'democracy' has very different senses, if by democracy be meant liberty ... the extension to each man in his own sphere of every privilege and of every franchise that he can exercise with advantage to himself and with safety to the State – then I must confess I don't see much to alarm us in the word democracy. But if by democracy be meant the enthroning of ignorance against knowledge, the setting up of vice in opposition to virtue, the disregard of rank, the forgetfulness of what our fathers have done for us ... then ... I ... am an enemy of democracy.[32]

Disraeli alleged that Gladstone wanted to import American principles, but Gladstone claimed that the proposed reduction in the borough franchise was 'a return to old English principles'.[33] That argument was undermined by his Tocquevillian assertion: 'You cannot fight against the future. Time is on our side.'[34] Although the Liberal government resigned after it was defeated on a reform amendment, Lord Derby then formed a Tory minority government which introduced its own reform bill in 1867. Disraeli claimed that the Tory reform bill had no tendency in the direction of democracy.[35] But Gladstone believed that the antics of the Tory leaders over reform undoubtedly accelerated the advent of household suffrage.[36] The episode illustrated the wide gap that existed in Britain between rhetoric about democracy and actual franchise reform.

In the second decade of the twentieth century, David Lloyd George in Britain and Woodrow Wilson in the United States were the leading champions of liberal progressivism. They also had much else in common. Both men were mid-Victorians by birth, lawyers by training and admirers of Gladstone and Lincoln. Wilson, at the age of 15, hung a portrait of Gladstone over his desk and he formed a Liberal Debating Club at Princeton in 1878.[37] In the same year, Lloyd George, aged 15, showed his first interest in politics when he read Gladstone on the eastern question.[38] Wilson and Lloyd George also admired Lincoln, who, as a lawyer-turned-politician, provided them with a role model.[39] Lloyd George came from a humble backwoods home like Lincoln and hero-worshipped Lincoln from when he was a boy in Wales.[40] When Lloyd George toured America, in 1923, he met Lincoln's son and visited Lincoln's birthplace and grave.[41] Woodrow Wilson was more circumspect in his praise of Lincoln because he was a Democrat from Virginia, which had been the heartland of the Confederacy. When Wilson spoke at Gettysburg, to mark the fiftieth anniversary of the battle, he made no reference to the Gettysburg Address, which Lloyd George regarded as the greatest speech that Lincoln ever made.[42]

Wilson frequently used the word 'democracy' in his speeches and writings. His partiality for the term reflected its new acceptability amongst the political élite around the turn of the century. Democracy even secured representation at the Capitol, in Washington, DC, where the pediment of the House of Representatives was adorned, in 1908, with Paul Bartlett's allegory, 'The Apotheosis of Democracy'.[43] Wilson's endorsement of democracy was tempered, however, by his great admiration for Edmund Burke.[44] In 1891, Wilson stated that although the people were the source of authority, they were not 'authority itself' – they could choose, but not control, their representatives. Wilson thought that the essence of democracy was not equality of power, but equality of opportunity.[45] He defined democracy as 'not so much a form of government as a set of principles' – the most radical form of constitutional action.[46] By that Wilsonian standard, Lloyd George was clearly a democrat, although he seldom employed the term 'democracy' in his speeches before the First World War. Wilson regarded Anglo-American democracy as an offspring of 'the great Germanic heritage of liberty'.[47] This theory was, however, undermined by Germany's actions in 1914.

The First World War led first Lloyd George, and then Wilson, to extend their democratic rhetoric from the home front to the international stage. In 1909, Lloyd George denounced the Tory peers who had rejected his budget in the Lords.[48] Five years later, he trained his oratorical fire on the German aristocracy. In September 1914, he claimed that victory for the Prussian junker would be 'the greatest catastrophe that has befallen democracy since the days of the Holy Alliance'.[49] His speech was widely admired, but it had no perceptible effect on Wilson, who pursued a policy of strict American neutrality. Wilson's desire for 'Peace without Victory' aroused the ire of Lloyd George who thought that it was a mockery to talk of self-determination and democratic governments while Germany was undefeated.[50]

The policy gulf between Wilson and Lloyd George in the early part of the war, partly reflected the lack of direct contact between them. In 1916 Colonel House considered Lloyd George 'as ignorant as ever about our public men and affairs'.[51] He was not unique in this respect, however, for no one in the American administration was personally known to anyone in the British government.[52] When Lloyd George became Prime Minister, in December 1916, Americans were struck, not by his commitment to democracy, but by his dictatorial powers. The American ambassador informed Wilson that 'The Prime Minister, by public consent, is nearer a dictator than any man in England since Cromwell'.[53] Lloyd George himself later admitted, that 'the nation in peril did not object to virtual dictatorship'.[54]

In 1917, foreign and domestic developments led Lloyd George to emphasize the democratic aspect of the allied struggle. The February revolution in Russia, which removed the tsar, freed Britain and France from the taint of alliance with an autocracy. Lloyd George told the new Russian premier that the war was 'at bottom a struggle for popular Government as well as for liberty'.[55] He developed this point to the Imperial War Cabinet on 20 March:

> The second aim which I hope will be achieved by this war is the democratisation of Europe. It is the only sure guarantee of peaceful progress. The menace to Europe did not come from its democratic countries; it came from military autocracy ... if Germany had had a democracy like France, like ourselves, or like Italy, we should not have had this trouble. Liberty is the only sure guarantee of peace and goodwill among the peoples of the world.[56]

Lloyd George's comments were made before the United States declared war on Germany and they foreshadowed Wilson's famous speech to Congress two weeks later. Lloyd George expected the allies to be led to victory by the British Empire which would then be, 'the first Power in the world' and also a 'democratic commonwealth of nations ... the truest representative of freedom – in the spirit even more than in the letter of its institutions'.[57]

The letter, as well as the spirit, of British institutions soon became more democratic. The recommendation of the all-party Speaker's Conference that all servicemen and women over 30 should be enfranchised on account of their contribution to the war effort was welcomed by Lloyd George.[58] He regarded the 1918 Reform Act – which tripled the size of the British electorate – as the most revolutionary reform in British history: 'We had long called ourselves a democratic country. Not until this measure was passed into law could it be truly said that our parliamentary representation was elected on a really democratic basis.'[59] The passage of the 1918 Reform Act enabled Churchill to tell MPs: 'We are elected on the widest franchise obtaining in any country in the world.'[60] In the United States, women did not obtain the right to vote in federal elections until the passage of the Nineteenth Amendment in 1920.

In the spring of 1917 a combination of political and military developments convinced Wilson that the United States could no longer stand aloof from the war in Europe. On 2 April, he told Congress:

> The peace of the world is involved and the freedom of its peoples, and the menace to that peace and freedom lies in the existence of autocratic governments backed by organized force which is controlled wholly by their will, not by the will of their people ... The world must be made safe for democracy. Its peace must be planted upon the tested foundations of political liberty.[61]

Wilson did not acknowledge that he had been influenced by Lloyd George, but he did admit that 'Webster, Lincoln, and Gladstone had announced the same principles'.[62] None of that trio, however, had employed the term 'democracy' with respect to international relations. Colonel House believed that Wilson had always held these convictions, but that 'until Russia joined the democratic nations he did not think it wise to utter them'.[63] Certainly Wilson welcomed the February 1917 revolution and the United States was the first country to recognize the new Russian government.[64] But the entry of the United States into the war engendered a wave of patriotism in America which stifled democratic dissent. The Russian-born anarchist, Emma Goldman, justified her opposition to the draft on the grounds that 'if America has entered the war to make the world safe for democracy, she must first make democracy safe in America'. This argument did not prevent her being convicted and imprisoned for her activities and then deported to Russia.[65]

In January 1918, Lloyd George, in a restatement of British war aims, observed that 'the adoption of a really democratic constitution by Germany would be the most convincing evidence that in her the old spirit of military domination had indeed died in this war'.[66] Wilson feared that Lloyd George had stolen his thunder, but House assured the President that his forthcoming address to Congress would again make him 'the spokesman for the Entente, and ... the liberals of the world'.[67] Yet Wilson's address to Congress – which included his famous 14 Points – marked a retreat from the democratic theme he had expounded only nine months before. He made only one specific reference to democracy – ironically, when he praised the Bolsheviks for insisting, 'in the true spirit of modern democracy', that the Brest-Litovsk negotiations should be held in public. His call for Russia to be welcomed 'into the society of free nations under institutions of her own choosing', enabled the Bolsheviks to suppress the Russian National Assembly without fear of American condemnation.[68]

By 1919 the democratic dimension to the political rhetoric of both Wilson and Lloyd George had largely evaporated. Lloyd George observed of Wilson: 'He talks a lot of sentimental platitudes, but he believes them.'[69] Lloyd George shed no tears when Wilson's ill-health forced him to retire from politics in 1920 and his final verdict was damming: 'Wilson was not a Lincoln.'[70]

Before and during the Second World War, the cause of democracy was championed by two patricians: Roosevelt and Churchill. They both had ministerial responsibility for the navy during the First World War and had briefly met in London, in 1919, but they had no further direct contact until 1939. Churchill expressed misgivings about Roosevelt's New Deal, but admired his personal fortitude in the face of adversity.[71] In the later 1930s, Roosevelt and Churchill in their speeches – many delivered on the radio – expressed a common antagonism to dictatorship and a shared belief in democracy. Roosevelt's commitment to democracy was evident from the start of his presidency, when he responded to the slump in the spirit of Al Smith's belief that 'All the ills of democracy can be cured by more democracy'.[72] Roosevelt regarded the New Deal as a triumph for democracy: 'We have come through a hard struggle to preserve democracy in America. Where other nations in other parts of the world have lost that fight, we have won.'[73] Roosevelt believed that his first term of office had proved that democracy could act in a crisis as effectively as dictatorship and he argued that the essence of democracy was not a weak executive, but free elections.[74]

Roosevelt also sought to propagate democracy abroad. At the 1936 Buenos Aires conference, he spoke of the need to justify democracy, by proving its practical efficacy:

> Democracy is still the hope of the world. If we in our generation can continue its successful application in the Americas, it will spread and supersede other methods by which men are governed

and which seem to most of us to run counter to our ideals of human liberty and human progress.[75]

By concentrating on the Americas – the traditional sphere of United States influence – Roosevelt avoided close involvement in the defence of democracy in Europe.

Churchill, by contrast with Roosevelt, placed less emphasis on democracy in his pre-war speeches on foreign affairs. His reticence partly reflected the situation in central and eastern Europe where there were many less-than-democratic states which were not yet part of the Nazi system. There were no such complications on the Atlantic seaboard and in 1936 Churchill warmly welcomed the opposition of the French, British and American democracies to the Nazis and Communists.[76] Churchill believed that his hostility to the dictators had influenced Roosevelt, but there is no direct evidence of this.[77] In 1938 Chamberlain's disregard for Roosevelt's peace initiative led Churchill to issue his own call to the democracies on both sides of the Atlantic:

> Have we not an ideology – if we must use this ugly word – of our own in freedom, in a liberal constitution, in democratic and Parliamentary government, in Magna Carta and the Petition of Right? ... Ought we not to produce in defence of Right, champions as bold, missionaries as eager, and if need be, swords as sharp as are at the disposal of the leaders of totalitarian states.[78]

Churchill made three broadcasts to America before the war. In his first broadcast, after the Munich agreement, he asked all those who cherished the ideals of the British and American constitutions to oppose racial persecution, religious intolerance, suppression of free speech, and the cult of war. He called on Britain and America to arm themselves with what the dictators feared most – ideas: 'People say we ought not to allow ourselves to be drawn into a theoretical antagonism between Nazidom and democracy; but the antagonism is here now. It is this very conflict of spiritual and moral ideas which gives the free countries a great part of their strength.'[79]

In 1939 Roosevelt tried to define the essence of a democratic society. He noted that the American Constitution of 1789 was not based on universal suffrage, but on regular elections and a free choice of ministers, which he described as 'this fundamental, or perhaps, in more modern language, I should call it this ideology of democracy'. He contrasted the guarantees for individual liberty provided by the Bill of Rights and trial by jury with the illiberal practices in the dictatorships.[80] A month later, Churchill echoed Roosevelt's remarks from a British perspective: 'In the British Empire we not only look out across the seas towards each other, but backwards to our own history, to Magna Carta, to Habeas Corpus, to the Petition of Right, to Trial by Jury, to the English Common Law and to Parliamentary Democracy.'[81] In a broadcast to America, Churchill contrasted the all-powerful position of Hitler with the horror of the English-speaking peoples for one-man power.[82] Only three months before, however, Churchill had written of Chamberlain's government: 'There never has been in England such a one-man Government as that under which we have dwelt for the last year.'[83] Churchill's opposition to the Munich agreement left him isolated until Chamberlain brought him into the cabinet at the outbreak of war in September 1939. Then Churchill candidly told the House of Commons that a war undertaken in the name of liberty and right required, 'the surrender for the time being of so many dearly valued liberties and rights'.[84] Such measures, he argued, would convince the world that the democracies were more than a match for the dicatorships.[85]

The neutrality of the United States during the first two years of the war, led Roosevelt to direct much of his democratic rhetoric to the home front, rather than abroad. He believed that the people would only defend democracy if it benefited them personally, consequently he regarded his programme of social and economic reform as 'a part of defense, as basic as armaments themselves'.[86] He thought that American democracy could thrive only if it provided security and hope for all its citizens: 'the white and the colored; the Protestant, the Catholic, the Jew'.[87] Roosevelt described the Battle of Britain as 'proof that democracy, when put to the test, can show the stuff of which it is made', yet he made few comments about the predicament of Britain.[88] In December 1940 he endorsed the Lend-Lease bill with the well-known phrase – 'We must be the great arsenal of democracy' – words which did not commit the United States to any direct military support for democracy abroad.[89] Nevertheless Churchill welcomed the Lease-Lend Act as a 'new Magna Carta' issued by 'the most powerful democracy'.[90]

Roosevelt's re-election for a third term broke with tradition and drew accusations of dictator-like tendencies, but his inaugural address reached new heights of democratic rhetoric:

> The democratic aspiration is no mere recent phase in human history. It *is* human history. It permeated the ancient life of early peoples. It blazed anew in the middle ages. It was written in Magna Carta ... In the Americas its impact has been irresistible ... Its vitality was written into our own Mayflower Compact, into the Declaration of Independence, into the Constitution of the United States, into the Gettysburg Address.[91]

Events, however, soon undermined the tide of transatlantic democratic discourse. When Hitler invaded the Soviet Union, in June 1941, Churchill immediately pledged British support since 'the Russian danger is ... our danger and the danger of the United States, just as the cause of any Russian fighting for his hearth and home is the cause of free men and free peoples in every quarter of the globe'.[92] Nevertheless the inclusion of the Soviet Union in the anti-Nazi front weakened the democratic credentials of the allies. Seven weeks later, Roosevelt and Churchill met off Newfoundland and signed the Atlantic Charter. This was drafted so as not to offend the Soviet Union and contained no reference to democracy. The charter did endorse two of Roosevelt's 'four freedoms' – freedom from want and freedom from fear – but did not refer to the other two – freedom of speech and religion.[93]

After the entry of the United States into the war, in December 1941, Churchill addressed a joint session of Congress:

> I am a child of the House of Commons. I was brought up in my father's house to believe in democracy. 'Trust the people' – that was his message ... Therefore I have been in full harmony all my life with the tides which have flowed on both sides of the Atlantic against privilege and monopoly, and I have steered confidently towards the Gettysburg ideal of 'government of the people by the people for the people'.

Churchill's father, Lord Randolph, had certainly been associated with the concept of 'Tory democracy', but he had largely avoided using the phrase and had stressed its Tory, rather than its democratic connotations.[94] Churchill himself had admitted that 'Tory Democracy was necessarily a compromise ... between widely different forces and ideas'.[95] Churchill's reference to Lincoln's Gettysburg Address was diplomatic, but unprecedented and rather unconvincing, for he did not mention the address in his long historical account of the American Civil War.[96]

Roosevelt thought that Britain's commitment to democracy was compromised by its continued rule over India, but Churchill refused to contemplate Indian independence until after the war was over.[97] In 1944, Churchill asserted, in a message to Roosevelt, that British imperialism 'has spread and is spreading democracy more widely than any other system of government since the beginning of time'.[98] Roosevelt did not respond and the two men had no public disagreeement on the matter before the President died.

After the war, events in Britain and Eastern Europe prompted Churchill to again deploy his democratic rhetoric to a transatlantic audience. At Fulton, Missouri, in 1946 , he declared that free and secret elections, freedom of speech and an independent judiciary formed the message of the British and American peoples to mankind: 'Let us preach what we practise – let us practise what we preach.'[99] Churchill was concerned not only with Stalin's Iron Curtain in Europe, but also with the potential threat to democracy posed by the Labour government in Britain.

During the debate on the Parliament bill in 1947, Churchill criticized the 'we are the masters now' mentality of the Labour government:

> Democracy is not a caucus, obtaining a fixed term of office by promises, and then doing what it likes with the people. We hold that there ought to be a constant relationship between the rulers and the people. Government of the people, by the people, for the people still remains the sovereign definition of democracy. There is no correspondence between this broad conception and the outlook of His Majesty's Government.[100]

Thus Churchill linked Labour with an unfavourable image of American democracy – government by caucus – rather than with the populist concept of American democracy coined by Lincoln, which had now become the basis for political authority even for the theoretically monarchist government of Britain.

The discourse of the six politicians examined in this study, suggests that the tide of democratic rhetoric and (more arguably) democratic practice flowed at a similar rate in both Britain and America. This was the case even when there was little or no contact between the two political élites. In the mid-nineteenth century, the language of explicit democracy – in the sense of universal suffrage – was not accepted officially either in America or in Britain. Both Lincoln and Gladstone employed the old language of liberty, rather than the new language of democracy, though they both enjoyed a posthumous reputation as democratic populists. Wilson and Lloyd George deployed the concept of democracy first in national, and then in international affairs. Their example was emulated and then overshadowed by two patrician champions of democracy: Churchill and Roosevelt. They defended the democratic system at home and abroad, and made it one of the key ingredients of Britain's and America's ideological offensive during the Second World War. But in their struggle with the dictators, Churchill and Roosevelt mixed the 'new' language of all inclusive democracy with the 'old' language of popular liberty.

British and American attitudes towards democracy were never an exclusively national product, but were much influenced by foreign developments. Thus in the spring of 1917, for example, Russia's liberal revolution encouraged the democratic language of Wilson and Lloyd George. More often, however, it was an ideological and military threat from abroad which prompted Britain and America to assert their democratic values. War boosted democratic discourse on both sides of the Atlantic, but it also led to the suppression of civil liberties in the interests of national security.

In 1954 Churchill observed to Eisenhower: 'The British and American Democracies were slowly and painfully forged and even they are not perfect yet.'[101] That was certainly true, for in Britain the old aristocratic élite retained much power and in America, blacks did not win effective legal equality until the 1960s.[102] Even today, the continued existence of an hereditary monarchy and peerage in Britain and the high costs of political campaigning in the United States illustrate how both nations remain undemocratic in important respects. Thus over the last century, the two countries have been united, less by a common system of democracy than by a common presumption of democracy. That presumption has disguised the very real shortcomings of democracy in Britain and America, and exaggerated the centrality of democracy in their political tradition. Nevertheless that presumption has also assisted the slow, but steady, democratization of both countries and has had profound and largely beneficial consequences for the rest of the world.

Notes

1. J. C. D. Clark, *The Language of Liberty 1660–1832: Political Discourse and Social Dynamics in the Anglo-American World* (Cambridge, 1994), p. 383.
2. Andrew Robertson, *The Language of Democracy: Political Rhetoric in the United States and Britain 1790–1900* (Ithaca, NY, and London, 1995).
3. David Herbert Donald, *Lincoln* (London, 1996).
4. Walter Bagehot, 'Mr Gladstone', in R. H. Hutton (ed.), *Biographical Studies* (London, 1881), pp. 94, 112.
5. Lord Charnwood, *Abraham Lincoln* (London, 1947), pp. 452–3.
6. Mark E. Neeley Jr, *The Fate of Liberty: Abraham Lincoln and Civil Liberties* (New York and Oxford, 1991), pp. 211, 214.
7. Richard Shannon, *Gladstone: Volume I 1809–1865* (London, 1982), p. 168; Goldwin Smith, *My Memory of Gladstone* (London, 1904), pp. 37–9.
8. Roy P. Basler (ed.), *The Collected Works of Abraham Lincoln* (New Brunswick, 1953), vol. 4, p. 240.
9. Keith Robbins, *John Bright*, (London, 1979), p. 164.
10. Shannon, *Gladstone*, p. 494: Gladstone to Sumner, 5 November 1863.
11. Basler, *Collected Works of Lincoln*, vol. 5, p. 388: Lincoln to Horace Greeley, 22 August 1862.
12. Harold J. Laski, *The American Democracy: A Commmentary and Interpretation* (London, 1949), p. 6.
13. Roy P. Basler (ed.), *Abraham Lincoln: His Speeches and Writings* (Cleveland, OH, 1946), p. 42.
14. Charnwood, *Lincoln* , pp. 452–3.
15. Basler, *Collected Works of Lincoln* , vol. 2, p. 532.
16. Charnwood, *Lincoln* , p. 74.
17. Donald, *Lincoln* , p. 59.
18. *Parliamentary Debates*, 3rd series, vol. 182 (1866), cols 1134–5.

19. Charnwood, *Lincoln*, pp. 116–17: Lincoln to Joshua Speed, 24 August 1855.
20. Basler, *Collected Works of Lincoln* , vol. 4, p. 240; Mark E. Neeley Jr, *The Fate of Liberty: Abraham Lincoln and Civil Liberties* (New York and Oxford, 1991), pp. 214–16.
21. Laski, *The American Democracy*, p. 17; Robertson, *The Language of Democracy*, p. 1.
22. John Bright and James E. Thorold Rogers (eds), *Speeches on Questions of Public Policy by Richard Cobden M.P.* (London, 1878), p. 582: speech at Rochdale, 18 August 1859.
23. See David P. Crook, *American Democracy in English Politics 1815–50* (Oxford, 1965).
24. Robert Blake, *Disraeli* (London, 1966), p. 419: Disraeli to Mrs Brydges Willyams, 8 December 1861.
25. John Vincent (ed.), *Disraeli, Derby and the Conservative Party: Journals and Memoirs of Edward Henry Lord Stanley 1849–1869* (Hassocks, 1978), pp. 219–20: diary entry for 23 June 1864.
26. Shannon, *Gladstone*, p. 553: Gladstone to Sumner, 25 August 1865.
27. Bagehot, *Gladstone*, p. 89.
28. *The Times*, 7 April 1866.
29. *Parliamentary Debates*, 3rd series, vol. 285 (1884), col. 106–7.
30. M. R. D. Foot and H. C .G. Matthew (eds) *The Gladstone Diaries vol. III 1840–47* (Oxford, 1974), pp. 24, 39.
31. W. E. Gladstone, 'Kin Beyond the Sea', in W. E. Gladstone, *Gleanings of Past Years* (London 1879), vol. 1, p. 203.
32. *The Times*, 7 April 1866.
33. *Parliamentary Debates*, 3rd series, vol. 183 (1866), cols 103–13, 145.
34. Ibid., col. 152.
35. Ibid., vol. 186 (1867), col. 7.
36. John Brooke and Mary Sorensen (eds), *W. E. Gladstone: Autobiographica* (London, 1971), pp. 92–3.
37. Patrick Devlin, *Too Proud to Fight, Woodrow Wilson's Neutrality* (London, 1974), p. 27; E. M. Hugh-Jones, *Woodrow Wilson and American Liberalism* (New York, 1948), pp. 6–7.
38. W. R. P. George, *The Making of Lloyd George* (London, 1976), pp. 80–81: David Lloyd George's diary entry for 12 July 1878.
39. George, *Making of Lloyd George*, pp. 79–80. For the posthumous influence of Lincoln see Merrill D. Peterson, *Lincoln in American Memory* (New York and Oxford, 1995).
40. Frank Owen, *Tempestuous Journey: Lloyd George His Life and Times* (London, 1954), p. 29.
41. *The Times*, 20 October 1923.
42. A. J. P. Taylor (ed.), *Lloyd George: A Diary By Frances Stevenson* (London, 1971), p. 141: diary entry for 5 February 1917.
43. Thomas P. Somma, *The Apotheosis of Democracy* (Delaware, 1994).
44. Devlin, *Too Proud to Fight*, p. 27.
45. Woodrow Wilson, 'Democracy', in A. S. Link (ed.), *The Papers of Woodrow Wilson, vol. 7 1890–92* (Princeton, NJ, 1969), pp. 347, 352.
46. Woodrow Wilson, 'Democracy and Efficiency', in A. S. Link (ed.), *The Papers of Woodrow Wilson, vol. 12: 1900–02* (Princeton, NJ, 1972), pp. 8, 20.

47. Wilson, 'Democracy', pp. 357, 368.
48. See, for example, *The Times*, 11 October 1909.
49. *The Times*, 20 September 1914.
50. David Lloyd George, *War Memoirs* 2 vols (London, 1938), vol. 1, p. 982.
51. Bentley B. Gilbert, *David Lloyd George a Political Life: Vol. II. Organizer of Victory 1912–1916* (London, 1992), p. 293.
52. Burton J. Hendrick, *The Life and Letters of Walter H. Page*, 2 vols (London, 1923), vol. 2, p. 253.
53. A. S. Link (ed.), *Papers of Woodrow Wilson, vol. 41: 24 Jan.–6 April 1917* (Princeton, NJ, 1983), p. 214: Walter Page to Wilson, 11 February 1917.
54. Tom Clarke, *My Lloyd George Diary* (London, 1939), p. 158: entry for 29 July 1932.
55. Lloyd George, *War Memoirs*, vol. 1, p. 970: Lloyd George to Prince Lvoff, 24 March 1917.
56. Ibid., p. 1050.
57. Ibid., pp. 1052, 1057.
58. *Parliamentary Debates*, 5th series, vol. 92 (1917), cols 489, 492.
59. Lloyd George, *War Memoirs*, vol. 2, p. 1174.
60. *Parliamentary Debates*, 5th series, Commons, vol. 114 (1919), col. 1254.
61. Link, *Papers of Woodrow Wilson, vol. 41* , p. 525: Wilson's speech to a joint session of Congress, 2 April 1917.
62. Charles Seymour (ed.), *The Intimate Papers of Colonel House: Volume II From Neutrality to War 1915–17*, (London, 1926), p. 473.
63. Charles Seymour (ed.), *Papers of Colonel House: Volume III Into The World War April 1917–June 1918* (London, 1928), p. 38: House to Sir Eric Drummond, 9 April 1917.
64. Link, *Papers of Woodrow Wilson, vol. 41*, p. 461: Diary of Josephus Daniels, 23 March 1917.
65. Brian Macarthur (ed.), *The Penguin Book of Historic Speeches* (London, 1996), p. 450.
66. Lloyd George, *War Memoirs*, vol. 2, p. 1511: Lloyd George's speech to the Trade Union Congress, 5 January 1918.
67. A. S. Link (ed.) *Papers of Woodrow Wilson, vol. 45: 11 November 1917–15 January 1918*, (Princeton, NJ, 1984), pp. 556–7: Diary of Colonel House, 9 January 1918.
68. Ibid., pp. 534, 537: Wilson's address to a joint session of Congress, 8 January 1918.
69. J. M. McEwen (ed.), *The Riddell Diaries 1908–23* (London, 1986), p. 268: entry for 11 April 1919.
70. Lloyd George, *War Memoirs*, vol. 1, p. 1009.
71. Winston S. Churchill, 'Roosevelt from Afar' in Winston S. Churchill, *Great Contemporaries* (London, 1949), pp. 293–303.
72. *New York Times*, 28 June 1933: Smith's speech at Albany, 27 June 1933.
73. B. D. Zevin (ed.), *Nothing to Fear: The Selected Addresses of Franklin Delano Roosevelt 1932–45* (Cambridge, MA, 1946), p. 69: Roosevelt's speech at Chicago, 14 October 1936.
74. Ibid., pp. 80–81: Roosevelt's message to Congress, 6 January 1937; ibid., p. 89: Roosevelt's second inaugural address, 20 January 1937.

75. Ibid., p. 78: Roosevelt's speech at Buenos Aires, 1 December 1936.
76. Robert Rhodes James (ed.), *Winston S. Churchill His Complete Speeches 1896–1963, vol. VI, 1935–1942* (New York, 1974), p. 5788: Churchill's speech in Paris, 24 September 1936.
77. Winston S. Churchill, *The Second World War, Volume I, The Gathering Storm* (London, 1949), p. 222: Churchill to Eden, 20 September 1937.
78. Winston S. Churchill, *Into Battle* (London, 1945), pp. 17–18: Churchill's speech at Manchester, 9 May 1938.
79. Ibid., p. 58: Churchill's broadcast to the people of the United States, 16 October 1938.
80. Zevin, *Addresses of F. D. R.*, pp. 176–8: Roosevelt's address to Congress, 4 March 1939.
81. Churchill, *Into Battle*, p. 100: Churchill's speech of 20 April 1939.
82. Ibid., pp. 126–8: Churchill's broadcast to the people of the United States, 8 August 1939.
83. Winston S. Churchill, *Step by Step 1936–1939* (London, 1939), p. 341: 'The Crunch, 24 March 1939'.
84. Churchill, *Into Battle*, p. 128b: Churchill's speech to the House of Commons, 3 September 1939.
85. Ibid., pp. 133–4: Churchill's broadcast, 1 October 1939.
86. Zevin, *Addresses of F. D. R.*, p. 166: Roosevelt's annual message to Congress, 4 January 1939.
87. Ibid., p. 221: Roosevelt's radio address, 19 July 1940; ibid., p. 245: Roosevelt's radio address, 4 November 1940.
88. Ibid., p. 230: Roosevelt's speech at Dayton, Ohio, 12 October 1940.
89. Ibid., p. 257: Roosevelt's radio broadcast, 29 December 1940.
90. Winston S. Churchill, *The Unrelenting Struggle* (London, 1942), pp. 78–9: Churchill's statement to the House of Commons, 12 March 1941.
91. Zevin, *Addresses of F. D. R.*, pp. 269–70: Roosevelt's third inaugural address, 20 January 1941.
92. Churchill, *The Unrelenting Struggle*, p. 180: Churchill's broadcast, 22 June 1941.
93. Cf. Zevin, *Addresses of F. D. R.*, p: 266: Roosevelt's speech at Washington, 6 January 1941.
94. See Roland Quinault, 'Lord Randolph Churchill and Tory Democracy 1880–1885', *Historical Journal*, 22 (1979), 141–65.
95. Winston S. Churchill, *Lord Randolph Churchill* (London, 1907), p. 821.
96. Churchill's account of the American Civil War was largely written between 1938 and 1940 and published in his *A History of the English-speaking Peoples, Volume IV, The Great Democracies* (London, 1958).
97. Lord Moran, *Winston Churchill: The Struggle for Survival 1940–65* (London, 1966), pp. 30–31.
98. Warren F. Kimball (ed.), *Churchill and Roosevelt: The Complete Correspondence III. Alliance Declining February 1944–April 1945* (Princeton, NJ, 1987), p. 140: Churchill to Roosevelt, 21 May 1944.
99. Winston S. Churchill, *The Sinews of Peace: Post-war Speeches* (London, 1948), p. 97: Churchill's speech at Westminster College, Fulton, Missouri, 5 March 1946.
100. Winston S. Churchill, *Europe Unite, Speeches 1947 and 1948* (London,

1950), p. 198: Churchill's speech in the House of Commons, 11 November 1947.
101. Anthony Montague Browne, *Long Sunset: Memoirs of Winston Churchill's Last Private Secretary* (London, 1996), p. 164.
102. For a recent perspective on this topic see Eric Foner, *The Story of American Freedom* (London, 1999).

CHAPTER EIGHT

Free Trade and the International Order: The Anglo-American Tradition, 1846–1946

Anthony Howe

In the last years of the Thirteen Colonies, a strong strand of economic liberalism, deriving in large part from Adam Smith, served as one of the vibrant linkages within Anglo-American culture.[1] Even before the *Wealth of Nations* had been published, Benjamin Franklin had urged that commerce should be 'as free between all the nations of the world, as it is between the several counties of England'.[2] Yet over the next century, no policy seemed more to divide Britain from her former subjects than that of free trade. For Britain's progressive adoption of free trade (including the abandonment of the Navigation Acts which many believed had fomented the American revolt), was matched by the new republic's increasing resort to protection, with the erection of a battery of tariffs and discriminatory duties.[3] This contrast proved enduring, for although at times it seemed that the United States might embrace free trade, for the most part, her policy into the 1930s remained one of unremitting protectionism.[4] Britain appeared similarly rigid in her attachment to free trade, a loyalty that provided one of the most important and long-lasting ideological characteristics of the British Liberal Party.[5] However much, therefore, historians have identified the emergence of a common liberalism between the two polities, for example, readily associating American Democrats with admiration for Gladstone, or the Edwardian New Liberals with American Progressives, this mutuality fell short of common adherence to free trade.[6]

American hostility to free trade was in turn the source of great anxiety among British Liberals, with Gladstone in 1890 already seeking to direct the United States towards the free trade responsibilities which he held properly belonged to the world's premier economic power.[7] Protectionism, if not quite sinful in the Gladstonian creed, was a dangerous disease against which he even felt it necessary to warn the grandson of Sir Robert Peel before he embarked for the United States in 1896. Thus, George Peel recalled that he had visited Gladstone, who 'adminstered to me, for some three or four hours altogether, what I could only regard as a prophylactic, an inoculation, against my contemplated contact with American realities. This took the form of an account ... of those principles of economic policy which had animated and guided Sir Robert Peel ... and, in turn, himself'. Peel added 'A few weeks later, in remote Nebraska, I was destined to sustain a converse "economic impact" from Mr William Jennings Bryan'.[8]

A similar homily contrasting British free trade with American protectionism awaited President Roosevelt on USS *Augusta* in Placentia Bay, Newfoundland in August 1941. For, when negotiations over the Atlantic Charter reached the delicate issue of trade discrimination, Winston Churchill 'could not help mentioning the British experience in adhering to Free Trade for eighty years in the face of ever mounting American tariffs ... All we had got in reciprocation was successive doses of American protectionism'.[9]

Yet by the time of this famous meeting, the roles of Britain and the United States had been significantly transposed. As one American policy-maker put it, '[while] we had reversed our international policies and begun to move vigorously in the direction of healthy international economic relations, Great Britain was in the process of moving away from the sound international policies which she had advocated and pursued'.[10] On the one hand, in 1931 Britain had at last succumbed to the pressure for protection and imperial preference after a sustained campaign launched in 1903 by Joseph Chamberlain and completed with due filial piety by his son Neville in the budget of 1932.[11] On the other hand, in the United States by 1941 a solid commitment to the abandonment of protectionism had become central to post-war economic planning, to an extent which sometimes dismayed Britain's leading policy-maker, Keynes. Keynes found in American proposals in 1941 'a dogmatic statement of the virtues of *laissez-faire* in international trade on the lines familiar forty years ago'.[12] Such free trade policies smacked woefully of a return to those defunct nineteenth-century pieties from which Keynes's career had been designed to rescue politicians. Despite Britain's abandonment of free trade, therefore, the free trade ideal was not dead. Rather, as Calleo and Rowlands tersely put it, 'it had simply moved to America'.[13] As a result, by the time Churchill and Roosevelt met in August 1941, the United States had become the leading proponent of multilateral trade, with one of her main objectives to wean Britain off the imperial preference she had adopted in 1932.

This neat contrast between British free trade and American protection before 1931, and between British imperial preference and American free(r) trade after 1931, belies a complex interaction between the two contrasting ideals. For just as Tariff Reform in Britain was no sudden eruption in 1931, so too 'the free trade element' in the United States was not simply confined, as Keynes once claimed, to State department officials, representing 'almost nothing but themselves'.[14] Rather, as this chapter seeks to show, the American free trade ideal was more deeply rooted than Keynes suggested. The tendency therefore to dismiss free trade as a policy of 'state' committed to internationalism and inimical to domestic American interests in important respects misconceives the free trade tradition in the United States.[15] This tradition, on the contrary, has both a long genealogy and a genuine domestic political resonance which have too often been neglected in studies of American foreign economic policy. As a result, despite the apparently overwhelming differences between British and American attitudes to the tariff question, there is a strong line of continuity linking Richard Cobden, the exemplar of British free trade in Victorian Britain and Cordell Hull, whose policies in the 1930s embodied America's decisive breach with protection.[16]

This genealogy may very schematically be broken down into four leading periods. First, between 1846 and c. 1872, there was in the United States a strong strand of free trade cosmopolitanism, tied very closely to the British model. Second, between c. 1872 and the turn of the century, free trade ideas were increasingly submerged not only by the growth of Republican protectionism but also by the strength of competing issues, above all, that of the currency question. For while money remained marginal in Britain, it took centre stage in American politics, and was, in some ways, say, the equivalent of Irish Home Rule in Britain in its impact on party fortunes.[17] Third, before 1914 the economic internationalist tradition revived, especially in the ideas of Woodrow Wilson and with the passing of the Underwood tariff of 1913. This left an important legacy. Thus, Cordell Hull's internationalism, the association of peace with trade, clearly derives from this period, although only put into practice in the 1930s. Fourth, from 1934 a new commitment to a freer trade international order became central to American commercial policy and from 1941 to American post-war planning. But the implementation of this ideal was still shaped in important ways by British as well as American policy-makers. The world trade edifice constructed by 1946 was a far cry from that of the 1840s but free traders in 1946 were able to recognize in the proposed International Trade Organization (ITO), the twentieth century's equivalent to Britain's Repeal of the Corn Laws in 1846. In the short term the ITO proved still-born but its goal of global free trade has proved strongly influential since 1946, imparting an idealistic flavour to the formation of the World Trade Organization (WTO) in 1995 and operating as a crucial, if variable, determinant of American foreign policy.[18]

In the first period, the British model of free trade culminating in the repeal of the Corn Laws in 1846 was in a sense derived from a shared late eighteenth-century vision of free trade. For whatever the power of protectionism in the early republic, the free trade ideal had remained resilient, epitomized above all in the Jeffersonian tradition of commercial policy.[19] Subsequently, free trade ideas had been powerfully expressed in the writings of economists such as John Taylor, Francis Wayland, Thomas Cooper and Condy Raguet (incidentally an important influence on Cobden himself), informing discussion in Congress and in the press. Similarly, while protectionists were far better able to unite to put pressure on Congress, free traders were not without influence, with, for example, the Philadelphia Free Trade Convention of 1831 preceding the conferences of the British Anti-Corn Law League by a decade.[20] Britain herself before the repeal of the Corn Laws in 1846 was not yet a free trade power – and this fact itself legitimated some influential expressions of American protectionism. But when the repeal of the Corn Laws in 1846 offered a powerful example of unilateral free trade (and the possibility of growing wheat exports to Britain), there was a significant body of American opinion ready to follow suit.[21] Thus, as James and Lake have argued, the reduced tariff duties in the Walker Tariff of 1846 were in some ways a direct response to British tariff liberalization.[22] After 1846 free trade enjoyed a growing ascendancy in the United States, and the Tariff Act of 1857 confirmed the trend to more moderate duties.[23] Stimulated by admiration for Cobden and Bright, there also emerged a clear group of American epigoni.[24] Among such we might single out W. C. Bryant, journalist and poet, a spectator at Anti-Corn Law League meetings in London in the 1840s and in 1865 the editor of the American imprint of Cobden's *Political Writings*.[25] By 1865 the first American Free Trade League (AFTL) had been formed, headed by Bryant and the New York lawyer Dudley Field, and it was soon publishing its own journal.[26] With the formation of the Cobden Club in Britain in 1866, a close network linking British and American free traders grew up, with the club publishing several tracts by American authors, and with the United States strongly represented among the club's honorary members – men such as Wells, John Bigelow and S. S. Cox.[27]

Among this group of adherents free trade won acceptance primarily on the grounds of intellectual authority and natural justice, with tariffs seen, as in Great Britain, not only as an artificial distortion of the economy but as a regressive form of taxation.[28] This perspective most strongly influenced D. A. Wells, at one time special commissioner for revenue (and a protectionist) but who was to become the embodiment of American free trade values.[29] Wells's report on government finance in 1869 was thus greeted by one free trader as 'our Bible in our future onslaughts on the monopolists. Its facts clinching the irrefragable truths of Free trade will in time demolish the citadel of Protection'.[30] Above all, the increasing burden of taxation as a result of the Civil War exerted a profound effect on the future history of free trade and protection. For, on the one hand, it confirmed free traders in their belief that the protective tariff was a war-induced aberration and that the *ante bellum* economy represented a period of prelapsarian principle and prosperity.[31] On the other hand the extent of government dependence upon tariff revenue now put in place the most effective obstacle to liberalization. For, as Brownlee has shown, even after tariff revenue was no longer needed, tariffs were left in place, the rewards to interest groups built up behind the Republican coalition.[32] Finding an acceptable alternative source of revenue was to prove one of the free traders' most enduring difficulties, while subsequent budget surpluses were to allow governments considerable latitude in the face of free trade pressures.

The second leading free trade emphasis, derived from Smith and Ricardo, urged the economic benefits of specialization and international interdependence. This seemed congruent with the exploitation of America's natural resources and comparative advantage in agricultural exports, rather than industrial development.[33] This also accentuated the link between free trade and its rural southern base, and towards identification with the Democrats. But free trade was never simply a southern planters' creed, and in fact suffered from its identification with the eastern seaboard and New York importers.[34] It should also be noted that many free traders were keen to distance themselves from the Democratic Party, for as G. W. Curtis, editor of *Harper's*, wrote in 1871, 'it is Tammany; whoever helps to bring it into power does not only freedom of trade but all liberty an immense injury'.[35] Arguably, therefore, as Goldstein has suggested, protectionism provided a much tighter identity for the Republican Party than did free trade for the Democrats.[36]

American cosmopolitanism, however, found other sources of strength; for example, it was fed by the Anglo-American peace movement, with its strong links with European free traders in the 1840s through men like Elihu Burritt, free trader and pacifist.[37] In the aftermath of the American Civil War, Burritt urged Wells to become the 'Cobden of America' while himself contemplating 'writing the history of Protection, of the wars it has engendered and its domestic and foreign tyranny'.[38] Similarly, keen American interest in international law was strongly powered by free traders. For example, Henry Wheaton, who provided the free traders' favoured textbook of international law, had been intimately involved in United States commercial diplomacy in the 1840s, while other free traders, such as Dudley Field, were strong campaigners for an international legal code.[39] Another early proponent of international law, Francis Lieber produced one of the most effective philosophical defences of free trade in 1870.[40] As in Britain, where Boyd Hilton has suggested free trade was powerfully influenced and complemented by arguments drawn from evangelical religion, there seems also to have been considerable theological involvement in the American free trade cause – with the most conspicuous example that of the Reverend Henry Ward Beecher, the brother of Harriet Beecher Stowe, although his support proved a mixed blessing.[41] Beecher provocatively attacked protection as anti-Christian; more conventionally the Reverend Joshua Leavitt asserted 'in the free trade movement, we have the laws of God, which He has imposed upon human progress in our favour'.[42] Finally, free trade harmonized with ideals of a *laissez-faire* Utopia, freedom from all forms of interference, the minimalist state and the point at which liberalism and pure individualism came together. This anti-statist ideal remained strong in the United States, although governmental economic intervention acquired growing legitimacy. However, the link between free trade and individual freedom exposed trade policy to vicarious slurs. For example, the well-known Pennsylvanian businessman, Joseph Wharton sought to arouse puritanical instincts by associating free trade with free love, a charge it seemed not wholly without foundation, when the Reverend Beecher achieved notoriety for alleged adultery in the 1870s.[43]

This cadre of free traders, inspired by the British model of free trade and Peelite–Gladstonian finance conducted an energetic educational and political campaign on behalf of a tariff for revenue only. Under the aegis of the AFTL, a number of regional associations were formed and educational crusades undertaken, for example, General Brinkerhoff and Professor A. L. Perry of Williams College conducted lecture tours as free trade evangelists in the early 1870s.[44] Even so, this movement, for all its vigour and impressive credentials, eventually dissipated its energies in the abortive Liberal Republican campaign of 1872. For men such as Carl Schurz, Horace White, and E. L. Godkin, who had campaigned for free trade, were eventually led indirectly into support for protection by the endorsement of Horace Greeley at Cincinnati in 1872.[45] This did not end the free trade movement but left it demoralized, divided and diminished. As R. R. Bowker, then secretary of the Brooklyn Free Trade Club and later one of America's most active free traders, noted laconically of this first Free Trade League, 'It went to Cincinnati but it did not come back'.[46]

In the succeeding years, in the second phase outlined above, American free traders were to be largely on the defensive as the protectionist tariff was consolidated.[47] For the most part, this reduced the free trade ideal to one of tariff revision, an attempt to moderate the severity of protection, as seen in campaigns for the Morrison Bill in 1876 and the

Wood Bill in 1878.[48] Similarly, in the election campaign of 1880, it proved impossible to canvass free trade as a national issue. Much of the impetus behind free trade was now extra-political, carried forward in the universities and in various campaigning groups. Significantly, in academic circles, there is probably a good case for arguing that the intellectual merits of free trade were in the ascendant – with leading economists such as Perry and Taussig strong and influential doctrinal free traders, ably seconded by W. G. Sumner at Yale and H. C. Adams at Cornell.[49] Adams, for example, hitherto little interested in more than pure finance, devoted a special course of lectures to the refutation of protection in 1884.[50] In addition, free-wheeling publicists such as David Wells and Edward Atkinson, aspiring to the parts of Cobden and Bright, played a vital role in keeping the English model of free trade before the public mind.[51] Their collective efforts spawned a number of associations ranging from the International Free Trade (IFT) Alliance set up in New York in 1876 to the Question Clubs organized by Atkinson in Boston.[52] Among pressure group activists, the energetic New York publisher and Mugwump R. R. Bowker, emerged at the centre of a series of leagues and crusades. In particular he set out to revive the AFTL in association with the New York Free Trade Club (NYFTC), with a view to 'fighting Republican protectionism' as well as converting the Democrats and the western farmers, to free trade or at least a revenue only tariff.[53] These objectives caused some dissension in free trade ranks. For they were opposed both by those such as Atkinson who regarded them as too ambitious, and those such as Earle who feared too great a watering down of the goal of 'absolute free trade' to which he had devoted the pages of *The American Free Trader* since 1882.[54] Yet by 1883, the compromise position of a revenue-only tariff (the Iowa platform) had enabled this movement to build up considerable national strength, with New York, Michigan, Nebraska, Detroit, Oregon and Atlanta among the organizations sending representatives to a national conference at Detroit in May 1883.[55] This successful revival of revenue reform sentiment in turn encouraged the departure of the Mugwumps, including Wells and Bowker, from the Republican Party in 1884, even if the strength of protectionism within the Democratic Party still prevented effective free trade policies or even free trade's prominence as an electoral issue in 1884.[56] Yet in 1885 the free trade momentum was kept up, with the Chicago Free Trade Conference achieving nation-wide attendance and publicity, with Wells elected chairman of the national Free Trade League, Bowker the head of its committee and with *The Million* as an effective propaganda organ.[57] This also provided the groundwork for the Democratic endorsement of free trade between 1886 and 1888.[58]

This period also saw a considerable broadening and reinforcement of the intellectual and political case for free trade. For example, it was no longer defended simply as crucial to agriculture but also to manufacturing industry as the dynamic growth of the American economy made exports essential to prosperity. This led to fear of a cycle of booms and gluts, to which free traders responded by urging free imports (especially of raw materials) while protectionists moved towards a search for opening markets through reciprocity treaties.[59] There was also a vigorous attempt to rebut the Republican link between high wages and protection by drawing attention both to the unequal distribution of wealth but also to real rather than nominal wages.[60] There was now a more concerted attempt to draw specific groups towards free trade, whether as farmers, manufacturers, industrial workers or consumers.[61] This period also saw the rise of the crucial platform point linking protection and political corruption, with tariffs resulting from powerful lobbying, not from an expert understanding of economic needs. It was widely asserted that tariffs benefited select groups of well-organized businessmen, and that the infant industry argument, however plausible in the 1840s, now served, if not to protect industrial senility, then at least to disguise burgeoning monopolistic powers.[62] Finally, the emergence of Henry George, linking free trade and the single tax, while alienating some conservative free traders, probably strengthened and helped popularize the wider cause of free trade.[63] This widespread movement, while falling short of its model, the Anti-Corn Law League, in both regional and national power, strongly sustained the Cleveland presidential campaign of 1888.[64] Yet Cleveland's defeat, albeit narrow, once more threw free trade back into a gradualist revisionist creed, not the battle of ideals which had been foreshadowed in 1888.

In this period, free trade as a political platform suffered from two major weaknesses. First, quite unlike the case in Great Britain, there is clear evidence that American voters tended to see themselves primarily as producers, not as consumers. This is understandable for whereas in Britain, the agrarian producers in question had been easily identified with a small group of aristocratic landowners, in the United States the producers embraced a far more multifarious series of urban and rural occupations. But significantly, even the members of the industrial workforce in the United States held a self-image of themselves as producers, earning wages, not as in Britain, as consumers, purchasing goods.[65] Hence much debate was focused on refuting the protectionist charge that foreign competition represented pauper labour, designed to pull down American wages.[66] Second, free trade was identified with Britain, and in the wake of the Civil War, there was a widespread Anglophobia readily drawn upon by economic nationalists. American free traders were easily traduced in this period as the recipients of 'British gold', while remarkably the relatively innocuous Cobden Club earned the reputation (as it did in Bismarckian Germany) of a powerful international free trade conspiracy designed to undermine Britain's economic competitors.[67] Free trade now became an 'UnAmerican activity' whose proponents would be easily lambasted as guileless victims of John Bull. As Atkinson put it in 1885, 'One of the chief obstructions to the progress of free trade in this country is the notion that Great Britain desires us to adopt it'.[68]

These underlying weaknesses of free trade deprived it of clear political definition and left Democrats lukewarm in their enthusiasm. Despite the promise of 1888, the 1890s were therefore to reveal the powerlessness of the free traders in American politics, just as the 1900s in Britain would reveal the impotence of the tariff reformers within the liberal state. On the ideological front, the free traders now focused on free raw materials as the essential basis of both lower consumer prices and as the basis for the export of American manufactured goods.[69] Propaganda work was still kept up by groups such as the New York Reform Club, while the National Association of Democratic Clubs still aspired to play the role of the Anti-Corn Law League in the 1894 election.[70] Following the Democratic success, the Wilson Tariff Bill of 1894 did reveal some readiness to pursue lower tariffs. But as its author admitted to James Bryce, it had returned from the Senate 'badly tattered in many of its most essential and democratic features'.[71] This outcome in fact heightened the free traders' sense of impotence against the power of vested interests, with the predominant tone set not by the Wilson free trade tariff but the twin peaks of protection enshrined in the McKinley Tariff of 1890 and the Dingley Tariff in 1897. 'We seem', as Charles Eliot, the president of Harvard, put it to Bryce, 'to be relapsing into the commercial barbarism of protection.'[72] The Republicans themselves increasingly aware of the importance of American exports, now directed their commercial diplomacy towards reciprocity in order to open markets to American goods. But reciprocity was derived from protection, and was not envisaged as a half-way house to free trade.[73] Similarly, the emerging doctrine of the 'Open Door' was by no means the equivalent to free trade, for it sought merely to guarantee equal access to foreign markets, which in practice could mean equal prohibition from, rather than free entry to, some trading areas. Free trade suffered a further severe blow when the Democratic Party took up the silver question in 1896, for this not only redirected energies away from tariffs but also alienated many keen gold standard free traders. Finally, the pessimism of many free traders in the 1890s was further deepened by America's growing imperial involvement, epitomised by the Spanish-American War of 1898. For men such as Worthington C. Ford and Edward Atkinson were keenly attached to the Cobdenite precepts of peace and non-intervention. The Treasury statistician, Ford, perhaps typified the public strengths and weaknesses of this generation of free traders, noted by Beatrice Webb in 1898 as 'alert, industrious, cultivated ... an Anglo-maniac ... a free-trader, a "gold standard" and a peace man'.[74] But by the turn of the century, the tariff had been eclipsed as a leading political issue and the morale of American free traders had sunk to its nadir.

From this low ebb, the free trade cause was to be only slowly reconstructed in the early twentieth century. A large part of its gradual revival derived from the coalescence between long-standing Boston free traders such as C. F. Adams Jr and W. L. Garrison with New England manufacturers increasingly alienated from Republican tariff policy. This first led in 1888 to the formation of the New England Tariff Reform (NETR) (from 1894, Free Trade [FT]) League.[75] This sought in particular to expose the link between tariffs and trusts but gradually broadened its platform.[76] By 1902 it had reincarnated itself as the second American Free Trade League, publishing the *American Free Trader* and in 1903 the *Free Trade Almanac*.[77] But in contrast to the earlier Free Trade League which had always sought to combine tariff revision with absolute free trade, the movement was advowedly gradualist, seeking simply tariff adjustment, and especially free raw materials, as the maximum possible given the configuration of domestic politics.[78] Free traders such as Garrison remained gloomy, particularly as Chamberlain's advocacy of tariff reform in Britain was now used against them. Garrison for example reported despondently to Bryce, the father confessor of American liberals,

> There is no free trade party here. The second generation since the war is grown up in the protection establishment, is used to it as the normal thing, continues to thrive in spite of it. The propaganda is less in evidence than formerly yet is carried on with a great deal of system.[79]

Despite this gloom, however, residual free trade sentiment in the United States was appropriately rallied in 1904 to celebrate the centenary of the birth of the apostle of free trade and friend of America, Richard Cobden. But whereas in Great Britain, that centenary had been the occasion for the reaffirmation of Cobden as the symbol of progressive new liberalism, in the United States Cobden's career was recalled as a distant beacon whose promise might hopefully draw the Democratic Party back to the advocacy of the fundamental ethical questions which underpinned the free trade cause.[80]

Interestingly, at this time the hopes of Garrison and other free traders really lay more with the Republicans taking up free trade rather than the Democrats, hopes however which were doomed to disappointment under Taft and Theodore Roosevelt.[81] The real impetus towards free trade therefore could only come from within the Democratic Party and, above all, it came from the growing readiness of Woodrow Wilson to take up this issue.[82] Wilson had been a committed free trader from his days as president of the Atlanta Young Men's Free Trade Club in the 1870s. But his growing attacks on the tariff-makers, combined with the publicity given to this issue by 'muckrakers' such as Ida Tarbell, strongly reaffirmed the goal of free trade as essential to free American politics from the power of vested interests.[83] In this vein, free trade became an integral part of political morality, as it had been preached by Cobden and Gladstone. However, this was not in itself enough to sustain free trade. Wilson, as others, was necessarily influenced by the realities of the American economy whose expansion now made necessary the growth of export markets, and among free traders, the recognition that increased exports necessitated increased imports. But the Democratic victory in 1910 was hailed as 'a wonderful insurrection against your tariff' and British free traders now looked on Wilson as the leader of a world-wide crusade for freer trade.[84] This reputation was consolidated by the Underwood tariff of 1913, hailed by the *Economist* as 'the heaviest blow that has been aimed against the Protective system since the British legislation of Sir Robert Peel between 1842 and 1846'.[85] The Underwood tariff, therefore, despite Lake's suggestion that this was a pragmatic response to the fear of British protectionism encouraged by tariff reform, had a vital domestic ideological dimension.[86] It should also be noted that an essential part of the package was fiscal. For free trade, as in Britain in the 1840s, was accompanied by income tax as the vital resource of government but one which now could claim to free the people from the rapacity of the trusts.[87]

But, above all, Wilson's pursuit of free trade was grounded on an implicit recognition that America was part of an international order in which free trade was the best guarantee of peace. This may be seen as part of a broader Anglo-American *rapprochement* in the Edwardian years for, as the ambassador Spring Rice noted, anti-English feeling was now much more muted than in the past (save, of course, among the Irish).[88] But central was the Cobdenite link between free trade and peace – a simple message yet one largely ignored in Europe in the later nineteenth century and only now taken to heart by leading Democrats. From this association would be constructed the third of Wilson's 14 Points, which sought the removal of all economic barriers and the reestablishment of equality of trade conditions as an essential means to permanent peace after the First World War. Interestingly, it was now largely through American influence that the idea of the liberal international economic order, based on the 'open door' proved so resilient during the First World War.[89] The 'open door' was not 'free trade', Eliot had earlier pointed out to Bryce, but it was a via media likely to satisfy protectionist and liberal powers.[90] Significantly too Cordell Hull's First World War rhetoric was grounded in the need for free trade as part of a peaceful world order: in 1916 he called for an international trade conference at the end of the war. He was also to be critical of the failure of the Versailles peace settlement in terms of trade policy.[91] Of course, the possibility of the restoration of free trade after the First World War was remote, but American influence had been exerted successfully against economic war after the peace, although domestically Wilson was unable to secure, as he wished, the continuance of the liberal policy of 1913.[92] Even so, the ideological linkage now made between free trade, peace, and American power was to be of enduring importance.

That importance, as is well known, was of no immediate consequence as America withdrew behind rising tariff walls. The Fordney-McCumber Act in 1922 saw average tariff rates rise from 27 per cent to 39 per cent, while the United States declared its tariffs autonomous, i.e. non-negotiable downwards, with the president empowered to add 50 per cent to duties in the case of countries which discriminated against her. In some ways this provided incentives to keep markets open but very much on American terms in what has been plausibly seen as 'a successful example of hegemonic predation'.[93] This trend was confirmed by the notorious Smoot-Hawley tariff in 1930.[94] But despite this apparent rise of economic nationalism, one should not ignore the post-war growth of important forces which promoted free trade, and which slowly drew the United States towards the position which Britain had occupied in the pre-war system. First, the economic impact of the war had reduced Britain to the position of debtor nation, for whom exports were now vital in order to repay the interest on debts to the United States. This added a powerful prudential argument to the free trade arsenal, even if it was by no means immediately effective.[95] Second, the extension of American industry during the war acted as a stimulus to retain her markets abroad, and there is growing evidence of business pressure for market expansion based on tariff reductions; at this point, significant sections of business opinion endorsed the goal of freer trade.[96] In some sectors, where the United States held a clear market lead and technological advantage, as in automobiles, this produced a powerful advocacy. In some ways Detroit in the 1930s played the part that Manchester had done in the 1830s, with the directors of General Motors, it was widely believed, doing much to promote the American free trade cause.[97]

Third, less materialistically, perceptions of foreign policy dictated a concern with peace, while a clear range of progressive opinion-forming bodies promoted the association of peace, prosperity and freer trade.[98] Foremost among these was the Carnegie Endowment for International Peace, led by Nicholas Murray Butler. Interestingly Butler had been a protectionist on principle in the 1900s but was by 1930 ready to assert that 'The name of Richard Cobden and his teachings grow more important, and not less, as the years pass'.[99] In addition, bodies such as Foreign Policy Association (FPA) and World Peace Foundation (WPF) exerted an important influence upon educated opinion, and offered a sustained and constructive critique of the economic nationalism behind American tariffs.[100] The impact of such groups could of course be counterproductive – certainly the attempt by the British MP Morrison Bell, under the patronage of Butler, to illustrate through his famous Tariff Map the danger of rising European tariff walls, had no effect on Senator Smoot with whom Bell optimistically left his map shortly before the infamous tariff was passed.[101]

Fourth, American economists in the inter-war years emerged as a significant part of the academic and policy-making community. Yet however agreed they mostly were on the desirability of free trade, they lacked political weight. Thus in 1930, 1028 economists famously condemned the Smoot-Hawley tariff, but they were ignored by politicians.[102] Yet increasingly economists gained influence within the bureaucracy, and became a vital force sustaining the case for American participation in a multilateral trading system, even if the administration of Franklin D. Roosevelt was to be deeply divided.[103] In addition, what were considered the excesses of Smoot-Hawley gave rise to two influential analyses of its political and international significance that did much to damage the image of American protectionism.[104]

Finally, the changing position of Great Britain belatedly reacted upon American policy. To a large extent in the 1920s Britain had been attempting to sustain an international order beyond her resources. In 1931, she finally acknowledged failure and in the Ottawa agreements of 1932 for the first time since the repeal of the Corn Laws in 1846, abandoned internationalism for the empire, a choice confirmed by the failure of the World Economic Conference of 1933.[105] Arguably in taking this course, British protectionist thinking had itself been influenced by the American example. Since the 1870s some of the most powerful arguments in favour of fair trade and tariff reform had derived from America – partly as an illustration of the failure of British free trade to secure imitation abroad but also increasingly as an example of what protection could achieve within a federation of states, to which some urged the British Empire should aspire.[106] Britain's reversion to imperial preference in 1932 was not in any simple sense a direct riposte to Smoot-Hawley but the drift of American tariff legislation in the 1920s had considerably narrowed the options facing policy-makers in Britain by 1930. For Britain's sometimes lone efforts to sustain international free trade had received little American encouragement and who, after Smoot-Hawley, could argue plausibly that protection in America was a dying cause? Rather as one Foreign Office (FO) official noted 'the cause of high protection in the US is likely to die even slower than free trade in this country'.[107] Even so, Britain's endorsement of protection in 1931 did much subsequently to sharpen American perceptions of the importance of free trade for world economic prosperity.

Those perceptions reached their fruition in the fourth period outlined above, a phase embodied primarily in the commercial diplomacy of Cordell Hull.[108] For, ironically, just after Britain had abandoned free trade, Cordell Hull, in his reciprocity trade agreements after 1934 embraced the goals of a freer world trading order. Hull, well-termed the 'cautious visionary', sought to guide the United States along the lines of international policy that Britain had abandoned in 1931. As a leading executive politician in an administration that proved suspicious of many of his goals, Hull's freedom of manoeuvre was necessarily limited. But Hull's commitment to free trade was of long standing, influenced by the writings of W. G. Sumner, by the example of Gladstone and the fiscal ideas of his Tennessee political mentor, Benton McMillin.[109] Hull's creed has been criticized for its simplicity but that was in part its importance – for he set out a general direction of policy, clearly contrasting with that of rivals such as Raymond Moley and George Peek and signifying a distinct break with the American past.[110] This provided a policy umbrella under which officials could gradually redirect American policy, while Hull himself was intimately involved in publicizing this new direction. At its core was the Reciprocal Trade Agreements Act of 1934 which removed tariffs from the arena of log-rolling in the Senate and gave the executive power to negotiate bilateral treaties cutting existing tariff rates by up to 50 per cent, together with the ability to grant unconditional most-favoured nation status.[111] This was the basis of Hull's wide-ranging design to contain economic nationalism and reconstruct a liberal trade order.[112] As one State Department memo put it, the trade agreements 'were the sole practicable way of repairing the ravages of super-protectionism and other forms of economic warfare'.[113] This policy was vitally sustained by officials such as Francis Sayre (Woodrow Wilson's son-in-law), and by the writings of a notable group of ideological free traders, including O. G. Villard.[114] But the reciprocity treaties of 1930s, comparable to those of Britain in the 1820s, were designed to boost world trade as distinctly an 'American interest'. As such they were increasingly to gain the support of Republicans as well as Democrats, acquiring by 1945 the political legitimacy previously accorded to protectionism. Finally, Cordell Hull's

trade programme necessarily involved relations with Britain. He showered British diplomats with memoranda on trade policy, sometimes
provoking resentful dismay at American lectures, as Ambassador Lindsay
put it, on 'the gospel of peace by trade' (1936),[115] and normally drawing
the response that British markets, despite Ottawa, still remained relatively open. Even so, Hull now sought to end (and certainly to prevent
the increase of) imperial preference and to create a more liberal trade
agreement between Britain and America.[116] This proved a slow process
but an Anglo-American trade agreement was eventually signed in November 1938. It did not immediately or decisively weaken preference but
it killed the illusion that the British Empire could be reshaped as an
effective economic and political whole.[117] It contained the implicit recognition that Britain's imperial strategy in the 1930s had forfeited
international goodwill, and that Britain could no longer afford that risk.
In this sense it marked a victory for Hull's international policy and
proved the harbinger of Anglo-American co-operation during the Second
World War.

To disentangle the complex skein of wartime economic diplomacy lies
beyond the scope of this chapter.[118] But, as we have noted above, when in
1941, the Atlantic Charter was negotiated one of the goals of American
policy was the endorsement of the world commercial republic once
preached by Paine and Cobden, together with the abandonment of imperial preference.[119] As a result, Article VII of the Mutual Aid Agreement,
as the British economist, and future biographer of Keynes, Harrod put it,
became 'the modern Free Trade Charter'.[120] But while the United States
was now committed to a more open trading order, the exact means and
direction of policy were not yet clear.[121] This uncertainty affected, above
all, the extent to which she would pursue bilateral negotiations, as in the
1930s, or now turn to attempt to construct a multilateral system, with
simultaneous negotiations among many powers. This occupied many
officials in lengthy wartime conferences but the eventual outcome, foreshadowed in the Anglo-American loan negotiations of 1945, was the
pursuit of multilateralism through the proposed ITO (International Trade
Organization), a permanent institution designed to supervise a non-
discriminatory system of world trade. In September 1946 this was
embodied in the Suggested Charter of the ITO and was the basis for
Anglo-American talks in London in October 1946.[122] One hundred years
after Britain had attempted to lead the world towards free trade by
example, the United States sought through this regulatory framework to
achieve the comparable goal, in an utterly different context, of encouraging the world's nations to seek prosperity through untrammelled commerce.

In adopting this goal, American politicians and policy-makers were
responding not simply to the 'free trade element' in the State Department

but were part of a continuous ideological tradition which had since 1846 (or since 1783) proclaimed the benefits for the United States of free trade between nations. For the reasons we have seen, those arguments had until the 1930s often remained those of a beleaguered minority, suspect for their adherence to the 'English model' of political economy. But it is noteworthy that in ultimately pulling the United States towards a multilateral system, the British nineteenth-century model of free trade was of central heuristic importance. First, leading officials such as Sumner Welles had valorized 'the trade policies of the British Empire during the latter portion of the 19th century [which] ... contributed enormously to the sane and prosperous condition of the world'.[123] As Patricia Clavin has shown, such 'lessons of the past' were uppermost in the minds of officials such as Herbert Feis, a former pupil of Taussig's, and now State Department adviser on international economics. In addition, information programmes run by the Department in 1945 regularly contrasted Britain's responsibility towards the international economy in the nineteenth century with the irresponsibility of American protectionism during the Depression.[124] Second, among British officials, while one should not describe them as 'Cobdenite', there was a clear sense that in 1931, the reversion to empire had marked a false turning. There was therefore a warm welcome for an American policy which, as Hall-Patch approvingly put it, 'was away from their old heresies ... and towards what our own policy had been until the 1930s'.[125] Finally, this view of 1931 powerfully influenced James Meade, and it was Meade's alternative to empire that was presented in the scheme for international commercial union in 1942, the most crucial document in shaping the post-war trading order, and the basis of what, after several transmutations, would become the proposed ITO in 1946.[126] Meade's scheme for an 'international commercial union' was designed to recreate the liberal, if flawed, pre-Ottawa economic order while carrying it forward to accommodate the new political and economic structures of the post-war world. It was this combination of older ideals and new models which entitled it to be seen, not as the product of 'mossback Cobdenites', but as the product of 'economists of modern outlook'.[127]

The leading obstacles to the success of multilateral trade were now twofold: residual American protectionism and the British desire to combine the new Keynesian goal of full employment with the old Chamberlainite goal of imperial preference. This is a well-known story but two aspects are worth noting. First, by 1946, American commitment to freer trade was far greater than in the past. This was partly the result of a decade of educational efforts by Hull and his associates and was clearly reflected in post-war American public opinion surveys on tariffs and trade, even if some states, such as Colorado, remained strongly protectionist.[128] Free trade in America could not aspire to become an uncontested issue as in Victorian Britain but by 1946 there were strong elements of a cross-party consensus as trade became part of 'the American dream'.[129] This was a tendency reinforced by the ideological overtones of the Cold War, allowing some to preach the message of Free Trade/Free World, and would be consolidated under Eisenhower in the 1950s.[130]

Ironically, it was in post-war Britain that free trade now seemed most remote – fervently supported by the Cobdenite remnant of the Liberal Party but otherwise adrift in a Britain described by the German 'social market' economist Roepke as an 'insufferable' mixture of 'Labour paradise and Colonel Blimp'.[131] Free trade had steadily lost the popular legitimacy it had enjoyed in the Edwardian period, with many Labour supporters critical of what one Labour MP described as a return to the mid-nineteenth century and many of its policy-makers, under the aegis of Bevin, still strongly attached to empire.[132] At the same time, the Conservative Party, especially through veteran tariff reformers such as Amery, vigorously defended imperial preference, while the Dominions remained a crucial constraint on British policy-makers in the post-war trade conferences. In this situation, Labour sought to combine its commitment to full employment with its obligations to the empire and its financial dependence on the United States. This did not prove an easy task, and it was the imperatives of American policy and wartime promises rather than the legacy of her own free trade past which drew Britain towards support for a new institutional framework for international free trade embodied in the proposed ITO in 1946.[133]

The ITO fell short of fruition – GATT (General Agreement on Trade and Tariffs) in 1947 was to be only a pale shadow of Meade's original conception of an international economic union, while Britain held tenaciously, and for a time successfully to imperial preference.[134] But the aspiration towards a liberal economic order had been powerfully and permanently restated in wartime Anglo-American discussions. In many ways the origins of that ideal go back to Cobden and Peel in 1846 who hoped that Britain's repeal of the Corn Laws would encourage, by the unilateral example of British free trade, international welfare and prosperity within the Pax Britannica. Over the succeeding century that contentious ideal had both attracted and repelled American intellectuals, interest groups, policymakers, and voters; but ultimately, in 1946, free trade had been endorsed as a goal of the Pax Americana. Ironically by that date, the British public debate on the merits of free trade had all but died. Even so, the theory and practice of British free trade between 1846 and 1946 had provided a vital political and diplomatic spur for a new stage in Anglo-American partnership. The United States had not only succeeded John Bull but also Richard Cobden.

Notes

1. J. Dorfman, *The Economic Mind in American Civilization*, 5 vols (London, 1947–59), vols 1 and 2; P. Conkin, *Prophets of Prosperity: America's First Political Economists* (Bloomington, 1980).
2. Quoted A. E. Eckes, *Opening America's Market: U.S. Foreign Trade Policy since 1776* (Chapel Hill, NC, 1995), p. 2.
3. For the theoretical origins of this contrasting trend, see P. McNamara, *Political Economy and Statesmanship: Smith, Hamilton and the Foundation of the Commercial Republic* (DeKalb, IL, 1998).
4. See *inter alia*, Eckes, *America's Market*; E. Stanwood, *American Tariff Controversies in the Nineteenth Century*, 2 vols (London, 1904); F. W. Taussig, *The Tariff History of the United States*, 1st edn (New York and London, 1888, 5th edn 1909); D. A. Lake, *Power, Protection, and Free trade: International Sources of U.S. Commercial Strategy, 1887–1939* (Ithaca, NY, 1988); J. Goldstein, *Ideas, Interests, and American Trade Policy* (Ithaca, NY, 1993).
5. A. Howe, *Free Trade and Liberal England, 1846–1946* (Oxford, 1997).
6. R. Kelley, *The Transatlantic Persuasion: the Liberal-Democratic Mind in the Age of Gladstone* (New York, 1969); K. Morgan 'The Future at Work: Anglo-American progressivism, 1890–1917', in H. C. Allen and R. Thompson (eds), *Contrasts and Connections: Bicenntennial Essays in Anglo-American History* (London, 1976), pp. 245–70; L. Martin and A. Wolfson, *The Anglo-American Tradition in Foreign Affairs* (New Haven, CT, 1956).
7. H. C. G. Matthew (ed.), *The Gladstone Diaries*, vol. 12 *1887–1891* (Oxford, 1994), pp. xlii–iii.
8. G. Peel, *The Economic Impact of America* (London, 1928), p. vii.
9. W. Churchill, *The Second World War: Vol.3 The Grand Alliance* (London, 1950), p. 387; L. S. Pressnell, *External Economic Policy since the War. Vol.1. The Post-War Financial Settlement* (London, 1986), p. 38; D. Reynolds, *The Creation of the Anglo-American Alliance, 1937–41* (Chapel Hill, NC, 1982).
10. Pasvolsky to Hull, 12 December 1941, Cordell Hull Papers, F366, Library of Congress (LC).
11. P. Williamson, *National Crisis and National Government* (Cambridge, 1992); Howe, *Free Trade*, pp. 283, 295.
12. *The Collected Writings of John Maynard Keynes, Vol. XXVI Activities, 1941–46* ed. D. Moggridge (Cambridge, 1980), p. 239.
13. D. P. Calleo and B. M. Rowlands, *America and the World Political Economy: Atlantic Dreams and National Realities* (Bloomington, 1973), p. 33.
14. *Keynes, Vol. XXVI*, p. 251, memo 31 December 1942.
15. This bias mars Eckes's *Opening America's Market*.
16. This was well noted in J. Pennar, 'Richard Cobden and Cordell Hull. A Comparative Study of the Commercial Policies of Nineteenth Century England and Contemporary United States' (PhD thesis, Princeton, 1953). A more recent study similarly identifies 'a Cobdenite–Hullite vision of peace and security through liberal economic institutions and expanding international commerce' as inspiring American trade policy since 1945, G. A. Pigman, 'Hegemony and Free Trade policy: Britain, 1846–

1914 and the USA, 1944–1990 (unpublished Oxford DPhil thesis, 1992).

17.   For example, R. Nugent, *Money and American Society, 1865–1880* (New York, 1968).

18.   R. Ruggiero, 'From Vision to Reality: the Multilateral Trading System at Fifty', WTO Press/94, 4 March 1998; S. Aaronson, *Trade and the American Dream* (Lexington, 1996); Eckes identifies Clinton with Cobden in *America's Market*, pp. 278–89. The ideas of Arthur Dunkel, Secretary-General of General Agreement on Trade and Tariffs (GATT) 1980–94 have also been linked to those of Cobden, J. Bhagwati and M. Hirsch (eds), *The Uruguay Round and Beyond* (Ann Arbor, MI, 1998), p. 193.

19.   D. S. Ben-Atar, *The Origins of Jeffersonian Commercial Policy and Diplomacy* (Basingstoke, 1993).

20.   Dorfman, *The Economic Mind*, vol. 2, p. 603; Stanwood, *Tariff Controversies*, ii, 296–302; cf. J. Pincus, *Pressure Groups and Politics in Antebellum Tariffs* (New York, 1977).

21.   J. Curtis, *America and the Corn Laws* (Manchester, 1841).

22.   S. C. James and D. A. Lake, 'The Second Face of Hegemony: Britain's Repeal of the Corn Laws and the American Walker Tariff of 1846', *International Organisation*, 43 (1989), 1–30.

23.   Taussig, *Tariff History*, 5th edn, p. 157; Eckes, *America's Market*, p. 25.

24.   This is well revealed by *The American Diaries of Richard Cobden* [1859] ed. E. H. Cawley (Princeton, NJ, 1952).

25.   J. Bigelow, *William Cullen Bryant* (Boston, MA and New York, 1890), pp. 182–3.

26.   American Free Trade League, miscellaneous leaflets etc. Newberry Library, Chicago; Library of Congress; and New York Public Library: *The League* (1867–68); *The Free Trader* (1868–69).

27.   Cobden Club Minutes, March 1868, February 1870, February 1873, Cobden Papers, West Sussex Record Office; J. Bigelow, *Retrospection of an Active Life*, 3 vols, (New York, 1909), vol. 2, pp. 445ff; vol. 3, pp. 470, 473–4; W. V. Cox and M. H. Northrup, *Life of S. S. Cox* (Syracuse, NY, 1899), ch. 29. Cox was the author of *Free Labour and Free Trade: The Lessons of the English Corn Laws Applied to the United States* (New York, 1880). New York free traders also formed in 1867–68 the Round Table, see *The Round Table Dining Club, Roster of Members* (New York, 1926).

28.   For example, *Platform and Constitution of the Brooklyn Free Trade League* (New York, 1869), pp.1–2; Dorfman, *Economic Mind*, vol. 3, 9, pp. 55–6.

29.   H. R. Ferleger, *D.A. Wells and the American Revenue System, 1865–70* (New York, 1942); F. B. Joyner, *David Ames Wells, Champion of Free Trade* (Cedar Rapids, IA, 1939): T. E.Terrill, 'David A. Wells, the Democracy and Tariff Reduction, 1877–1894', *Journal of American History*, 56 (1969–70), 540–55.

30.   A. L. Perry to D. A. Wells, 31 December 1869, Wells Papers, reel 3A, Library of Congress.

31.   Topically, protection was presented as a new form of fiscal slavery, see manifesto, American Free Trade League, 21 April 1869, copy in R. R. Bowker Papers, New York Public Library (NYPL).

32. W. E. Brownlee, 'Economists and the Tax System in the USA', in M. O. Furner and B. Supple (eds), *The State and Economic Knowledge* (Cambridge, 1990), pp. 401–35.
33. For Ricardian arguments, Dorfman, *Economic Mind*, vol. 2 and Conkin, *Prophets of Prosperity*; see too, F. Lieber, *Notes on the Fallacies of American Protection*, 4th edn (New York, 1870).
34. Harold F. Williamson, *Edward Atkinson, the Biography of an American Liberal, 1827–1905* (Boston, 1934), p. 79; for the distribution of free traders in Congress, A. W. Nitsch, *Record of the Action of the Members of the House of Representatives on the Tariff Question during the 41st Congress* (New York, 1870).
35. Curtis to Wells, 31 August 1871, Wells Papers, NYPL.
36. Goldstein, *Ideas*, p. 79.
37. C. Phelps, *The Anglo-American Peace Movement in the Mid-Nineteenth Century* (New York, 1930); M. Ceadel, *The Origins of War Prevention: The British Peace Movement and International Relations, 1730–1854* (Oxford, 1996).
38. Burritt to Wells, 14 May 1869, D. A. Wells Papers, Library of Congress, Reel 1.
39. E. F. Baker, *Henry Wheaton, 1785–1848* (Philadelphia, 1937); Dorfman, *Economic Mind*, vol.3, p. 56 on Amasa Walker; C. L. Brace, *Free Trade as Promoting Peace and Goodwill* (New York, 1879).
40. F. Freidel, *Francis Lieber Nineteenth Century Liberal* (Baton Rouge, LA, 1947).
41. As a publicist, Beecher was said to be strong on generalities but weak on detail, Wells to Atkinson, 20 September 1884, Atkinson Papers, Massachusetts Historical Society, Boston. In 1886 he published *Why I am a Free Trader* (New York). Links between evangelicalism and American political economy would repay study. See also Goldstein, *Ideas*, pp. 86–7.
42. On Beecher's oratory, J. Bigelow, *A Substitute for the Tariff upon Imports* (New York 1908), p. 54; for Leavitt, *The Free Trader* (March 1868), p. 111. Lieber also believed religion would help the free trade cause, 'for it is nought but the realization of the angelic Good will towards man to the productive sphere and the material world of exchange'. To Wells, 1 April 1869, Wells Papers, reel 1, Library of Congress.
43. Dorfman, *Economic Mind*, vol. 2, p. 16; for the Beecher *cause célèbre*, see J.A. Garraty and M. C. Carnes, *American National Biography*, 24 vols (New York and Oxford, 1999), vol. 2, pp. 467–9.
44. Dorfman, *Economic Mind*, vol. 3, pp. 56–9; R. Brinkerhoff, *Recollections of a Lifetime* (Cincinnati, 1900), pp. 194–5.
45. J. G. Sproat, *'The Best Men' Liberal Reformers in the Gilded Age* (New York, 1968) esp. pp. 76–87.
46. Bowker to A. L. Earle, 11 October 1875 quoted E. McCurg Fleming, *R. R. Bowker, Militant Liberal* (Norman, 1952), p. 97.
47. See especially, T. E. Terrill, *The Tariff, Politics and American Foreign Policy, 1874–1901* (Westport, CT, 1973).
48. Taussig, *Tariff History*, 5th edn (1909), p. 191; Terrill, *Tariff*, pp. 25–30.
49. Dorfman, *Economic Mind*, vol. 3, *passim*; Goldstein, *Ideas*, pp. 85, 88–90.
50. Printed syllabus of lectures, 4–18 March 1884 (copy in University of Chicago Library). Adams intended his lectures to be 'aggressive, not

defensive'; he believed most students to be free traders but unwilling to desert the Republican Party for it. See Adams to D. A. Wells, 20 January, 27 February and 28 March 1884, Wells Papers, Box 1, NYPL.

51.　Sproat, 'The Best Men', p. 179; Joyner; Wells; Wells Papers, passim; Williamson, Atkinson, introduction by F. W. Taussig, p. xlii.; Atkinson's role after 1875 was, however, a much reduced one given his business commitments, and his changing views as to what free traders could achieve, ibid., p. 92.

52.　W. G. Sumner's Lectures on the History of Protection in the United States (New York, 1895) comprised lectures first given for the IFT Alliance; Williamson, Atkinson, pp.149–50.

53.　For the formation of the NYFTC in 1877, E. P. Wheeler, Sixty Years of American Life. Taylor to Roosevelt, 1850–1910 (New York, 1917), pp. 150–51; for the AFTL, Bowker Papers, passim, e.g. Bowker to H. J. Philpot (Iowa), 29 July 1883, to Earle, 23 July and 10 October 1883, Box 89; Bowker to Wells, 30 June 1883, Wells Papers, NYPL, Box 1. Williamson, Atkinson, pp. 135–42. Atkinson to the dismay of many free traders now sought to work for ('Peelite') revenue reform through the protectionist Democrats such as Randall. Wells to Bowker, 23 October 1885, Bowker Papers, Box 65; Atkinson to Nordhoff, 26 May, to Bowker, 16 October 1885, Atkinson Papers, Letterbooks ff. 264, 493.

54.　Atkinson to Wells, 12 August 1885, Wells Papers, reel 7; Earle to Bowker, 15 October 1884, Bowker Papers, Box 21.

55.　American Free Trader, 1 (7) (1883), Bowker to Wells, 30 June 1883, Wells Papers, NYPL.

56.　Terrill, Tariff, p.101; Williamson, Atkinson, p.138.

57.　Proceedings of National Conference of free traders and revenue reformers, Chicago, 1885, under the auspices of the AFTL, 11 & 12 Nov. (New York, 1885); the Cobdenite civil servant Sir Louis Mallet was much struck by the 'ability, vigour and earnestness' of the Chicago proceedings, Mallet to Wells, 4 October 1886, Wells Papers, reel 7, LC; Bowker, passim; Wheeler, Sixty Years, p. 165

58.　'I cannot resist feeling that progress is being made most rapidly in the free trade cause. We are getting discussion and that is a great thing. The democratic convention resolutions come pretty well up to the mark.' Wells to Bowker, 31 August [1886], Bowker MSS, Box 65; Terrill, Tariff, ch.5.

59.　Dorfman, Economic Mind, vol. 3, 131ff.; Terrill, Tariff, pp. 77–86, 168–71; a Manufacturers' Tariff Reform League was formed in New York in 1884.

60.　Free Trade: The Best Protection to American Industry (New York, 1884); T. G. Shearman, Free Trade: The Only Road to Manufacturing Prosperity and High Wages (New York, 1888).

61.　G. McAdam, The Protective System. What It Costs the American Farmer (New York, 1884); James Means, Oppressive Tariff Taxation (Boston, MA, 1885); J. S. Moore, The Champion Tariff Swindle of the World. Friendly Letters to American Farmers and Others (New York, 1888); J. B. Sargent, The Tariff, Manufacturers, and the People (New York, 1886).

62.　Terrill, Tariff, p. 59; W. G. Sumner, History of Protection; F. W. Taussig, The History of the Present Tariff, 1860–1883 (New York and London, 1885).

63. Dorfman, *Economic Mind*, vol. 3, pp. 142–9; for approval of George, see T. G. Shearman to R. R. Bowker, 28 September 1887, Bowker MSS, Box 59; his newspaper, *The Standard* proved one of the most effective free trade advocates, Wheeler, *Sixty Years*, p. 180; Earle to Bowker, 10 November 1887, Bowker MSS, Box 21, cf. Atkinson to Wells, 24 December 1885 in Bowker MSS, Box 65.

64. J. Reitano, *The Tariff Question in the Gilded Age: The Great Debate of 1888* (University Park, PA, 1994).

65. Goldstein, *Ideas*, p. 102, cf. Howe, *Free Trade*, p. 135.

66. E.g. Wells, *The 'Foreign Competitive Pauper Labor' Argument* (New York, 1883); T. G. Shearman, *The 'Pauper Labor' of Europe* (New York, 1886).

67. J. H. Patton, *Our Tariff: Why Levied and Why Continued and a Sketch of the Cobden Club* (New York, 1887); E. Crapol, *America for the Americans: Economic Nationalism and Anglophobia in the Late Nineteenth Century* (Westport, CT, 1973); for some good illustrations, Eckes, *America's Market*, pp. 39–40, 61. Even among free traders, 'American facts' were considered preferable to English tracts, C. E. Ferguson to G. McAdam, 13 March 1883, Bowker MM, Box 90. In 1906 *The Nation* (NY) recalled that 20 years ago, 'no presidential election passed without the dread that from the overflowing coffers of the Cobden Club "British gold" in enormous quantities would be provided to swamp our prosperity and republic together.' 83, 23 April, 156.

68. Atkinson to Moreton Frewen, 21 December 1885, quoted Williamson, *Atkinson*, p. 150.

69. Terrill, *Tariff*, ch. 8.

70. *Reform Club. Tariff Reform Committee. Annual Report, 1890*; Address of the National Association of Democratic Clubs, Feb. 1894 (typescript), W. E. Russell Papers, Box 20, Massachusetts Historical Society, Boston. Wilson was the club's president.

71. Wilson to Bryce, 4 July 1894, MS Bryce USA 21, f. 247, Bryce Papers, Bodleian Library, Oxford; F. S. Summers, *William L. Wilson and Tariff Reform: A Biography* (New Brunswick, 1953); Terrill, *Tariff*, ch. 8; Goldstein, *Ideas*, pp. 108–11.

72. C. E. Eliot to J. Bryce, 18 June 1897, MS Bryce USA 1, f. 33.

73. Reciprocity was first introduced in the McKinley tariff. See J. F. Kenkel, *Progressives and Protection: The Search for a Tariff Policy, 1866–1936* (Washington, DC, 1983); E. S. Kaplan and T. W. Ryley, *Prelude to Trade Wars: American Tariff Policy, 1890–1922* (Westport, CT, 1994); Terrill, *Tariff*, p. 168ff; P. Wolman, *Most-Favoured Nation: The Republican Revisionists and US Trade Policy, 1897–1912* (Chapel Hill, NC, 1992); Lake, *Power, Protection and Free Trade*; Goldstein, *Ideas*, p. 114, sees reciprocity as part of a 'great mercantilist tradition'.

74. *Beatrice Webb's American Diary, 1898*, ed. D. A. Shannon (Madison, WI, 1963), p. 38, 20 April 1898.

75. This had begun life as the Massachusetts Tariff Reform League in 1885; among other publications of the NETR(FT)L, see W. L. Garrison, *Republican Reciprocity* (Boston, MA, n.d. ?1896); A. B Farquhar, E. Atkinson and H. N. Shepard, *Arguments against the Dingley Bill* (Boston, MA, 1897); H. W. Lamb, *Whom does Protection Protect?* (Boston, MA, 1898);

C. Warren, *Do Protective Tariffs Give More Work to the Workingman?*
(Boston, MA, 1898).

76. *Inter alia*, W. L .Garrison, *Trusts and Tariffs* (Boston, MA, 1899); H. W.
     Lamb, *Tariff Trusts* (Boston, MA, 1899); B. W. Holt, *The Tariff the
     Mother of Trusts* (Boston, 1899).

77. In 1906 Bowker gave the funds of the defunct NYFTC to Garrison,
     Bowker to Garrison, 27 December 1906 (copy), Bowker MSS, Box. 2.

78. S. W. Mendum, 'Free Coal and Free Beef' (*The Free Trader*, bulletin no.
     3, 15 January 1903).

79. Garrison to Bryce, 23 July 1903, MS Bryce USA4, f. 336.

80. *Richard Cobden Centennial: Speech of C. F. Adams at the dinner of the
     Free Trade League*, Boston, 3 June 1904; L. R. Ehrich, *Protection and
     the Democratic Party* (Boston, 1903); Garrison to O. G. Villard, 13 July
     1904, Villard Papers, bMS Am 1906 (11), Houghton Library, Harvard
     University.

81. Goldstein, *Ideas*, pp. 116–18; R. C. Baker, *The Tariff under Roosevelt
     and Taft* (Hastings, NB, 1941). Ironically, Roosevelt had been an honor-
     ary member of the Cobden Club in the 1880s. In April 1906,
     Massachusetts Republicans in Congress acted as a focus for tariff revi-
     sion. *The Nation*, 5 April 1906, p. 275.

82. W. Diamond, *The Economic Thought of Woodrow Wilson* (Baltimore,
     MD, 1943); Dorfman, *Economic Mind*, vol. 3, 335–42.

83. I. Tarbell, *The Tariff in Our Times*, 1st edn (New York, 1906) 5th edn
     (New York, 1911); Woodrow Wilson, Address on the Tariff, 3 January
     1912 in *The Papers of Woodrow Wilson*, ed. A. S. Link (Princeton, NJ,
     1966–) vol. 23 (1977), 1911–12, pp. 637–50.

84. *The Free Trader*, 18 July 1912; see also ibid., 16 August 1909; F. W.
     Hirst to F. W. Taussig, 24 December 1912, Taussig Papers, Box 1, File
     Iron 2/2, Harvard University Archives.

85. Quoted in Lake, *Power, Protection, and Free Trade*, p. 155.

86. The British ambassador regarded it as 'only the first instalment of a
     broad and comprehensive scheme of legislation', Spring Rice to Sir
     Edward Grey, 6 November 1913 [no.364 Comm.] FO 368/884, PRO.

87. Brownlee, 'Tax System', p. 404. But reliance on tariffs for revenue
     greatly inhibited the pace of tariff reform, E. A. R. Seligman to Bowker,
     4 February 1910, Bowker MSS, Box 59.

88. Spring Rice to Sir Edward Grey, 19 May 1913, FO371/1958, PRO.

89. Diamond, *Economic Thought*, pp. 162–92; G.-H. Soutou, *L'or et le
     sang: les buts de guerre économique de la Premiere Guerre mondiale*
     (Paris, 1989), pp. 840–43.

90. 16 June 1915, MS Bryce USA 1, f. 136.

91. See especially W. R. Allen, 'The International Trade Philosophy of Cordell
     Hull, 1907–1933', *American Economic Review*, 43 (1953), 101–16;
     C. Savage to Hull, 2 June 1943, with copy of speech, 8 July 1916,
     Cordell Hull papers, F156, Library of Congress.

92. Wilson to Taussig, 12 May 1919, Taussig Papers. Taussig counselled
     against stirring up needless controversy on this issue.

93. J. A. Conybeare, *Trade Wars: The Theory and Practice of International
     Commercial Rivalry* (New York, 1987), ch. 10.

94. For a revisionist account, Eckes, *America's Market*, ch. 4.

95. C. P. Parrini, *Heir to Empire: United States Economic Diplomacy, 1916–*

1923 (Pittsburgh, PA, 1969), pp. 6, 234–5; Eliot to Bryce, 2 November 1920, MS Bryce USA 1, f. 265.

96. Joan H. Wilson, *American Business and Foreign Policy, 1920–1933* (Lexington, KY, 1971); Sir A Geddes to Lord Curzon, 30 December 1921, FO371/7262; C. Hamlin (Federal Reserve Board) to F. W. Taussig, 9 January 1933, Taussig Papers, Box 6.

97. G. H. Thompson at the FO noted 'US motor manufacturers ... have been bitter opponents of the new Hawley-Smoot tariff bill', 3 July 1930, FO371/14280, f. 117; Oswald Villard likewise reported to F. W. Hirst the work of General Motors in promoting lower tariffs, 31 October 1935, Villard Papers, bMS Am 1323, Houghton Library, Harvard University. See also C. P. Kindelberger, *The World In Depression, 1929–39* (London, 1973), p. 234.

98. Cf. those 'peace progressives' who treated tariffs simply as a domestic issue, R. D. Johnson, *The Peace Progressives and American Foreign Relations* (Cambridge, MA, 1995), pp. 192–3.

99. N. M. Butler, *Across the Busy Years*, 2 vols (New York and London, 1939–40), vol. 1, p. 376.

100. E.g. *Recommendations of the Committee on Commercial Policy* (New York and Boston, MA, March 1934, FPA and WPA).

101. C. M. Bell, *Tariff Walls* (London, 1930), pp. 164–5.

102. Eckes, *America's Market*, pp. 132–4; Signatories included Taussig, Clair Wilcox, author of *A Charter for World Trade* (New York, 1949) and Paul Douglas, see *America in the Marketplace* (New York, 1966), p. 86; see also H. R. Mussey, 'Free Trade and the United States', *The Nation*, 9 September 1931, pp. 250–52.

103. W. J. Barber, *Designs within Disorder. Franklin D. Roosevelt, the Economists, and the Shaping of American Economic Policy, 1933–1945* (Cambridge, 1996), pp. 154–5.

104. J. M. Jones, *Tariff Retaliation* (Philadelphia, 1934); E. E. Schattschneider, *Politics, Pressures and the Tariff* (New York, 1935), cf. Eckes, *America's Market*, pp. 34–5, 116, 125, 128.

105. I. M. Drummond, *Imperial Economic Policy, 1917–1939* (1974); P. Clavin, 'The World Economic Conference, 1933: the Failure of British Internationalism', *Journal of European Economic History*, 20 (London, 1991), 489–527.

106. E.g. W. F. Ecroyd, *The Policy of Self-Help* (London, 1879); 'It is, Eliot wrote to Bryce, rather amusing to see Chamberlain trotting out in England all the arguments which have so long done duty for Protection in the U.S.', 16 March 1904, MS Bryce USA 1, f. 55.

107. G. H. Thompson, memo 27 November 1930, FO371/14280, f. 226.

108. C. Hull, *The Memoirs of Cordell Hull*, 2 vols (New York, 1948); M. A. Butler, *The Cautious Visionary: Cordell Hull and Trade Reform, 1931–37* (Kent, OH, 1998).

109. Hull, *Memoirs, passim.*

110. Hull, 'Call off the Tariff War!' *The Nation*, 16 December 1931, pp. 667–9.

111. D. Irwin, 'From Smoot-Hawley to Reciprocal Trade Agreements', in M. Bordo, C. Goldin, and E. White (eds), *The Defining Moment: The Great Depression and the American Economy in the Twentieth Century* (Chicago, 1998).

112. See especially, A. W. Schatz, 'Cordell Hull's Search for Peace, 1936–38', *Journal of American History*, 57 (1970), 85–103.

113. Draft, 17 June 1936, Hull Papers, F385.

114. See especially Sayre's correspondence with E. W. Smith of General Motors, January–April 1936, Sayre Papers, Box 1, Library of Congress; Sayre to Hull, 10 April 1940, Sayre Papers, Box 2, Library of Congress; draft speeches, 1934–39, Boxes 15 and 16, *passim*; F. B. Sayre, *America Must Act* (Boston, MA and New York, 1936); Villard Papers, Harvard, *passim*.

115. Lindsay to Eden, 5 February 1936 [copy], BT11/591, PRO.

116. B. M. Rowland, *Commercial Conflict and Foreign Policy: A Study in Anglo-American Relations, 1932–38* (New York, 1987).

117. C. Kreider, *The Anglo-American Trade Agreement* (Princeton, NJ, 1943); I. M. Drummond and N. Hilmer; *Negotiating Freer Trade: The United Kingdom, the United States, Canada and the Trade Agreements of 1938* (Waterloo, Ont., 1989). *The Economist* hailed the agreement as 'the largest operation in trade liberalisation that has ever been undertaken' (31 December 1938).

118. See *inter alia*, Pressnell, *External Economic Policy*; A. P. Dobson, *The Politics of the Anglo-American Economic Special Relationship, 1940–1987* (Brighton, 1988); R. B. Woods, *A Changing of the Guard: Anglo-American Relations, 1941–46* (Chapel Hill, NC, and London, 1990); R. N. Gardner, *Sterling-Dollar Diplomacy in Current Perspective* (1956; new edn New York, 1980); Burk, in this volume, ch. 13.

119. Hull's adviser Pasvolsky feared that preference 'will contribute powerfully to a stagnation of world commerce in general', Pasvolsky to Hull [memo on the possible conflict between British and American views of post-war economic policy], 12 December 1941, Hull Papers, F366. See Pressnell, *External Economic Policy, passim*.

120. *Free Trader*, May–June 1946, p. 173; Pressnell, *External Economic Policy*, pp. 5–7ff.

121. D. C. Watt, *Succeeding John Bull* (Cambridge, 1984); W. Kimball, 'Lend-Lease and the Open Door', *Political Science Quarterly*, 86 (1971), 232–59.

122. Gardner, *Sterling-Dollar Diplomacy*, p. 269ff.

123. Sumner Welles, *Where Are We Heading?* (New York and London, 1947), p. 14.

124. P. Clavin, 'The Lessons of the Past', in A. J. Marrison (ed.), *Free Trade and its Reception, 1815–1960* (London, 1998), pp. 287–307.

125. Memorandum, FO 3 August 1945, R. Bullen and M. Pelly (eds), *Documents on British Policy Overseas*, series 1, vol. 3 (1986), p. 3.

126. S. Howson (ed.), *The Collected Papers of James Meade*, vol. 3 (London, 1988); cf. J. Odell and B. Eichengreen, 'The United States, the ITO, and the WTO', in A. Krueger (ed.), *The WTO as an International Organisation* (Chicago, 1998), pp. 181–209.

127. E. Penrose, *Economic Planning for the Peace* (Princeton, NJ, 1953), pp. 89–90, 349; cf. W. Diebold who attributed the failure of ITO to its 'antediluvian tendencies' in his *The End of the ITO* (Princeton, NJ, 1952), p. 35.

128. For one British attempt to gauge American opinion, J. A. Stirling, 'The Probable Attitude of the USA towards a Liberal Trade Policy', 2 December 1942, T160/1378/18003/021/1, PRO.

129. See especially Aaronson, *Trade and the American Dream*.
130. K. W. Stiles, 'The Ambivalent Hegemon: Explaining the Lost Decade in Multilateral Talks', *Review of International Political Economy*, 2 (1995), pp. 1–26.
131. W. Roepke, *Briefe, 1934–1966: der innere Kompass*, ed. E. Roepke (Zurich, 1976), p. 91.
132. F. Trentmann, 'The Erosion of Free Trade: Political Culture and Political Economy in Great Britain c.1897–1932', (Harvard PhD thesis, 1998); J. Kent, *British Imperial Strategy and the Origins of the Cold War, 1944–49* (Leicester, 1993).
133. See especially, Gardner, *Sterling-Dollar Diplomacy, passim*.
134. As the Cold War tempered American anti-imperialism, so too her economic aid to Britain helped sustain the British empire. See W. R. Louis and R. Robinson, 'The Imperialism of Decolonization', *Journal of Imperial and Commonwealth History*, 22 (1995), 462–511.

CHAPTER NINE

Irish Nationalism and Anglo-American Relations in the Later Nineteenth and Early Twentieth Centuries[1]

Alan O'Day

> All the emigrants who are now leaving the country carry with them the most determined hatred of British power. Those whom they leave behind sympathise in their feelings, and whenever the opportunity occurs, the Irish abroad and a large portion of the Irish at home will be ready to aid any attempt that can strike a blow at that power.[2]

> We cannot afford, either as a matter of decency or as a matter of interest, to allow professional or hereditary Anglophobists to endanger the understanding between England and America which is the best guarantee now 'in sight' for the peace and progress of the world.[3]

Undoubtedly the profound feature of the twentieth century is the close affinity of language, culture, political traditions and military co-operation of the two principal Atlantic democracies. This fusion enabled the 'Anglo-Saxon' nations to triumph in the world wars while the British capitalist economic system refined under American tutelage saw off its Marxist rival in Eastern Europe during the 1990s. These and other victories allow an Anglo-American alliance to enter the next millennium with an optimism that borders on a triumphalism perhaps not seen since the headiest days of Roman civilization. But, this union of the heart as well as of the mind seemed anything but inevitable in the decades preceding the First World War. Moreover, Isaac Butt's observation in 1866 that ex-patriot Irish Catholics were driven by intense Anglophobia, devoted to the emancipation of their homeland from British rule and prepared to use their money, enthusiasm and votes in America to resist any *rapprochement* between Great Britain and the United States still retains a residual significance.

Michael Davitt's characterization of Irish-America as 'the avenging wolfhound of Irish nationalism' has modern scholarly endorsement.[4] F. S. L. Lyons identified the famine of the 1840s as a watershed for 'the long-standing and deep-rooted hatred of the English connection was given not only a new intensity, but also a new dimension ... this hatred, this bitterness, this resentment were carried overseas, and especially to America'.[5] 'The political consequences, 'of this unending exodus of a permanently antagonised population were literally incalculable' he insists. That outcome, in his estimation, was to make the Irish situation an international concern, to influence Anglo-American relations and to provide the finance essential to the operations of subsequent national organizations. In a recent assessment of the American element in the contemporary conflict in Northern Ireland Andrew Wilson stated,

> large-scale emigration created an Irish diaspora which became an integral part of the historical development of their native land. Nurturing an intense anglophobia, they vowed revenge for the suffering they had endured. Nationalists in Ireland soon realised the potential of the vast immigrant population in America and began to tap its power and wealth to sustain the drive against British rule.[6]

The Irish, of course, were not the sole ethnic interest complicating Anglo-American understanding. Woodrow Wilson's often quoted remark in May 1914, 'some Americans need hyphens in their names, because only part of them has come over',[7] is an apt reminder of the complexity of the social and political fabric of the United States resulting from recurrent streams of European immigration.

Proportionate to size and population Ireland contributed more people to the United States than any other country and the Irish were the most prominent group with a political agenda until 1914, therefore making a apt case study in the impact of ethnic politics on the policy of the United States. Moreover, this allows for an additional glimpse of the extent and form the ethnic or national identity of the Irish has taken. These matters are viewed within perspectives formulated by Milton Esman, Don Handleman and Herbert J. Gans, reflecting the 'new' or 'situational' sociological school rather than the older polarities of 'assimilationist' and 'pluralist' accounts of American immigrant behaviour. Esman observed that the ability of diasporas to influence the course of events is conditioned by their access to resources, the opportunities offered by the host society and degree of internal solidarity in the ethnic cohort.[8] As will be argued, the Irish fit this paradigm. Handleman has identified four states of immigrant identity.[9] These he terms, an ethnic category (a loose level of incorporation, where there is a perceived cultural difference between the group and outsiders), an ethnic network (where there is regular interaction between the group members, allowing the network to distribute resources among its members), ethnic association (where members develop political organizations to express common goals) and an ethnic community (which possesses a permanent, physical or more appropriately in this case a mentally bounded territory, over and above its political organizations). Gans pioneered the concept of 'symbolic ethnicity', a new form of ethnic behaviour where people can find their identity by 'affiliation' with an abstract collectivity which does not exist as an interacting group.[10] It consists of a love for and a pride in a tradition that can be felt without having to be incorporated in everyday life. He distinguishes between expressive and instrumental functions of identity, pointing out that the first increasingly became the larger dimension with ethnicity emerging as more of a 'leisure-time activity and losing its relevance, say to earning a living or regulating family life'.[11] No doubt the vast majority of Irish people were able to slip into one more or more of Handleman's categories, shifting between them over time in many instances and doing so in ways outlined by Gans.

It then is not simply a question of being Irish or distancing oneself from an Irish identity but of picking and choosing when one wished to exhibit an Irish identity and the substance of this identity. This framework resolves a recent sterile commentary on the historiography of the diaspora and its reliance on what the author sees as an antiquated concept of 'community' though she is wedded to an outdated 'pluralism'.[12] The Irish could be a 'community' in varying senses; Gans's notion of an ethnic 'aggregate' rather than a 'group' meets the problematic question of what constitutes a 'community' while his emphasis on the context in which ethnicity finds expression adeptly bridges the gap between the assimilation and pluralist schools. The crucial question is whether ethnic identity, no matter how delineated, translated into anything tangible and, for the purposes of the current discussion, the limits such an elusive identity placed on diaspora influence over Anglo-American relations.

Irish political problems were, and to a limited degree remain, a source of discord in Anglo-American affairs. At the beginning of October 1910 John Redmond promised,

> One object for which we shall work after home rule comes is a closer Anglo-American understanding. There is no doubt that a formal agreement between Great Britain and America cannot be secured until the Irish question is settled, for the anti-British feeling among the Irish-Americans is too strong to permit it.
>   But this feeling will change when local self-government is given to Ireland, and we shall do our best to strengthen the Empire by bringing Britain and America closer together.[13]

In April 1917 Robert Lansing, the American Secretary of State, seem to confirm this, observing privately for David Lloyd George's benefit, 'the only circumstance which seems now to stand in the way of absolutely cordial co-operation with Great Britain by practically all Americans who are not influenced by ties of blood directly associating them with Germany is the failure so far to find a satisfactory method of self-government for Ireland'.[14] The American role in the talks over Northern Ireland is a latter-day manifestation of an Irish thorn potentially ready to lacerate the cordial relationship between Britain and the United States.[15] Ireland as a problem afflicting Anglo-American relations reached an apogee between 1916 and 1921 only reappearing on stage occasionally thereafter. Following the outbreak of the Second World War, Winston Churchill considered retaking by force, if necessary, the Treaty Ports in the Éire but was cautioned against such a course by the government of the United States.[16] However, following American entry into the conflagration, its government, was vastly less tender hearted about the neutrality of Éire than was His Majesty's – an ironic twist on earlier Irish and Irish-American presumptions.[17] The present chapter assesses the place of the Irish dimension in the age of growing Anglo-American understanding.

Most commentators have adopted an 'assimilationist' perspective, attributing the waning of Irish-American nationalism to the effects of assimilation and/or the resolution of Ireland's political status in 1921–22. Lawrence J. McCaffrey succinctly outlines this frequently repeated hypothesis:

> The disintegration of the Irish cultural empire is the result of (1) the decline in Irish emigration to the United States, (2) the economic and social mobility of Irish-Americans, (3) the fallout from the Civil War in Ireland, (4) a change in the character of Irish nationalism, and (5) a fading Irish identity in the United States.[18]

Kerby Miller reaffirmed this observation,

> in retrospect, Irish-American nationalists ... were very fortunate that in the end, in 1916–21 they finally succeeded in helping to free most of Ireland politically, through Irish-American financial support. For essentially they were fighting what had appeared a losing battle against time, dwindling numbers of new emigrants, and powerful forces working for ideological as well as behavioural assimilation in America.[19]

Modern specialist works also advance this viewpoint. F. M. Carroll, for instance, suggested that the creation of the Irish Free State allowed Britain to 'confidently expect a genuine rapprochement between herself and the one English-speaking country outside the Empire, the United States'.[20]

Much of the existing literature treats the Irish as a socially distraught group torn from their moorings in the Old World and suffering psychological dislocation. This emphasizes the internal psyche of the Irish with a concomitant tendency to stress the ethnic cohesion of the group in the period before assimilation takes root. Surprisingly, the political culture of the diaspora has received less systematic attention within this perspective and comments about it habitually begin with an expectation that the Irish were politicized, Anglophobic and uncritically supported the self-government aspirations of their countrymen. Two of the more interesting analyses of diaspora politics are Matthew Jacobson, *Special Sorrows*, and T. N. Brown, *Irish-American Nationalism, 1870–90*, the last having exercised a significant spell over subsequent writings. The first argued that the manifestation of nationalism in the United States was paramount to the diasporic understanding of itself as well as being at least as important as its flowering in Ireland. According to Jacobson, 'collective emigration nourished a political culture based on the ideas of injury and displacement ... allegiance to the old centres of experience translated into an emergent, New World zeal for Old World nationalisms...'.[21] He underlined this connection, stating

> The political culture ... contained an element of compelling obliga-
> tion: by nationalist lights, the emigrants not only ought to dwell
> upon the nature of the calamity, by which they now found them-
> selves in a state of exile, pilgrimage, or wandering in North America,
> but they should recognise as well the unique vantage point from
> which they might now serve the nation they had left behind.[22]

Moreover, migration across the sea exacerbated national identity in two ways. First, as Patrick Ford observed, it brought together disparate peoples, releasing them from 'the littleness of countryism into the broad feeling of nationalism', anticipating what is often termed 're-tribalisation'.[23] According to Jacobson this allowed 'for the reinterpretation of Old World experiences in national terms rather than in simply local ones'.[24] Second, T. N. Brown championed the view that Irish-American nationalism was more virulent than its parent in Ireland, arising from the internal needs of the diaspora. 'It sprang also from the experience of life in the United States', he contended.[25] Leadership, Brown noted, came from a second generation who 'were fiercely active in the cause. They wanted to be respected as Americans and this ... gave immigrant nationalism its dynamic thrust'.[26] And, in his estimation, 'American plutocracy became a new Irish passion. No longer did England seem unique in cruelty. Nevertheless John Bull remained the most compelling symbol of Irish frustration'.[27] All this receives an apt summary from Jacobson who observed 'Irish nationalism took root and flourished in a variety of forms both in the tightly packed ghettos of the major urban centres of Boston and New York, and in smaller, more remote communities like Butte, Denver and Sacramento'.[28] Among the various groups in America, 'Irish nationalism was perhaps the quickest to take hold and the most prolific in its organisation expression'.[29] These and other explanations are consistent with the comments by Lyons cited above, but they do not offer a satisfactory explanation for the varying levels of ethnic identification by even the same individuals or shed light on the ineffective performance of the Irish-America pressure groups on Anglo-American relations.

The hypothesis advanced by McCaffrey, Brown and others is superficially attractive – it fits the chronology and is consistent with the decline in immigration – but it is unconvincing on three grounds. First, the Irish exercised little genuine political influence at any phase, including moments of a more favourable demographic situation. Second, the Irish Catholic ethnic community, including the descendants of immigrants in the United States, actually was becoming larger, more cohesive and self-conscious just at the point when the effects of falling immigration/incorporation were supposedly undermining it.[30] Third, if as most observers indicate, the Anglo-Irish settlement in 1921 effectively truncated mass Irish-American interest in the homeland, this result cannot but seem inconsistent with the image of an Anglophobia and a militant nationalism which was stronger in the New World than in the Old. It would be more reasonable to anticipate increased resentment and renewed political militancy in the wake of the partition of the island, especially as Irish-American Catholicism gathered force in the face of attacks like those mounted by the American Protective Association, the Immigration Restriction League and the Anti-Saloon League. Here would appear to be a confirming illustration of what J. Milton Yinger described as the complementary process of assimilation and dissimilation taking place simultaneously.[31] Moreover, Brown's and Jacobson's stress upon the uniqueness of the situation of Irish-Americans neglects the fortunes of the diaspora in Great Britain and elsewhere which appears remarkably similar both in terms of timing and political performance.

America's Irish as a prop to the movement at home proved to be a damp squib. In the eyes of the leadership in Ireland their compatriots in America had three broad functions; to garner the finance necessary for the national struggle at home; to muster moral support behind Ireland's claims; and to exert pressure on the policy-makers in the United States to use their resources in ways designed to injure British interests if she did not accede to Irish self-government. In the first and second instances the programme achieved limited results but in the third it had little to show for the effort prior to 1914 and not much more thereafter. If history is often a story about success, this is one of failure, a failure that at first glance must seem very curious in view of the alleged nationalist commitment and political acumen of the Irish in America.

Irish-American political failure has a threefold explanation: an illusion built on a demographic and coherent community that never existed; the ambivalence of the leadership of both the Irish national movement at home and in America about the functions of the diaspora and Irish-American support for an Anglo-American *rapprochement* at the turn of the century. In short, it is suggested, a very considerable section of Irish-America did not differ markedly from Anglo-Saxon Americans. This is not to say that the outlook of Irish-Americans was identical to unhyphenated Americans for concern about Ireland was sometimes triggered for specific purposes. This outcome fits what is called 'voluntary' ethnic identification.[32] At the same time a clear distinction must be made between political and other kinds of transatlantic Irish-American communal association.

It is certainly difficult to assess the size and character of the 'ethnic Irish' community in America and its influence on Anglo-American relations is even more puzzling. Definitions of the concept 'diaspora' frame subsequent writings but because what constitutes the notion has been elastic; discussions of how the Irish responded as individuals or as an aggregate are often at cross-purposes not least because the distinction between the individual and the group are frequently blurred.[33] Most observers tend to resort to a demographic catalogue in order to establish the extent of the group for which Gans's term 'aggregation' may be more appropriate.[34] Ward and Carroll, as noted above, posit the figure of 20 million Irish-Americans in 1920, an obvious overestimate, with the second, observing that they may have represented nearly 19 per cent of the entire population and 'were a very remarkable and powerful element of American society'.[35] A substantial Irish population settled in America prior to the Great Famine. Three million more arrived between 1845 and 1891. In 1861 approximately 1 611 000 Irish-born lived in the United States representing 5.12 per cent of the total population; by the turn of the century census enumerators counted 1 615 419 Irish-born in the United States or 2.13 per cent total. In 1910 this reached 4 504 360 Irish-born or with one parent born in Ireland. While the 'Irish' clearly were a substantial element, it is essential to keep them in perspective.

Modern scholarship emphasizes the religious, spatial and class segmentation of the diaspora. Few Protestants, the majority of American Irish, were attracted to political nationalism and thus the cohort can be confined more realistically to Irish Catholics who numbered something like 3.5 million in 1890 and approximately 8 million in 1920, less than half of Carroll's figure. In spite of Brown's contention that the second generation Irish were fiercely nationalistic, the ethnic cohort born in the United States was less disposed to take an active interest in Ireland just as the longer the period of residence the more apt the migrants were to reduce or cease their remittances to the old country. Most the leaders of national organizations were immigrants; American-born Irish were more likely to take up prominent positions in urban Irish-American political machines which usually expressed support for national aspirations but gave very little practical aid to the advancement of these goals. The ratio of American-born to Irish-born in 1900 was about three to one. Generational differentiation is vital in another respect; though the Irish outdistanced other immigrants in acquisition of American citizenship and in electoral participation, a significant number ranging from a quarter to a third of the foreign-born influx did not gain naturalization and therefore could not affect the electoral process.[36] The whole question of the citizenship of a number of Irish-born men arrested by the British authorities reared its head on several occasions. Additionally, women were excluded from the franchise and an unusually high percentage of Irish-born migrants were female. Moreover, the Irish were dispersed geographically, often separated by very huge distances indeed. The President of the United Irish League of America in 1905 doubted the value of conducting a widespread recruiting drive because 'distances in the west are so great between places worth visiting, and the railroad rates so high that it would hardly pay to employ an organiser west of Chicago or Indiana. The Irish in this state, outside of Chicago, have little national spirit and are mostly devoted to sectarian societies'.[37] In 1910 there was resistance to holding the biannual convention of the League in Chicago again because in the view of the Secretary, 'I don't think we could get 20 from New England to go'.[38] Even within cities with considerable Irish populations like New York, Philadelphia and Chicago diffusion was typical thereby further weakening ethnic cohesiveness. Dennis Clark argues that the political impact of the Irish in Philadelphia was moderated by differences of class and internal migration within the city.[39] While it is no doubt true that a coherent sense of identity can exist independent of physical proximity, in the absence of positive or negative factors enforcing this commonality, distance is likely to prove a barrier to the three elements J. Milton Yinger cited as essential for the existence of 'full ethnicity'. These he maintained are self-identification, identification by others and shared activities.[40] In sum the size of the ethnic group, variable over time and space, is not coterminous with the numbers of Irish enumerated in census returns or even of Irish-Catholics.

Exact estimation is impossible but surely for present purposes the effective potentially politicized group ordinarily did not exceed more than 2 million (including women), a figure that contracted (or sometimes expanded) and, as has been observed, active participants numbered many fewer. Nevertheless, the Irish were a considerable factor; where they were situated geographically and socially, their political organization and motivation were as important as aggregate size. But by 1910 the Irish were not the largest diasporic group – Germans, with the inclusion of those originating in Austria-Hungary were almost twice as numerous and people from Russia-Finland and Italy, though arriving later, were a substantial component of the American population and increasing more rapidly than the Irish. Third in rank order behind Germans and Irish peoples were persons born in the rest of the United Kingdom. This British element was in reality much the largest segment in America as a consequence of nearly 200 years of continuous immigration. Irish demands, thus, had to be measured against the concerns of competing interests.

The Irish are usually seen as heavily involved in American politics, particularly in the urban Democratic Party machines, and committed to the cause of their homeland. This picture at least is supported by contemporaries. In 1916 the British Ambassador to Washington, Sir Cecil Spring-Rice, observed that the Irish are 'the best politicians in the country'.[41] The limits of Irish effectiveness have been cited for Philadelphia; a study of Chicago emphasizes the group's tendency to interpret political power as a device to advance the ethnic interest by securing employment for members rather than for ideological purposes, a point reinforced across a broader spectrum by Steven P. Erie's, *Rainbow's End*.[42] Erie argued that nationalism and working-class radicalism became linked in the early 1880s, thereby presenting a challenge to Irish urban political machines.[43] Therefore, according to him, they were cautious about giving free rein to nationalism and the dominant theme of post-1900 machines was to damp down working-class discontent. From another angle Gans underlined this symbiosis. He pointed out that urban political life, especially among the working classes, was structured by and through ethnicity; ethnic political activity took place around working-class issues rather than ethnic ones.[44] By 1914 Irish dominance of urban machines in many cities had begun to crumble as it would do further during the inter-war years. Furthermore, the implication of Erie's research is that until the 1890s political patronage was too meagre to act as a lever for group cohesion while thereafter the rewards though certainly more munificent aided individual not group advancement. The Irish did as well outside the big cities where they were politically strong.[45] Incentives, then, for long-term group solidarity were relatively weak though, of course, individuals and a section of the Irish had every reason to foster a common identity. In this wider political context it is, therefore, difficult to accept the frequently stated contention that Irish-Americans seemed unanimous in their support of some kind of self-government for Ireland, although they often disagreed vigorously over the form such self-government should take – home rule within the empire or independence – and the method through which it should be achieved – constitutional reform or revolutionary action. He maintains that the majority of Irish-Americans took their political opinions on Irish affairs from the columns of the nationalist newspapers, notably *The Gaelic American* and *The Irish World*. Nearly every city in the north and middle-west had an Irish-Catholic newspaper; perhaps 500 000 families subscribed to these at the close of the nineteenth century. *The Irish World* then had a circulation of 125 000, *The Boston Pilot* some 75 000 and other journals reached figures of between 20 000 and 50 000. Substantial though this circulation is, Irish-Catholic newspapers only reached a minority of the ethnic cohort. Contrary to what is so often alleged, the politicized Irish were much narrower than the apparent potential size of the ethnic cohort.

How important was Irish-American financial support for Irish nationalism? Gans offered a point of departure for the discussion when he opined: 'Old countries are particularly useful as identity symbols because they are far away and cannot make arduous demands on American ethnics; even sending large amounts of money is ultimately an easy way to help unless the donors are making major economic sacrifices'.[46] Daniel O'Connell established the American Repeal Association but after a brief flourish it dissolved in acrimony. The Irish Republican Brotherhood (Fenians) formed in 1858 was initially an American creation. By 1866 it had collected some half a million dollars to purchase arms for an insurrection in Ireland but little of this bounty ever reached the homeland. In the same year Fenians instigated a raid into Canada in expectation that their seizure of territory north of the border would be endorsed by the government of the United States. The American authorities, however, simply closed the frontier to Fenian reinforcements with the result that the insurgents were quickly mopped up and during the 1870s President Grant closed down any prospect of support for its operations. Over the next two decades Irish-Americans provided funding for various political movements in Ireland, particularly Charles Stewart Parnell's parliamentary party. The situation did not brighten up in the period between 1900 and 1914, though, considerable sums of money were forwarded for the operations of the Irish Party. The actual total collected for the whole era for political purposes defies accurate calculation. In reality, only limited amounts of money flowed into any branch of the national movement and that stream of cash was erratic. It has been asserted that the Fenians received $500 000 between 1858 and 1866; the 'skirmishing fund' of the Clan na Gael raised $50 000 by 1877, some $635 873 was collected for the Irish National League from

April 1883 to January 1890. The chief agency for soliciting money in the United States was the Irish National League of America (founded in April 1883) which was dismissed by Brown as nothing more than 'a propaganda and money-collecting agency' and as an 'irrelevance'.[47] The effectiveness of the organization was hampered throughout the 1880s by the bitter feud between the dominant Chicago wing controlled by Alexander Sullivan and John Devoy, which ended in public scandal in 1889. As well, Sullivan sponsored the dynamite campaign in Great Britain between 1883 and 1885, causing Parnell substantial embarrassment. The split in national ranks occasioned by the Parnell divorce scandal in 1890 led to an immediate collapse of the American organ. The anti-Parnellite, Irish National Federation of America formed in May 1891 had 150 branches in 1893 but virtually disappeared thereafter.[48] Its operating funds were of a modest order, falling to $5500 in 1894 and merely $2000 the following year.[49] A hypothetical $50 000 could have been raised in the early 1890s, but this sum was probably a considerable exaggeration.[50] In reality Irish political movements received little Irish-American money in the 1890s.

It is uncertain what sums were sent to the Irish party between 1901 and 1914. There can be no doubt that Irish leaders treated American contributions seriously. Reunification of the movement in 1900 was motivated, in part, by hopes of securing renewal of American cash. In nearly every year one or more prominent figures toured the United States soliciting money. John Redmond himself visited America in 1883, 1886, 1895, 1899, 1901, 1902, 1904, 1908 and 1910. T. P. O'Connor, John Dillon and Joseph Devlin were also regular transatlantic travellers. O'Connor's trip in 1909, for instance, had sometimes discouraging results.[51] Ward provides a partial catalogue of the sums raised. According to his figures $61 665 ($100 000 by Carroll's calculations) from Redmond's tour was contributed between October 1902 and August 1904; the convention in Philadelphia in 1906 pledged at least $60 000, T. P. O'Connor's mission in 1909 yielded more than $60 000 and there was the substantial sum resulting from Redmond's trip in 1910 which amounted to $100 000. This is not a complete list but and it should be treated with reserve, especially as the O'Connor mission is known to have fallen below expectations. Carroll points out that the scandal over funds contributed in 1902 left the chief money-raising body, the United Irish League of America, wounded until 1910.[52]

Party accounts and the correspondence in the Redmond papers paint a considerably less rosy picture. Efforts to open Irish-American pocketbooks for the general election of 1900 fell flat. Alfred Webb, the Treasurer of the United Irish League, disclosed to Redmond that a total of £8715 2s. 3d. came into the election fund but merely £608 1s. 1d. was from the United States and Canada (just over £1525 was raised in Great Britain and more than £6109 in Ireland while Australian contributions were more than half that of the North Americans).[53]

Attempts to solicit money were confronted by numerous difficulties. Redmond's chief confidant in the United States, John O'Callaghan, reminded him in May 1901, 'no member of the party has been west of the Rocky mountains since you were there yourself in 1883 or 1884' and endorsed the Irish leader's observation that 'there is a great unattached body of Irish opinion in America'.[54] A prominent New York Irishmen in January 1902 observed, 'it has been like pulling teeth to get any of the wealthy Irishmen to take any interest or to do anything'.[55] Another correspondent in the same month admitted, 'it is only fair to confess that the movement seems to provoke no popular support'.[56] Redmond expressed disappointed at the state of fund raising and then in March was of opinion that the movement in America was 'not progressing'.[57] In April O'Callaghan who had become Secretary of the United Irish League, reported that he would have liked to send an organizer to Montreal but dare not because the 'anti-Boer war stance [is] unacceptable there'.[58] Webb in May 1903 complained, 'so far we have received nothing of importance from America for the Parliamentary Fund this year'.[59] In August O'Callaghan's estimate of the state of the movement outside its traditional bastions was confirmed by the President of the League. In addition he noted,

> there is also the great state of Texas, which has a large Irish population, lying utterly fallow. Nothing has been done to work it up since Parnell's time. There is, however, an advantage in this, which also applies to the Pacific states that the people have not been drained out of contributions, but when they give, they will give liberally.[60]

Matters did not improve much before 1910. In August 1905 O'Callaghan inveighed, 'Boston and Philadelphia will have to do the most towards completing the balance [of fund-raising] ... New York and Chicago seem to be beyond redemption and the hides of men there seem to be so thick that it is impossible to penetrate them by criticism'.[61] Contributions towards the expenses incurred in the general election of 1906 were unimpressive.

The United Irish League of America functioned mainly in Boston where O'Callaghan lived but even there it had few members. In August 1907 one observer noted, 'I met John O'Callaghan, *entre nous* and the whole of the U.I.L. of Boston. Their organisation fitted easily into the corner of a small tap-room. But what a figure they cut on paper!'[62] Later the American Association for the Recognition of the Irish Republic received more than $10 million for the relief fund and bond certificates, though of this impressive total only a fraction reached Ireland. A size-able portion of this money was contributed out of humanitarian rather than political instincts. The size of the collections in 1910 and again the much more substantial sum raised during the Anglo-Irish War should be seen as exceptional. Over the long-haul, Irish-Americans were relatively stingy when plied to finance political causes.

Although the impress of Irish-America in the political sphere is decid-edly indifferent, this is not to say that it turned its back on the old country. A comparison of political contributions with the resourcing of other aspects of Irish life is illuminating. In three areas, especially, Irish-American financial support was huge – remittances to family members left behind, contributions to alleviate rural distress and funds sent home for religious purposes. These contributions, though, presuppose famil-ial, religious and local loyalty rather than a national or ethnic commitment. Arnold Schrier draws attention to the imbalance between these flows of funds and sums raised for political usage.[63] The practice of sending money home did not become widespread until the migra-tions of the 1840s. In 1849 Earl Grey, Secretary for War and the Colonies, asked the Emigration Commissioners to establish the extent of funds transmitted by all migrants to North America during the preceding year; 1848, then, is the first year for which information was assembled.[64] This information is for sums remitted to the United King-dom as a whole not just for Ireland though perhaps 90 per cent of the money was destined for the Emerald Isle.[65] It was estimated that in that year alone at least £460 180 was remitted from the United States. Although the official statistics are flawed, it seems, none the less, that more than £34 million, or an average of £850 000 per annum between 1848 and the later 1880s was sent. Inclusion of other estimates leads Schrier to accept a figure of more than £1 million per year as the likely sum.[66] He observes that between 1852 and 1872 emigrants' remittances exceed by nearly £1 750 000 the whole of government expenditure for poor relief in Ireland. By 1880 one agency alone in Boston was remit-ting over $180 000 annually from servant girls. Indeed, one of the features of the flow was that a large proportion, possibly eight out of ten, who sent money home were women. Times of distress occasioned especially sizeable remittances. In 1879 over £1 million was sent, a sum which expanded to more than £1 700 000 in 1880, reaching a peak of over £2 200 000 in 1884. By the 1890s more than $5 million a year was being remitted via American postal money orders.[67]

This money was transmitted for further family emigration, payment of rent, reduction of accounts in local shops, and to enable parents or relatives to obtain comforts beyond their immediate means. It was reported, for example, that a large portion of the rent paid between

1860 and 1864 came from America. Similarly, in 1880 it was observed by a parish priest that in County Kerry many tenants paid rents with money received from children in the United States, something that was still prevalent in the western County of Mayo at the end of the century.[68] In one area of County Donegal, 'if you said that everybody in Irishowen paid the rent at one time or other with American money it would not be an exaggeration'.[69] Shopkeepers regularly advanced credit in anticipation of clients settling accounts on receiving remittances. In 1861 one proprietor proclaimed that from the advances made on the strength of American money he had 'never lost a penny that way'.[70] In one district of County Clare some half of 180 new houses constructed between 1851 and 1900 were the fruit of American money. Because the accounts are not broken down by region and religion there is no way to separate Catholic and Protestant generosity but, as well, there is not any suggestion that one confession was more munificent than the other, though it seems that the poorer and rural people generally received remittances more faithfully than the better-off.

Humanitarian assistance was a second major area of Irish-American involvement with the old country. At the close of the 1870s Ireland experienced a series of poor harvests with corresponding concerns of a renewal of the famine, especially among the smallholders of the West. In October 1879 the Irish National Land League was formed to combat landlordism. Parnell, who had established a reputation as a 'Young Turk' among Irish national parliamentarians, mainly on the issue of 'obstruction' in the House of Commons was chosen President of the new association. He agreed to undertake a fund-raising mission to North America, landing in New York on 2 January 1880. His tour for which the best description is by Michael Davitt, *The Fall of Feudalism in Ireland* (1904), lasted until 11 March 1880 when Parnell returned home to fight the general election called while he was visiting Montreal.[71] Parnell had four purposes in North America – promotion of the self-government cause; to discuss the policy of 'activism' in the House of Commons; to solicit funds for the political operations of the Land League; and humanitarian assistance to relieve distress at home.

This mission illustrates the distinction between broadly based support, including that by Americans generally, for humanitarian relief and the more limited sympathy enlisted for nationalist political aspirations. His arrangements and venues were managed by the Clan na Gael, a revolutionary organization with a primarily political agenda. A key Clan figure such as Dr William Carroll thought that 'charity should have been kept separate from politics and such is the general feeling in Phila[delphia], especially among our friends the Newspapers'.[72] Parnell's mixture of the two elements has obscured the functions of the mission

and the prime reason for its success. Solicitation of funds for the relief
of distress soon became the pre-eminent object of the tour. Even prior
to disembarking from his ship he granted an interview to the *New York
Herald* in which he stated that though the original purpose had been
political, he now meant to give primacy to the relief of agrarian distress.
This was reiterated at the outset of the tour and confirmed with the
issue of a circular by Parnell and John Dillon on 30 January from the
Office of the Irish Famine Relief Fund, pleading,

> We beg to enclose you copy of an Appeal which we have issued to
> the American People. The circumstances of the case are of so
> pressing and so terrible a nature, that we trust they will form a
> sufficient excuse for addressing you.
>   We would venture to suggest the immediate formation of a Re-
> lief Committee in your City, composed of gentlemen of all
> Nationalities, so that an opportunity may be afforded every citizen
> of assisting us to keep our people alive until the Government of
> England comes to their relief.
>   All money sent to Drexel, Morgan & Co., will be cabled promptly
> to Ireland, and used within a week, in saving the Peasantry of the
> West of Ireland from death by starvation.[73]

Throughout his mission Parnell explained that the movement's political
agenda was not simply relief but to alter the land system which he
claimed was responsible for the distress. That outcome he held could be
gained by the force of public opinion on the British Parliament which
Americans had a vital role in shaping. To that end, as he stated to the
House of Representatives, in early February, 'I do not seek to embroil
your government with the government of England; but we claim that
the public opinion and sentiment of a free country like America is
entitled to find expression wherever it is seen that the laws of freedom
are not observed'.[74] These themes were elaborated during his two stops
in Canada as well, showing that Parnell did not address only American
and presumably more receptive audiences but took the message into the
heart of the empire. The public demonstrations always had Catholic
priests but frequently included clergy of other denominations, state and
local politicians who had no connection with the Irish community on
the platforms.

  Parnell's mission raised approximately £72 000, including about
£12 000 for the Land League, and was an evident success, though this
was, in fact, the smallest of the four funds begun to aid the peasants.
Contributions for humanitarian aid vastly outstripped sums for political purposes, especially when the receipts of the four funds are collated.
A second American fund started by the proprietor of the *New York
Herald*, James Gordon Bennett, obtained even larger donations. Parnell
appealed to Americans generally and not just to the Irish, even if the

last were the greater portion of the constituency. His speeches were usually reported verbatim in the local press. Many were printed in *The Irish World* and some in other ethnic newspapers. Parnell's prominence, the novelty of the tour and its humanitarian purpose ensured fairly intense coverage though typically, each speech was reported only in the local press of the city where he spoke. Aside from readers of the *Irish World* and a handful of similar newspapers, few Americans would have been aware of the mission's overall progress. Newspapers frequently were sympathetic to the humanitarian purposes; there was some endorsement of Parnell's views on reforming the land system as well, but enthusiasm for the wider political agenda of self-government was much more restrained. This political aspect of the tour was only introduced at the close of each speech which was mainly directed to the need for generous contributions to relieve distress.

Parnell's trip certainly had great value in publicizing rural distress and it elevated his reputation at home and abroad. But it is easy to exaggerate its longer-term political significance. Two decades later Davitt wrote:

> the political value of the mission to the league movement was enormous. Active sympathy for its objects was awakened throughout America, and all the bitter memories of landlord oppression and insolence were revived in the hearts of our exiled people, soon to help us to enlist the active co-operation of hundreds of thousands of Irish-American Land-Leaguers in the combat against the landlord and Castle enemy of the old country.[75]

This verdict has received modern affirmation with one writer observing that the mission was a 'a sort of pilgrimage in which the ties binding Irishmen on both sides of the Atlantic were reaffirmed and strengthened' and that this support, moral and financial, forced 'the British government to deal with an "Irish nation" whose boundaries extended beyond the shores of Ireland itself'.[76] Such judgements contain a grain of truth but overestimate Irish-American solidarity and conflate the humanitarian and political ends.

Between 1916 and 1921 there was a comparable spell of fund-raising, including the solicitation of money for the Irish Relief Fund which collected $50 000 by July 1916, contributions directly to the Irish White Cross, the Irish Victory Fund which received some $887 000 by the end of 1920 though only $115 000 found its way to Ireland, and Eamon de Valera's bond drive raising some $5 500 000 though again only a small portion reached the homeland. It was no easy matter to disentangle political from humanitarian motives though, as in the case of Parnell's mission, much of the money was secured because of the latter.

A third and less easily quantified financial involvement were sums contributed for religious needs. Throughout every part of the country there was a mushrooming of cathedrals, churches, chapels, convents, monasteries, seminaries, parochial houses, espiscopal palaces, schools, colleges, orphanages, hospitals and asylums. Catholic bishops in a joint Pastoral in 1859 enthused, 'in every part of the country we see churches rising up that rival in beauty of design and elegance of execution the proudest monuments of the zeal, the piety, and the taste of our forefathers'.[77] In 1868 *The Freeman's Journal* believed that since 1800 £5 690 995 had been expended on the erection of Catholic buildings, estimating the annual expenditure of the Church at £762 030.[78] Construction remained a priority for another decade and though the pace slowed after 1880, the costs of maintenance and other expenses were considerable.[79] Many of these ambitious works exceeded the financial capacity of the locality or diocese. The needs were met, in part, by the priest assembling the names of emigrants from the locality to whom he then wrote personally. Clerical soliciting for contributions was an integral part of life at home and abroad for the Irish, something certainly facilitated by the large numbers of clergy who following ordination in Ireland went overseas in the service of god and church in 'Ireland's spiritual empire'.

It is impossible to cite exactly how much money was collected or the number of churches or other religious constructions owing existence to Irish-American dollars but it surely was substantial.[80] In part such moneys along with other remittances offset the outflow of capital from Ireland which reached a peak during the last quarter of the nineteenth century. Writing in 1906 to refute allegations of extravagance on church buildings, Father O'Riordan claimed that some £4 million had been spent for this purpose with about £1 million contributed from abroad, mainly by Irish-Americans.[81] His figures were compiled to refute Sir Horace Plunkett's allegations of ecclesiastical extravagance and are too low. Extending the more reliable calculation published in *The Freeman's Journal* in 1868, the Church probably spent at least £8 million up to 1921 with £1½ to £2 million being raised in North America.[82] Some half dozen churches in a small part of County Galway were financed by this means before 1900 in what appears to be a typical example of opportunistic fund-raising.[83] In 1877 the bishop after complaining about the scale of the cathedral at Queenstown observed, 'I have got nearly £3,000 from the priests I sent to Australia. I am now thinking of sending out two more to America to collect'.[84] In 1910 the then bishop was obsessed with the still considerable sums required for the as yet incomplete cathedral. He observed that people at home were financially exhausted and collections already had been taken up in the United States three times. During the long agricultural downturn in the last quarter of the nineteenth century Catholics' share of national income, according to Emmet Larkin, dropped while at the same time the proportion in the hands of the Church rose,[85] a factor, which if true, was made possible by contributions from abroad. Liam Kennedy convincingly undermines Larkin's figures, arguing that the financial burden is overstated but agrees that the total cost was not insubstantial and thereby indirectly confirming the hypothesis concerning overseas remittances.[86] Whatever the actual sums collected, it is certain that up to 1914 these outstripped political contributions by a huge margin. Unlike remittances and humanitarian assistance, such solicitations, of course, were confined to Catholics. An Irish identity could be invoked for some, mainly non-political, purposes. This functioned best in symbolic situations where the desires for individuality were combined with feelings both of community and conformity through the exercise of personal choice, something pointed to as crucial in contemporary manifestations of ethnicity.[87]

Irish-Americans proved largely impotent as an influence on American foreign affairs. In 1866 a resolution was introduced in the House of Representatives urging the Department of State to recognize the Irish nation as a belligerent which was promptly ignored by the Secretary of State.[88] A second Fenian incursion into Canada in May 1870 ended with the perpetrators receiving long prison sentences for violation of American neutrality laws. Between 1876 and 1896 the near balance between the Republican and Democratic parties, especially with large Irish populations in the key states of New York, Pennsylvania, New Jersey and Massachusetts, afforded the Hibernian element an exceptional opportunity. This period coincided with a considerable number of Anglo-American diplomatic issues. Also, 15 Irish-Americans (11 Democrats) held seats in the House of Representatives and three sat in the Senate for some portion of the 1880s, though they did not constitute a unified bloc on Irish matters. Opponents of Great Britain were not necessarily pro-Irish in the American context. In 1883 the Secretary of State, James G. Blaine, who had a 'general dislike for all foreigners, and especially the English' declared:

> it was a disgrace to permit the United States to be made the refuge for the scum of Europe ... There had been of late too much 'demagogy' on the part of the Government in dealing with the Irish element in New York. It must not be forgotten that although it dominated the State and City of New York it was a foreign element and in no sense an American one, and that as such it might become a very dangerous one to American institutions.[89]

Yet, when the Republicans lost the White House in 1884, Blaine and some other Republicans openly courted the Irish electorate. Some Irish-American spokesmen, including Alexander Sullivan, supported the

Republicans though many others, such as, John Boyle O'Reilly, kept faith with the Democrats. As the *Saturday Review* in 1883 observed. 'the Irish were influential enough to be flattered, but by no means able to determine the policy of the United States'.[90] Joseph P. O'Grady found little evidence of capacity to exert an impact on foreign relations during the 1880s.[91] Indeed, he suggests that some American leaders used Irish-Americans for their own political purposes rather than the reverse.[92]

The failure of the Bayard-Chamberlain Treaty in 1888 and the Arbitration Treaty in 1897 to secure the approval of the Senate were greeted enthusiastically by Irish-American groups but the real reason for the defeat was embedded in wider American politics. When the Boer War began in October 1899, Irish-Americans had a further opportunity to seek to injure British interests. The Secretary of State, Hay, turned aside these efforts and on the eve of the conflict he professed that the 'one indispensable feature of our foreign policy' was a 'friendly understanding with England'.[93] The then Governor of New York, Theodore Roosevelt, openly supported Great Britain. When a Fenian inquired about his attitude if a further invasion of Canada were launched, Roosevelt warned that the militia would be called out and he would 'clap them all in jail'.[94] Even Charles Callan Tansill's uncritical account, admits that 'in the field of national politics the Irish-American pressure group had much to learn about propaganda and procedure'.[95] Ward acknowledges the 'nuisance value' of the Irish but notes the futility of their opposition to the several negotiations for treaties between the United States and Great Britain throughout the Edwardian years, observing that these only enjoyed a measure of success when they chose to 'support Americanism, and the prerogative of the Senate'.[96] He points out that they had little bargaining power with Republican administrations unsympathetic to their Anglophobia and their anti-imperialism.[97] Thus the Venezuelan boundary dispute was resolved in 1899, the Hay-Pauncefote Canal Treaty approved in 1901, but the Arbitration Treaty in 1904 stumbled. Still an Arbitration Treaty succeeded in 1908 'notwithstanding an enormous number of petitions against the treaty from the Clann na Gael [*sic*] and other Irish societies'.[98] In 1911 a British official characterized these groups as emitting 'much "hot air" as they would say in the US'.[99]

There were always prominent Americans ready to align themselves with the idea of self-government in Ireland. Roosevelt and William Howard Taft are two such notable examples and leading politicians, including Presidents, met Irish leaders when they visited the United States.[100] Many people in the United States retained a strong sense of Anglophobia, resulting from the Revolutionary and 1812 wars, boundary disputes with Canada, a dislike of monarchy and aristocracy, and suspicions of British economic competition. As one leading Irish-American figure observed, 'Home Rule is very popular with nearly all classes in the United States, as it is generally looked upon as an American idea, owing to the Federal relations of the different states to the central government'.[101] Additionally, the agitation in Ireland against landlord-ism struck a responsive chord among Americans of all descriptions. Irish influence did not advance remarkably with the election of the Democrat, Woodrow Wilson in 1912, who enjoyed Irish electoral sup-port. In a ceremony on 16 May 1914 for the unveiling of the congressionally financed monument of John Barry, Wilson unleashed his famous attack on hyphened Americans cited above.

It is often alleged that Irish-American pressure had some force between 1916 and 1921. During this time the British government, it is maintained, was sensitive to American opinion and therefore anxious to achieve a settlement in Ireland. Carroll and Ward, in particular, argue for this proposition, suggesting that Lloyd George pressed on for a resolution of the Irish situation in order to assuage America.[102] The evidence for this contention is tenuous. Diplomatic correspondence from the British embassy in Washington emphasized the Irish dimen-sion, as might be expected, and it figured to an extent in the exchanges between key leaders in Great Britain, but the ebb and flow of events on the ground scarcely reveals obeisance to American views. The formula adopted by the British leadership was shaped by four factors – the crisis of 1912–14 ending with the passage of the Government of Ireland Act, its suspension until one year after the conclusion of the European War along with a stated promise to amend the legislation so as to accommo-date the Ulster demand; the deteriorating political and military situation on the ground after 1919; and the constraints of a Conservative domi-nated coalition in the aftermath of the general election of 1918.[103] There is ample testimony in official, public and private correspondence about each of these facets but not much evidence to indicate that the government took more than cursory notice of American government opinion, particularly after the autumn of 1918. As Stephen Hartley observed, the Foreign Office officials, influential senior civil servants, including Maurice Hankey, and Conservative members of the cabinet, summarily dismissed American pressure.[104] What did change after 1916 was that the cabinet devoted time to consideration of the American dimension and that some figures in the Conservative Party were con-verted to seeking an Irish solution in order to abet better Anglo-American relations. But American considerations played only a limited part in British government calculations. The execution of the leaders of the rebellion was done contrary to American concerns, the refusal to treat captives as prisoners of war also flaunted American views, while the execution of Roger Casement at the beginning of August, too, ran counter to pleas for clemency by officials in America. Similarly, the introduction of legislation enabling conscription in Ireland contravened American advice while the worst excesses by British military personnel in Ireland took place between 1919 and 1921. In autumn 1920 Terence MacSwiney was allowed to die on hunger strike and Kevin Barry was hanged just before the American elections. By 1921 Congressional interest in Ireland was fast fading.

There is a difficulty in distinguishing between a crescendo of Irish-American rhetoric and the reality of politics on the ground. Despite a chorus of support for Germany from Irish-American organizations at the outbreak of the war, Daniel Boyle, an Irish party MP, in 1915 found little pro-German sympathy among ordinary Irish-Americans.[105] In spite of numerous Irish-American leaders throwing their weight behind the Republican candidate standing against Wilson in the presidential election of 1916, he actually increased his vote in most areas with large Irish populations.[106] An analysis of the Irish vote in the election shows that though Wilson did not receive their vocal support he did gain their vote. Another study reveals that, in an Irish district of Buffalo, Wilson enlarged the Democratic candidate's share of the vote from three to one in the 1908 and 1912 contests to five to one in 1916.[107] Irish-Americans responded to American issues rather than to the aspirations of Ireland, while the Catholic Church sought to distance itself from partisan politics. The bulk of Irish labour leaders were pro-Wilson and bread and butter matters eclipsed ethnic or religious sentiment among the rank and file.[108] The extensive correspondence of Senator Walsh shows that Irish-Americans throughout much of the country did yeoman work to re-elect Wilson.[109] The Irish vote as an *Irish* vote was not a significant factor in the presidential election of 1920.[110] A study of seven states indicates that the Irish were not significant in providing abstentions, except possibly in Massachusetts; they were not directly or disproportionately responsible for the swing against the Democratic candidate.[111] While Irish organizations campaigned against the League of Nations, Irish-American voters were not swayed by this propaganda but reacted to American economic questions and local considerations.

Wilson, of course, had little sympathy for Irish-American agitation. Ward points out that for many years until 1916 Congress had shown only minor interest in Ireland.[112] Resolutions for home rule died in 1908, 1909 and 1913 without even been discussed in committee. Wilson (and the United States) refused to endorse the demands of Sinn Fein plenipotentiaries at the Versailles Conference. In the end the final negotiations on self-government owed nothing to American interest – and the terms of the treaty incorporated Great Britain's domestic requirements.

Nationalist activists in America created a ruckus all out of proportion to their numbers but their impact on the affairs of Great Britain and the United States was limited. A reformulation of Ward's conclusion about the impact of Irish-Americans on the relations of the United States with Britain is in order. Irish-American organizations retained a nuisance value but were only effective and on the winning side when their Anglophobic views coincided with American ideas and policy more generally. Irish-America was not well organized for political purposes, though it had more bite in certain places, Boston being an obvious example. But the Irish were an energetic political element in only a handful of eastern states along with an equally small number of cities in the interior. Moreover, as Carroll notes, there was a native American counter-response to Irish-American agitation.[113] Because of their superior social station and access to the press, leading American critics of the Irish were better able to influence opinion. What Irish-Americans, as contrasted with Nationalist organizations and ethnic newspapers, felt about the growing harmony between their adoptive land and the hereditary enemy cannot be ascertained from a brief survey, but they were not well positioned to be more than a minor impediment. The Irish dimension worked more effectively for humanitarian than for political purposes. Thus, except for brief moments, Anglo-American accord before and during the First World War had been established on a secure footing, to the chagrin or otherwise of one group of hyphened-Americans.

The paradigm of Irish-America's inability to log substantial political success despite a supposedly high level of ethnic identity and commitment to the homeland arises from a misunderstanding of how ethnicity functions in an adopted land where the hurdles to incorporation are comparatively low and the group largely sought resolution of grievances through non-ethnic parties and institutions. With the aid of sociological theorizing on ethnicity, it is now possible to arrange the empirical evidence in ways revealing more clearly why the Irish had a very limited political impact. This is only partly attributable to the progressive weighting of the Irish towards those born in the United States or to upward social mobility, though these are not irrelevant, but partly to internal dynamics of a diaspora which lacked the attributes to form cohesive self-sustaining communities overseas even at its numerical peak. If remittances serve as some measure of identification/loyalty, daughters, who remained largely outside the political arena, had a greater propensity to sustain links with the home or homeland than their brothers and a good measure of that enthusiasm was channelled into religious institutions. This aids in explaining the paradox of subsiding political commitment at a moment when religious association was accelerated and is largely consistent with the observations of Esman, Handleman and Gans among others. The Irish in America, or more accurately a significant section of the 'aggregation', were approaching the point where 'symbolic ethnicity' rather than activity commitment best describes their situation. As Gans noted, financial contributions, particularly for non-political ends, satisfied much of the need to be 'Irish'. It can be added as a postscript that the timing and outcomes for the diaspora in Great Britain were virtually identical, suggesting that internal rather than external factors were at work in both instances in about equal proportion and that there was nothing unique about the conditions stimulating a particular form of Irish nationalist commitment in the United States. The rapid acceptance of the Anglo-Irish Treaty, the collapse of support for republicanism, and the lost of interest in Ireland after 1921 confirm not the strength but the relative weakness of the potential of political nationalism throughout the period.

Notes

1. I wish to thank the research committee of the University of North London for financial assistance. Also, I want to acknowledge the help of Peter Alter, John Broad, George Boyce, Barbara Gauntt, Donald and Shirley Ginter, Sheridan Gilley, Terry Gourvish, David Howell, Michael Hurst, John Hutchinson, Donal Kerr, Jonathan Moore, Margaret Mullally, Andrew O'Day, Colonel Helen E. O'Day, Roger Swift, Charles Thomas, F. M. L. Thompson, Gabrielle Ward-Smith, and the members of group four under the leadership of Kevin B. Nowlan in the project, 'Governments and Non-Dominant Ethnic Groups in Europe, 1850–1940' sponsored by the European Science Foundation (ESF), along with Christoph Mülberg now in Bonn and Genèvieve Schauinger in Strasbourg from the ESF. Roland Quinault made valuable comments on the original text.
2. Isaac Butt, *Land Tenure in Ireland; A Plea for the Celtic Race*, 3rd edn (Dublin, 1866), p. 11.
3. *New York Times*, October 1899, quoted in Alan J. Ward, *Ireland and Anglo-American Relations 1899–1921* (London, 1969), p. 47.
4. Quoted in Lawrence J. McCaffrey, *The Irish Diaspora in America* (Washington, DC, 1976), p. 130.
5. F. S. L. Lyons, *Ireland Since the Famine*, 4th imp. (London, 1976), p. 19.
6. Andrew J. Wilson, *Irish America and the Ulster Conflict 1968–1995* (Belfast, 1995), p. 4.
7. Quoted in Ward, *Ireland and Anglo-American Relations*, p. 70.
8. Milton J. Esman, 'Diasporas and International Relations', in J. Hutchinson and A. D. Smith (eds), *Ethnicity* (Oxford, 1996), pp. 316–20.
9. See, ibid., p. 6.
10. Herbert J. Gans, 'Symbolic Ethnicity: The Future of Ethnic Groups and Culture in America', *Ethnic and Racial Studies*, 1, 1 (January 1979), 8–9.

11. *Ibid.*, p. 9; see, also, Mary C. Waters, *Ethnic Options: Choosing Identities in America* (Berkeley, Los Angeles and Oxford, 1990), p. 147.

12. Mary J. Hickman, 'Alternative Historiographies of the Irish in Britain: A Critique of the Segregation/Assimilation Model', in R. Swift and S. Gilley (eds), *The Irish in Victorian Britain: The Local Dimension* (Dublin, 1999), pp. 236–53. This peculiar, not to say acrimonious, essay seems to have been constructed for a personal and political agenda and is intellectually slipshod. Her conclusions would apply equally to writings on the American Irish.

13. *Daily Express*, 5 October 1910.

14. Quoted in Francis M. Carroll, *American Opinion and the Irish Question 1910–23* (Dublin, 1978), p. 90.

15. Stephen Hartley, *The Irish Question as a Problem in British Foreign Policy, 1914–18* (London, 1987), pp. 198–9.

16. Wilson, *Irish America and the Ulster Conflict*, p. 15.

17. Robert Fisk, *In Time of War: Ireland, Ulster and the Price of Neutrality 1939–45* (London, 1983), pp. 455–68.

18. Lawrence J. McCaffrey, 'A Profile of Irish America', in D. N. Doyle and O. D. Edwards (eds), *America and Ireland, 1776–1976: The American Identity and the Irish Connection* (Westport, CT, 1980), pp. 86–7.

19. Kerby Miller, *Emigrants and Exiles: Ireland the Irish Exodus to North America* (New York, 1985), p. 554.

20. Carroll, *American Opinion and the Irish Question*, p. 1.

21. Matthew Frye Jacobson, *Special Sorrows: The Diasporic Imagination of Irish, Polish and Jewish Immigrants in the United States* (Cambridge, MA, 1995), pp. 2–3.

22. Ibid., p. 15.

23. Quoted in ibid., p. 19.

24. Ibid., p. 20.

25. Thomas N. Brown, *Irish-American Nationalism, 1870–1890* (Philadelphia and New York, 1966), p. 20.

26. Ibid., p. 24.

27. Ibid., p. 63.

28. Jacobson, *Special Sorrows*, p. 24.

29. Ibid.

30. Alan O'Day, 'Irish Diaspora Politics in Perspective: The United Irish Leagues of America and Great Britain, 1900–14', *Immigrants and Minorities*, 18 (July/November 1999), 214–39; also published in Donald M. MacRaid (ed.), *The Great Famine and Beyond: Irish Migrants in Britain in the Nineteenth and Twentieth Centuries* (Dublin, 2000).

31. J. Milton Yinger, 'Toward a Theory of Assimilation and Dissimilation', *Ethnic and Racial Studies*, 4, 3 (July 1981), 249–64.

32. Waters, *Ethnic Options*, p. 147.

33. Yinger, 'Toward a Theory of Assimilation and Dissimilation', p. 255.

34. Gans, 'Symbolic Ethnicity', p. 16.

35. Carroll, *American Opinion and the Irish Question*, p. 3.

36. Steven P. Erie, *Rainbow's End: Irish-Americans and the Dilemmas of Urban Machine Politics, 1840–1985* (Berkeley, Los Angeles and London, 1988), pp. 28, 33, 53, 91, 94–100.

37. John F. Finerty to John O'Callaghan, 11 December 1905, John Redmond Papers, National Library of Ireland, MS 15,213 (5).

38. 11 March 1910, ibid., MS 15,213 (12).
39. Dennis Clark, *The Irish in Philadelphia: Ten Generations of Urban Experience* (Philadelphia, 1973), pp. 126–44.
40. Yinger, 'Toward a Theory of Assimilation and Dissimilation', p. 249.
41. Quoted in Carroll, *American Opinion and the Irish Question*, p. 29; quoted in Lawrence J. McCaffrey, 'Irish-American Politics: Power With or Without Purpose?' in P. J. Drudy (ed.), *The Irish in America: Emigration, Assimilation and Impact* (Cambridge, 1985), p. 169.
42. Michael F. Funchion, 'The Political and Nationalist Dimensions', in L. J. McCaffrey, E. Skerrett, M. F. Funchion and C. Fanning (eds), *The Irish in Chicago* (Urbana, IL and Chicago, 1987), pp. 61–97; Thomas H. O'Connor, *The Boston Irish: A Political History* (Boston, MA, 1995), pp. 95–165; Erie, *Rainbow's End*, pp. 57–66, 85–91.
43. Erie, *Rainbow's End*, p. 50, 104.
44. Gans, 'Symbolic Ethnicity', p. 3.
45. Also, see, Steven P. Erie, 'Politics, the Public Sector and Irish Social Mobility: San Francisco, 1870–1900', *Western Political Quarterly*, 31 (June 1978), p. 287.
46. Gans, 'Symbolic Ethnicity', pp. 10–11.
47. Brown, *Irish-American Nationalism*, p. 161.
48. David Brundage, '"In Time of Peace Prepare for War": Key Themes in the Social Thought of New York's Irish Nationalists, 1890–1916', in R. H. Bayor and T. J. Meagher (eds), *The New York Irish* (Baltimore, MD and London, 1996), p. 325.
49. Carroll, *American Opinion and the Irish Question*, p. 210, n. 13.
50. Ibid., p. 7.
51. Ibid., p. 16.
52. Ibid., p. 8.
53. Alfred Webb, 'Analysis of General Election Fund 1900', John Redmond Papers, National Library of Ireland, MS 15,231 (2).
54. O'Callaghan to Redmond, 16 May 1901, ibid., MS 15,213 (3).
55. T. St John Gaffney to Redmond, 7 January 1902, ibid., MS 15,236 (9).
56. W. Bourke Cochran to Redmond, 7 January 1902, ibid., MS 15,236 (2).
57. Quoted in Ward, *Ireland and Anglo-American Relations*, p. 15.
58. O'Callaghan to Redmond, 13 April 1902, Redmond Papers, MS 15,213 (4).
59. Webb to Redmond, 11 May 1903, ibid., MS 15,231 (3).
60. John F. Finerty to Redmond (copy), 20 August 1903, ibid., MS 15,213 (5).
61. *Ibid.*, 11 August 1905, MS 15,213 (7).
62. Quoted in William O'Brien and Desmond Ryan (eds), *Devoy's Post Bag 1871–1928* (Dublin, 1953), vol. 2, p. 358.
63. Arnold Schrier, *Ireland and the American Emigration 1850–1900* (Minneapolis, MN, 1958), p. 103.
64. Ibid., p. 104.
65. Ibid., p. 106.
66. Ibid., p. 105.
67. Ibid., p. 108.
68. Ibid., p. 112.
69. Quoted in ibid., pp. 112–13.
70. Quoted in ibid., p. 113.

71. Michael Davitt, *The Fall of Feudalism in Ireland* (London, 1904), pp. 193–210.
72. O'Brien and Ryan, *Devoy's Post Bag* (Dublin, 1948), vol. 1, p. 486.
73. Quoted in ibid., p. 480.
74. *Congressional Record* (2 February 1880), vol. 10, pt 1, pp. 664–5.
75. Davitt, *Fall of Feudalism*, p. 210.
76. Michael V. Hazel 'First Link: Parnell's American Tour, 1880', *Eire–Ireland*, 15 (Spring 1980), p. 24.
77. Quoted in E. R. Norman, *The Catholic Church and Ireland in the Age of Rebellion 1859–1873* (London, 1965), p. 1.
78. Ibid., p. 15.
79. Liam Kennedy, *Colonialism, Religion and Nationalism in Ireland* (Belfast, 1996), p. 107.
80. Ibid., p. 110.
81. M. O'Riordan, *Catholicity and Progress in Ireland*, 4th edn (London, 1906), p. 19.
82. For a useful discussion of expenses see, Desmond Keenan, *The Catholic Church in Nineteenth-Century Ireland: A Sociological Study* (Dublin, 1983), pp. 226–39.
83. Schrier, *Ireland and the American Emigration*, p. 120.
84. Quoted in Emmet Larkin, 'Economic Growth, Capital Investment and the Roman Catholic Church in Nineteenth-Century Ireland', *American Historical Review*, 72 (April 1967), p. 864.
85. Ibid., p. 865.
86. Kennedy, *Colonialism, Religion and Nationalism in Ireland*, p. 106.
87. Waters, *Ethnic Options*, p. 151.
88. Charles Callan Tansill, *America and the Fight for Irish Freedom 1866–1922: An Old Story Based Upon New Data* (New York, 1957), p. 36.
89. Quoted in ibid., pp. 79, 84.
90. *Saturday Review*, 61 (1883), p. 303.
91. Joseph Patrick O'Grady, *Irish-Americans and Anglo-American Relations, 1880–1888* (New York, 1976), pp. 283.
92. Ibid., p. 274.
93. Quoted in Tansill, *America and the Fight for Irish Freedom*, p. 118.
94. Quoted in ibid., p. 114.
95. Ibid., p. 120.
96. Ward, *Ireland and Anglo-American Relations*, pp. 68–9.
97. Ibid., p. 59.
98. Quoted in ibid.
99. Quoted in ibid., p. 66.
100. Carroll, *American Opinion and the Irish Question*, pp. 9–10.
101. Finerty to Redmond, 11 December 1903, Redmond Papers, MS 15,136 (2).
102. Carroll, *American Opinion and the Irish Question*, pp. 149–76; Ward, *Ireland and Anglo-American Relations*, pp. 113, 227, 258.
103. See, Alan O'Day, *Irish Home Rule 1867–1921* (Manchester, 1998), pp. 266–306.
104. Hartley, *Irish Question as a Problem in British Foreign Policy*, p. 194.
105. Also, see Edward Cuddy, 'Irish-Americans and the 1916 Election: An Episode in Immigrant Adjustment', *American Quarterly*, 21 (Summer, 1969), p. 237.

106. William M. Leary, Jr, 'Woodrow Wilson, Irish Americans, and the Election of 1916, *Journal of American History*, 54 (June 1967), pp. 70–72.
107. Cuddy, 'Irish-Americans and the 1916 Election', p. 236.
108. Ibid., p. 238.
109. Ibid., p. 242.
110. Ward, *Ireland and Anglo-American Relations*, p. 224.
111. R. A. Burchell, 'Did the Irish and German Voters Desert the Democrats in 1920? A Tentative Statistical Answer', *Journal of American Studies*, 6, 2 (1972), p. 156–7.
112. Ward, *Ireland and Anglo-American Relations*, p. 117.
113. Carroll, *American Opinion and the Irish Question*, pp. 9–13.

CHAPTER TEN

Was there an Anglo-American Feminist Movement in the Earlier Twentieth Century?

Christine Bolt

Emily Balch, a distinguished American academic and pacifist, once remarked that 'If Europeans seem to Americans to find it too difficult to believe, too difficult to act, Americans seem to Europeans too naive, impulsive and idealistic, not to say sentimental, exaggerated, unstable, puzzling, incalculable'.[1] Judgements such as Balch's are not uncommon. So why, then, should anyone expect to find an Anglo-American women's movement either before or after 1900?

At first sight, the prospects do not look promising. I have commented elsewhere on the differences between the pioneering British and American feminists, and have noted that these differences related directly to their two countries' distinctive social and political circumstances.[2] Notable among the factors shaping activism in the United States were its federal political system, practical coalition parties and assertive courts. Additionally, reformers had to rise to the challenge of America's huge terrain and accompanying sectional contrasts, its elevation of race over class divisions and its mounting religious and ethnic tensions. In Britain, the key determinants of outlook and action were a unitary political system, a pervasive class-consciousness, a strong establishment, and an imperial outlook which gave a particular flavour to pronouncements on race. Although American and British reformers were themselves seldom parochial, they were well aware of their contrasting environments, and hence of the dangers involved in extending too overt a welcome to foreign agitators, tactics and ideas. After all, it was hard enough to unite activists in national crusades of any duration, let alone in transnational collaborative ventures.

Another factor that put limits on Anglo-American co-operation was the strong sense of superiority that sustained British and American feminists alike. Accordingly, British women took pride in their nation's mature culture and their own political expertise, usually exercised through existing channels and institutions, while feminists in the United States gloried in their democratic ethos, social freedom and ability to devise an

elaborate network of women's organizations. Furthermore, the particularly close transatlantic connections sustained before and after the American
Revolution by kinship, cultural and economic ties, declined in importance from the 1850s. In the decades that followed, as Thistlethwaite has
pointed out, the British and American economies ceased to complement
each other, and British capitalists increasingly regarded the United States
as a competitor. American democracy provided less inspiration for British
radicals, the West drew American attention from the Atlantic economy,
and mass immigration created a more polyglot American population.[3]

None the less, from the nineteenth century to the First World War the
British and American women's movements did have much in common,
and shared in the fluctuating 'special relationship' between the United
States and Britain. The first phase of organized feminism began and
peaked around the same time in the two countries, whose activists saw
themselves as leading the rest of the world in the struggle for women's
emancipation. American feminists travelling to Europe stopped first in
Britain, where a shared language made it easy not only to observe and
publish reports on British reform operations, but also to work in them.[4]
For their part, British feminists found publicity and insights, friendship
and funds in the United States.

In both countries, initially middle-class campaigners were shaped by a
liberal political tradition that served to thwart revolutionary pressures yet
celebrated opportunity, freedom and progress: a tradition that encouraged equal rights claims and put fewer obstacles in the way of political
protests than women encountered in continental Europe. In both countries, an individualistic Protestantism likewise helped to drive women
towards reform, and as reformers they influenced significant shifts in
social thought, besides being affected by and contributing to arguments
over race, class, industrialization, urbanization, political democratization
and imperialism. In both countries, the women's movements became
more complex over time, more radical on sexual and economic issues,
more determined to establish feminism as an international cause and
more willing to deploy assertions about women's distinctiveness to achieve
their egalitarian objectives. And from the end of the nineteenth century
they benefited from the formal *rapprochement* between the United States
and Britain that arose out of foreign policy needs and was justified with
reference to large claims about the destiny of the Anglo-Saxon race. As a
result, contemporaries tended to see a sort of unity among Anglo-Saxon
women, and to identify an Anglo-American egalitarian feminism which
contrasted with the continental European, maternalist variety.

However, it is my belief that the connection between the American
and British movements climaxed with the securing of national suffrage,
and that they pulled apart steadily during the inter-war years of the

twentieth century. Consequently, the two movements were very different from each other when they were revitalized in the 1960s. Moreover,
even in the period from 1900 to the First World War, when Anglo-
American feminist ties in the mounting suffrage fight were very strong,
there were clear contrasts between the activists.

This process of disengagement and these contrasts are traced fully in
my forthcoming book on the centrifugal force of race, class and internationalism in the twentieth-century British and American women's
movements.[5] It is the purpose of the present chapter to introduce some
part of my story, looking first at the final phase of suffragism; and then
at aspects of Anglo-American involvement in internationalism during
the 1920s and 1930s. Internationalism has been chosen to illustrate my
argument because feminists recognized the importance of foreign affairs
in the post-war world, and invariably emphasized their desire to work
for peace. Given their perception and their elevated hopes, internationalism was the area where co-operation between American and British
activists might have been expected to be most pronounced. But in fact,
the international arena frequently served to demonstrate the enduring
or emerging strength of national loyalties and considerations, for by the
1920s no goal so clear and badly wanted as the vote drew the world's
women together.

Suffragism, 1900–28

Early twentieth-century suffragists in the United States and Britain,
after long campaigns which had produced elaborate propaganda and
organization without bringing victory, were resolved to diversify their
arguments and tactics. They therefore took their message from parlours
and halls to the streets and political constituencies, and reached out to
hitherto neglected sources of support, especially among the working
class. In the process, they agonized over divisions within their own
ranks, and pondered the wisdom of abandoning political bipartisan-
ship, the value of seeking to coerce the party in power and the best way
of influencing cautious and unsympathetic political leaders. They were
also formally united from 1904 in the International Woman Suffrage
Association (IWSA), a body which they dominated and which was
headed until 1923 by Carrie Chapman Catt of the United States, and
from 1923 to 1946 by Britain's Margery Corbett Ashby. Yet the very
closeness of British and American suffragists only threw into stark relief
the real differences that remained between them.

The American crusader for peace, labour rights and the vote, Florence
Luscomb, has left us an interesting account of her time observing

British suffrage activities in 1911, when she was headed for the IWSA conference in Stockholm. Luscomb studied both branches of the British campaign, 'so we could copy their ideas in Boston'. She was personally anxious to learn from her hosts, having been drawn into suffragism as a college student by the example of English militants; and despite her preference for the tactics and leaders of the Women's Social and Political Union (WSPU), she avoided snap judgements formed on the strength of one-sided information. Accordingly Luscomb was full of admiration for the 'clever & telling work' of the Actresses Franchise League: indeed, she thought that all the English societies 'organized on professional lines' were 'unqualifiedly successful', and that the Americans should institute them. She similarly applauded the way that the suffragettes kept themselves newsworthy by their various 'stunts', and she appreciated their harassment of Liberal politicians opposed to the vote.

On the other hand, Luscomb noted that an American woman employed by the militant camp had felt it necessary 'to learn to speak and dress English, which is very different from American indeed'. Although they were welcome in English militant ranks if they had come to work rather than observe, Luscomb and her companions were 'given the glad hand' only by their American contact, and they were uncomfortably conscious of English class prejudices and assuptions of superiority. Having attended a training session for English suffrage speakers, Luscomb had more respect for comparable sessions in the United States, and she believed that American methods were generally better at preventing 'a lack of harmony and cooperation' among campaigners. Generally, the American visitors did not feel at home. A House of Commons session revealed 'utter cold bloodedness to women', while English workers were deemed to be a 'poor looking lot, very ill fed and uneducated in appearance, and sloppily dressed'. There was a dearth of pretty women, cold drinking water and good food, whereas there was all too much 'British weather – blooming, blarsted, bloody!'[6]

Irritants of this kind, though petty in themselves, are a reminder of the deeper political differences between Britons and Americans. It was especially difficult for Americans to accept that militants in Britain, with its slow movement towards democracy, and political style in which tradition, formality and class snobbery played a large part, were leading the political arm of the women's movement and attracting the attention of feminists throughout the world. After all, it was not only Luscomb who was turned to militancy by the British example but also such leading American suffragists as Alice Paul, Lucy Burns, Doris Stevens, Mary Beard and Harriot Blatch. When Elizabeth Cady Stanton and her daughter, Harriot Blatch, were at the heart of British suffrage militancy during the 1880s, there had still been a tendency for British radicals to apologize for their country's backwardness, as compared with America.[7] In the decades before the First World War, that tendency had largely gone. The attitude of Mrs Pankhurst is a case in point.

Militancy's most charismatic figure recognized that American audiences might relish hearing her account of British politicians behaving badly, and she went in person to appeal to Americans' known generosity, as did other English militants, among them Christabel and Sylvia Pankhurst, and Mrs Cobden-Sanderson. These transatlantic contacts, as Sharon Strom has shown, introduced American suffragists to the merits of open-air meetings: a tactic used by moderates and militants alike in Britain but little tried in America before about 1908.[8] The visits in turn rewarded British militants with hospitality, personal encouragement, fresh inspiration and money. However, Mrs Pankhurst combined gratitude with self-congratulation when she toured the United States. Writing to Luscomb in 1914, she paid tribute to her backing for the WSPU and acknowledged how cheering it was 'to have these marks of sympathy from other countries'. She then proceeded to stress that England was 'the storm centre of the world wide women's movement', before conceding that women found 'the very worst kind of opposition' there, 'probably because in an old civilization like ours the power of vice & corruption of every kind is very great. If we win here it means the women's victory all over the world'.[9] The American actress and writer, Elizabeth Robins, who lived in England, supported the WSPU until 1912, and explained the British suffrage scene to Americans – notably in her 1913 book, *Way Stations* – similarly suggested that the battlefield was now 'English soil, but the issue belongs to the human race'. She also agreed with Pankhurst that the Americans 'have taken fire from the English torch'.[10]

Activists in the United States took their own view of things. Its militants were themselves initially inclined to the common view of their countrywomen that the British persecution of suffragettes 'could never happen here! Our men would never treat us so'. (Incidentally, such a view was not confined to Americans. In the words of one Welsh suffragist, 'I fancy the Saxon has not the courtesy of the Celt to women'.) American women accepted that British suffragettes had been driven to extreme tactics by politicians' intransigence, and they admired the protesters' bravery and commitment. Conversely, American campaigners were restrained by knowledge of militancy's disruptive impact on British suffragism, and by awareness of the draconian responses it had evoked from the British government. Nor had memories faded of the recent American suppression of violent labour protests, while the American respect for property was as strong as ever. Most importantly, Strom reminds us, American suffragists clearly recognized that state

constitutional amendments enfranchising women required the endorsement of voters, many of whom might be alienated by militant tactics
brought over from Britain.[11] Hence, as one veteran who had worked in
both countries recalled, the militant suffrage movement in the United
States was 'not so much a question of doing damage as of getting
publicity. There was no window breaking and no destructive fires' of
the kind resorted to by the British.[12]

The fact that American militancy was adopted in the course of the
First World War, while British militants abandoned their campaign at
its outset, made American suffragettes vulnerable to charges about their
patriotism. Despite their shared interest in the vote, American and
British feminists were, in fact, differently affected by the war. After
1914, suffragists in Britain were increasingly concerned to grasp the
novel opportunities created by war work and a coalition government no
longer dominated by old political enemies. They were too distracted to
give much support to their militant sisters in the United States,[13] whose
divided suffragists were only slowly drawn into peace, relief and prepar-
edness groups, carried on their campaigning without pause and were
obliged to continue dealing with the carefully calculating President
Woodrow Wilson. The American militants' adoption of the British
tactic of holding the party in power responsible for female enfranchisement was denounced by moderates as inappropriate in the American
setting, where the two major parties might share control of the different
branches of government. And American anti-suffragists, influenced by
an extremely strong national cult of domesticity, condemned militancy
as the indulgence of Britain's conservative society women and as a
dangerous foreign import.

In the years before the First World War, American observers had
often been as sympathetic with the Irish suffrage movement as they had
been with the English, combining their concern with an interest in the
home rule struggle. During the war, the pronounced patriotism of the
two principals of British suffragism – Mrs Pankhurst and Mrs Fawcett –
could sometimes strain relations with more pragmatic American contacts. Mrs Catt, for example, was prepared to downplay her initial
pacifism in a calculated bid to make suffragism palatable to a president
embroiled in war. When she did attempt to reassert her peace sympathies through IWSA, which had its headquarters in London, she quickly
found herself in conflict with and contained by Mrs Fawcett.

Catt and Fawcett were, of course, similarly versatile and prudent
organization women, who were on cordial terms.[14] Although Fawcett
never saw the need to cross the Atlantic, she was delighted to chair the
1920 mass meeting at Central Hall, Westminster, that welcomed Catt to
England and celebrated the American women's suffrage victory. Yet

there remained a distance between them that was compounded after 1918 by the need of Fawcett and her successors in the National Union of Societies for Equal Citizenship (NUSEC, 1919) to push for the enfranchisement of British women under 30 years old. All American women had gained the vote through the Nineteenth Amendment, ratified in 1920, and as the American radical Crystal Eastman remarked in 1926, when she was resident in Britain, it 'seemed an anachronism to be going to a suffrage meeting'. While she praised the verve of the suffrage speakers she heard, she was dismayed by the 'strong conservative trend in England', which was behind moves to raise the voting age.[15] The gulf was further widened by different American and British roles in feminist internationalism, to which I shall now turn.

Feminist internationalism

British and American women committed to international co-operation and campaigning during the 1920s and 1930s had various women's organizations to choose from: among them were the International Council of Women (1888); the Women's International League for Peace and Freedom (WILPF, 1915); IWSA (renamed in 1926 the International Alliance of Women for Suffrage and Equal Citizenship); the Open Door International (1929) and the World Woman's Party (1938). Three additional bodies co-ordinated the operations of these societies: namely the Joint Standing Committee of Women's International Organizations (1926); the Liaison Committee of Women's International Organizations (1931) and the Disarmament Committee (1931). Since, as the flamboyant American feminist, Doris Stevens, observed, 'the subjection of women is world-wide', it seemed reasonable to maintain that 'this subjection can be removed finally and permanently only through international co-operation'.[16] From such co-operation, women believed, came the pooling of ideas, a sense of proportion about domestic problems, increased visibility in the world's affairs, and strengthened bonds of sisterhood.

Feminists with pacifist leanings were especially drawn to the international women's groups. Taking exception to the social order made by men and dominated by force, they thought that women, as the industrious makers of homes, the rearers of children and the chief victims of war, should exert themselves to find more rational ways of resolving international quarrels. But in Britain and the United States alike, the First World War experiences of such activists had reminded them of the risks involved in linking or equating the women's movement and other causes. Most bruisingly, suffragists had divided in 1915 over the peace–suffrage connection, with the linked British and American peace women having to find new organizational outlets in WILPF and its national sections. The nature of the connection between pacifism and feminism continued to be debated by women throughout the inter-war years, with women on both sides of the Atlantic being accused of lacking patriotism and practicality when they associated themselves with peace efforts.[17]

None the less cosmopolitan American and British feminists, who were often drawn from comparably privileged and liberal backgrounds, lobbied and published, set up meetings and marches, made powerful friendships among themselves and contacts among politicians, and strove to persuade international bodies like the League of Nations to take more account of women's interests. This might mean seeking independent nationality rights for married women, debating labour legislation, looking into the situation of women refugees, investigating the traffic in women and children, mobilizing women's representatives in support of disarmament, or warning of the dangers accompanying the rise of the dictators. Along the way, women from each country found themselves either resisted by international agencies fearful of offending member states, or used by them to publicize objectives that the women would not necessarily have given priority. As Britain's Helena Swanwick ruefully put it, she was assigned at the league 'a sort of rag-bag of miseries and forlorn hopes'; or as America's Mildred Scott Olmsted more positively expressed it, activists came to see 'the connection between peace and freedom and minorities and the right to self-determination as all parts of the whole' – to see, that is, 'the inter-relatedness of all social problems'.[18] Acceptance of diverse goals seemed inevitable once female internationalists were no longer united by their disfranchisement. Since the upheavals of world war had persuaded the United States, Britain and many European states to extend votes to women, an undue focus on the vote during the inter-war years would only have underlined the obvious differences of circumstance and outlook between white Western women and their sisters in other parts of the world.[19]

There were differences, too, among British and American feminists, and they had an unfortunate habit of breaking through the formal record of collaboration. Such differences were partly the inevitable result of their two countries' contrasting social, economic and political conditions after 1918. In the United States, activists were affected by a period of economic expansion and political reaction, succeeded in the 1930s by a depression that was the worst in the world and a political response to it that showed the dynamism of a reunited and liberalized Democratic party. Following the American rejection of League of Nations membership, they were also faced with isolationist pressures which mounted with the collapse of the international economy and the growing conviction, in certain quarters, that the United States had unworthily entered the First World War as a result of the self-interested manoeuvres of munitions manufacturers and international bankers. In Britain, by contrast, the post-war years were economically difficult for women from the outset and, while British membership of the league gave them one advantage in internationalism, the strength of conservatism between the wars worked against feminists who had traditionally looked for encouragement to a more interventionist liberalism and socialism.

An additional strain for campaigners on both sides of the Atlantic came from the marked chill that affected Anglo-American relations as the United States emerged from the First World War 'as a competitor on a global scale', while Britain struggled to reassert its power, unsuccessfully in the 1920s but with some success after America 'retreated into economic isolationism' in the 1930s.[20] John Moser's recent study of Anglophobia in the United States from 1921 to 1948 provides a stimulating reminder of the hatred that was directed by some sections of American public opinion against the British Empire, social system and prominent politicians. A real 'special relationship' between the United States and Britain, Moser argues, was impossible until it was clear that in any transatlantic alliance, America 'would be the dominant power'.[21]

Under these circumstances, it is perhaps not surprising that just as British and American suffragists had been divided between and among themselves by their diverse degrees of commitment to pacifism during the First World War, so post-war feminists in the United States and Britain were divided over how far to pursue peace and women's rights through international channels and how far to proceed through national agencies. Hence American activists, drawing on a stronger tradition of organized female consumerism than existed in Britain, asserted their power as consumers in the prosperous 1920s and brought pressure to bear on government for tariff reductions. They likewise displayed a distinctive concern for Latin American women, and rallied to an opportunity not straightforwardly presented to British women of backing the Kellogg-Briand Pact of 1928, designed to outlaw war. In the following decade, they played a leading part in agitating for an inquiry into 'the munitions industry's influence on foreign policy'. And between 1939 and 1941 they were obliged to respond to an 'America First', militantly conservative and largely female branch of pacifism which did not have an equivalent in Britain. Among British women activists, while there was during the 1920s some opposition to war profiteering comparable to that which peaked in the United States during the 1930s, the focus was primarily on the operations of the League of Nations, on female emancipation in various parts of the empire and on the relative merits of pacifism and anti-Fascism.[22]

American feminists were obviously disadvantaged by their geographical and political distance from the headquarters of international endeavours at Geneva. Alice Paul of the National Woman's Party (NWP) therefore urged a British collaborator on nationality questions in the 1930s to get European women to act 'without our having to work from this Hemisphere as we are so far away'.[23] She was convinced that 'Our greatest difficulty in doing anything [in Geneva] ... lay of course in the fact that we were outside of the League'. This outsider status provoked animosity, and Carrie Catt felt obliged to warn an English ally that 'whatever you hear in Geneva about the United States or anybody in it is pretty sure to be a big, black lie'.[24] Furthermore, the importance of American money in keeping international organizations going was acknowledged but not always applauded, since the power of the purse might incline those who wielded it to assume the power of command.[25] Accordingly, one wealthy and assertive American internationalist, Alva Belmont, in 1929 confided to Paul that 'I do not believe ... we will get any assistance at all from England. They take the position that they are friendly to us, but are very jealous of our power and will not in any way assist us to increase it'.[26]

However, British jealousy of their powerful ally, though it did exist, cannot alone explain the inter-war tensions between British and American feminists. Reformers in the two countries had competed in doing good since the nineteenth century, and their tradition of accepting observers and collaborators from overseas still continued. Thus, for instance, Elizabeth Robins, Hazel Hunkins-Hallinan, Betty Gram and Crystal Eastman were able to work in the British movement after the First World War, and Ray Strachey, the half-American historian of that movement and biographer of Millicent Fawcett, was an ardent Anglophile who once confided to Fawcett that she thought 'Englishness ... and the characteristics of it' was 'one of the solidly good things in the world'. The American-born British MP, Nancy Astor, modelled her consultative Committee of Women's Organizations on the Women's Joint Consultative Committee that she had observed during her 1922 trip to the United States.[27] And other British feminists made similarly instructive and successful visits.

Notable among them was IWSA's Margery Corbett Ashby, who paid tribute to the immense kindness of the women she encountered in 1925, when she was asked to speak all over the United States and felt she could have gone on doing so indefinitely. Her reception encouraged further tours in 1934 and 1937. In the course of these travels, Corbett Ashby may have retained an element of British pride, enjoying her 'distinguished visitor' status and reporting the 'touching ... admiration for England' that she encountered. She even informed her devoted mother that after one meeting 'they said no American woman could make such a finished speech, so well constructed & expressed'. Moreover, as a staunch supporter of the League of Nations, Corbett Ashby both reproached and patronized her American hosts by telling them that not only were they 'shirking their responsibilities' by not joining the league, but that 'far too much fuss was being made about [the] ... fact & that the League would go on quite well without them'.

On the other hand, awareness of American generosity drew Corbett Ashby across the Atlantic; and when in 1925 she 'struck three other money raising campaigns & ... [found] it difficult to push in', she was deeply grateful that Harriot Stanton Blatch kindly came to her rescue and offered to seek funds for the IWSA. During her visits Corbett Ashby formed many useful contacts and renewed her close links with American feminists such as M. Carey Thomas, whom she saw as 'a wonderfully able woman', and Carrie Catt, who remained in regular touch and during the 1940s was still paying tribute to the English woman's 'long years of steadfast hard work ... [for] the women's movement'. In addition, Corbett Ashby left chauvinism behind when she used her lectures to equate the causes of feminism and pacifism. To this end, she attempted to alert American women to the creeping menace of Fascism, stressed that 'Anglo-American co-operation is essential to world peace' and highlighted 'the splendid work of American women's organizations in educating their home opinion on the great issues of world policy'.[28]

Yet undermining the accumulated goodwill between British and American campaigners in the inter-war years was the determined bid of affluent radicals from the National Woman's Party (NWP) of the United States to export their opposition to protective legislation for women. They took their case to the national and international associations of women, and to Geneva; and they began with Britain, as Crystal Eastman recounted. In 1925 she celebrated the creation in London of 'the first national group of what is bound to become a world-wide Equal Rights Committee', formed to 'guard the rights of women and watch over their real interests in all international agreements, treaties and "conventions", and to advocate and proceed with the full program of Equal Rights for men and women throughout civilization'.[29]

The debate over protective legislation in the workplace had disturbed British feminists and labour women alike before it had surfaced in the United States, because Britain's prior industrialization had politicized the issue there as early as the 1840s. But in the 1920s, reanimated by NWP shock troops on the international scene, it became more disruptive in class terms, dividing British labour women who favoured protection from bourgeois feminists who stressed the importance of freedom. The British were not polarized by any equivalent of America's proposed Equal Rights Amendment, which was introduced by the NWP and allegedly threatened hard-won protective laws for women,[30] thereby alienating the powerful network of social reformist feminists who were mobilized in bodies like the League of Women Voters (LWV, 1920). Nevertheless, the protection question soon had Britain's activists at odds at home and abroad.

Matters came to a head internationally at the IWSA conference of 1926, when the NWP applied for membership with a view to finding a platform for its equal rights position and undermining the influence of the LWV, which represented American women in the alliance. Although its application was turned down, the NWP won support from nine out of the 12 British delegates who were attending the conference. In Britain, sympathy for the American radicals was considerable in NUSEC; the Women's Freedom League (1907); and the Six Point Group (SPG, 1921), which withdrew its own bid for membership of IWSA as a gesture of solidarity. Some British women then backed the NWP as it continued its campaign for equal rights treaties through new international organizations and at international gatherings.

The diplomatic Corbett Ashby attempted to keep the peace between feuding American feminists and to contain the fallout in Britain. She was, however, disappointed in her hope of sustaining 'unofficial co-operation' between IWSA and the NWP, since the radical Americans were well aware that Mrs Catt had worked behind the scenes to retain the LWV's unchallenged authority in IWSA, even threatening to remove American financial assistance for the alliance if the NWP was admitted. To make matters worse, and notwithstanding Catt's friendship with Corbett Ashby, the dispute encouraged transatlantic feminist friction. In essence, it made the American leader very conscious of the advantages of her time as head of IWSA, when she had 'held every rein in my own hands': a control, Catt felt, that the British had always resented.[31]

Corbett Ashby was equally incapable of quelling support for the NWP in Britain. While internecine feminist fights were routinely condemned by all concerned as a 'terrible waste of time & energy', British allies of the NWP admired the vigorous leadership of women like Alice Paul and Doris Stevens. Lady Rhondda of the SPG was

> absolutely clear that the torch of the militants which has been handed from one side to another of the Atlantic time & again during the last century is now in the hands of the Woman's Party & I would follow you if I were the only woman in Europe to do it. But I should not be the only woman.

Rhondda, like NWP members, was convinced that most women activists were not feminists but social reformers, 'interested in a dozen things besides equality'. Unfortunately for those of her radical persuasion, social reformist feminists were similarly fond of getting their own way, with IWSA principals allegedly 'blackening the name of the N.W.P.' and Rhondda expressing the opinion that only a visit to England by Paul and Stevens could improve matters.[32]

Thus after the First World War, as Susan Becker has shown, the dispute over equal rights inadvertently precipitated 'a schism in the international women's movement'.[33] The issue undoubtedly plunged American and British feminist internationalists into widely publicized wrangling which was not helpful to the fortunes of their respective women's movements, and which also put a strain on Anglo-American feminist relations. But its nature should not be misrepresented, as feminist quarrels so often are. On this occasion, British and American women were divided according to principle as well as by nationality, and principled differences may have value. They are certainly not just a feature of reform campaigns run by women. As one observer wrote philosophically to the editor of the *New York Times*,

> while appreciating your point that it would be much better for all women to agree, wouldn't it be much better if all men could agree? Yet no one expects them to, or condemns them because they don't, as it is clearly recognized that progress will always result in controversy, until an ideal state is reached.[34]

The dispute was, none the less, peculiarly trying at the international level because, as Rhondda acknowledged in 1928, 'international feminism is still a bit difficult to arouse interest in except in the already educated'. In this situation, the British preoccupation with women in India, Hong Kong or the white dominions served to point up an imperial connection of which Americans disapproved, just as the increasing tendency of radical American feminists to pursue internationalism through pan-American endeavours, underlined the distinctive overseas concerns of the United States. And during the 1930s especially, the tendency of pacifism to take precedence over feminism, and to encourage isolationism rather than internationalism, was difficult for any but the most determined feminist-internationalists to resist.[35]

Conclusion

British and American feminists continued to work together during the 1920s and 1930s but found no objective with the unifying power of the vote – urged before 1914 with cordiality at international gatherings and pursued nationally as local circumstances allowed. To some extent, their loosely connected movement was uncoupling. The United States and Britain were both affected by the traumas of the First World War, post-war recovery, political instability and economic depression. Yet their experience of these forces was very different, aggravating the divergences that had always existed between British and American feminists and had happily been muted in more progressive times, when the advance of suffragism had generated extraordinary optimism and the power balance between the two countries had been more equal. Throughout the inter-war years, activists in the United States and Britain alike struggled to give permanent significance to their enfranchisement and to capture the allegiance of younger women. But as they did so, race, class and international differences in particular surfaced to erode their former links and to strenghten their preference for their own ways of working. That feminists did not, under such difficult circumstances, contribute to the inter-war tensions that beset the larger Anglo-American relationship is one of their major achievements.

Notes

1. Quoted in M. Randall, *Improper Bostonian: Emily Greene Balch* (New York, 1964), p. 308.
2. C. Bolt, *The Women's Movement in the United States and Britain From the 1790s to the 1920s* (London and Amherst, 1993), and C. Bolt, *Feminist Ferment: The 'Woman Question' in the USA and England, 1870–1940* (London, 1995).
3. F. Thistlethwaite, *America and the Atlantic Community: Anglo-American Aspects* (New York, 1963), pp. 174–6.
4. See, for instance, E. Pethick-Lawrence, *My Part in a Changing World* (London, 1938), p. 308.
5. See C. Bolt, *Sisterhood Questioned? Race, Class and Internationalism in American and British Feminism, c.1880s–1980s* (London, forthcoming).
6. Florence Luscomb's journal, Florence Luscomb Papers, Schlesinger Library, Radcliffe College, Cambridge, Massachusetts; see also 'Personal Recollections of Suffrage Campaigning', and article in *St Louis Post-Dispatch*, 5 March 1976, both in the Luscomb Papers.
7. S. Holton, '"To Educate Women into Rebellion": Elizabeth Cady Stanton and the Creation of a Transatlantic Network of Radical Suffragists', *American Historical Review*, 99 (1994), 1112–36, especially 1119.
8. S. H. Strom, 'Leadership and Tactics in the American Woman Movement: A New Perspective from Massachusetts', *Journal of American History*, 62 (1975), 307–10.
9. Mrs Pankhurst to Florence Luscomb, 8 July 1913 and June 1914, in Florence Luscomb Papers.
10. A. John, *Elizabeth Robins: Staging a Life, 1862–1952* (London, 1995), pp. 142–72, quotations from p. 104.
11. Article on Doris Stevens from *Time and Tide*, London, 26 October 1928, in Doris Stevens Papers, Schlesinger Library, Radcliffe College, Cam-

bridge, Massachusetts; K. Cook and N. Evans, '"The Petty Antics of the Bell-Ringing Boisterous Band"? The Women's Suffrage Movement in Wales, 1890–1918', in A. J. John (ed.), *Our Mothers' Land: Chapters in Welsh Women's History, 1830–1939* (Cardiff, 1991), p. 165; Strom, 'Leadership and Tactics', 306–7.

12. Article entitled 'Memories of the Militant Movement in the United States', from *The Women's Bulletin*, 2 May 1958, in Doris Stevens Papers.
13. See ibid.
14. C. Murphy, *The Women's Suffrage Movement and Irish Society in the Early Twentieth Century* (Hemel Hempstead, 1989), pp. 50–51; D. Rubinstein, *A Different World for Women: The Life of Millicent Garrett Fawcett* (Columbus, 1991), ch. 16 and pp. 231–2; R. Jeffreys-Jones, *Changing Differences: Women and the Shaping of American Foreign Policy, 1917–1994* (New Brunswick, 1995), ch. 2; R. B. Fowler, *Carrie Catt: Feminist Politician* (Boston, 1986); R. Wiebe, *Self-rule: A Cultural History of American Democracy* (Chicago and London, 1995), pp. 152–5 and 167–70 on Catt; and C. Bolt, *Sisterhood Questioned?*, ch. 3, on the broad impact of the First World War on the American and British women's movements.
15. Rubinstein, *A Different World for Women*, p. 258, and chs 19 and 20; L. B. Costin, 'Feminism, Pacifism, Internationalism and the 1915 International Congress of Women', *Women's Studies International Forum*, 5 (1982), 301–15; B. W. Cook (ed.), *Crystal Eastman on Women and Revolution* (Oxford and New York, 1978), pp. 177–81; C. Law, *Suffrage and Power: The Women's Movement, 1918–1928* (London and New York, 1997), ch. 9.
16. Quoted in Cook, *Crystal Eastman*, p. 197.
17. J. Vellacott, 'Feminist Consciousness and the First World War', *History Workshop*, 23 (1987), 81–101; Rubinstein, *A Different World for Women*, p. 217f.; S. Oldfield, *Spinsters of this Parish: The Life and Times of F. M. Mayor and Mary Sheepshanks* (London, 1984), ch. 9; A. Wiltsher, *Most Dangerous Women: Feminist Peace Campaigners of the Great War* (London, 1985), ch. 4; J. Vellacott Newberry, 'Anti-War Suffragists', *History*, 62 (1977), 411–25; B. J. Steinson, *American Women's Activism in World War One* (New York, 1982), ch. 1; H. H. Alonso, *Peace as a Women's Issue: A History of the U.S. Movement for World Peace and Women's Rights* (Syracuse, 1993), chs 2 and 3; D. G. Daniels, *Always a Sister: The Feminism of Lillian D. Wald. A Biography* (New York, 1995), ch. 9; Pethick-Lawrence, *My Part*, ch. 21; C. R. Marchand, *The American Peace Movement and Social Reform* (Princeton, NJ, 1972), ch. 6; Randall, *Improper Bostonian*, ch. 6; J. T. Smith, 'Rent, Peace, Votes: Working-Class Women and Political Activity in the First World War', in E. Breitenbach and E. Gordon (eds), *Out of Bounds: Women in Scottish Society, 1800–1945* (Edinburgh, 1992), pp. 181–4.
18. H. Swanwick, *I Have Been Young* (London, 1949), p. 385; C. Foster, *Women for all Seasons: The Story of the Women's International League for Peace and Freedom* (Athens, GA, 1989), p. 123; C. Miller, 'Lobbying the League: Women's International Organizations and the League of Nations' (DPhil thesis, University of Oxford, 1992); C. Miller, 'Geneva – the Key to Equality: Inter-War Feminists and the League of Nations', *Women's History Review*, 3 (1994), 219–45; L. J. Rupp, *Worlds of Women:*

The Making of an International Women's Movement (Princeton, NJ, 1997), *passim*; J. Alberti, *Beyond Suffrage: Feminists in War and Peace, 1914–28* (London, 1989), ch. 8.

19. M. Bosch with A. Kloosterman (eds), *Politics and Friendship: Letters from the International Suffrage Alliance, 1902–1942* (Columbus, OH, 1990), pp. 142–3, 175f.; L. Rupp, 'Constructing Internationalism: The Case of Transnational Women's Organizations, 1888–1945', *American Historical Review*, 99 (1994), 1571–1600.

20. P. J. Cain and A. G. Hopkins, *British Imperialism: Crisis and Deconstruction, 1914–1990* (London, 1993), especially p. 4 and ch. 5; P. S. Bagwell and G. E. Mingay, *Britain and America: A Study of Economic Change* (London, 1987), chs 9 and 10; D. Beddoe, *Back to Home and Duty: Women Between the Wars, 1918–1939* (London, 1989).

21. J. E. Moser, *Twisting the Lion's Tail: Anglophobia in the United States, 1921–48* (London, 1999), Introduction and *passim*; quotation from p. 7.

22. Jeffreys-Jones, *Changing Differences*, pp. 35–6, 73, 98; M. Ceadel, *Pacifism in Britain, 1914–45* (Oxford, 1980) provides a full account of the ideas and activists of British pacifism, but has little to say about the British section of WILPF – except (p. 319) that it had 'no clear policy'; M. Pugh, *Women and the Women's Movement in Britain, 1914–1959* (London, 1992), pp. 105–7; Alberti, *Beyond Suffrage*, ch. 8; J. Liddington, *The Long Road to Greenham: Feminism and Anti-Militarism in Britain since 1820* (London, 1989), pp. 132f.; G. Bussey and M. Tims, *Pioneers for Peace: Women's International League for Peace and Freedom, 1915–1965* (London, 1980), *passim*, but especially p. 144; Randall, *Improper Bostonian*, p. 307, and chs 13–15. The Kellogg-Briand Pact was complicated for European women by the desire not to seem hostile to the rival Soviet peace initiative: see Oldfield, *Spinsters of this Parish*, pp. 250–51.

23. Alice Paul to Dorothy Evans, 2 April 1934, Alice Paul Papers, Schlesinger Library, Radcliffe College, Cambridge, Massachusetts.

24. Alice Paul to Doris Stevens, 9 October 1930, Doris Stevens Papers; Carrie Chapman Catt to Kathleen Courtney, 13 December 1932, in Committee on the Cause and Cure of War Papers, Schlesinger Library, Radcliffe College, Cambridge, Massachusetts.

25. Charles Chatfield, *For Peace and Justice: Pacifism in America, 1914–1941* (Knoxville, TN, 1971), p. 95; Rupp, 'Feminism, Pacifism, Internationalism', p. 1579.

26. Mrs O. H. P. Belmont to Alice Paul, 16 September 1929, Alice Paul Papers.

27. B. Harrison, *Prudent Revolutionaries: Portraits of British Feminists between the Wars* (Oxford and New York, 1987), pp. 70, 179 for quotations; p. 75 on Astor.

28. See letters amd press cuttings relating to Corbett Ashby's USA tours of 1925, 1934 and 1937; Carrie Chapman Catt to Corbett Ashby, 14 August 1942 and 19 August 1946; letter of Corbett Ashby to the Prime Minister, n.d. [1935]; and 'Message to the USA', n.d. [1938]: all in Margery Irene Corbett Ashby Papers, Fawcett Library, London; see also Catt to Corbett Ashby, 9 February 1928, in Committee on the Cause and Cure of War Papers.

29. Cook, *Crystal Eastman*, p. 165.

30. The NWP in fact argued that it was not 'opposed to industrial legisla-

tion', merely advocating 'the removal of sex in protective laws': see *Equal Rights*, 20 October 1923, p. 285.

31. S. D. Becker, *The Origins of the Equal Rights Amendment: American Feminism between the Wars* (Westport, CT, and London, 1981), pp. 165–71, especially on Catt's role in the equal rights dispute: Catt quotation taken from p. 167; Cook, *Crystal Eastman*, pp. 155–72; P. Graves, *Labour Women: Women in British Working-Class Politics, 1918–1939* (Cambridge, 1994), pp. 139f.; Alberti, *Beyond Suffrage*, pp. 204–10; letter of Margery Corbett Ashby to Alice Paul, 15 December 1925, in Alice Paul Papers.

32. See letters of Rhondda to Alice Paul and Doris Stevens, and Rhondda to Helen Archdale, 1926–31, in Doris Stevens Papers.

33. Becker, *The Origins of the Equal Rights Amendment*, p. 186.

34. Mrs Stephen Pell to the editor, *New York Times*, 20 December 1933, in Alice Paul Papers.

35. See Alonso, *Peace as a Women's Issue*, pp. 125–6, on the overshadowing of women's concerns by general foreign policy issues in American peace organisations during the 1930s; and Rhondda to Helen Archdale, 4 June 1928, in Doris Stevens Papers. The whole range of British and American women's activities in inter-war internationalism is discussed in Bolt, *Sisterhood Questioned?*, ch. 4.

CHAPTER ELEVEN

Public Face and Public Space: The Projection of Britain in America before the Second World War

Fred M. Leventhal

In the aftermath of the First World War, politicians and publicists struggled to define a new image for Britain as they came to terms with a world in which its economic and imperial dominance was increasingly called into question. In 1932 Sir Stephen Tallents, a visionary propagandist who was then serving as secretary of the Empire Marketing Board, warned fellow countrymen of the danger of neglecting the projection of national personality. In the altered circumstances of the post-war world, self-promotion abroad was, he proclaimed, imperative if Britain were to continue to play a significant international role. In identifying those attributes of national character that appealed most strongly to other countries, Tallents cited such institutions as the monarchy and the navy, cultural icons like the English Bible, Shakespeare and Dickens, and qualities like the tradition of justice and the reputation for fair play. Britain should 'project upon the screen of world opinion such a picture of herself as will create a belief in her ability to serve the world under the new order as she served it under the old'.[1]

It was partly to remedy a perceived publicity deficiency *vis à vis* the totalitarian powers that the British Council was launched in 1934 to promote a wider appreciation of British civilization abroad. In view of retrospective American antipathy to propaganda during the First World War, the Foreign Office imposed a ban on official publicity in the United States, restricting its cultural operations to a small press bureau in New York, known as the British Library of Information.[2] Thus, when the noted Boston museum curator W. G. Constable appealed to the British Council for a sponsored exhibition of watercolours to foster Anglo-American cultural relations, he was informed that the organization was barred from activity in America. The council concurred in the British Ambassador's view that

> we should do more harm than good, due to the fact that we are known to be a semi-official propaganda organisation and that such propaganda and of such organisations the Americans have a deep

distrust. Others with whom the matter has been discussed agree
with the Ambassador's views, saying that Messers Hitler and Mus-
solini are doing quite enough for Great Britain without any help
from us.[3]

Anxiety that cultural projection should not be perceived as propaganda
was clearly warranted. An October 1939 poll revealed that 40 per cent of
Americans interviewed believed that the United States had been a victim
of 'propaganda and selfish interests' in entering the First World War.[4]

Sir Ronald Lindsay, long-time British emissary in Washington and an
astute observer of American opinion, appreciated the delicacy of Anglo-
American relations, strained by post-war American disenchantment with
Europe, cancelled war debt payments, and resurgent isolationism, especially in the hinterland. Anglophilia might pervade the eastern academic
and social establishment, but anti-British sentiment was rampant among
Irish-Americans, Jews hostile to the restrictive immigration policy in
Palestine, and liberals who decried England as class-ridden and oppres-
sively imperialistic. Even American internationalists, usually supportive
of British interests, balked at Chamberlain's appeasement of Hitler.
Americans were, as Lord Lothian (Lindsay's successor in Washington)
acknowledged, 'peculiarly ready to suspect all and sundry attempting to
use undue influence. The British are held to be great adepts at the
subtlest arts of propaganda and capable of luring innocent Americans
into their traps'.[5]

Not even the monarchy, invariably and paradoxically an object of
fascination for Yankee republicans, was immune from criticism. As
Prince of Wales, Edward garnered media attention and popularity during two highly publicized visits to the United States, while his abdication
in order to marry his American mistress merely enhanced his romantic
aura. Although Lindsay upheld the prohibition against overt propaganda,[6] he urged a psychological initiative as a way of generating
American goodwill towards England:

> The late King George broadcasting to his Empire, Mr Baldwin's
> speech in the House on the abdication crisis, the Stratford Shake-
> speare Company, *Goodbye, Mr Chips* by [James] Hilton, Noel
> Coward's film *Cavalcade*, the successes of Great Britain, the calm-
> ness and dignity of her people, these are the things that move
> America.[7]

Among other initiatives, the Ambassador endorsed a substantial British
contribution to the New York World's Fair of 1939 through an exhibit
that emphasized British cultural achievements.

While British officials remained punctilious about propaganda even
after 1939, they came to recognize the benefit of American moral and
material support as the prospect of war with Germany loomed ever

more menacingly and mobilized the British Broadcasting Corporation (BBC), the Department of Overseas Trade, and the Ministry of Information in a campaign to cultivate American opinion. Officials also welcomed spontaneous initiatives by novelists, film-makers, American broadcasters and, more sceptically, lecturers – who frequently turned out to be leftists critical of imperial policies – to convey ingratiating images of Britain. In this campaign the British could count on the tacit goodwill of President Roosevelt, facing his own uphill battle to overcome neutralist sentiment in Congress, not to mention large sections of the nation, and of interventionists like the journalist William Allan White. Roosevelt readily acknowledged the impact of such literary works as Jan Struther's *Mrs Miniver* (1939), Alice Duer Miller's *The White Cliffs* (1940), and Eric Knight's *This Above All* (1941) in enlisting American sympathies.[8] In the months before Pearl Harbor, the best-selling novels in the United States were emotionally charged depictions of contemporary Britain: Knight's *This Above All*, James Hilton's *Random Harvest* and Richard Llewellyn's evocative *How Green Was My Valley*. All were adapted into commercially successful films which compounded their impact, as were *The White Cliffs [of Dover]* and *Mrs Miniver*, a Hollywood travesty of Struther's pre-war *Times* women's columns.[9] These movies followed upon the earlier commercial success of *Cavalcade*, *South Riding* and *Goodbye, Mr Chips*. Many of them featured established British actors, like Robert Donat or Ronald Colman, Walter Pidgeon, who was actually Canadian, or the Anglo-Irish Greer Garson, who epitomized for American audiences English characteristics of good breeding, politeness and restraint. These books (and their cinematic spin-offs) dealt, sometimes obliquely, with class relationships but usually stressed the permeability of social barriers, especially in wartime.

In contrast to the First World War propaganda focus on Hun atrocities, the British now sought to project positive images of themselves and to stress affinities with their North American cousins. What seemed crucial to Foreign Office policy-makers no less than to cultural arbiters was to ensure that Britain was presented abroad in a favourable light. While rearmament efforts and resistance to Fascism needed greater emphasis – especially after Munich – the propagation of shared political and cultural values was perceived as an even more potent weapon in winning American hearts. As one official commented,

> We must keep it all on the high moral plane & must try so to talk that an American looking at Europe will not see ... a welter of power politics but rather the simple clear cut issue of 'Liberty (with a capital L) versus Tyranny'. Only then will he realise that we have common cause with America, and one which is founded on spiritual values and ideals.[10]

While it was no longer appropriate – or politically correct – to portray
Britain as steeped in archaic traditions, holding sway over an empire on
which the sun never set, it was equally clear that American anglophilia
was deeply enmeshed in nostalgia for a romanticized past, a sentiment
unabashedly exploited in the three cultural events to be examined here:
the British Pavilion at the New York World's Fair, the visit of King
George VI and Queen Elizabeth to the United States in 1939, and the
exhibit of British war art at the Museum of Modern Art in 1941. It was
essential to show that Britain could adapt to modern times, that it was
no less democratic than the United States and that significant strides
had been made in eliminating social inequities. It was as relevant to
American national identity as to Britain's that common values of free
speech and equal justice under law be vindicated. Social hierarchy and
élitist institutions were tolerable only if economic disparities were miti-
gated by state action, if class barriers did not impede the advancement
of the talented and ambitious. But at the same time it would have been
a betrayal of its heritage to suggest that Britain had become so 'Americanized' that its distinctive characteristics had been effaced. The very
threat to survival that Hitler posed made its immutable features, its
landscape and political institutions, the pageantry of its traditions, all
the more potent as symbols of the durability of Anglo-Saxon civilization. For these reasons, official and more popular projections of British
culture tended to stress both continuity and change, a linkage calculated
to reassure Americans that their imagined Britain would not vanish
even as it adjusted to the exigencies of wartime.

Once the New York World's Fair received the sanction of the International Bureau of Exhibitions in May 1937, the British consented to
participate, although confusion abounded as to which government department was responsible for planning their contribution.[11] What they
did agree on was how to reconcile the depiction of the past with the
fair's theme: 'building the world of tomorrow'. The Foreign Office
suggested a pavilion that would represent the British way of life, 'its
foundations, development, enduring qualities, dignity, and harmony',
while testifying to 'our adaptability to a changing world'.[12] Lindsay,
echoing the emphasis on continuity, urged that it 'typify Old England',
not merely because this would be popular with Americans, but because
traditional institutions and industries were Britain's strongest suit. While
endorsing a display of industrial goods, he was more sceptical about a
housing exhibit, since British standards fell below American expectations, but his misgivings were ignored in the determination to show
how Britain was improving the lives of its inhabitants.[13]

The World's Fair authorities designated a commanding site on Constitutional Mall, the central avenue of the fair grounds, for the British

Pavilion, appropriate for America's 'closest kinsman among nations'.[14] The *New Statesman*, sneering at imperial pretension, claimed that 'the building has little but size, respectability and a charming garden to commend it', but the official World's Fair guidebook described it as 'huge and majestic'.[15] Since this was intended to be the most massive international exhibition yet held, the British tailored their role accordingly, less to avoid being outdone by other nations, than because it offered an ideal venue in which to celebrate Britain's contribution to civilization and the increasingly vital friendship between the two nations.

Throughout the pavilion, history, tradition and standards of workmanship were paraded, while the American fascination with the British past was fully exploited. In the so-called Court of Honour, decorative panels and shields depicted the historic heraldry of Britain, complemented by antique plate from the City livery companies. A royal room emphasized 'the manner in which Britain's history has centred round her kings' with large paintings, one of which symbolized the age of colonization with a colonist on a boat bearing aloft a banner of the United States.[16] Adjacent to the royal room visitors could see replicas of the Crown jewels, plus royal swords, sceptres and other ornaments of the regalia. Several halls were devoted to heavy machinery and shipbuilding, while British superiority in the manufacture of fine woollens, china and leather goods were amply documented, all conveying an image of solidity and quality. An exhibit largely organized by Sir Kenneth Clark, Director of the National Gallery, contained a sampling of twentieth-century painting from Augustus John, Wilson Steer and W. R. Sickert to Paul Nash, Stanley Spencer and Graham Sutherland, testifying not only to the breadth of Clark's taste but also to stylistic continuity in British art. His comments, characteristically understated, never intimated artistic genius or radical innovation. 'Charm, freedom, a native elegance, and poetry are more natural to English painters', he noted, 'than power of composition.'[17]

Although much of the British Pavilion was devoted to re-creations of the past or to material achievements, Public Welfare Hall pointed to

> another and a newer Britain – a country where great schemes of social security, financed by contributions from employer, worker, and Government, protect the working population against the worst evils of sickness, bereavement, unemployment, and old age.[18]

Viewers were assured that substandard housing was rapidly vanishing from a Britain in which garden suburbs proliferated. While conceding that slums and 'grimy industrial cities' had not yet been entirely eradicated, the displays drew attention to new housing, maternity and child welfare services, and employment exchanges, without mentioning distressed areas, derelict mines and factories, labour camps or the dole. With a nod to the American faith in limited state intervention, the guidebook noted that 'in the town of today public and private effort in combination are steadily and surely carrying through a process of social transformation'.[19] Public Welfare Hall, thematically tendentious, demonstrated that Lindsay may have been correct to advocate an exhibit that would 'typify Old England'. Most observers, unfamiliar with actual industrial conditions may have been convinced by the distorted image of social progress, but more discerning visitors must have recognized that the purported age of universal welfare had not yet dawned.

For Americans, the most awesome exhibit was probably Magna Carta Hall, where the cardinal document of British constitutional history was on view, strategically positioned next to a genealogy of George Washington, revealing his descent from King John and 25 of the barons. Nothing could have demonstrated more effectively how inextricably linked were the political cultures of the two nations, especially since the World's Fair was ostensibly devised to commemorate the sesquicentennial of Washington's inauguration. To reinforce its propaganda impact, a pamphlet explicating Magna Carta was disseminated to schools throughout the United States, with a forward by John C. Fitzpatrick, editor of Washington's writings.[20] As if its implications were not abundantly clear, the *New York Times* pronounced that 'this precious parchment ... is as much our heritage as Britain's'.[21]

When wartime risks made it inadvisable to transport the sacred document back across the Atlantic after the fair closed in October 1939, the Foreign Office readily seized upon a ceremony presenting it to the Library of Congress for the duration of the war 'for a little legitimate and valuable publicity'. Officials also suggested that the Ambassador's speech on that occasion 'contain by inference some reminder that the principles it enshrines must be vindicated anew by each generation. The moral', it was noted, 'is rather obvious'.[22]

It might be supposed that the huge popularity of the British Pavilion – more than 14.3 million visits by the end of the 1939 season[23] – would have been grounds enough to reopen it in 1940, but financial constraints initially prompted a decision to dismantle the structure. When the fair's impresario, Grover Whalen, claimed that the British Pavilion was 'an admirable asset from the point of view of propaganda', he was summarily informed that 'the propaganda aspect of the matter could be dismissed at once, as it was not our intention to indulge in attempts on American soil to persuade the United States that their interest lay in giving support to Great Britain'.[24] Not that withdrawal would itself fail to generate some propaganda advantage, as one Treasury official pointed out:

> If there is any criticism of our refusal to incur expenditure in
> keeping the British Pavilion open, the fact that we are concentrat-
> ing all our efforts on fighting to save democracy provides a complete
> answer which we think would be generally accepted, and indeed
> respected in America.[25]

However, once France consented to reopen its pavilion and the World's
Fair authorities to underwrite exhibits, British officials, at risk of 'appearing either rather sanctimonious or mean', decided that it was
politically expedient to 'conform our action to that of the French'.[26]

Of all the visitors to the British Pavilion, none were more highly
celebrated than King George VI and Queen Elizabeth, who made a
whirlwind stop on the way from Washington to the Roosevelt country
home at Hyde Park in June 1939, arriving by motorcade from the
Battery. Plans for the first visit to the United States by reigning British
monarchs had been in the works ever since the coronation, but the
largely social – and indeed private – aspects of the royal tour acquired
political overtones by June 1939. Roosevelt's initial proposal for a
purely private visit, shielding the monarchs from the glare of publicity
and from queries about diplomatic implications, was illusory. The British Embassy feared that if the occasion were monopolized by the
President, it might incur the wrath of overlooked American interests –
political and regional – which contended for their share of royal attention. As plans evolved, it became an official state visit, but a very brief
one – lasting only four days. Lindsay saw some advantage in its brevity,
a way to defuse political connotations. Had the American interlude
been the principal purpose of the journey, it would have 'given rise to
every possible misunderstanding'. Even though no conceivable diplomatic undertakings could emerge from a royal visit, it was important to
reinforce 'favourable emotional factors' whose benefit would redound
in the 'warm feelings of the people' and in improved Anglo-American
relations.[27]

The official announcement of the forthcoming trip was positively
reported in American newspapers, assuring a cordial welcome 'despite
the fact that the American people feel convinced their own government
and nation must travel its own way'.[28] But press response was by no
means universally enthusiastic: the Hearst papers were cool, and the
Chicago Tribune decidedly hostile. The palace was disturbed by an
article in *Scribner's Magazine* entitled 'Selling George VI to the U.S.',
which claimed that a large part of the country 'still believes that Edward,
Duke of Windsor, is the rightful owner of the British throne, and that
King George VI is a colorless, weak personality, largely on probation in
the public mind of Great Britain, as well as of the United States'.[29] Less
serious, because unpublicized, were private communications to the State

Department from those hoping to intercede behind the scenes. A New York politician, deriding the visit as a 'publicity stunt for the World's Fair', feared that it would be exploited by 'the tireless and powerful people who are perpetually seeking to get us into an alliance with England'.[30]

In the end, its success exceeded all expectations. The tone of the visit was set during the train journey across Canada, where the British monarchs frequently abandoned formal protocol and mingled with people informally. Full coverage of the transcontinental trip by American newspapers paved the way for an ebullient welcome when they arrived at Niagara Falls on 7 June, *en route* to Washington for a White House state dinner, an embassy reception, and tours of Mount Vernon, Arlington and a Civilian Conservation Corps camp. In both Washington and New York, where the streets were thronged with cheering crowds, the king and queen scored a remarkable personal triumph. The first glimpse by Americans of British royalty may have dispelled some of the magical aura, but observers were dazzled by the queen's radiant smile, unfazed by the oppressive heat, the crowds or personal fatigue, and newspapers described her appearance and outfits in lavish detail. Eric Knight reported to an English friend that

> the American people, very suddenly and unreasoningly, merely went mad and riotously crazy over the Queen, and as a result England today – almost overnight – now stands in popular estimation in the position she did several years ago. In admiration of this one woman, America has somehow blinded herself to Chamberlain, has forgotten Munich, and now sees only the strong British nation again.[31]

Not surprisingly, the reticent and unglamorous king attracted less attention. Yet the most memorable part of the visit was not its ceremonial aspects, or even the unflagging good spirits of the royal pair, but the 30 hours of what Roosevelt disingenuously referred to as 'very simple country life' at Hyde Park.[32] Here they were treated to two dinners with the Roosevelt family and selected friends, a Sunday morning service at the tiny village Episcopal church, and the publicized picnic where the king consumed his first hot dog. Photographs of the royal couple in country attire, enjoying a cookout with America's first family, emblazoned on front pages of newspapers throughout the country, struck a more responsive chord than the uniforms and tiaras and obligatory toasts at the state dinner. 'To the American people', the President told his guest, 'the essential democracy of yourself and the Queen makes the greatest appeal of all.'[33]

If the youthful monarchs triumphed as goodwill ambassadors, trading on the American fascination with royalty, it was evident that by the time of their visit the President felt impelled to instil some courage in the beleaguered British, admittedly in an avuncular spirit. As he wrote to his old friend, the Harvard historian R. B. Merriman,

> I wish the British would stop this 'We who are about to die, salute thee' attitude. Lord Lothian was here the other day, started the conversation by saying he had completely abandoned his former belief that Hitler could be dealt with as a semi-reasonable human being, and went on to say that the British for a thousand years had been the guardians of Anglo-Saxon civilization – that the sceptre or sword or something like that had dropped from their palsied fingers – that the U.S.A. must snatch it up – that F.D.R. alone could save the world ... I got mad clear through and told him that just so long as he or Britishers like him took that attitude of complete despair, the British would not be worth saving anyway. What the British need today is a good stiff grog, inducing not only the desire to save civilization but the continued belief that they can do it. In such an event they will have a lot more support from their American cousins.[34]

At Hyde Park the two leaders found time for a private conversation that convinced George VI that Britain had a reliable friend in the White House, Roosevelt having confided – erroneously it transpired – that 'if London was bombed U.S.A. would come in'.[35]

The Foreign Office, initially apprehensive given the king's inexperience and diffidence, was delighted with the success of the trip, which they believed had dispelled any lingering notion that the British monarchy was 'in any way stuffed shirt'. The geniality of the visitors elicited a desire among both press and public to demonstrate 'America's sympathy towards the democratic ideals represented by the British monarchy'.[36] Letters to President and Mrs Roosevelt generally brimmed with adulation towards the visitors, but there was some venting of spleen, ranging from outrage at the inclusion on the menu of such plebeian food as hot dogs, to indignation over the appearance of black performers at the White House state dinner, to revulsion over 'this begging trip of the King and Queen'.[37] While the royal visit had no tangible impact on entrenched isolationist sentiment, it did achieve the desired psychological effect. Warning that it would be dangerous to assume that the British government 'had America politically "in the bag"', Lindsay was none the less confident that 'our hidden reserves have been immensely strengthened'.[38]

Five months after the royal visit and two months after the war began, Kenneth Clark formed the War Artists' Advisory Committee, whose purpose was to hire artists to record both military and civil aspects of the war, either through salaried service with the armed forces or by means of official commissions for paintings and drawings that the committee would purchase and subsequently exhibit. For Clark, it was an opportunity to extend state patronage to artists, enabling them to perform national service while practising their own craft.[39] As in the case of Council for the Encouragement of Music and the Arts (CEMA), the forerunner to the Arts Council also founded in the early weeks of the war, it would testify to the importance the state placed upon the civilizing arts and the need to preserve them in time of national emergency.[40] Eventually, the committee's roster included not merely such established artists as Muirhead Bone, William Rothenstein, Stanley Spencer and Paul Nash, who had performed similar duties during the previous war, but Clark's younger protegés, like Graham Sutherland, John Piper and Henry Moore. Following an invitation from Alfred Barr, Director of New York's Museum of Modern Art in September 1940, the committee agreed to send some 75 'of the very best war artists' work for exhibition to New York'.[41]

Although the initiative for the exhibit came from America, its British organizers were quick to perceive its propaganda value, and justified it on that basis when proposals were submitted to the government's Overseas Planning Committee in October 1940.[42] The Director-General of the Ministry of Information suggested using picture captions 'to give some even tendentious comment upon the war, so long as we do not lapse into direct propaganda'.[43] Eventually, some 110 oils and watercolours were selected, supplemented by First World War pictures borrowed from the National Gallery of Canada. Because of shipping delays,[44] the exhibit could not open until May 1941, six months later than originally scheduled, and by then it had expanded to include other paintings, photographs, posters, cartoons, architectural designs and examples of camouflage, as well as films.[45]

In his introduction to the published catalogue, Herbert Read contended that the exhibit was emblematic of national identity. Anticipating that American audiences might regret the lack of bombastic battle scenes, he observed that 'though the English are energetic in action, they are restrained in expression. Our typical poetry is lyrical, not epical or even tragic ... Our typical painting is the landscape'.[46] In his speech at the opening, Lord Halifax, the new ambassador, reiterated the theme that these works of art provided insight into national character:

> You will not find heroics here. What you will find are unmistakable records of that calm and determined resolution with which the ordinary folk of Britain meet the varying hazards of this most grim war; and those who see these pictures will feel a deeper understanding of the quality of the British people.[47]

Portraits of servicemen were chosen to reflect a cross-section of ranks and social backgrounds, while Moore's justly acclaimed shelter drawings epitomized the populism that underlay the exhibit, intended to appeal to American democratic sensibilities. Several paintings represented a neo-Romantic response to bomb damage, rooted in the tradition of landscape painting. The naturalistic 'Withdrawal from Dunkerque', by unknown artist Richard Eurich, attracted considerable attention; its treatment of the disaster was subdued in tone and in colour, suffusing catastrophe with charm.[48] Pictures and photographs of ruined buildings – especially the unscathed dome of St Paul's surrounded by smoke from bombs – expressed a sense of national architectural heritage, linking the English people with their history.

Press reviews were generally positive, although most conceded that the exhibit contained little work of the highest quality. *The New Yorker* praised the absence of propaganda and emphasis on horror for its own sake, the reticence and general air of dignity.[49] The *New York World Telegram* found in the paintings an expression of 'strong faith in the English way of life, their unifying conviction that it must and will be maintained'. For its critic, the downed enemy planes depicted by Nash and others 'become the symbols of the victory of human courage over this tyranny'.[50] The entire exhibit, another critic exclaimed, 'constitutes a great boost for Britain and for British art'.[51]

Since it was impossible to transport the collection to England when the Museum of Modern Art (MOMA) show ended in September 1941, it toured Canada and the United States for several years, gradually trickling back across the Atlantic in several shipments between 1944 and 1946. In contrast to the crowds who enjoyed the royal visit and the New York World's Fair, its impact was doubtlessly more selective – limited to museum-goers – although, unlike those events, Americans all over the country saw the collection, displayed mainly at university galleries. Over 13 000 attended the MOMA show during its first two weeks, but when the exhibit opened at the San Francisco Palace of the Legion of Honor in March 1942, it drew 2000 on the first day.[52] Now that the United States had entered the war, its message had lost any unpalatable propagandistic overtones. Here, in the words of one commentator, was

> a collection of art which is an embodiment of a definite policy, the concrete results of a determination to continue the worthwhile in spite of apparent discouragement, the exemplification of the right to express what we think and feel, a policy we cherish and for which we are willing to die.[53]

It is impossible to measure precisely the impact of such cultural episodes or to determine what factors influence public opinion. These three events were symptomatic of a broader projection of British culture in America before and during the Second World War, in which films, print journalism, broadcasting and fiction were also significant. Furthermore, if American attitudes were shifting, they were certainly not doing so uniformly. Sentiment about Britain continued to show regional, ethnic and class differences. None the less, it seems fair to suggest that a cumulative process, taking place from the late 1930s to the early 1940s, transformed an isolationist America into Britain's closest ally and foreshadowed the cultural 'special relationship' that has characterized the years since 1945. Lindsay's 'hidden reserves' had not only been immensely strengthened but, after 1941, they were to be fully deployed.

Notes

1. S. Tallents, *The Projection of Britain* (London, 1932), pp. 11–14, 37, 39.
2. R. A. Butler claimed that many MPs did not understand why the British Council did not function in America, whereas left-wing critics, like Harold Laski, were able to operate with impunity. Foreign Office Minute, 16 February 1939, PRO FO 371/22827/A1143.
3. W. G. Constable to Charles Bridge, 3 April 1939; Bridge to Constable, 14 April 1939, PRO BW 63/22/USA/28/1.
4. H. Cantril and M. Strunk (eds), *Public Opinion 1935–1946* (Princeton, NJ, 1951), p. 202.
5. Lord Lothian to Lord Halifax, 22 September 1939, PRO FO 115/3418/299/89/39. Also see K. R. M. Short, '*The White Cliffs of Dover*: Promoting the Anglo-American Alliance in World War II', *Historical Journal of Film, Radio and Television*, 2 (1982), 3–5.
6. It was the British Embassy that enforced the ban. Sir Robert Vansittart disclosed that 'the reason that we do not attempt propaganda in the USA is the firm & invincible opposition of the Embassy. This is an old bone of contention between us at the Foreign Office & Sir Ronald Lindsay & his predecessors'. Foreign Office Minute, 16 February 1939, PRO FO 371/22827/A1143.
7. Sir Ronald Lindsay to Anthony Eden, 22 March 1937, PRO FO 371/20651/A2378.
8. Roosevelt told Jan Struther that *Mrs Miniver* helped to bring Americans into the war. The book was a Book-of-the-Month Club selection. On Jan Struther and *Mrs Miniver*, see A. Light, *Forever England: Femininity, Literature and Conservatism between the Wars* (London, 1991), pp. 113–55. *The White Cliffs* sold 300 000 copies in the United States. On Alice Duer Miller and *The White Cliffs*, see Short, '*The White Cliffs*', pp. 6–12. *This Above All*, which headed the best-seller list for several months, greatly impressed Eleanor Roosevelt, who mentioned it in her 'My Day' column on 9 May 1941 and invited Eric Knight to Hyde Park. See Eleanor Roosevelt to Eric Knight, 7 June 1941, Eleanor Roosevelt Papers, Box 1608, Franklin D. Roosevelt Library, Hyde Park.
9. See J. Richards and D. Sheridan (eds), *Mass Observation at the Movies* (London, 1987); Short, '*The White Cliffs*', pp. 12–23.

10. David Scott, Foreign Office Minute, 8 February 1939, PRO FO 371/ 22827/A1143.
11. Despite its reluctance to assent to so lavish an expenditure, the Treasury approved the sum of £350 000, half of which was to be spent on buildings. Treasury to Department of Overseas Trade, 1 March 1938, PRO FO 371/21537/A1634.
12. Memorandum on British exhibit [n.d., 1937], PRO BT 60/51/2.
13. Memorandum of conversation between Lindsay and R. S. Hudson, 14 October 1937, PRO BT 60/51/2. Hudson was the Minister for Overseas Trade and Chairman of the Advisory Committee. See N. J. Cull, 'Overture to an Alliance: British Propaganda at the New York World's Fair, 1939–1940', *Journal of British Studies*, 36 (July 1997), 325–54.
14. G. Harding, 'World's Fair, New York', *Harpers Magazine*, **179** (July 1939), p. 200. See 'The Official Participation of the United Kingdom in the New York World's Fair, 1939', PRO FO 371/22787/J12885.
15. *New Statesman*, 10 June 1939, p. 891; *Official Guide Book. The World's Fair 1940*, p. 61.
16. New York World's Fair, *Guide to the Pavilion of the United Kingdom, Australia, New Zealand, and the British Colonial Empire* (1939), p. 11.
17. *Guide to the Pavilion*, p. 88. Fifty-nine artists were represented in the exhibit, which included 96 oil paintings, 53 watercolours and drawings, 136 prints, and 5 pieces of sculpture. PRO BW 63/12/WA/28/1. Clark was originally scheduled to go to New York to hang the pictures himself, but in the end Professor Constable of the Boston Museum of Fine Arts deputized. Kenneth Clark to Lionel Fandel-Phillips, 12 September 1938; Fandel-Phillips to Hudson, 18 October 1938, PRO BW 63/12/USA/28/1. The post-World's Fair circulation of the exhibit was handled by the Department of Overseas Trade since it was 'a fixed and inviolate rule that the British Council under no circumstances operate in the USA because of the deadly dangers arising from American susceptibilities to what is considered any form of British propaganda'. F. R. Cowell to A. A. Longden, 22 November 1939, PRO BW 63/22/USA/28/1.
18. *Guide to the Pavilion*, p. 20.
19. Ibid., p. 24.
20. Ibid., pp. 81–4; *Magna Carta Hall, British Pavilion, New York World's Fair, 1939*, 6 pp. Also see Cull, 'Overture to an Alliance', pp. 342–44. The Foreign Secretary intervened personally to persuade the Dean of Lincoln Cathedral to lend its copy of Magna Carta after the request was initially refused. Hudson to Halifax, 24 June 1938, PRO FO 371/21538/ A5069; Halifax to Dean of Lincoln Cathedral, 28 June 1938, PRO FO 395/639/P148/31/150.
21. *New York Times*, 25 April 1939.
22. Cowell to A. B. Fletcher, 20 October 1939, PRO FO 371/22788/78–80/ A7262.
23. Figures quoted in Cull, 'Overture to an Alliance', p. 346; PRO BT 60/52/ 4.
24. Memorandum by J. A. Balfour, 3 October 1939, PRO FO 371/22788/ J12885.
25. E. Hale to A. Mullins, 4 December 1939, PRO FO 371/22788/138–9/ A8458.
26. Scott to Hudson, 23 November 1939, PRO FO 371/22788/J12885. Also

see Lothian telegram, 15 November 1939, PRO FO 371/22788/134/A8134 and Balfour memorandum and Foreign Office Minute, 16 November 1939, PRO FO 371/22788/A7005.

27. Lindsay to Sir Alexander Cadogan, 1 November 1938, PRO FO 371/ 21548/A8828.

28. Lindsay to Cadogan, 16 November 1938, Royal Archives (hereafter RA) PS/GVI/PS 030400/003/01/024. Material in the Royal Archives had been made available with the gracious permission of Her Majesty Queen Elizabeth II.

29. Josef Israels II, 'Selling George VI to the U.S.', *Scribner's Magazine*, 195 (February 1939), 16–21.

30. John D. Moore to Cordell Hull, 22 October 1938, National Archives (hereafter NA) 841.001/George VI/265.

31. Eric Knight to Paul Rotha, 15 June 1939, Paul Rotha Collection, University Research Library, Los Angeles.

32. Franklin D. Roosevelt (hereafter FDR) to George VI, 17 September 1938, RA PS/GVI/PS 03400/003/01/001.

33. FDR to George VI, 2 November 1938, RA PS/GVI/PS 03400/003/01/015.

34. FDR to Roger B. Merriman, 15 February 1939, Roosevelt Papers, PSF: Diplomatic, Box 32. The Foreign Office itself was growing restive amid the post-Munich self-abnegation. As one key official put it,

> The sovietesque orgy of self-criticism in which we have been indulging for the last six months does us no good in the States & however behindhand we may be with our war-planning, any visitor to the US is more than justified in emphasising the fact that the old virtue has not gone out of us & we are even now an exceedingly formidable proposition to tackle. (Scott, Foreign Office Minute, 7 February 1939. PRO FO 371/22827/A1143)

35. The king's notes, quoted in J. W. Wheeler-Bennett, *King George VI: His Life and Reign* (London, 1958), p. 391.

36. Foreign Office Minute, 3 July 1939, PRO FO 371/22801/A4443.

37. Bradley E. Stafford to Eleanor Roosevelt, 9 June 1939, Eleanor Roosevelt Papers, Box 989. Mrs Roosevelt also received a handful of anonymous hate letters mostly condemning the appearance of Marion Anderson and other black entertainers at the White House.

38. Lindsay to Halifax, 20 June 1939, PRO FO 371/22801/A4443; Lindsay to Halifax, 12 June 1939, PRO FO/414/276/A4139.

39. See M. Secrest, *Kenneth Clark: A Biography* (London, 1984), pp. 151–3; P. Curtis, Preface to *World War Two*, Tate Gallery Liverpool (1989), pp. 2–4.

40. See F. M. Leventhal, '"The Best for the Most": CEMA and State Sponsorship of the Arts in Wartime, 1939–1945', *Twentieth Century British History*, 1 (1990), pp. 289–317.

41. A. H. Barr to Clark (telegram), 9 September 1940; War Artists' Advisory Committee (WAAC) Minutes, 12 September 1940, Minute Book, War Artists Archive, Imperial War Museum (IWM), GP/46/24/4A.

42. 'Proposals submitted to the Overseas Planning Committee for Final Approval, 25 Oct. 1940', War Artists Archive, IWM, GP/46/24/4A.

43. Director-General to E. M. O'R. Dickey, 1 November 1940, War Artists Archive, IWM, GP/46/24/4A.
44. In December it was erroneously reported that the paintings had been lost at sea. *Daily Telegraph*, 4 December 1940; Longden to Dickey, 8 January 1941, War Artists Archive, IWM, GP/46/24/4A.
45. Notes on Meeting about 'Britain at War' Exhibition, 30 January 1941, Museum of Modern Art, War Artists Archive, IWM, GP/46/24/4A.
46. M. Wheeler (ed.), *Britain at War* (New York, 1941), p. 12.
47. *New York Times*, 23 May 1941.
48. *New York Herald Tribune*, 1 June 1941; *New York Times*, 1 June 1941. The British Press Service reported that Eurich's painting 'has been frequently reproduced'. Telegram to Ministry of Information, 11 June 1941, War Artists Archive, IWM, GP/46/24/4A.
49. *The New Yorker*, 31 May 1941.
50. *New York World Telegram*, 31 May 1941.
51. *New York Herald Tribune*, 1 June 1941.
52. Museum of Modern Art, Britain at War file 42(4).
53. *The Argonaut* (San Francisco), 10 April 1942.

CHAPTER TWELVE

Commitment and Catastrophe: Twentieth-Century Conservative Historiography in Britain and America

Reba N. Soffer

The deeply felt political commitments that had informed the writing of history in America and Britain during the first four decades of the twentieth century intensified in response to the radically altered exigencies of the Cold War. This was especially true for conservatives on both sides of the Atlantic. Convinced that the unprecedented directions taken in the post-war world were fundamentally misconceived, they produced patriotic and cautionary lessons in which history corrected by example. The virtues of an idealized national past, imagined differently in each country, became their test for evaluating the forms and contents of the present as well as for prescribing the future. A few historians, influential far beyond their numbers, resurrected and redefined a conservative historiography. They did not perceive of themselves as political propagandists. Instead, they believed that the historically demonstrated rectitude of conservatism provided an objective perspective for historical understanding. Until supplanted by the more coherent, if fractious, neo-conservatism of the Radical Right in the 1970s, these historians acted individually and often idiosyncratically, rather than as an identifiable group, to shape historical scholarship and to affect national and international policy. In Britain, Herbert Butterfield, Geoffrey Elton and Max Beloff wrote within a continuous 200-year-old tradition that accepted common assumptions about the infirmities of human nature and their disastrous consequences. Unlike Britain, America had no consistent conservative legacy that persisted from earlier centuries. In order to fashion cohesive principles in the absence of a living heritage, conservatives such as Peter Viereck, Russell Kirk and, above all, Daniel Boorstin produced an often personal but still perspicuous conservative historiography based upon American exceptionalism. Elton, Beloff, Viereck and Kirk were aggressively conservative, while Butterfield and Boorstin adopted and used conservative ideals combatively without identifying, or perhaps even recognizing, themselves as conservatives.

Any discussion about the meaning of conservative historiography on both sides of the Atlantic has to consider both similarities and differences in the national concepts of conservatism. If there was one principle accepted by most post-war Anglo-American conservatives, it was that institutions, traditions, practices and habits survived and deserved deference because they had intrinsic merit and because they restricted irrational human nature and its potentially destructive effects. In Britain, conservative historians started with a deep distrust of human nature that separated them from liberals and socialists. American conservative historiography, although also distrustful of humanity's darker side, was a much more eclectic amalgam that included liberal and populist interests. That eclecticism was based upon broad agreement that American history was determined by inimitable American conditions: the separation of church and state, religious pluralism, a classless society, social and geographical mobility, the constant influx of immigrants, and the establishment of an industrial plutocracy in place of a paternalistic landed aristocracy. While British conservatives, including historians, emphasized liberty, with its connotations of a political meritocracy guiding the inchoate, American conservatives and their historical advocates were dedicated to a democratic society characterized by equal opportunity. The Americans believed in the given historicity of a vast and heterogeneous geography, massive waves of immigration that populated those spacious lands, and social and economic mobility. American conservatives shared with their British counterparts the historical search for stability, order, continuity and the institutional preservation of freedom. But, standing apart from the British, the Americans applauded, enthusiastically, two specifically American attributes: exceptionalism and the rich mixture of peoples creating their own history.

After the Second World War, American conservatism became increasingly difficult to distinguish from liberalism. Both Peter Viereck and Russell Kirk, stymied by the lack of an authentic conservative intellectual legacy in their national history, superimposed an ordered Burkean conservatism upon recalcitrant American development.[1] Lionel Trilling commented, famously, in 1950 that liberalism was 'not only the dominant but even the sole intellectual tradition'.[2] Charles Dunn and David Woodward recently tried to refute Trilling by continuing the Viereck and Kirk explanation of American conservatism as part of European and especially British experience. Although they struggle valiantly to find a distinctive definition, they arrive only at 'a defense of the political, economic, religious, and social status quo from the forces of abrupt change, that is based on a belief that established customs, laws, and traditions provide continuity and stability in the guidance of society'.[3] While this definition may describe conservative preferences, it hardly illuminates the American context. Even George Nash, the most thoughtful and sympathetic exponent of post-war conservatism, conceded 'that conservatism is inherently resistant to precise definition' and that conservatives 'probably never would' construct a unified conservative philosophy.[4] The difficulty in identifying conservative principles was due in part to the absence of a Conservative Party in American public life. The election of Richard Nixon in 1968 finally made the Republican Party appear to be conservative, but his administration, especially in its adventurous foreign policy, satisfied liberal rather than conservative requirements. Until a coalition of disparate groups supporting Ronald Reagan agreed upon a more explicit creed, Potter Stewart's view of pornography as something that he could not define but knew when he saw it, described American impressions about conservatism.[5]

While American conservatives attempted without great success to find roots, British conservatives held fast to principles developed during the nineteenth century in reaction against liberalism. Those principles repudiated free will, rational individualism and a utopian willingness to believe that desirable progress could actually occur to emphasize instead national institutions and traditions as necessary brakes against the unpredictable effects of flawed human nature. British conservatism promoted a moral and stable community by vesting authority in a social hierarchy that included Crown and Church. Throughout the nineteenth and until the third decade of the twentieth centuries, conservatives generally maintained that hierarchy on the basis of traditional landed wealth, membership in the Church of England, and identification with the national constitution. After 1867, they were supported often by working-class electors whose particular local interests took precedence over both political dialectics and class affiliation.

Unlike the British, American working classes in the late nineteenth century leaned to the left and rejected the policies of the wealthy and powerful to deplore the expanding gulf between rich and poor and the inequity suffered by ethnic immigrants. By the twentieth century, in contrast to working-class perceptions as well as to those of the Progressive historians who found a historical record marred by injustice, conservatives continued to see America as an open society with increasing economic independence for its citizens. The left increasingly became the target for conservative attack, especially at the end of the Second World War, because leftist internationalism championed collectivism and central planning. To post-war conservatives in Britain and America, the left was preparing the way for a communism as totalitarian as defeated fascism.

American conservatives after the Second World War opposed not only the left but liberalism, too. Was Irving Kristol correct to define a conservative as 'a liberal mugged by reality?'[6] That autobiographical reflection describes Kristol and Norman Podhoretz, editor of *Commentary*, who stampeded from the far left to the far right when they found the discord of the post-war world unnerving. The attraction of conservatism may have been its 'capacity to picture a natural, spontaneous order ... and to blame the disruption of that order on liberal élites and their policies and ideas'. Post-war American conservatism was aimed especially at the New Deal and its domestic and international legacy.[7] Liberal 'cosmopolitanism' became even more dangerous to the conservatives when strengthened by the diaspora of left-wing intellectuals into America in flight from fascism and communism.[8]

Differences between American and British conservative historians, much greater than their similarities, become more transparent when their work is set within historiographical traditions that reflected and attempted to accommodate the emergence of the twentieth-century British and American nations. It is striking that American historians of America stayed awake at night worrying about the meaning of history while their British counterparts slept soundly. More than 100 books have been written on American historiography in this century, but there are few studies of British historical writing and the majority of those are written by scholars of Britain who are not British.

At least two explicitly American phenomenon explain why American historians were so preoccupied with each other in marked contrast to the British. The first was determined by academic practice and the second by intellectual convention. Academic practice was created by the substance, content and emphases of graduate training in history. Within rapidly proliferating American universities, twentieth-century graduate students were generally required to take a historiographical seminar which taught them to read historians as well as the history they wrote. But systematic graduate training in history, casually and reluctantly introduced within British universities only after the Second World War, did not include historiography. The second phenomena, American intellectual convention, was rooted in the first half of the twentieth century, when both pragmatism and admiration for the objectivity of scientific method led to suspicion of speculative systems as disguised 'ideology'. To deal with thought empirically and avoid deceptive abstraction, Americans studied specific works of historical writing and distilled ideas from their content.[9] Unlike their American colleagues, few British historians expected history to benefit from scientific models, but they did believe in objective truth that could be revealed by a dispassionate study of facts. Their ideal of emotional neutrality was often confounded by heated and truculent quarrels about the uses of evidence, but British historians were rarely perturbed by disputes about the nature, contents and uses of history.

The British historian's attitude towards historiography, until at least the 1960s, depended in great part upon the homogeneous qualities of academic life and the smallness of Britain. These historians shared family and class backgrounds and values, were educated in the same few schools and universities, and tended to spend the rest of their lives in the institutions that had taught them. Part of an exclusive and almost incestuous community, they were confined to a crowded island that could be swallowed up by California. Familiarity, combined with innocence about historical introspection and admiration for English development, bred indifference to what their colleagues thought about history. American historians, in marked contrast, came from remarkably disparate backgrounds and were often separated from each other by thousands of miles. Public and personal power in America was fragmented among many local, regional and state interests, representing diverse social, ethnic, religious and educational constituencies. In conspicuous contrast, Britain was governed by a homogeneous cadre, educated largely within two élite universities.

While America was just beginning its climb to world power in the late nineteenth century, Britain was already *the* hegemonic industrial empire. Residues of the living past persisted in every English village and town to testify to the stability and endurance of a people whose qualities of mind and will enabled them to succeed so conspicuously. An agreement that history could be misappropriated to become part of contemporary political struggles led the British to concentrate study and teaching in the centuries before the nineteenth. No matter what their political inclinations, established historians tended to admire their own history as a continuous story of moral and material achievement. From the conservative Bishop Stubbs in the 1880s through such twentieth-century liberals as A. L. Smith and even socialists such as R. H. Tawney, professional historians subscribed to similar scenarios about national success. The British believed that their history demonstrated an ability to solve social, economic and political problems without domestic disorder. That ability, they believed, was derived from the rule of law, a judicious constitution, responsible institutions, the cultivation of national character, education directed towards the public good and the favour of a God who, fortunately, was English.

Unlike the British, the dissimilar and often rootless American historians wanted to discover a 'usable past' in their relatively new and still unsettled continent. An examination of the writing of their peers and predecessors led them to conclude by the 1930s that American historical writing had alternated between interpretive currents of conflict and consensus. The conservative, eastern establishment of nineteenth-century aristocratic gentleman amateurs, who reached their apotheosis in Henry Adams, initially discovered consensus as a reassuring explanation of a common unity and order in what was largely an expanding and mobile agrarian population. When history became the professional province of university-trained scholars, living after the 1880s in a world increasingly industrial and plutocratic, consensus was challenged by the 'New' or Progressive view introduced by liberal and occasionally radical scholars, such as Charles and Mary Beard, who were raised in small-town and rural America and trained in middle-American and western universities. In opposition to their predecessors, they responded to their immediate world by reading the American story as a drama of recurring and rending conflict. Both the consensus and the conflict schools assumed that history had a practical, even contemporary application, and that part of the historian's task was to confirm the singular qualities of American experience.

In burgeoning public universities all over inter-war America, students and faculty without the advantages of birth or wealth heard historians expand political history to its social and economic milieu as part of ordinary people's experience. At the State University of Iowa as early as 1933, Arthur Schlesinger introduced a course on 'Social and Cultural History of the United States', the first of its kind anywhere in America.[10] In the 1920s and 1930s, younger historians turned increasingly to the particular lives of such historically neglected groups as dirt farmers, immigrants, cowboys and native Americans. At the same time, British historians continued to study and teach high politics and the constitution in their few privileged universities to a select group of students. Even liberal historians regarded the British constitution as the most appropriate subject for university study.[11] Only in the 1960s did social, and later still cultural, history appear in British historical writing and teaching.

In twentieth-century America until the 1950s few American historians were recognized as conservatives because liberal historians often adopted conservative principles of historical interpretation such as: 'consensus' historiography; or rejection of the idea of progress and its assumptions about human perfectibility; or opposition to collectivism; or the appreciation of power and its uses. Peter Novick perceptively identifies Richard Hofstadter and Louis Hartz, as well as Boorstin, as the three leading consensus historians.[12] Boorstin is a conservative consensus historian, but Hofstadter and Hartz fall into the liberal consensus camp. Hofstadter, like the conservatives, dismissed progressive models and advocated the pragmatic necessities of power to curb collectivism, especially in its communist guise. Hartz's consensus was based on his conviction that in the United States, instead of distinctly liberal and conservative dichotomies there was only consistent liberalism.[13] Additionally, the conservative reading of the twentieth century as a 'tragic' history was accepted by many liberals such as Arthur Schlesinger Jr, and even by historians on the far left such as William Appleman Williams, who had difficulty reconciling the holocaust and the atomic bomb with traditional liberal and socialist faith in progress and rationality.[14] Although liberals and conservatives appeared to share hermeneutic strategies, similar rhetoric concealed disparate motives and conclusions.

Political discourse and historiography in America and Britain took a critical turning after the Second World War. In post-war America, the elderly and discarded conservatism of the late nineteenth century had its face lifted to be born again as American triumphalism. Since America was undeniably the greatest of superpowers, militarily, politically and economically, American history, as the justification for that status, became increasingly important for American conservatives. For their British counterparts, the Second World War and its consequences were not a source of rejuvenation but rather of premature ageing. Britain emerged from the Second World War as a diminished, post-imperial nation, with a problematic future in the councils and markets of the world. The scale and depth of horrors, beyond the holocaust and the atomic bomb, included for conservatives a Labour victory, the establishment of the welfare state and the rise of an aggressively communist Soviet Union. Their assessment of their own time and their place within it led to increased pessimism.

British conservative historiography was prepared to be pessimistic because it accepted that human nature was beyond redemption and that human aspirations and any possibilities for carrying out those aspirations were bound to fail. The corruption of human nature solved the problem of evil, whether seen through a Christian lens, as Herbert Butterfield did, or from the secular perspective of Geoffrey Elton and Max Beloff. For the religious and secular pessimist alike, the historical record demonstrated that when humans exercised their free will they almost always chose disastrously. British conservative historians turned to history to show that the best means of constraining corruption, whether private, public or international, was through reconciliation, compromise and a balance of powers. Their post-war agenda stressed the restraint of power and the avoidance of that hubris which trusted centralized planning.

After the Second World War, conservative historians in Britain such as Winston Churchill or George Kitson Clark, continued to write the same cautiously optimistic history they had written decades earlier. At the same time, Peterhouse in Cambridge became especially conspicuous for its distinguished collection of historians and for its polemical commitment to a newer, more militant conservative historiography.[15] The Peterhouse group were not the only conservative historians in Britain, but they became the most widely influential. Herbert Butterfield, their founder, repudiated as insufficiently polemical by the next generation of Peterhouse neoconservatives, gave conservatism an Augustinian basis in moral depravity and its inevitable conclusion in human helplessness. At the same time, Geoffrey Elton, first at the University of London and then at Clare College, Cambridge, provided a similar conservative view of history with mundane roots.

What did influential post-war British and American conservative historians – Butterfield, Elton, and Beloff, Kirk, Viereck and Boorstin – have in common? They shared two conspicuous attributes. First, with the exception of Butterfield, born in 1900, they came into the post-Great War world between 1914 and 1921 to experience traumatically the depression, Hitler's war, and an intense Cold War fear of communism. And they were each from backgrounds that would normally have excluded them from positions of power or influence. Instead, largely as a result of ability and of speaking to an audience that found them congenial and often inspirational, they moved comfortably and easily from the marginal periphery to positions near the centre.

Peter Viereck described McCarthyism as the 'revenge of the noses' that 'for twenty years of fancy parties were pressed against the outside window pane'.[16] Can that description be applied to American and British conservatism in general and to conservative historians in particular? In Britain, those who held conservative views looked out of their windows at a pleasant countryside which largely belonged to them. American conservatives were drawn from too many affiliations and disparate classes to fit any generalization. What about the conservative historians in both countries? Their similarities are more striking: they became passionate defenders of a welcoming national establishment which gave them fame and authority. Their gratitude may have been crucial to their use of history against threats to the national fortress.

After Dunkirk, Butterfield mounted the parapets by rewriting his famous denunciation of *The Whig Interpretation of History* (1931). The result, his patriotic *The Englishman and his History* (1944), discovered a Whig tradition that was 'a moderate pace of reform, a cautious progress to whatever end may be desired: a whiggism which, abhorring revolutionary methods, seems now mildly left-wing, now almost indistinguishable from conservatism'.[17] As he pointed out four years later, between the 'fanaticisms of right and left' a conservative kind of whiggism had steered 'the country through perilous seas, measured the limits of what was practicable and prevented catastrophe by a maturer kind of political wisdom'.[18] In 1992, two years before his death, Elton published *The English*, a personal tribute to the 'country in which I ought to have been born' where 'the centuries of a strong monarchy and a powerful system of legal rights left the twentieth century a legacy of the toleration of variety and respect for the rights not of Man but of English men and women'.[19]

What made them all initially outsiders? Butterfield was a lower-middle class Methodist scholarship boy. He achieved a central role in Cambridge, a conservative influence on contemporary policy studies, especially in America, and gave a polemically conservative reading to the relationship between Christianity and history. Elton was a Jewish refugee from Hitler's Prague who became one of the few historians in Britain to found an international school of disciples. Elton's admiration of high politics, expressed in his Tudor studies, carried a conservative message within Britain, America and Australia. Max Beloff came from a family of Russian Orthodox Jewish immigrants, never assimilated into Anglo-Jewry. Educated at St Paul's School and Oxford, Beloff was historical adviser to the Anglo-Russian section of the Committee on Reconstruction during the Second World War. Then, he taught American history at Oxford where he was elected Gladstone Professor of Government and Public Administration. He also became principal-designate of the new University College of Buckingham, now the University of Buckingham. Among his 19 books, there is a study of Thomas Jefferson, written in 1948, the same year that Boorstin turned to Jefferson to exemplify American pragmatic conservatism. Beloff's *The Balance of Power* (1967) testifies to a typical conservative concern shared by conservative historians in Britain, 'the rise and fall of states and empires and the governance of men'.[20]

On the American side, Boorstin, born in Atlanta, Georgia, was a Jewish outsider as a student in the then Protestant communities of Harvard, Oxford and Yale. Boorstin took two degrees as a Rhodes Scholar at Oxford, in history and in law, and was admitted to the English bar. At Yale, he was awarded a doctorate in legal history and then spent the greater part of his academic career at the University of Chicago. Peter Viereck, also educated at Harvard and Oxford, was the son of George Sylvester Viereck, the German-American apologist for the Kaiser in the First World War who, in 1940, defended Hitler's Germany. Viereck's conservatism was, in part, a rejection of his father's principles.[21] During the war, he served in Africa and Italy with the army's psychological propaganda branch. A Pulitzer-prize winning poet in 1948, Viereck remained at Mount Holyoke College as a professor of history. Russell Kirk began on the 'wrong side of the window-pane', too. The son of a railroad engineer, he grew up in small-town Michigan, attended Michigan State College, took a Master's degree in history at Duke, and after his military tour in the Chemical Warfare Service, eventually earned a doctorate at St Andrews in Scotland. Although Kirk never held a permanent academic position, he was a visiting professor at universities all over the United States and wrote a 'From the Academy' column for the *National Review* until 1980. In addition to a spate of books and journalism defining and defending his 'Bohemian Tory' brand of conservatism, he wrote Gothic novels.[22] Viereck and Kirk both felt ideological and aesthetic ties to Europe and to British and European conservatism, while Boorstin repudiated foreign ideologies as alien and unnecessary to the understanding of American history.

Were the conservative historians on both sides of the Atlantic always conservative? Butterfield, Elton and Viereck were conservatives as undergraduates. Beloff was a conservative as a schoolboy, a socialist at university and a liberal after the war. In 1979, after retiring from Buckingham he joined the Conservative Party because Labour had opposed the creation of an independent university of Buckingham and because the Liberals, who in his view were moving increasingly to the left, also refused to champion Buckingham. Margaret Thatcher, in contrast, was a steadfast supporter. In 1981, he entered the House of Lords for the Conservative Party and became the insider's insider as an adviser to the Conservative Party Research Department. Although Kirk voted for Norman Thomas in 1944, he had long been a convert to conservatism as a result of writing his Master's thesis on John Randolph of Roanoke.[23] Only Boorstin, who has denied that he is a conservative, dramatized his outsider status by his pre-war politics. In *The Mysterious Science of the Law* (1941), Boorstin treated Blackstone and the common-law traditions as bourgeois justifications of unjust property rights.

Boorstin best reveals the anomalous, eccentric character of American conservative historians. A pre-war member of the Communist Party, he subsequently named three of his Harvard colleagues as fellow Communists before the House Un-American Activities Committee. Reinventing consensus history to give American exceptionalism a new meaning that could be used as a noetic weapon in the Cold War, his work became a historical demonstration of the practical institutions and the special environment that have produced the American 'experiment'.[24] Beginning with *The Lost World of Thomas Jefferson* (1948) Boorstin spent his long, productive career explaining that the whole of American history could be understood as an exceptional national narrative based upon institutions and values resulting from a direct and constructive confrontation with American nature and geography. He rejected systems of ideas, such as the Enlightenment, because they were 'homogenized stereotypes' that ignored what particular eighteenth-century Americans were really doing.[25] It apparently never occurred to him that the institutions he trusted to transmit permanent values might also represent special interests or that the traditions those institutions protected were perpetuated more by inertia than by merit. An enduring strength of the American tradition for Boorstin was the provision of opportunities for assimilated outsiders, such as himself. Those opportunities and his own considerable skill in recreating the texture of American life earned Boorstin the Bancroft Prize in 1958 for his *The Americans: The Colonial Experience*. His appointment as Librarian of Congress was a canonical recognition of the ultimate insider.

Although all were respected members of inner circles, these conservative historians were concerned above all with their responsibilities as historians. Butterfield, Elton, Beloff and Boorstin all repudiated belief in progress and in the historical possibility of human perfection because they believed them to be fundamentally irresponsible positions. Yet they still wanted to believe that a knowledge of history provided a means of discovering intelligibility within apparent randomness. A crucial difference between British and American conservative historians was that, unlike the pessimistic British, the Americans were committed to the indeterminacy of empiricism. That meant that their world was not sharply divided 'between good and evil, virtue and corruption, democracy and capitalism'.[26] American conservatives, who generally avoided such abstractions as 'human nature', began rather with an emphasis upon experience rooted in the uniqueness of American circumstances. For the American conservative historians, their public responsibilities were carried out by constructing a parable of American success around the assimilation of successive flows of peoples into a fecund and fruitful landscape.

In British life until the 1950s, there were no waves of immigration except for the Irish who were theoretically British. The new groups, like the Irish before them, were hardly assimilated. British conservatives, even in top positions within the Foreign Office, remained relatively ignorant of non-British peoples because few lived amongst them. British conservative historians also found their country to be singular, but for very different reasons, and they attempted to fulfil their public responsibility by demonstrating that singularity. Beloff tried to prove that the characteristic themes of English history were order, an independent judiciary and the central role of Whitehall over Westminster.[27] Butterfield searched for evidence that national survival depended on co-operation with Providence, and in English history he discovered a national aptitude for such co-operation.[28]

The American conservative historians in the three decades between the ending of the war and the appearance of neo-conservatism shared with their British colleagues the evolutionary search for stability, order, continuity and the institutional preservation of freedom. But they diverged sharply from their British colleagues by accepting three additional, distinctly American themes: the inappropriateness of ideology as a determining force in American history; the Progressive belief in a steady and consonant development of specially American institutions and values; and, the melting pot of peoples transforming their common lives. To illustrate the negligible role of ideas, the consistency and unity of characteristically American history, and the importance of immigration, Boorstin, in 1958, 1965 and 1973, published his massive three-volume study *The Americans* on the colonial, national and democratic experiences. Boorstin insisted that our

> most important and most representative thinkers have been more interested in institutions than in ideologies. For an ideology is something fixed and rigid ... But institutions live and grow and change. They have a life of their own as a philosophy cannot; and our major accomplishments have been in the realm of institutions rather than in thought.

Boorstin saw the historian as 'the high priest of uniqueness' who made clear the process and the outcome.[29] From his emphatically waste-not, want-not, can-do view of American history, Boorstin explained that:

> Perhaps the intellectual energy which American Revolutionaries economized because they were not obliged to construct a whole theory of institutions was to strengthen them for their encounter with nature and for the solution of their practical problems. The effort which Jefferson, for example, did not care to spend on the theory of sovereignty he was to give freely to the revision of the criminal law, the observation of the weather, the mapping of the continent, the collection of fossils, the study of Indian languages, and the doubling of the national area.

While Europeans were prepared to kill each other over conflicting theories, Americans were constantly making and remaking their world. To Boorstin, 'the sparseness of American political theory' was due less to a conscious refusal of American statesmen to think about philosophical problems 'than to a simple lack of necessity'.[30]

Liberal historians assert that Boorstin's treatment of the American Revolution has left out the ideals, the principles, the passion and the revolution. Bernard Bailyn considers the ideas of the American Revolution as logical weapons in the hands of reasonable people who organized and acted on experience. Unlike Boorstin, Bailyn found that the political awareness of Americans was formed by the literature of English

politics and that the pre-Revolutionary period was the most creative of
all periods in American political thought. By 1776, the traditional
words and concepts of the Enlightenment and of English libertarianism
had been reshaped into American radicalism, by adjusting ideas to
reality through a uniquely American spirit of pragmatic idealism.[31]
Both liberal and conservative historians found 'pragmatism' to be specifically American, but for the conservatives it was a pragmatism based
on institutional practice rather than on the validity of any set of ideas.

That aspect of Boorstin's work which has attracted the greatest criticism has been his discussion of the Civil War. Hofstadter argued against
Boorstin that the division was a major test of institutions and ideas
which collapsed tragically.[32] Are Hofstadter's criticism and Bailyn's implicit criticism warranted? Boorstin described the war as a federal conflict
based on each section's appraisal of the 'givenness' of the 'totality' of its
own culture. Instead of relying upon abstractions or slogans, each side
made its case by citing those 'facts' which characterized their region.
Like the American Revolution, the debate that occurred between North
and South was essentially legalistic in that each side thought that it
represented the Constitution. Boorstin's stress upon a legal structure
reflected his own background in law and legal history, and his conservative belief in the superiority of evolving law over rigid opinion. The
Civil War, for Boorstin, was about issues marked by long series of
compromises, beginning with the Declaration of Independence and the
Constitution. When the Civil War was over, he contended, federal
institutions were strengthened.[33]

In keeping with his belief in the adaptability of law, institutions, and
the American people, Boorstin, too, changed with the times. In *The
National Experience* (1965), he condemned the South for adopting the
European weakness of abstract thought; for slavery; and for an inability
to move with improving times. Although the Civil War itself is never
discussed in *The National Experience* or in its successor, *The Democratic Experience* (1973), Boorstin is unequivocal in his judgement
about guilt. It was slavery, the South's 'Peculiar Institution', that bifur-
cated 'the life, the hopes, and the destiny of Southern communities ...
"The South" became the most unreal, most powerful, and most disastrous oversimplification in American history'.[34] The progressive and
flexible North emerges as the true representative of American pragmatic
traditions which change the country while retaining its best traditions.

Boorstin's generation were cold warriors who developed their American version of conservatism in a flight from the left to a patriotic
affirmation of American unity and values. A pragmatic and passionate
belief in American exceptionalism and historical opportunity tempered
their conservative perceptions. The British conservative historians were

also moved by their fear of the Cold War, but they belonged to a more well-defined, darker conservative allegiance. Unlike their triumphalist American colleagues, their bleaker pessimism and the reality of their vitiated nation left diminished faith for the future. When both post-war revisions of conservatism were abandoned first in America and then in Britain during the Reagan and Thatcher years, a neo-conservative, more aggressive generation emerged and its progeny of historians turned away from the characteristically conservative observance of community, hierarchy and social order.

In the late 1960s, extraordinary events compelled American histori-ans to confront their own lives and times. Both liberal and conservative historians were brought up short by cumulative trauma that trans-formed thinking about history. For the conservatives, a post-war interpretation of a unified, harmonious and extraordinary history, based upon unique evolving and equitable institutions, became very difficult to sustain. The escalation of the Vietnam War, the Watts riots and the civil rights revolution, the assassination of Kennedy, the campus disor-ders and the emergence of an anarchistic youth movement, the appearance of the 'Radical Right,' and belligerent feminism could not be explained within post-war American historiography. In Britain, books like A. J. P. Taylor's *The Origins of the Second World War* (1961) and E. P. Thompson's *The Making of the English Working Class* (1963) more than events challenged historians to reconsider the purposes and mean-ing of historical study. Whether or not there was a post-war political agreement between the Labour and Conservative parties during the 1950s and early 1960s, the Keynesian policies followed by the Labour Minister Hugh Gaitskell and continued by his Conservative successor, R. A. Butler, as well as the systematic connections established between Whitehall, employers and their employees, flourished as the standard of living rose. In contrast to the turmoil in America, there was little searing confrontation in the streets, in Parliament or in common-rooms. But in an economy increasingly global, Britain, a country in relative decline, had to address its own history more critically. From the late 1970s, discontent occurred in Britain as well as in America, and a new coali-tion of the far right developed in the wider community, in the halls of government, and in the academy. But on both sides of the pond, mili-tant conservative historians rushed to the market to return in the cross-dressing of classical, nineteenth-century liberals. It remains to be seen whether their slightly worn finery testifies to a new and flamboy-ant style for conservatism or rather to a postmodern version of the emperor's old clothes.

Notes

1. P. Viereck, *Conservatism Revisited. The Revolt against Revolt, 1815–1949* (New York, 1949) and *idem, Conservatism. From John Adams to Churchill* (Chicago, 1953); R. Kirk, *The Conservative Mind. From Burke to Eliot* (Chicago, 1953).
2. L. Trilling, *The Liberal Imagination* (New York, 1950), p. ix.
3. C. Dunn and D. Woodward, *American Conservatism from Burke to Bush. An Introduction* (New York, 1991), p. 31.
4. G. Nash, *The Conservative Intellectual Movement in America since 1945* (1976) [reissued Wilmington, NC, 1996], pp. xiii–xiv, 170.
5. The Supreme Court justice Potter Stewart, in *Jacobellis v. Ohio*, 378 U.S. 184 (1964), 197.
6. Kristol acknowledges this definition. Discussion with the staff of *The Public Interest*, 19 March 1998.
7. J. L. Himmelstein, *To the Right. The Transformation of American Conservatism* (Berkeley, CA, 1990), pp. 62, 77.
8. See D. Hollinger's percipient *In the American Province. Studies in the History and Historiography of Ideas* (Bloomington, IN, 1985), esp. ch. 4.
9. I am grateful to Stan Katzman for this insight.
10. J. Higham, *History: Professional Scholarship in America* (Baltimore, MD, 1965), p. 194.
11. See R. N. Soffer, *Discipline and Power. The University, History and the Making of an English Elite, 1870-1930* (Stanford, CA, 1995).
12. P. Novick, *That Noble Dream. The 'Objectivity Question' and the American Historical Profession* (Cambridge, 1989), p. 333.
13. See R. Hofstadter, *The American Political Tradition* (New York, 1948) and L. Hartz, *The Liberal Tradition in America* (New York, 1955).
14. W. A. Williams, *The Tragedy of American Diplomacy* (New York, 1959); A. Schlesinger, *The Vital Center* (Boston, MA, 1949).
15. See R. N. Soffer, 'The Conservative Historical Imagination', *Albion* (Winter, 1995); *idem*, 'Twentieth-Century Conservative Historiography in Britain', in B. Stuchtey and P. Wendt (eds), *British and Germany Historiography, 1750-1950. Traditions, Perceptions, and Transfers*, (Oxford, 1999); and *idem*, 'The Long Nineteenth Century of Conservative Thought', in G. K. Behlmer and F. M. Leventhal (eds), *Singular Continuities: Tradition, Nostalgia, and Identity in British Culture*, (Stanford, CA, 2000).
16. P. Viereck, 'The Revolt Against the Elite', in D. Bell (ed.), *The Radical Right* (New York, 1955), p. 162.
17. H. Butterfield, *The Englishman and his History* (Cambridge, 1944), p. 92.
18. H. Butterfield, *Lord Acton* (London, 1948), p. 20.
19. G. Elton, *The English* (Oxford, 1992), pp. xii, 234–5. See, too, *idem, Return to Essentials. Some Reflections on the Present State of Historical Scholarship* (Cambridge, 1991).
20. M. Beloff, *An Historian in the Twentieth Century. Chapters in Intellectual Autobiography* (New Haven, CT, 1992), pp. 18–19. Lewis Namier, also a conservative, was closer to conservative American historians than to his British colleagues in his dismissal of ideas and of intellectuals. In *Vanished Supremicies. Essays on European History, 1812–1918* (New York, 1958), Namier saw Hitler and the Third Reich as the 'most

gruesome' culmination of belief in the idea of progress and in intellectuals rather than in the 'heritage of rooted institutions', p. 176. Unlike Butterfield, Elton and Beloff, he never approached the inside and his unrequited longing for a fellowship at Balliol was hardly appeased by his chair of modern history at Manchester University. See L. Colley, *Lewis Namier* (London, 1989). Namier never achieved the impact that he sought and although the Namierite school was often discussed, only John Brooke was a disciple. See L. Namier and J. Brooke's *The House of Commons, 1754–1790*, 3 vols (Oxford, 1964).

21. Nash, *Conservative Intellectual Movement*, p. 58.
22. See R. Kirk, *The Sword of Imagination. Memoirs of a Half-Century of Literary Conflict* (Grand Rapids, MN, 1995), and *idem, Confessions of a Bohemian Tory* (New York, 1963).
23. Nash, *Conservative Intellectual Movement*, p. 63.
24. R. H. Pells, *The Liberal Mind in a Conservative Age. American Intellectuals in the 1940s and 1950s* (New York, 1985), p. 318.
25. D. Boorstin, *America and the Image of Europe. Reflections on American Thought* (Cleveland, OH, 1960), p. 77.
26. D. W. Noble, *The End of American History. Democracy, Capitalism, and the Metaphor of Two worlds in Anglo-American Historical Writing, 1880–1980* (Minneapolis, MN, 1985), p. 10.
27. Beloff, *An Historian in the Twentieth Century*, pp. 35–7.
28. Butterfield, *The Englishman and his History*, p. 2.
29. D. Boorstin, *America and the Image of Europe*, pp. 52, 66.
30. D. Boorstin, *The Genius of American Politics* (Chicago, 1953), p. 95.
31. B. Bailyn, *The Ideological Origins of the American Revolution* (Cambridge, MA, 1971).
32. R. Hofstadter, *The Progressive Historians* (New York, 1968), pp. 461–62.
33. Boorstin, *The Genius of American Politics*, pp. 118, 122, 131.
34. D. Boorstin, *The Americans: The National Experience* (New York, 1966), p. 170.

CHAPTER THIRTEEN

War and Anglo-American Financial Relations in the Twentieth Century

Kathleen Burk

Nervos belli, pecuniam infinitam

(Cic. *Phil.* v. ii. 5)

The theme of this chapter is summed up by Cicero: infinite money, the sinews of war. War-making requires unending supplies of money. Happy is the country which has access to such supplies; almost as happy is the country which has access to a country which can provide such supplies. But complicated are the relations between two such countries. War accelerated Great Britain's[1] decline from, and America's rise to, global power. Furthermore, at the same time it facilitated the transfer of power from one to the other. Indeed, the overarching structure of Anglo-American relations during the twentieth century has been the – perhaps unprecedented – transferral of power from one Great Power to another without being forced to it by defeat in battle. The intention in this chapter is to give a snapshot of the two countries at the outset of the twentieth century, and then briefly to trace the downward trajectory of Britain's independent war-making power, from 1900 to the present day. The chapter will begin with the Boer War, where turning to the United States was a matter of convenience, continue with the First World War, where it was a matter of strategic necessity, and the Second World War, where it was a matter of dire necessity, and end with the very different settings of the Cold and Falkland Wars. Beginning with convenience, this chapter will end with convenience.

Central to British power since the eighteenth century has been economic and financial strength. Voltaire in Letter no. 10 of his *Lettres sur les Anglais* tells the following story:

> When Louis XIV made Italy tremble and his armies, already masters of Savoy and Piedmont, were about to take Turin, Prince Eugene had to march from the middle of Germany to relieve the Duke of Savoy. He had no money, without which cities cannot be taken or defended, so he had recourse to English merchants [i.e., the City of London]. In just half an hour he was lent fifty million. With that he relieved Turin [and] beat the French ... [2]

What the City could do for a foreign prince it could easily do for a British one. Indeed, one could argue that British power has been peculiarly dependent on financial power. Certainly it used its great economic resources to finance that weapon of empire, the Royal Navy, but beyond that it used its financial power as a weapon in itself. Britain might subsidize other states' armies to fight for or with her: the soldiers of Hesse to fight for her during the American War of Independence, or the Prussians against Napoleon. What was crucial was the fact that there was both private sector and public sector finance: the private sector might finance Prince Eugene, the public sector the Hessians. When the two worked together there was, for over two centuries, no financial power in the world to match it.

At the outset of the twentieth century, then, Great Britain was not only a Great Power, it was the supreme international power, with 'an empire on which the sun never set', the largest navy in the world to defend it, and the most advanced financial system in the world to support it. What, conversely, was the position of the United States? It was certainly *not* a Great Power, although the potential was there. It was large: without counting Alaska and Hawaii it stretched the distance from London to Teheran. It was increasingly an economic powerhouse, with steel production twice that of Great Britain. Its navy was growing, and it had a substantial merchant marine, both important in view of its growing imperial possessions as well as its long-standing foreign trade. And, relevant to the theme of this chapter, New York City was an increasingly important capital market, although most of its funds were devoted to internal development rather than to foreign investment.

As the century opened, Great Britain was engaged in a fight with the two Boer republics in South Africa, the Transvaal and the Orange Free State, over British attempts to annex them. The war had begun in October 1899, when it was assumed that it would be over by Christmas, but the grievous defeats suffered by the British Army in December 1899 ensured that its duration would be rather longer. During the early months of the war, it had been financed by means of Treasury bills, that is, by short-term borrowings, usually for three, nine or 12 months. However, this could only be a temporary expedient, and by early 1900 the government needed to borrow; in January 1900 the Chancellor of the Exchequer decided to tap the New York money market, the first time since the Seven Years War (1756–63) that the British had looked abroad for funds. Why did they do this?[3]

The Treasury habitually looked to the City of London whenever it needed to borrow, consulting the Governor of the Bank of England and certain notable merchant bankers, usually a Rothschild, a Baring, sometimes a Morgan and, during this period, Sir Ernest Cassel. Should they issue more Consols (these had originated in 1751, when Henry Pelham at the Exchequer had grouped together a number of funds into the 'three per cent consolidated annuities'), which are never redeemed and therefore add to the permanent national debt? Should they issue medium-term bonds? What interest rate would the City accept? During the Boer War the government had to borrow five times, and each time the Permanent Secretary to the Treasury, Sir Edward Hamilton, consulted his 'representative City men'.[4] He did so in January 1900, but the answers he received failed to satisfy him. The City wanted the government to continue to issue Treasury bills: they were as good as cash, since they were always saleable, and had the 'sanctity of tradition', and therefore the government would be able to negotiate a lower interest rate.[5] This argument, of course, was attractive to the Treasury, but they had other concerns as well.

They were concerned, first of all, not to add more to the permanent debt of the country, and therefore favoured a medium-term loan – medium-term because they hoped that it would fall due soon after they had defeated the Boers, and that the Transvaal, the main gold-producing region of southern Africa, would then help to pay it off. Second, the Chancellor wanted more gold. Supplies from the Rand had nearly stopped with the outbreak of the war, and diminishing supplies of gold were causing 'tightness', as he put it, in the money market. And third, they wanted some international demonstration of support for the war effort.[6]

As it happened, turning to the New York money market would solve these problems, and the Chancellor did so for four of the five loans issued during the war. The Chancellor worked through the House of Morgan, with its unrivalled placing power in the United States, and certainly New York took all that the Chancellor was willing for America to have – and would have eagerly taken much more. Second, New York provided new gold, which London needed in place of the lost supplies of Transvaal gold. And third, the willingness of Americans to loan to the British government was taken as a demonstration of American support for the British position in southern Africa, a counterbalance to, for example, the fulminations of German public opinion against it.[7]

It can be argued, then, that American financial power was instrumental in helping Great Britain to fight the Boer War, but it was not necessary: rather, it was convenient for the British government to draw on it because it would solve certain economic and political problems. Indeed, the turn to the United States was felt to be regrettable in the Treasury: as Hamilton, the Permanent Secretary, wrote in his diary, 'I don't much like the idea. It looks so much as if we had ... to go cap in hand to America to enable us to carry on the war'. However, with that clearsightedness for which the Treasury is notable, he added that 'On the other hand, there are threats of tight terms here; and the only way of preventing excessive tightness is to get gold. So there are direct advantages to be attained by our negotiating with our American friends'.[8]

Yet Hamilton saw the longer-term implications, too, writing in 1901 about British financial dependence on the United States that 'Our commerical supremacy has to go sooner or later; of that I feel no doubt; but we don't want to accelerate its departure across the Atlantic'.[9] Borrowing from the United States during the Boer War did not do so, except in the sense that it enhanced the position of the New York money market as well as of the House of Morgan, who were now, respectively, the creditors and agents of the most powerful creditor country in the world. Acceleration would come with the next episode, the First World War, in which the strategic necessity for Great Britain to turn to the United States for financial aid led directly to the reversal of positions between them.[10]

When the war broke out on 4 August 1914, Great Britain intended to fight in its traditional manner: it would blockade the Continent and subsidize British allies, but not engage in large-scale fighting itself. Within a week, however, the decision had been taken to raise a mass army, and with this decision Britain's financial power was irredeemably compromised. The problem was, a new mass army required clothing, weapons and provisions, only some of which were immediately available in Great Britain itself. The government instead turned to the largest neutral power, which was also the most powerful industrial economy accessible to the Entente Powers, the United States. Beginning with an order for rifles in October 1914, within two years 40 per cent of all British spending on the war was being spent in North America.[11] Great Britain was not only purchasing supplies for its army and navy and for its civilian population in the United States: it was also financing or guaranteeing in North America the purchases of France, Russia, Belgium, Italy, Rumania and Greece. In due course the burden almost bankrupted Britain.

A government attempting to supply its population from domestic resources can do so in a number of ways: it can raise taxes, or print money, or borrow or even commandeer goods. However, purchasing goods abroad requires an ability to buy the currency of that country with hard currency of one's own. Great Britain's problem was that it had to buy ever-increasing numbers of dollars. It shipped gold to buy dollars, forced its citizens to turn over American shares in exchange for British government bonds so that the government could sell the shares for dollars, and borrowed dollars on Wall Street. By the date of American entry into the war in April 1917, Great Britain was within three weeks of defaulting on American payments. Once the United States entered the war, Great Britain hoped and expected that the United States would take over the financing of British purchases, and those of its allies in the United States, and relieve her of the burden.[12]

How did the US government view all of this? In the first place, it saw Great Britain as it had been for over a century, the supreme economic power: why should the United States pay Great Britain's bills? The Americans feared being taken advantage of by the crafty Europeans – and indeed, in some sense they had cause, because the British certainly wanted the United States to assume as large a share of the financial burden as possible. Great Britain assumed that a major war interest of both countries was to maintain British financial power. As A. J. Balfour, the Secretary of State for Foreign Affairs, wrote to E. M. House, President Wilson's confidential adviser, 'we seem on the edge of a financial disaster which would be worse than a defeat in the field', adding that 'You know that I am not an alarmist: but this is really serious'. The United States, while not wishing Great Britain to crash in flames, saw no reason why American interests should be sacrificed to British interests which were, as it saw matters, unconnected with the war.[13] The British were desperate; indeed, Lord Northcliffe, newspaper magnate and the head of the British War Mission in the Unites States, wrote to a London colleague in July 1917 that 'We are down on our knees to the Americans'.[14] Without American financial and other aid, Great Britain would be simply unable to continue fighting the war on anything like the same scale as heretofore and might be forced to negotiate a disadvantageous peace with a Germany still in occupation of Northern France. The two countries, however, eventually agreed, after a show of British brinkmanship, that the United States should indeed shoulder much of the burden of the purchases of Great Britain and its allies in the United States by loaning – not granting – them billions of dollars. This was the genesis of the war debts.[15]

But elements in the American government determined to exploit what all assumed to be temporary British financial dependence on the United States in order to further American interests. Certainly the US Treasury wished the dollar to replace the pound as the supreme international currency, and for New York to displace London as the world's major financial centre.[16] President Wilson, too, planned to use American strength against British weakness, in his case to enforce his plans for the Versailles Peace conference: as he wrote in July 1917, at the height of the desperate British fight for American financial aid, 'England and France have not the same views with regard to peace that we have by any means. When the war is over we can force them to our way of thinking, because by that time they will, among other things, be financially in our hands'.[17] None of these plans worked immediately; but the idea that the Americans, not the British, should set the international economic agenda began a path which future US governments trod, and by the Second World War the American use of the financial weapon would be, from the British point of view, merciless.

As stated above, Great Britain turned to the United States for financial resources during the First World War increasingly out of strategic need. At the outset of the war, and indeed for the first year, Great Britain was able to find the dollars it needed at home but, as the pressure mounted, had increasingly to turn to the United States. By April 1917 the need was perceived as vital. But this all took place within the context of continuing British power. Great Britain would not have *lost* the war through lack of financial resources – but would have had to have fought it differently, and could not have continued to subsidize its allies. Perhaps there would have been a negotiated peace, as President Wilson wished. To fight the war Great Britain wanted to fight, it needed American financial resources – but it is arguable that Britain would not have stopped fighting had it lacked them.

A fundamental consequence of the First World War was that the United States and Great Britain exchanged positions as international financial powers. Great Britain had been greatly weakened by its financial efforts on behalf of itself and its allies, and emerged from the war an international debtor. The United States, conversely, had greatly benefited from the war, both in industrial development and in financial receipts – by 1925 it held about 45 per cent of the world's entire stock of gold. The United States was now the supreme international financial power and the major international creditor.[18]

During the inter-war period Great Britain became more and more conscious of its relative financial weakness. It feared the outcome as war became increasingly likely in the late 1930s, since it seemed probable that it would not this time have access to American funds. The US Congress, backed by public opinion, had decided that Americans should have little or nothing to do with political affairs in Europe, including those connected with Great Britain, and Congress passed during the 1930s a series of Neutrality Acts forbidding countries which had not paid their war debts access to aid from the United States in any future war. This included Great Britain. As for the British side: the American attempts to exploit British weakness for American gain, and particularly the American habit of giving advice but not acting itself, had burned itself into the minds of policy-makers. A supreme example of this was Prime Minister Neville Chamberlain, who in December 1937, in response to a Far Eastern crisis, wrote to his sister that 'It is always best & safest to count on *nothing* from the Americans except words'.[19] But Anthony Eden and Winston Churchill did not agree, and others such as the British Treasury had to hope that when war came, as they knew it must, the Americans would change their minds: if they did not, Great Britain was probably doomed.

And, of course, when war came the Americans *did* change their minds: Eden and Churchill had been right. But so had been Chamberlain, because the American government set out from the beginning to exact a price for their aid. Not money this time: no more war debts. But Lend-Lease, that 'most unsordid act' in Churchill's words, came with a heavy price. In the immediate term, Great Britain was forced to sell assets in the United States, Courtauld's American Viscose Corporation, at a rock-bottom price to a consortium of American bankers, who promptly sold it on for millions more: the reason for this was to convince Congress that Great Britain was making every effort to raise funds itself.[20] It was also forced to run down its reserves to the point that by March 1941 they stood at only £70 million above the Currency Reserve.[21] This was also done to influence Congress, but it served as well to placate the President, who refused to believe that Great Britain had as few assets as was claimed. As he commented, after a quick glance at a US Treasury estimate of British dollar resources in December 1940, 'Well, they aren't bust – there's lots of money there'.[22]

Negotiations took place over the following months for the Master Lend-Lease Agreement, and it was here, as well as during the negotiations for the Atlantic Charter in 1941, Bretton Woods in 1944 and the American Loan in 1946, that great pressure was applied. As Dean Acheson, member of the State Department and future Secretary of State, wrote in 1941, since British bargaining power was greatly diminished, now was 'their only chance to do it'.[23] Great Britain had to promise to abandon a number of policies which it had adopted over the previous years to safeguard its economy and trade, policies which the United States saw as damaging to its own national interests. The price for lend-lease aid – that is, for access to goods such as food and munitions, and to the money to pay for them – was 'the Consideration', always capitalized: Great Britain was to be forced to abandon discriminatory tariffs in general and Imperial Preference in particular, and to give up exchange controls.[24] For the Americans, this would give their own businessmen a level playing field, and foster international peace through free trade. For the British, this would open up their markets to the overwhelming dominance of American industrial might and of the dollar and, in short, would threaten their own traders and the economic health of the country. But they had no choice: they could only hope that the worse would not take place.

As the war went on and the United States became increasingly conscious of its immense power, it increasingly took decisions which benefited its own interests and damaged those of Great Britain. This, of course, is what states do, and it was precisely what Great Britain had done in *its* days of power, and continued to do as far as possible. Yet the belief persisted on the British side that relations between the two states should somehow be different, that the United States should not forward its own interests by taking advantage of British weakness during a war in which they were fighting shoulder to shoulder. It is not too much to say that British officials and politicians were angered and even hurt by the US government's acting as the Great Power which Great Britain had encouraged it to become.[25]

Great Britain to many American officials had in fact become an unwelcome encumbrance – goods which went to it could not go to American forces, and the planning of campaigns had sometimes to accommodate British strategic requirements and wishes in ways with which the Americans did not always agree. More worryingly, a number of US officials in the armed forces and the Treasury, among others, realized the potential of using lend-lease as leverage. In September 1944, for example, the chief of supply services for the US military urged that lend-lease be used to force the British to turn over their bases in the Pacific to the United States, to convert the 99-year leases in the Atlantic to permanent transfers, to agree to unconditional landing rights for American military *and* commercial aircraft at British bases around the world, and to prevent them from blocking American access to strategic materials in the Middle and Far East. The US Treasury also wanted to use the wartime leverage: they intended to dominate the international financial system after the war, and therefore needed to eliminate Great Britain as a viable rival. Consequently they set out increasingly to limit what Great Britain could claim was a war need, eligible for lend-lease aid: the idea was to force Great Britain to use up her reserves so that she would have little room for manoeuvre after the war and would have to assent to American plans.[26]

During the war Great Britain received from the American government about $20 billion in lend-lease aid, $27 billion if the aid given to the Commonwealth and empire are included; it in turn provided $6 billion in reverse lend-lease aid to the American government. Great Britain saw this as a joint endeavour, and perceived it as 'mutual aid'; the Americans, however, perceived it as the United States making up a deficit in British supplies, and saw themselves as not only entitled, but required, to keep a close eye on what supplies the British wanted and why. This close scrutiny also enabled policy-makers to fine-tune supplies if they wished to extract a concession from the British. And clearly they did – repeatedly.[27]

The tale is not altogether a pretty one, and historians over the past decade or so have increasingly documented the naked ambition of the

Americans and the sometimes futile defensive measures taken by the British.[28] But it is salutary to remember that for those who lived through the war, the balance appeared rather different. One particularly memorable comment was made by R. S. Sayers, in his official history of British financial policy during the war. Before detailing some of the negotiations, the American demands and the shifts to which the British were driven, he warned his British readers against their natural reaction:

> It is a story, above all else, of unexampled generosity on the part of the American nation. Unless this all-important fact is remembered throughout, these chapters are bound to convey a false impression, an impression insulting alike to the Americans who gave and the British who strove to justify acceptance of the colossal stream of munitions, of food, of aircraft and of materials to sustain both direct war production and civilian life in these islands.[29]

Sayers's comment about sustaining both direct war production and civilian life in Great Britain underlines one of the themes of this chapter: by the Second World War American financial aid was not just a convenience, as in the Boer War, or a strategic necessity, as in the First World War, but a *dire* necessity if Great Britain was to remain in the war at all. This is not to say that it was little more than a military satellite of the United States: certainly until American forces came on stream in mid-1943, the relationship was not unequal. Not only had Great Britain decrypted the enigma machine, enabling it and its allies to read and interpret German signals intelligence, not only had Great Britain stood alone and fought off the might of Germany, but until mid-1943 it simply had more forces in the field. But had Japan not bombed Pearl Harbor, had the United States remained neutral, even benevolently neutral, during the war, Great Britain's position would have been stark indeed, and all of those reversed road signs in East Anglia, carefully pointing in the wrong direction in order to confuse the German invaders, might have come into their own.

In August 1945 the war was over, but Great Britain's position was, if anything, worse. On 20 August the White House announced the termination of lend-lease, and British ministers and officials, who had been hoping that some arrangement might be made to aid the reconversion of the economy, were left, in Sayers's words, 'gasping for breath'.[30] The only path open to Great Britain was to apply for a loan, and negotiations for such a loan took place in Washington from September to December 1945, with J. M. Keynes as the lead negotiator for Great Britain. Keynes had hoped for a grant; then he hoped for an interest-free loan; finally he was offered a loan only 75 per cent as large as that for which he had hoped, and which carried an interest rate of 2 per cent.

In exchange Great Britain had to concede changes in its foreign economic policies which the United States had been attempting to achieve at least since 1932: it had to promise that within a year of Congress agreeing to the loan, the pound sterling would be fully convertible; it also had to promise the elimination of Imperial Preference, which the Americans saw as a restriction on trade between the empire and Commonwealth and the rest of the world. These negotiations can be considered the last of the wartime negotiations, since they were meant to provide Great Britain with the funds to enable it to deal with economic problems arising from the war. But it is also the case that the American negotiators came with perceptions of Great Britain formed in the pre-war period, in the sense that the United States still very much saw Great Britain as dangerous competitor rather than ally. In spite of their triumphalist rhetoric, the United States still walked unsurely abroad, and the pull from Congress, reflecting public opinion, was to bring the boys home and to get back to business. And in the business world, too, Great Britain was still a competitor, and a ruler of closed markets. The point of the loan for many American officials was to prise those markets open.[31]

But the stage and the scenery were to change: for the Americans a new villain – the Soviet Union – would change their perception of Great Britain. While no country could displace the right of the United States to play the role of hero, Great Britain now assumed the role of trusted sidekick. What did commercial rivalry matter in the face of the rise of world communism? A new war – the Cold War – was now upon them, and the fear engendered by the Soviet Union encouraged for the last time direct American financial aid to Great Britain. This arose out of Great Britain's participation in the European Recovery Program as a recipient of Marshall aid.[32]

The Marshall Plan was intended to facilitate the reconstruction of Europe, both economically and politically. The American government had become increasingly alarmed at the evidence of hunger and increasing chaos; both France and Italy had large Communist parties; Germany had to be helped, or at least allowed, to recover but without threatening France; and the economies of the European states had to be helped to recover, both for their own sakes and to lessen the threat of communism in some, and to provide markets for American goods, lest recession hit the American economy. Consequently, over the period 1948 to 1952 the United States government granted in the region of $14 billion to the 16 participating countries, an amount which should be multiplied by at least ten to convey the magnitude of the amount in current prices. The funds, of course, were not without strings. The American government had as its primary geopolitical goal at least the economic integration of

Europe, a goal supported by various requirements as to government planning, manufacturing productivity schemes, fairer taxation policies and not voting for Communists.

How did Great Britain fit into the scheme? First, it immediately took the lead in organizing the other European countries in the manner required by the United States – thereby beating the French – and helping to ensure that some sort of common reconstruction plan emerged from all of the negotiations. It saw itself as, and worked to ensure that it was perceived and treated by the United States as, a partner in this endeavour, not as merely another European country. This was tricky to achieve, since as a result of the policy of making the pound fully convertible in July 1947, imposed by the Americans as the price for the earlier (1946) loan, Great Britain had suffered a sterling crisis of very serious proportions in July–August 1947, just as the Marshall Plan discussions were getting under way. This crisis jolted the Americans into recognition of Great Britain's financial weakness, and it in fact received the largest tranche of Marshall aid of all of the participating countries, about $2.7 billion, in spite of the fact that the British economy was already performing at a far higher rate of production than that of any of the other former belligerents.

And what, in return for this financial aid, did the United States require of Great Britain? The fundamental requirement was that it act as the leader of Europe. The American government wanted the European countries to integrate first, their economies and second, their political systems. While not many knowledgable American officials really believed that the outcome could be a United States of Europe in the American mould, nevertheless they all believed that there could, and should, be a Europe without tariff or currency barriers, a huge single market, as had obtained in the United States for a century and a half. Furthermore, as a single political entity, Europe would provide a strong barrier against the westward expansion of the Soviet Union. Great Britain, as the strongest and wealthiest of the European countries, as the victorious allied power, indeed as the one European country still a Great Power, should, the American government believed, take the lead in such an endeavour.

And what was the British response? It was a comprehensive rejection of the American plans. Great Britain fought implacably against the proposals for its integration and that of its dependencies into a European economic organization. It had, after all, an empire and Commonwealth on which the sun still never set, and from these worldwide responsibilities stemmed its claim to be a global power.[33] Furthermore, the British government believed that it was not safe to be perceived as merely a European power. Because the European countries were unreliable as allies, Great Britain only felt safe when allied with the United States, in spite of all of the problems experienced during the Second World War; as a Minute recording a discussion in January 1949 between senior Treasury, Foreign Office, Dominions Office and Board of Trade officials put it,

> Since post-war planning began, our policy has been to secure close political, military and economic co-operation with U.S.A. This has been necessary to get economic aid. It will always be decisive for our security ... We hope to secure a special relationship with U.S.A. ... for in the last resort we cannot rely upon the European countries.[34]

Great Britain feared that if the United States saw it as only a European power, rather than as a world power, the American government would no longer treat it as a partner, even if only a junior one. In this fundamental geopolitical requirement, Great Britain was immovable: it sometimes conceded on small points, but never the larger one. For better or worse, Great Britain did not see its interests as only, or even primarily, lying in Europe, and nothing that the United States offered, or threated, moved it.

The question then becomes, why did the United States grant Great Britain the huge tranche of Marshall aid, when the British refused to accord their policies with the American government's main goal? The answer, of course, is that there was a Cold War on. In fact, the war seemed so threatening to so many European countries that they agreed with Great Britain in its goal to convince the Americans to agree to a peacetime alliance, and in April 1949 was signed the agreement for the North Atlantic Treaty Organization (NATO).[35] For the historians of both British and American foreign policy, April 1949 marks a watershed. 'No entangling alliances', the first American president, George Washington, warned his countrymen; 'no permanent friends or permanent enemies, just permanent interests', British tradition responded. NATO assumed entanglement, and certainly assumed both permanent friends and permanent enemies. The United States and the Great Britain were now permanent allies.

And within only a year of becoming allies, with Marshall aid came the last bit of crude financial aid to Great Britain from the United States. But instead of receiving aid for four years, as did the other European recipients, the US Congress cut off Marshall aid to it a year earlier than planned: British financial reserves had inconveniently risen too high for Congress to believe that Great Britain needed any more American taxpayers' money. From now on, the few American offers of financial aid came in the form of loans, and there were not many of these offered. Most were in the form of short-term credits from the

Federal Reserve Bank of New York to the Bank of England in support of the pound, such as during the middle 1960s or in June 1976,[36] credits which needed to be repaid. One of the few offers of a loan government-to-government came in the autumn of 1967 as the United States, then in the throes of the Vietnam War, tried to restrain Britain from withdrawing its troops from east of Suez. But the loan was to be short-term, the cost to Britain too great, and it was refused.[37]

As the two countries remained close allies, aid when given was and is given in kind and in policies, not in money. Britain since the Second World War has not been as strong economically as it ought to have been in order to fulfil its role, at first as a Great Power and now as a regional power with world-wide interests. It turned itself into a nuclear power, but since the Nassau Conference in 1962 Britain has received its delivery systems from the United States, certainly in the case of Polaris at an extremely low price.[38] In return the United States has control of the island of Diego Garcia in the Indian Ocean, from which Britain obligingly threw out the native inhabitants; it has the use of bases in Britain itself, from which, for example, it flew the planes which bombed Libya in spite of an outraged British public opinion; it has the control of a base on Ascension Island.

The Ascension Island base was crucial to British victory in the last war to be discussed in this chapter: the Falklands War in 1982 against Argentina. At some cost to its interests in Latin America, the United States, eventually, publicly supported Britain. This was not because President Ronald Reagan was besotted with Prime Minister Margaret Thatcher's blue eyes, her legs, or even her mind, ideology and determination, all of which were put forward as factors in newspaper commentary during the war. Rather, the United States supported its NATO ally, because a failure to do so would have sent a dangerous signal to the Soviet Union as well as undermining European faith in American willingness to support them. It also supported the Thatcher government because it was a Conservative government: the US government feared that if Britain lost the war, the government would fall and be replaced by a Labour government which would be anti-NATO, anti-Europe and anti-nuclear. But the United States did not support Britain with finance; rather, it provided aid in kind. It provided hardware, including various missiles: there were, for example, Sidewinder air-to-air missiles for the Harrier jump jets. These Sidewinders were supposed to replenish Britain's NATO stocks, but the assumption must be that some found their way to the South Atlantic. There was help with refuelling the task force, and the provision of some intelligence information, the latter by the eventual repositioning of an American intelligence satellite. But probably the most important assistance was provided right from the beginning with the British use of Wideawake Airfield on Ascension Island in the Azores, the only way in which British aeroplanes could have made the long journey from Britain to the South Atlantic. The island itself was British property and a refusal by the United States of British use of the facilities would have had enormous repercussions, possibly affecting the Americans' own use of the more important American base on the *British*-owned island of Diego Garcia.[39]

Within the context of the theme of this chapter, did American aid during the Falklands War count as strategic necessity or convenience? Clearly, it was both: almost certainly the task force would not have turned around in mid-ocean and steamed back to Britain had the United States refused to back it publicly. For one thing, a substantial amount of hardware had already been shipped to the British, thanks to the Anglophiliac Secretary of Defense, Casper Weinberger, and for another, the Conservative government, and especially Thatcher, were too committed to the recovery of the Falkland Islands to pull back once events were in motion.[40] Therefore the American aid was convenient but not vital – unless the assumption is made that the British government was prepared to gamble unreasonably with the lives of its soldiers and sailors, given that war is always a gamble.

The point is that the United States and Great Britain have been formal allies continually for over 30 years, and intermittently allies for 30 years before that – and allies to the death from 1941 to 1945. They were, and to an extent still are, held together by shared values and interests and, even more important, shared enemies. As allies, it is in the interest of each that the other should be strong, although not so much stronger that dragooning or even bullying is attempted. From 1917 to the present, the United States has been stronger financially than Great Britain, and during the various wars in which they have fought together[41] the United States has attempted simultaneously to support the British war effort and to force the British to accede to American policy goals, both wartime and peacetime.

Sometimes the United States has succeeded, but sometimes it has not, for Great Britain, too, has had its own strengths. It had the empire and Commonwealth, which for the United States since 1945 provided at least two advantages. First, this was territory for which Great Britain had the responsibility to keep out enemies, such as Communists, since territory which Britain oversaw was territory with which the United States did not have to bother. Second, such territory was very useful for bases and for intelligence listening posts.[42] Great Britain has a well-trained professional army, a navy of immense experience with which the US Navy has worked closely since the Second World War, and a Foreign and Commonwealth Office and diplomatic corps of high ability and immense continuity of experience. The two countries on the whole share many of the same interests, and will continue to do so as long as the United States has global responsibilities and Great Britain has global interests; they will consult and discuss and sometimes act together. In short, financial strength is not everything, but it is immensely useful when trying to fight a war: it was fortunate for Great Britain that when it needed help, the bank manager agreed to make those loans without actually insisting on the keys to the house.

Notes

1. Britain was commonly known as Great Britain both domestically and internationally until about the 1960s, during which the terminology changed to Britain. The same convention will be followed in this chapter.
2. Voltaire, *Letters on England* (Harmondsworth, 1980), p. 51.
3. For details on the series of Boer War loans see Kathleen Burk, *Morgan Grenfell 1838–1988: The Biography of a Merchant Bank* (Oxford, 1989), pp. 111–25.
4. Sir Edward Hamilton Diary, 9 December 1903, Add. MS 48681, British Library (BL), London.
5. Hamilton Diary, 4 February 1900, Add. MS 48676, BL.
6. Hamilton Diary, 31 July 1900, Add. MS 48676, BL. For an outline of the Boer War from the standpoint of economics and imperialism see D. J. Fieldhouse, *Economics and Empire 1830–1914* (London, 1976), pp. 354–62.
7. Hamilton Diary, 2 August 1900, Add. MS 48676, BL. Dawkins to Milner, 16 August 1900, Box 177, Milner Papers, Bodleian Library, Oxford. J. P. Morgan and Co. to J. S. Morgan and Co., 9 August and 8 August 1900 (second letter), MS 21, 802/9, Morgan Grenfell Papers, Guildhall Library, London. According to A. J. P. Taylor, privately the German government tended towards neutrality rather than opposition to the British position. A. J. P. Taylor *The Struggle For Mastery in Europe 1848–1918* (Oxford, 1954), pp. 388–9.
8. Hamilton Diary, 31 July 1900, Add. MS 48676, BL.
9. Hamilton Diary, 14 April 1901, Add. MS 48678, BL.
10. For details on the Anglo-American financial relationship during the First World War and its implications for the power relationship see Kathleen Burk, *Britain, America and the Sinews of War 1914–1918* (London, 1985), *passim*.
11. Or as J. M. Keynes put it for the cabinet, 'Of the £5,000,000 which the Treasury have to find daily for the prosecution of the war, about £2,000,000 has to be found in North America.' Cab. 42/23/7, Public Record Office (PRO), London.
12. J. M. Keynes, 'Statement of Resources and Liabilities in America', 17 March 1917, T. 172/422, fos 2–4, Treasury Papers, PRO. For borrowing see Kathleen Burk, 'J. M. Keynes and the Exchange Rate Crisis of July 1917', *Economic History Journal*, 2nd series, 32, 3 (August 1979), 406–7.

13.   A. J. Balfour, Secretary of State for Foreign Affairs, to Sir William Wiseman, Head of the British Military Mission and of MI6 in the US, to be passed on to Col. E. M. House, confidential adviser to President Woodrow Wilson, 28 June 1917, FO 800/209. Andrew Bonar Law, Chancellor of the Exchequer, to William Gibbs McAdoo, US Secretary of the Treasury, 23 July 1917, in Elizabeth Johnson (ed.), *The Collected Writings of John Maynard Keynes. Volume XVI. Activities 1914–1919: The Treasury and Versailles* (London, 1971), pp. 255–63. 'American financial policy will be dictated by a desire to cooperate to the fullest extent possible with the several powers making war in common against Germany, but America's cooperation cannot mean that America can assume the entire burden of financing the war.' McAdoo to A. J. Balfour, 12 July 1917, State Department, *Foreign Relations of the United States, 1917, Supplement 2, the World War*, (Washington, DC, 1932), pp. 543–5.

14.   Lord Northcliffe to Geoffrey Robinson, 1 July 1917, File 1917, Northcliffe Papers, *The Times* Archives, London.

15.   See Burk, 'J. M. Keynes and the Exchange Rate Crisis', 412–14 and *idem*, 'The Diplomacy of Finance: British Financial Missions to the United States 1914–1918', *The Historical Journal*, 22, 2 (1979), 363–6. The loans by the American government to Britain totalled $4.8 billion.

16.   House to Wiseman, 25 August 1917, 90/26, William Wiseman Papers, Yale University Library.

17.   Wilson to House, 30 April 1917, Box 121, E. M. House Papers, Yale University Library.

18.   US Bureau of the Census, *Historical Statistics of the United States, Colonial Times to 1957* (Washington, DC, 1969), p. 624 for the statistic on gold. Kathleen Burk, 'Money and Power: The Shift From Great Britain to the United States', in Y. Cassis (ed.), *Finance and Financiers in European History 1880–1960* (Cambridge, 1992), p. 363.

19.   Neville Chamberlain to Hilda Chamberlain, 17 December 1939, 18/1/1032, Neville Chamberlain Papers, Birmingham University Library. Quoted in William R. Rock, *Chamberlain and Roosevelt: British Foreign Policy and the United States, 1937–1940* (Columbus, OH, 1988), p. 48.

20.   Kathleen Burk, 'American Foreign Economic Policy and Lend-Lease', in A. Lane and H. Temperley (eds), *The Rise and Fall of the Grand Alliance, 1941–45* (Basingstoke, 1995), p. 54.

21.   R. S. Sayers, *Financial Policy 1939–45* (London, 1956), p. 496 (table 7: Gold and dollar reserves).

22.   Quoted in David Reynolds, *The Creation of the Anglo-American Alliance 1937–41: A Study in Competitive Co-operation* (London, 1981), p. 154, based on the manuscript diary of Henry Morgenthau, the Secretary of the Treasury, and in Warren Kimball, *The Most Unsordid Act: Lend-Lease, 1939–1941* (Baltimore, MD, 1969), p. 103, based on the files of Philip Young.

23.   Quoted in Reynolds, *Creation of the Anglo-American Alliance*, p. 274. For a lucid description and analysis of the Anglo-American negotiations see L. S. Pressnell, *External Economic Policy Since the War. Volume I: The Post-War Financial Settlement* (London, 1986), *passim*, which, despite its title, covers the period from 1941.

24.   Pressnell, *External Economic Policy*, ch. 3.

25. Burk, 'Lend-Lease'; Randall Bennett Woods, *A Changing of the Guard: Anglo-American Relations, 1941–1946* (Chapel Hill, NC, 1990).

26. Burk, 'Lend-Lease', pp. 58–9.

27. Sayers, *Financial Policy*, table 5: US lend-lease aid to the British Empire to 31 August 1945 and table 8: UK reciprocal aid to 1 September 1945. Burk, 'Lend-Lease', pp. 57–9.

28. See Woods, *Changing of the Guard*; Pressnell, *External Economic Policy*; Alan P. Dobson, *US Wartime Aid to Britain 1940–1946* (London, 1986); and Burk, 'Lend-Lease'.

29. Sayers, *Financial Policy*, p. 375.

30. Ibid., p. 480.

31. Donald Moggridge (ed.), *The Collected Writings of John Maynard Keynes. Volume XXIV. Activities 1944–1946: The Transition to Peace* (London, 1979), pp. 420–628; Richard Gardner, *Sterling-Dollar Diplomacy in Current Perspective* (New York, 1980), pp. 188–254.

32. Melvyn Leffler, 'The United States and the Strategic Dimensions of the Marshall Plan', *Diplomatic History*, 12, 3 (Summer 1988), 277–306.

33. Kathleen Burk, 'Britain and the Marshall Plan', in C. Wrigley (ed.), *Warfare, Diplomacy and Politics: Essays in Honour of A. J. P. Taylor* (London, 1986), pp. 210–30.

34. R. W. B. Clarke, 'Policy towards Europe', 5 January 1949, in Sir Alec Cairncross (ed.), *Anglo-American Economic Collaboration in War and Peace 1942–1949* (Oxford, 1982), p. 208.

35. Martin H. Folly, 'Breaking the Vicious Circle: Britain, the United States, and the Genesis of the North Atlantic Treaty', *Diplomatic History*, 12, 1 (Winter 1988), 59–78; Alex Danchev, 'Taking the Pledge: Oliver Franks and the Negotiation of the North Atlantic Treaty', *Diplomatic History*, 15, 2 (Spring 1991), 199–220; Sir Nicholas Henderson, *The Birth of NATO* (London, 1982); and Lawrence S. Kaplan, *NATO and the United States: The Enduring Alliance* (Boston, MA, 1988).

36. Robert Solomon, *The International Monetary System 1945–1981* (New York, 1982) and Kathleen Burk and Alec Cairncross, *'Goodbye, Great Britain': The 1976 IMF Crisis* (London, 1992).

37. And consequently Britain went ahead and devalued the pound. Alec Cairncross and Barry Eichengreen, *Sterling in Decline: The Devaluations of 1931, 1949 and 1967* (Oxford, 1983), ch. 5.

38. Lawrence Freedman and John Gearson, 'Interdependence and Independence: Nassau and the British Nuclear Deterrent', in K. Burk and M. Stokes (eds), *The United States and the European Alliance since 1945* (Oxford, 1999).

39. Lawrence Freedman and Virginia Gamba-Stonehouse, *Signals of War: The Falklands Conflict of 1982* (London, 1990); Michael Charlton, *The Little Platoon: Diplomacy and the Falklands Dispute* (Oxford, 1989); Nicholas Henderson, *Channels and Tunnels: Reflections on Britain Abroad* (London, 1987), pp. 83–108, and idem, *Mandarin: The Diaries of An Ambassador 1969–1982* (London, 1994), pp. 442–76.

40. Hugo Young, *One of Us: A Biography of Margaret Thatcher* (London, 1989), pp. 247–92.

41. For example, the Gulf War. See Lawrence Freedman and Efraim Karsh, *The Gulf Conflict: Diplomacy and War in the New World Order* (London, revd edn, 1994).

42. Jeffrey T. Richelson and Desmond Ball, *The Ties That Bind: Intelligence Cooperation Between the UKUSA Countries – the United Kingdom, the United States of America, Canada, Australia and New Zealand* (Boston, MA, 1990).

CHAPTER FOURTEEN

America and the Representation of British History in Film and Television

D. L. LeMahieu

In the late twentieth century, scores of cinema and television productions represented the British past to a mass American audience. Six of these productions won the Academy Award for Best Motion Picture, including *Lawrence of Arabia* (1962), *A Man for All Seasons* (1966) and *Gandhi* (1982). Television serials such as *The Forsyte Saga*, *Elizabeth R* and *Upstairs, Downstairs* attracted substantial audiences in America, as did the films of Merchant/Ivory during the 1980s. If in schools and universities, courses in British history suffered from diminishing enrollments, visual depictions of the British past enjoyed wide appeal. Film and television probably informed more Americans about British history than any other medium of communication.

Some have claimed that these costume dramas reinforced an ideology of social and political conservatism. Class and hierarchy, these commentators argue, so permeated these productions that they became a celebration of the class system. Powerful evidence supports this contention. Again and again, the dress, manners, politics, cultural taste and social prejudices of a privileged élite attract detailed, loving attention. Artfully photographed scenes luxuriate in conspicuous consumption: the imposing country house, the manicured lawn, the deer park, elegant aristocrats at a glittering occasion. If some critics accused these dramas of nostalgia, the compensatory emotion of a declining power, others indicated how they reinforced orientalist assumptions, even and perhaps especially when claiming to challenge the imperial legacy.[1]

Yet, 'conservatism' proves to be an elusive term, especially when transposed from one national context to another. This chapter, which treats selectively both fictional and factual representations of the British past, appropriates the term 'conservatism' but defines and explores its American context in three different ways. First, if clearly about class and social hierarchy, British historical dramas also buttressed values deeply embedded in the American tradition. A second, quite distinct conservatism emerged from those programmes that offered striking historical parallels from the British past to the convulsions of the late 1960s and early 1970s in the United States. Finally, British historical drama conserved an immediate experience of the past that few other media could match. The unfolding of these visual narratives permitted American audiences impatient with written history to reexperience more palpably the indeterminicies of what one observer called 'futures past'.[2]

Perhaps not surprisingly, British historical dramas of the 1950s and 1960s often explored themes central to the American experience. During an era when Westerns such as *High Noon* (1952) and *Shane* (1953) vivified the complexities of 'mythic individualism' in America, British films also commented upon the dilemmas of personal autonomy and civic engagement.[3] In particular, two celebrated productions by the director David Lean explored the tensions and ambiguities of courageous outsiders. In *The Bridge on the River Kwai* (1957), Alec Guinness portrays a British army officer, Colonel Nicholson, who in the middle of the Second World War defies the orders of a Japanese prison camp commander to force British officers to work alongside their men. These prisoners must construct an important Japanese railway bridge deep in the jungles of Siam. In the first third of the film, Nicholson emerges as a difficult but extraordinarily principled character, who endures weeks of terrible punishment to uphold tenets of the Geneva Convention. Yet, Nicholson's eventual triumph over the Japanese commander proves to be lethally ironic, when in the latter half of the film he decides to make the bridge an emblem of British pride. British commandos, assisted by a cynical American played by William Holden, blow up the bridge in a spectacular but ambiguous final scene, in which Nicholson realizes his folly only at the last possible moment.[4]

In this American-produced film, Lean presents two variations on the formula of heroic individualism. Nicholson demonstrates that stubborn adherence to a social code proves admirable only in quite specific contexts. As a defender of his officers early in the film, Nicholson earns the admiration of his men; as a misguided upholder of British racial pride, he becomes an exasperating impediment to the allied war effort. Heroism and irrationality occupy the same ground. Conversely, not unlike the hard-boiled detective, William Holden's wise-cracking cynicism early in the film distances him from the shibboleths of nationalism and military glory; an impostor and a hedonist, Holden's character, named Shears, disgusts British officers, whose contempt for him curiously prefigures that which American war veterans showered upon Vietnam protesters a decade later. Still, by the end of the film, Holden sacrifices himself for the cause, demonstrating his adherence to traditional values after all.

Lawrence of Arabia (1962) offers an even more ambiguous portrait of the heroic individual. As Michael Anderegg has noted, three paradoxes of Lawrence's character dominate this puzzling film. First, Lawrence continually demonstrates an extraordinary physical endurance; he traverses vast stretches of desert on foot; he suffers torture without complaint; he fearlessly leads Arab warriors into battle. Yet, in his portrayal, Peter O'Toole includes gestures and mannerisms clearly intended to portray Lawrence as weak, effeminate and masochistic. As with other films from this period, Lean codes Lawrence's sexuality in a manner that, if by current tastes stereotypical, many considered daring for its era. Second, Lawrence embodies both the strengths and limitations of British imperialism. Pledged to unify the Arabs against the Turks, he also willingly serves British interests antithetical to Arab needs. Lean clearly distances Lawrence from the more cynical manipulations of British imperial ambitions. Still, by casting the roles of leading Arabs with Western actors, including Alec Guinness, the film remains well within the conventions of orientalism. Third and finally, Lawrence both welcomes and eschews self-promotion. Shy and self-denying, he also revels in the publicity that followed his adventures. The American reporter in the film, clearly modelled on Lowell Thomas, initially admires but soon comes to distrust him. As with Nicholson and Shears in *Bridge on the River Kwai*, Lean provides no clear moral guidance about his heroic antagonists.[5]

Unlike the films of David Lean, *A Man for All Seasons*, released in 1966, possessed an unambiguous moral and a protagonist unencumbered by glaring weaknesses. The film's screenwriter, Robert Bolt, considered Thomas More 'a hero of selfhood'.[6] While the drama explores the conflict between religious and state authority, it centres upon More's measured opposition to the opportunists who surround him. Cromwell persistently tries to entrap More into a damaging statement of political opposition to the king. Richard Rich, whose vaulting ambition provides a striking contrast to More's humanism, eventually perjures himself to convict More in one of the film's more electrifying scenes. When, his conviction assured, he learns that Rich has been appointed Attorney-General for Wales, he remarks with pained astonishment, 'For Wales? Why, Richard, it profits a man nothing to give his soul for the whole world ... But for Wales!'[7] The film tries to render More's martyrdom a reluctant rather than fanatical act of a devoted Christian. The scenes with his protesting family prove some of the most affecting in the film. He argues with his clever daughter about the centrality of law; he comforts without patronizing his uncomprehending wife. Like Gary Cooper in *High Noon*, More does not relish the personal cost of duty. A box-office success which won six Academy Awards, including best picture, *A Man for All Seasons* was released in the United States at a time when thousands of college students began invoking a higher authority in their opposition to the draft. Though historians continue to slate the film for its historical inaccuracies, it was only in part about sixteenth-century England. Robert Bolt constructed a parable for his own time.

The 1970s witnessed a number of important changes in the presentation of British history to American viewers. First, as British film production declined, its television programmes enjoyed remarkable prosperity in the United States. The recently formed Corporation for Public Broadcasting and the Public Broadcasting System, excoriated by the Nixon Administration for its perceived left-wing bias, welcomed British programming as politically innocuous, a decision criticized by the Carnegie Commission in 1979.[8] Then, too, for the major oil companies, the historical dramas and classic serials of British television presented a relatively inexpensive opportunity for improving public relations during a period when petrol shortages, soaring retail prices and astronomical corporate profits enraged American consumers. With an assured demand for their product, Mobil and Exxon could impress an upscale, politically influential segment of the American public at remarkably little cost.[9]

It was also during this period that the mood of American culture darkened, as the duplicity of high government officials about the Vietnam War became compounded by the scandals of Watergate. Notions of conspiracy became increasingly respectable; corruption penetrated the core of American power. A number of British television serials during the 1970s reinforced suspicions about central authority. *The Six Wives of Henry VIII* (1971) presented an image of court not dominated by an eccentric but lovable monarch, as in Alexander Korda's famous film of the 1930s, but a milieu infused with intrigue, apprehension and fatal miscalculation. Though Keith Michell creates a multidimensional Henry, the king's shifting political and emotional allegiances precipitate a series of vividly enacted individual tragedies. For any number of characters, misalliance meant arrest, torture and death: *The Six Wives of Henry VIII* revived the inner meaning of Renaissance *fortuna* for American audiences.

This unsentimental portrait of the Tudor court was revisited in the opening episode of *Elizabeth R*, first shown in the United States in 1972. The young Elizabeth, played with admirable toughness and vulnerability by Glenda Jackson, confronts a number of conspiracies meant to deny her the throne. Declared the 'bastard Elizabeth' by her half-sister Mary, Elizabeth must disavow both her religion and treasonous rebellions raised in her name. Thrust into the Tower after the failure of Wyatt's Rebellion, she staves off immediate execution in a riveting scene that highlights both her grasp of English law and a stubborn will to survive. As with *The Six Wives of Henry VIII*, the first episode of *Elizabeth R* re-creates a polity full of menace for the righteous and unwary.[10]

Although *Chariots of Fire*, which won the Academy Award for Best Motion Picture in 1981, represents a notable shift in mood and tone, it also contains scenes of a corrupt Establishment. Two Masters of Cambridge colleges, acidly portrayed by Lindsay Anderson and John Gielgud, embody the casual anti-Semitism and complacent snobbery of an antiquated élite. Yet, the story centres on two figures, both social outsiders, who rise to individual heroism and athletic glory despite such obstacles. Abrahams hires a professional trainer and pursues his athletic goals without regard for the Master's code of amateurism. Gielgud considers this single-minded quest of individual glory as 'too plebeian'; Abrahams proclaims that 'I have the future'. Liddell, the Scottish Presbyterian who refuses to compete on Sunday even if it means missing an Olympic event he longs to win, must resist pressure from the Prince of Wales and other high officials to preserve his religious principles. Like Thomas More, but with far less at stake, he places 'God before Country'. As other commentators have noted, *Chariots of Fire* might easily be interpreted as a parable of Thatcherism; hard-working and dedicated social outsiders triumph over the stifling traditions of British paternalism.[11]

A number of films and television programmes about the late Victorian and Edwardian period in British history contrasted vital and appealing lower-class characters with their more languid, or artificial upper-class counterparts. In Joseph Losey's film adaptation of L. P. Hartley's *The Go-Between*, released in 1971, a beautiful upper-class women played by Julie Christie pursues an illicit love affair with a handsome lower-class farmer Ted Burgess, but must eventually marry Lord Trimingham, an affable but charmingly dense character. Described as 'a big hitter' and 'the best shot with a gun', the farmer Burgess, played by Alan Bates, embodies a Lawrentian vitality in a film that conveys palpably the heat of an unusually hot summer.[12] In a similar fashion, Alan Bridge's film adaptation of Rebecca West's *Return of the Soldier*, released in the United States in 1982, contrasts the instinctive empathy, vulnerability, and spiritual depth of the lower middle-class Margaret, played brilliantly by Glenda Jackson, with the neurotic brittleness of the passionless Kitty, again played by Julie Christie. In both films, a love affair of great naturalness and intensity must be terminated for reasons of class and social propriety. In both films, the artificial world of upper-class respectability contrasts sharply with the unpretentiousness of social outsiders.[13]

Indeed, the outsiders in these dramas often prove the most appealing characters. In the BBC's adaptation of John Galsworthy's *The Forsyte*

Saga, the television series that initiated the entire Edwardian sub-genre in the late 1960s, Young Jolyon's revolt in the early episodes against his family's materialism and complacency stands in welcome counterpoint to Soames's extraordinary possessiveness. Young Jolyon creates art to satisfy an inner desire for beauty; Soames collects art to increase his personal fortune. Jolyon, played by Kenneth More, tries to live spontaneously and rejects the tyranny of keeping up appearances; Soames, as portrayed by Eric Porter, calculates every move to maintain his social standing. Only in the concluding episodes, adapted from Galsworthy's later and more sentimental instalments of the saga, does Soames soften considerably.[14]

In the 1986 adaptation of *A Room with a View*, a father and son, the Emersons, embody an instinctive egalitarianism which their fellow English travellers in Florence find, as E. M. Forster originally described it, 'so ungentlemanly and yet so beautiful'. Without even a proper introduction, they offer to exchange their rooms with Lucy Honeychurch and her travelling companion Charlotte Bartlett, played by Maggie Smith. In Sante Croce, Mr Emerson interrupts the lecture of Reverend Eager to protest his claim that the church 'was built by faith'. 'Built by faith indeed!' Emerson exclaims, 'That simply means the workmen weren't paid properly.' The Emersons reject the notion that art somehow contains a greater or more revered truth than life itself. In these and other examples, they vault the conventional barriers of social class that separate individuals from authentic human passions.[15]

The issue of social class and conservatism in these Edwardian dramas thus involves some ambiguity. If many of these productions emphasize overwhelmingly the social preoccupations of a tiny élite, what they portray may not be necessarily what they endorse. For it is the outsiders and individualists within the social system that clearly attract the viewer's attention and empathy. These dramas may have been popular in America in part because they permitted audiences to glimpse the private lives of British élites while still identifying with characters and values more characteristic of the later twentieth century. To be sure, many of these productions were adaptations of earlier works, but usually by authors, such as E. M. Forster and Rebecca West, who satirized rather than extolled social inequality. Television and film permitted a visually literate audience to enter the drawing rooms of a vanished élite without leaving their values at the door.

British historical dramas also embodied another form of conservatism important for Americans, involving the controversial issues of both gender and patriotism. The women's movement of the 1970s, stronger in America than in Britain, represented only one aspect of a profound social transformation involving both men and women. Continuing a trend begun during the Second World War, the extraordinary prosperity of the 1960s allowed both Britain and America to expand greatly educational opportunities for a burgeoning generation of the young. The rising expectations of this generation manifested itself not only in the Youth Culture of the 1960s, which proved largely ephemeral, but in the changing patterns of work and family life during the 1970s and 1980s. The rapid expansion of the service economy during an era of stagflation, combined with the postponement of marriage and children among the better educated, helped transform the relationship among men and women both in the public and private sphere. This complex transformation, which the feminist movement both reflected and helped forge, manifested itself in a variety of cultural activities.

British historical dramas provided audiences with both a pedigree for contemporary feminism and, more subtly, encouraging illustrations of enlightened relationships among men and women. First, these productions often involved women engaged in revolt against male domination. In the early episodes of the *Forsyte Saga*, for example, Irene endures her loveless marriage to Soames Forsyte with barely concealed contempt. When he rapes her, she leaves him, only to return after the accidental death of her lover, the architect Bosinney. Though eventually Irene finds happiness in marriage to Young Jolyon, she remains an elusive character, in part because she is always portrayed externally, as a beautiful, passive object much admired by men. Moreover, her implacable rejections of Soames's repeated attempts at forgiveness or reconciliation helped transform him into a sympathetic character. More a *femme fatale* than a feminist, Irene remains well within the male gaze.[16]

The suffragettes offered a far less equivocal example of rebellion. *Shoulder To Shoulder*, first broadcast in 1974, focused on the heroic efforts of women to gain the vote before the First World War. In a six-part series that included unblinking portrayals of the deep splits within the movement, *Shoulder to Shoulder* uncovered a hidden history of political action that the series producers clearly hoped would inspire contemporary feminists. 'I don't think the media have treated the women's movement very kindly', one of the show's producers, Verity Lambert, told the *Sunday Times* in 1974. 'We aimed for a series of feminist programmes.'[17] Perhaps the most dramatic and effective episode traced the radicalization of Lady Constance Lytton. Outraged at the special treatment titled suffragettes received in prison, Lytton disguised herself as a commoner and endured repeated forced feedings at significant cost to her personal health. These striking visual depictions of women fed against their will, in one instance juxtaposed with a voiceover of the

House of Commons debate on the practice, provided the suffragettes with new historical stature. Scrupulously researched and only rarely sentimental, *Shoulder To Shoulder* restored the dignity and courage of women such as Emily Wilding Davison, who threw herself under the king's horse at the Derby in 1913, or Sylvia Pankhurst, who rejected the upper-class prejudices of her sister and mother, and sought to organize working-class women in the East End of London. 'It's ... easier to be a feminist in 1975', Susan Brownmiller wrote in a review of the series, 'for today we know there are glorious precedents.'[18]

Yet, it was not simply women who discovered role models among the Edwardians. These productions also provided striking examples of enlightened men who regarded women not as subordinates or possessions, but as equal partners in a relationship of mutual respect. In *A Room with a View*, for example, the young and engagingly spontaneous George Emerson implores Lucy Honeychurch not to marry Cecil, the absurdly self-conscious aesthete to whom she's engaged. 'He's the type who's kept Europe back for a thousand years', George warns. 'Every moment of his life he's forming you, telling you what's charming or amusing or ladylike, telling you what a man thinks womanly; and you, you of all women, listen to his voice instead of your own.' Like his father, George believes in a natural egalitarianism between the sexes that acknowledges and nurtures what Forster called 'the holiness of direct desire'. Cecil, on the other hand, represents a traditional, stifling paternalism that forces women to adopt artificial identities. By the end of the story, George and Lucy form a new kind of partnership in marriage, where passionate commitment need not compromise individual autonomy. For all its airiness and charm, *A Room with a View* delivers a feminist message no less powerful than *Shoulder to Shoulder*.[19]

Both *The Forsyte Saga* and *Upstairs Downstairs* provide contrasting models of the masculine treatment of women. In *The Forsyte Saga*, Soames's possessiveness and insensitivity towards both Irene and his second wife Annette, whose marriage to him resembles a business deal more than a love affair, contrasts sharply with the behaviour of his cousin, Young Jolyon, who understands and respects women. Jolyon's instinctive humanity encompasses the women in his life, whereas Soames's deep pessimism informs his encounters with all individuals, male and female. Only with his daughter Fleur, who shares many of his characteristics, does Soames demonstrate his strong need for trust and affection.[20]

In *Upstairs Downstairs*, James Bellamy's string of failed relationships stands in counterpoint to his father's successful marriages to Lady Marjorie and, after her death on the *Titanic*, to Virginia, a Scottish widow. In the early episodes, James impregnates Sarah, the rebellious under-house parlour maid, then stands by idly as the family solicitor, Sir

Geoffrey Dillon, announces a socially convenient arrangement that prevents their marriage and separates them permanently. During James's floundering marriage to Hazel, it is Richard and not his son, who best understands her needs and frustrations. As Hazel lies dying from influenza, James spends the evening at a society ball with Georgina, his attractive cousin. Outraged, Richard berates his son for his indifference. Unlike James, he treats women with unfailing courtesy, and communicates with them in ways his son cannot.[21]

The relationship of characters such as George Emerson and Lucy Honeychurch in *A Room with a View*, like the suffragette campaigns depicted in *Shoulder to Shoulder*, shared at least one important trait in common. Both involved revolts against a traditional hierarchy in which men occupied a privileged position. In the public sphere, the suffragettes fought for a more democratic franchise which another outside group, the working class, achieved in the nineteenth century. In the private sphere, feminism championed relationships of greater equality and mutual respect. Once again the Edwardians provided contemporary audiences with historical precedents worth pondering. The struggle against traditional paternalism could not be won in a single generation. Like the attack on class privilege, the women's movement was part of a much larger democratic revolution. British historical dramas provided contemporary American audiences, both male and female, with a valuable perspective that cushioned the shock of the new.

Because the Edwardian period ended in the national tragedy of the First World War, these dramas addressed another issue of enormous concern. The First World War shattered the idyll of upper-class Edwardian life. It discredited cherished nineteenth-century ideals, accelerated the relative economic decline of Great Britain and, above all, decimated an entire generation of youth and promise. Although this fall from grace might possess special meaning to an American audience recently traumatized by the Vietnam War, it also came to possess a larger, emblematic significance. The First World War became the first of many experiences in the twentieth century of youthful idealism betrayed by political reality.

Vera Brittain's *Testament of Youth* told the story of a young, middle-class woman from the North of England whose life changed utterly because of the war. Her career at Oxford needed to be postponed when she became a nurse, an experience that taught her in numbing detail the grim realities of modern warfare. Her great love, the gifted Roland Leighton, was killed by a sniper shortly before a Christmas leave. Her musically talented brother died of wounds within months of the Armistice. His closest friend became blinded then, after Vera committed herself to him, died in hospital. Returning to Oxford, she discovered that undergraduates showed little interest in her experiences. She became a socialist and a pacifist. 'All those with whom I had really been intimate were gone ... ', she wrote, 'the world was mad and we were all victims.'[22]

Like the book itself, the BBC's six-part adaptation of *Testament of Youth* glided over some interesting complications to Vera Brittain's powerful cautionary tale. The original diary from which she wrote the book in 1933, contains a number of militantly patriotic passages: only later did she impose pacifistic sentiments upon her wartime experiences. The portrayal of her own sufferings involves disturbing elements of triumphalism; no one, it seems, endured as much as she. As P. D. James observed, 'Vera Brittain was intelligent, courageous, determined, high-minded, and idealistic; one only wishes one could like her more'. Despite these ambiguities, however, *Testament of Youth* provided a powerful feminist perspective on a war that, in fact, most suffragettes supported.[23]

Other dramas developed similar themes. *Return of the Soldier* opens with a nightmarish sequence on a battlefield, where a woman in shadows leans over an immobile body, as soldiers pass without noticing. In this dream landscape, children in white suddenly jump into view, and play among the shell craters. At the very end of the film, the central character, now cured of the amnesia that blissfully insulated him from the unhappiness of his adult life, strolls at a distance towards the camera while on the soundtrack a whistle, followed by the sharp report of a rifle, prefigure his doom. In this story about past and present, innocence and experience, the war becomes a metaphor of unpalatable truth best left ignored.[24]

Upstairs Downstairs devoted an entire season of episodes to the First World War. In August, 1914, Richard Bellamy refuses to drink a toast to war: 'From battle and murder and from sudden death – Good Lord, deliver us.' After a train of enthusiastic departing troops leaves a railway station, another returns full of casualties, including a young soldier who dies shortly after Georgina tends to him. Edward, the footman, returns from the war shell-shocked and describes to Richard the grisly death of his closest friend. Rose's fiancé, Gregory, dies. Hazel has a brief affair with an airman, later killed in battle. In France, Georgina and James discuss the war in a flower garden, now converted to a cemetery. On leave, James tells his family at dinner that 'there can't be any dispute, any argument, that's worth so many lives'. The dead, he fears, 'died for nothing'.[25] These and other events from the Edwardian dramas of the 1970s and 1980s help make the First World War a metaphor for pacifism. The anti-war sentiments of the 1960s helped resurrect the generation of 1914.

The First World War also served another function. It became a watershed that separated the Edwardians from later modernity. After the horrors of the Great War, the period before 1914 became a privileged sanctuary, an era of lost greatness, forever separated from the remainder of the century. Both *The Forsyte Saga* and *Upstairs Downstairs* pursued the Edwardians into the 1920s. *The Forsyte Sage* offered a far more sympathetic portrayal of its ruthless central character in episodes dealing with post-war England. Faithful to Galsworthy's own change of heart, Soames became a representative of the old values in a shabby world of national decline. What seemed permanent and inexcusable about Edwardian Britain proved to be ephemeral and more forgivable after the war.[26] In *Upstairs Downstairs* Hudson, Mrs Bridges and Rose embody values of loyalty and service jeopardized by a more democratic post-war world. Servants leave without notice, elegant dinner parties give way to raucous gatherings of flappers, the new master James squanders his fortune on the American stock market, and commits suicide. The house is sold. A world has been lost.[27]

With their overwhelming emphasis on the social preoccupations of a tiny élite, these productions might easily be seen as paternalistic and traditionally conservative. Yet, as we have seen, they also involved elements of egalitarianism, feminism and pacifism that necessarily qualifies this view. These historical dramas may have been conservative, but not in the usual sense. They conserved and made more legitimate selected elements of the social agenda of the 1960s. By making social outsiders often their more sympathetic characters and, conversely, by satirizing the pretensions of wealth, they demonstrated the limitations of traditional social hierarchy, as well as revealing its glamour. By dramatizing the struggles of Edwardian women for greater autonomy and social respect, they provided a valuable pedigree for contemporary feminism. By vivifying the suffering and terrible costs of modern war, they affirmed the values of peace. These dramas acted as ceremonies of accommodation between a tumultuous decade and its more circumspect successors.

Historical films and television productions involved a third, more elusive form of 'conservatism'. These dramas recuperated the sensual immediacies and temporal uncertainties of a past too easily smothered by written history. Film transforms history into the present tense; history 'is' rather than 'was'. This re-experiencing, of course, never reproduces the event itself; it simulates rather than replicates. Still, costume dramas offer sights and sounds of remarkable verisimilitude. Located in one point of space/time, the attentive viewer becomes absorbed into another moment, a separate place, right now. This technological illusion, so assimilated by this century that its wizardry no longer astonishes, retains analogues of course from media of earlier periods. Literacy and print affected temporal consciousness in ways no less transcendent of conventional boundaries. Yet, arguably, electronic technology surpasses the imagination's ability to replicate in intricate detail the immediacy and uncertainties of the personal encounter.

The immediacy of film and television also helps recapture and conserve a past where the future remained unrealized, a condition of possibility. Historical events once again regain their spontaneity. As in any unfinished dramatic production, the viewer wonders 'what happens next?' One action prefigures another; characters react to one another unpredictably; a crisis begs for resolution. The viewer seeks closure to the unfolding narrative.

This recuperation of a future in the past often re-creates in detail the political and ethical predicaments of historical figures. The viewer becomes a privileged observer to the unanticipated complexities of leadership. To cite but one specific example: dressed in prison garb, Gandhi is brought before General Smuts. Smuts offers him sherry or perhaps some tea; Gandhi declines, remarking with quiet irony that he has 'dined in the prison'. Smuts enters into negotiation. He will recommend to the House that the government will 'repeal the Act that you have taken such "exception" to'. But, Smuts adds, such a recommendation might also involve severe, even absolute, restrictions on all future Indian immigration. In close-up, Gandhi pauses, looks down at the floor. 'Immigration was not an issue on which we fought', he replies. 'It would be wrong of us to make it one now that we ... ' Another pause, 'we are in a position of advantage.'[28] In all its fictionalized specificity – the elegantly furnished office of a high official, the authentically rendered uniforms, the ambient sounds of horses' hooves and military drill outside the opened windows – the scene recaptures and brings alive Gandhi's suppleness and flexibility. Smuts sets a trap; Gandhi deftly avoids it, while quietly not humiliating his defeated opposition. In this scene and others, the film unfolds sequentially the political accommodations of Gandhi's moral strategies.

This scene from *Gandhi* can be repeated; every detail will remain the same now as in 1982, when the film first appeared, and will remain the same as long as the film can be preserved. Nevertheless, the film as a work of art shares with 'history' as events at least one crucial feature. For everyone who sees the film, the initial or 'naïve' viewing eventually becomes a lost experience, strange and different. Even if new and different 'naïve' viewers might be recruited, as videotape now so easily allows, they see the film differently. As historicists long ago recognized, the precise same text attains constantly revised meanings with the passage of time. The representation of British history on film and television in the later half of the twentieth century remains provisional.

Notes

1. See, among others, T. Brennan, 'Masterpiece Theatre and the Uses of Tradition', in D. Lazere (ed.), *American Media and Mass Culture: Left Perspectives* (Berkeley, CA, 1987), pp. 373–83; A. Higson, 'Re-presenting the National Past: Nostalgia and Pastiche in the Heritage Film', in L. Friedman (ed.), *Fires Were Started: British Cinema and Thatcherism* (Minneapolis, MN, 1993), pp. 109–29. Raphael Samuel challenged this patronizing view of the heritage movement, though his own analysis of historical dramas tended to rehearse the same criticisms as those he condemned. See R. Samuel, *Theatres of Memory. Volume I: Past and Present in Contemporary Culture* (London, 1994).
2. R. Kosellnick, *Futures Past: On the Semantics of Historic Time*, K. Tribe, trans. (Cambridge, 1985), pp. 267–8.
3. The phrase 'mythic individualism' comes from R. Bellah, R. Madsen, W. Sullivan, A. Swidr and S. Tipton, *Habits of the Heart: Individualism and Commitment in American Life* (New York, 1985), p. 146.
4. See M. Anderegg, *David Lean* (Boston, MA, 1984), pp. 91–102; see also G. Pratley, *The Cinema of David Lean* (New York, 1974), pp. 129–38.
5. Anderegg, *Lean*, pp. 114–16. On Lean, see K. Brownlow, *David Lean* (London, 1996).
6. R. Bolt, 'Preface', in *A Man for all Seasons: A Play by Robert Bolt* (New York, 1962), p. xiii.
7. Ibid., p. 92. The play is different from the film in a number of ways, though these words are the same for both.
8. Carnegie Commission, *A Public Trust: The Report of the Carnegie Commission on the Future of Public Broadcasting* (New York, 1979), pp. 159, 320–21; W. Porter, *Assault on the Media: The Nixon Years* (Ann Arbor, MI, 1976), pp. 143–55; R. Avery and R. Pepper, 'An Institutional History of Public Broadcasting', *Journal of Communication*, 30, 3 (1980), 131–3; R. Blakely, *To Serve the Public Interest: Educational Broadcasting in the United States* (Syracuse, NY, 1979), pp. 191–228. Some of what follows can also be found in D. L. LeMahieu, 'Imagined Contemporaries: Cinematic and Televised Dramas about the Edwardians in Great Britain and the United States, 1967–1985', *Historical Journal of Film, Radio and Television*, 10, 3 (1990), 243–56.
9. P. Mareth, 'Public Visions: Private Voices', *Sight and Sound*, 46, 1 (1976–77), 16; L. Rosenbaum, 'Money and Culture', *Horizon*, 21, 5 (1978), 24–9; P. Kerr, 'Classic Serials – to be Continued', *Screen* 23, 1 (1982), 18–19; 'Mobil Gushes Up Record $10 Mil for TV Production Next Season' *Variety*, 8 June 1983, pp. 31, 54.
10. For one American response to *Elizabeth R*, see M. Hakell, 'That Woman in Every Woman', *Vogue*, 159, 4 (1972), 78.
11. G. Eley, 'Distant Voices, Still Lives: The Family is a Dangerous Place: Memory, Gender, and the Image of the Working Class', in R. Rosenstone (ed.), *Revisioning History: Film and the Construction of a New Past* (Princeton, NJ, 1995), pp. 22–3.
12. For an early version of the script, see H. Pinter, *Five Screenplays* (New York, 1973), pp. 285–367. For some good analysis of the film, see D. Grossvogel, 'Losey and Hartley', *Diacritics*, 4, 3 (1974), 51–6; F. Hirsch, *Joseph Losey* (Boston, MA, 1980), pp. 129–39; M. Ciment, *Conversations*

with Losey (London, 1985), pp. 303–16; N. Sinyard, *Filming Literature: The Art of Screen Adaptation* (New York, 1986), pp. 71–81.

13. For an interesting analysis of the film, see V. Young, 'The Fine Art of Film Adaptation', *Hudson Review*, 38, 4 (1986), 645–7.

14. *The Forsyte Saga*, BBC, 26 parts, produced by D. Wilson; in USA, PBS, 5 October 1969 to 29 March 1970. On the adaptation of the saga for television, see especially D. Wilson, '"The Forsyte Saga" on Television', *The Listener*, 30 November 1967, p. 697; D. Wilson, 'The Television Saga', *EBU Review*, 129, (1971), 31–5.

15. The script follows the novel closely. For the quoted material, see E. M. Forster, *A Room With a View* (rpt New York, n.d.), pp. 132, 27.

16. There is an extensive interpretative literature on Galsworthy. I found especially useful: D. H. Lawrence, 'John Galsworthy', in Edgell Rickword (ed.), *Scrutinies by Various Writers* (London, 1928), pp. 52–72; V. S. Pritchett, *Later Appreciations* (New York, 1964), pp. 282–8; J. Gindin, *John Galsworthy's Life and Art* (Basingstoke, 1987).

17. V. Lambert in *Sunday Times*, 31 March 1974, p. 35. See also G. Brown in *Washington Post*, 5 October 1975, p. 5 of TV Channels section. *Shoulder To Shoulder* was produced by the BBC and shown in the United States on 'Masterpiece Theatre', PBS, 5 October to 9 November 1975. It was rebroadcast in the United States in 1988.

18. S. Brownmiller, 'TV Series Exalts British Feminists', *New York Times*, 19 October 1975, II, p. 27. The two episodes of special importance are 'Lady Constance Lytton' by D. Livingstone, and 'Outrage!' by H. Whitemore. On the suffragettes in film, see M. Norden, 'Women's Suffrage Films as a Genre', *Journal of Popular Film and Television*, 13, 4 (1986), 171–7.

19. *A Room With a View* (film); (book) pp. 194, 240. On feminism and *Room*, see A. Kopkind, 'A Room with a View', *The Nation*, 16/23 August 1986, pp. 122–3. See also L. Trilling, *E. M. Forster* (Norfolk, CT, 1943), pp. 97–112; B. Finkelstein, *Forster's Women: Eternal Differences* (New York, 1975), pp. 65–88; C. Summers, *E. M. Forster* (New York, 1983) pp. 77–104.

20. On the changed attitude of Galsworthy towards Soames, see M. Seymour-Smith, 'The Galsworthy Saga', *Spectator*, 18 August 1967, pp. 188–9; I. Hamilton, 'The Stark Man Behind the Forsytes', *Illustrated London News*, 24 January 1967, pp. 26–7.

21. *Upstairs, Downstairs*: 'A Pair of Exiles' by A. Shaughnessy; 'Peace Out of Pain' by A. Shaughnessy.

22. Quotations from V. Brittain, *Testament of Youth* (New York, 1980), pp. 464, 376. *Testament of Youth*, BBC and London Film Productions, produced by J. Powell; in USA, 'Masterpiece Theatre', PBS, 30 November to 28 December 1980.

23. A. Bishop, '"With Suffering and through Time": Olive Schreiner, Vera Brittain and the Great War', in M. Smith and D. MacLennan (eds), *Olive Schreiner and After: Essays on Southern African Literature in Honour of Guy Butler*, (Cape Town, 1983), p. 84; P. D. James, 'The Women Who Went to the War', *Times Literary Supplement*, 5 May 1978, p. 492; Brittain, *Testament*, p. 290.

24. For a good analysis of the original story by Rebecca West, see the 'Introduction' by V. Glendinning to R. West, *Return of the Soldier* (New York, 1980), pp. 1–8.

25. *Upstairs, Downstairs*: 'The Sudden Storm' by J. Hawkesworth; 'Women Shall Not Weep' by A. Shaughnessy; 'If You Were the Only Girl in the World' by J. Hawkesworth; 'The Glorious Dead' by E. J. Howard; 'Another Year' by A. Shaughnessy.

26. J. Galsworthy, *Swan Song* (New York, 1928), pp. 30–31, 45, 86, 148, 199, 225, 352–3. For how the public reacted to this change, see V. Markovic, *The Reputation of Galsworthy in England, 1897–1950* (Belgrade, 1969), pp. 122–4.

27. *Upstairs, Downstairs*: 'Laugh a Little Louder, Please' by R. A. Sisson; 'All the King's Horses' by J. Paul; 'Whither Shall I Wonder?' by J. Hawkesworth.

28. J. Briley, *Gandhi: The Screenplay* (New York, 1982), pp. 54–5. The screenplay differs in many ways with the actual film.

CHAPTER FIFTEEN

Discord or Accommodation?
Britain and the United States in
World Affairs, 1945–92

Peter L. Hahn

Two issues pervade the vast literature on Anglo-American diplomatic relations during the Cold War. First, scholars who examine the fundamental nature of the Anglo-American relationship debate whether it was 'special' and what factors or persons made it so. Second, scholars have implicitly studied the connection between Britain's decline from great power status after the Second World War and the United States's concurrent rise to superpower status. Whether these two parallel developments were related causally or merely coincidental – and whether America's rise was resisted or resented by the British – are among the central queries posed by historians of Anglo-American relations.[1] This chapter conducts an overview of Anglo-American official relations during the Cold War first by surveying the major schools of interpretation of the relationship as it evolved and as it was shaped by diplomatic issues around the globe and, second, by surveying major international developments that influenced the relationship.

The genesis of the idea that a special relationship linked the United States and Great Britain is usually attributed to Winston Churchill. The wartime Prime Minister and post-war eminent statesman, a man of mixed British-American parentage, vigorously promoted a close partnership as a means of advancing British security interests, namely by convincing a reluctant United States to become involved in war and cold war on Britain's side. Churchill coined the phrase 'special relationship' and declared its actual existence as a way of achieving his objective. In his own historical writing, he painted a picture of Anglo-American common purpose and close collaboration to fulfil his quest for the same.[2]

Taking their cue from Churchill, many historians assert that United States–British relations became 'special' after 1940. Such a special relationship is attributed to common security perils in Germany and the

Soviet Union, cultural and linguistic affinity, shared democratic tendencies, business connections, and personal friendships between leaders
and prominent citizens. 'While the origins and durability of the relationship are to be found in common fears and interests', C. J. Bartlett
concludes, 'once in being the alliance could often be distinguished by
intimacy, vitality and comprehensiveness well beyond the norm.' Because 'cultural values have pulled in the same direction as national
interest', David Dimbleby and David Reynolds observe, the United
States and Britain became linked through an enduring 'double bond'. In
stressing the durability of the special relationship, Alan P. Dobson
observes that even in the 1990s 'the quality of the relationship does not
have to be devalued just because it operates at a less exalted level in
world affairs'.[3]

Not surprisingly, not all scholars agree with the special relationship
thesis. Revisionist scholars stress that beneath the veneer of collaboration against the axis powers and Soviet Russia lay deep rivalries and
disagreements over tactical military planning, British imperialism, commercial concessions and policy toward Europe, Asia, Latin America and
the Middle East. Many revisionists focus their attention on the Second
World War era and observe numerous serious conflicts within the Western alliance over major wartime and post-war issues. Other revisionists
find evidence of deep discord between American and British approaches
to the vital issues of the early Cold War.[4]

Revisionism permeates numerous case studies of Anglo-American
policy at specific points of crisis or in certain regions of the world.
Richard Neustadt documents the mutual misperceptions that bred Anglo-
American tension during the Suez Crisis of 1956 and the Skybolt
controversy of 1962. Several studies demonstrate that the two powers
repeatedly clashed over US containment policy toward Communist China
from the 1940s to the 1970s and over US decisions during the Korean
War. Anita Inder Singh finds that Britain failed in an effort to modify
US policy toward India and Pakistan in the early post-war period, and
Nigel John Ashton detects deep strategic dissonance in British and US
policy towards the Middle East in the late 1950s. William D. Rogers
stresses that the United States and Britain found no common ground for
diplomatic action in Latin America in the 1980s.[5]

Between the orthodox and revisionist divide, several historians stake
out a moderate or post-revisionist view that despite American and
British disagreements on certain major issues, the two powers shared a
remarkably close, unusually friendly and mutually beneficial relationship after 1940. Although the relationship was not free of differences
on specific foreign policy issues, such tensions never eroded the fundamental agreement about the need to function as close partners on behalf

of common security imperatives. Several scholars document that after early sparring over the issue of control of nuclear technology, the two allies, prodded by the Soviet launching of the *Sputnik* satellite, formulated a close nuclear partnership in the late 1950s. Although Britain diminished in importance relative to other allies in military and political terms, Samuel F. Wells notes, Anglo-American collaboration in intelligence and nuclear matters remained close throughout the Cold War era. David Dimbleby and David Reynolds caution that the Anglo-American relationship declined slightly during the late twentieth century as US and British security interests diverged, but they conclude that a special relationship continued, undergirded by shared national security interests, military and intelligence collaboration, common culture and history, travel and tourism, and personal friendships.[6]

An assessment of the Anglo-American relationship during the Cold War sheds light on the scholarly debate on the special relationship thesis. The post-war Anglo-American relationship developed through four stages. From 1945 to 1956, the two powers established a close working partnership in the Cold War against the Soviet Union, but lacked complete uniformity of policies toward every area of the world. Conflict in one region, the Middle East, generated serious friction in the relationship in 1956. From 1957 to 1963, American and British leaders repaired the strain in the relationship and renewed their close co-operation on Cold War issues. By contrast, the Anglo-American relationship experienced a serious breach from 1963 through the 1970s. Divergence of fundamental security interests and disagreement on issues ranging from Vietnam to European integration weakened the sense of partnership that had dominated previous decades. The last decade of the Cold War, on the other hand, witnessed the re-emergence of a special relationship based on common security objectives.

The special relationship forged against the axis peril in the Second World War survived into the post-war period. British and American officials viewed the Soviet Union as a common peril that threatened their joint strategic, political and economic interests in Europe and other regions. As Cold War tensions escalated after 1947, the two powers renewed a close working partnership in Europe. To restore economic activity in Western Europe, they merged their occupation zones in Germany into the so-called 'Bizonia'. In response to Britain's suggestion that it assume the responsibility for safeguarding the pro-Western governments of the Eastern Mediterranean, the United States promulgated the Truman Doctrine, providing $400 million in aid to shore up the governments of Greece and Turkey. British officials eagerly co-operated with the Marshall Plan, a massive US aid programme to resuscitate the capitalist economies of Western Europe in order to re-integrate them into the international marketplace and to deter them from adopting socialist models for post-war development. During the Soviet blockade of Berlin, British and American officials worked closely to formulate a united response (the airlift) and the British welcomed American bombers to their bases. In 1949, Britain and the United States led the effort to establish the NATO alliance, which linked them and other powers into a binding mutual defence treaty. Through joint effort, they formulated a plan to rearm Germany and reintegrate it into NATO on terms acceptable to France. On a fundamental level, the two powers built a special relationship on the basis of their common anti-Soviet containment policy.[7]

This bond was invigorated in the early 1950s by close personal ties between leaders in the two states. Churchill, the architect of the special relationship of the Second World War, returned as Prime Minister in 1951. 'My hope for the future is founded on the increasing unity of the English-speaking world', he told Eisenhower in 1953. 'If that holds all holds. If that fails no one can be sure of what will happen.' Meeting Churchill at Bermuda in late 1953, Eisenhower wrote, 'was for me a sort of homecoming, a renewal of an old and close relationship'.[8]

To be sure, there were points of contention between the United States and Britain during the first decade of the Cold War, but in effect much of the discord resulted from disagreement over how to implement their agreed strategy of containment. In 1945–46, there were certain wrinkles in the transition from wartime to post-war partnership. For example, the termination of Lend-Lease aid, which required Britain to seek a major loan from the American government, generated friction even as the two powers co-operated in fiscal diplomacy designed to advance their mutual interests. British officials complained when the Truman administration, in contradiction of a secret wartime Churchill–Roosevelt agreement, suspended the sharing of atomic secrets with the British, in line with the McMahon Act of 1946. In the early 1950s, US officials, eager to promote European integration, encouraged Britain to join the Common Market, but British officials, anxious to avoid the image that they were a mere regional power, resisted. Such surface quarrels did not undermine the special relationship.[9]

Despite shared views with regard to European matters, Britain and the United States disagreed more about Asia. In general, the British viewed Asian communism as less threatening than did the Americans. To US regret, the government in London recognized the People's Republic of China (PRC) in January 1950. While British officials generally endorsed the US military effort in Korea and placed British forces at the

United Nations' (UN) disposal, they privately concluded that Truman exaggerated the stakes in Korea, and when Truman hinted that he might use atomic weapons to defeat the Chinese army, Attlee raced to Washington to dissuade him from widening the war. In 1951, British officials diluted the terms of US-proposed United Nations resolutions aimed at the PRC. In 1954, Britain directed the Geneva summit meeting on Indo-China to a plan for a settlement in Vietnam whose terms US officials profoundly disliked, and in following years it expressed concern with the Eisenhower administration's defiance of those terms. A war in Indo-China would be 'a bigger affair than Korea', Eden told Dulles, 'which could get us nowhere'. And while both states were charter members of the Southeast Asia Treaty Organization (SEATO), they had divergent views about its purpose, viability and membership. On the other hand, despite Anglo-American differences on major issues in Asia, the British persuaded the Truman administration to provide funds to stabilize non-Communist regimes in several Southeast Asian states.[10]

In the Middle East, a pattern developed during the first decade of the Cold War of Anglo-American co-operation on fundamental security issues mixed with competition over certain matters. As the Cold War escalated in the late 1940s, American and British officials affirmed that they shared common strategic aims in the region and that they should collaborate to preserve those interests. British and American military strategists who planned hypothetically for war against the Soviet Union considered it imperative to maintain British military-base facilities in Egypt. American and British contingency war plans posited that a massive Western strategic air offensive from Egyptian airfields against vital targets in the Soviet Union would be essential to victory. At the Pentagon talks of October–November 1947, US and British strategists affirmed that the United States would endorse Britain's maintenance of a military position in the Middle East as a means of resisting Soviet expansionism.[11]

On the basis of such strategic accord, the two powers collaborated in opposing perceived Soviet expansionism along the so-called 'northern tier' of the region. In close accord with British officials, US officials took initiatives to bolster Iran, Turkey and Greece against Soviet expansion. The United States in effect accepted traditional British responsibility for containing Russian power along its south-western frontier, a duty the British could no longer fulfil. Through the early 1950s, US officials recognized Iraq as a British responsibility and did nothing to undermine British military, political and economic dominance designed to keep that state free of Soviet control.[12] To shore up Western security interests behind the northern tier states, the United States and Britain also formed a partnership with regard to Egypt during the early Cold War.

Commercial rivalry briefly revived in the late years of the world war, but in the late 1940s the United States consistently supported Britain's effort to maintain its base in Egypt against local resistance.[13]

In the 1950s, US and British officials continued to co-ordinate their strategic policies in the Middle East. With France, they jointly formulated the Tripartite Declaration of 1950 to promote intra-regional peace and stability and prevent an arms race among local powers. The United States and Britain also promoted the Middle East Command, alternatively known as the Middle East Defense Organization, a proposed regional defence pact based in Egypt. When the government in Cairo refused to co-operate, the two Western powers jointly promoted a security arrangement, eventually known as the Baghdad Pact, that linked four regional powers and Britain, and indirectly the United States, for most of the decade.[14]

American and British officials also co-operated in identifying common policy objectives in the Middle East and in formulating joint initiatives to reach those objectives. For example, officials from Whitehall and Foggy Bottom teamed up to draft the Alpha Plan, a comprehensive blueprint for settlement of the Arab–Israeli conflict, and to sell that plan to Egypt and Israel in 1954–55. Tension arose over US pressure on the British to evacuate their military base in Egypt, but American officials relented when Britain resisted, and the two Western powers were in close agreement when Britain signed a base pact with Egypt in 1954. London and Washington carefully co-ordinated their negotiations with Nasser in 1955 over joint financial aid to Egypt's Aswan dam project, and their so-called Omega initiative of early 1956, designed to reduce Nasser's prestige and power in part by gradually retracting their offers of aid for the Aswan scheme. The Alpha Plan, the Aswan dam aid offer, and the Omega initiative all bore the imprint of Anglo-American co-operation.[15]

Although they quarrelled over the details, officials generally worked closely to address the problem of revolutionary turmoil in Iran in the early 1950s. Mohammed Mossadegh, who displaced the pro-Western Shah Mohammed Reza Pahlavi, steered his country towards neutralism, expropriated British oil-producing facilities and imperiled common Anglo-American security interests. Britain initially proposed military action to unseat Mossadegh, but the Truman administration discouraged such a step, leading to renewed tension. Soon after taking office in 1953, however, Eisenhower authorized US officials to conduct covert operations, in close conjunction with the British, to remove Mossadegh from office and restore the Shah to power. Tension that developed over the spoils – as Eisenhower compelled Britain to surrender its monopoly over Persian oil – did not detract from the unified fundamental purpose in the joint Anglo-American approach to Mossadegh.[16]

The fundamental accord on Middle East security issues was occasionally broken by differences over certain regional issues. Significant disagreement centred on Palestine, where Bevin wished to establish a binational state and opposed a massive influx of Jewish immigrants from Europe. For a variety of political, cultural and moral reasons, Truman endorsed large-scale Jewish immigration and supported the partition of Palestine into two states. Flashpoints of conflict flared when Truman publicly demanded that Britain allow large-scale immigration in August 1945, when he implicitly endorsed Jewish statehood in October 1946, when he endorsed partition in November 1947, when he promptly recognized the Jewish state in May 1948 and when he resisted the Bernadotte Plan's provisions for redrawing the borders of Israel over Israeli objections in late 1948–early 1949. Registering sharp disapproval of Truman's actions, Bevin publicly suggested in August 1945 that the President wanted Jews to migrate to Palestine because he did not want them in America; and in protest to Truman's October 1946 call for statehood Attlee sent Truman a handwritten letter that, in the words of William Roger Louis, 'still radiates white-hot anger'. In British eyes, Israeli military superiority over Britain's Arab protegés was made possible by American political sustenance. In February 1949, Bevin denounced US policy as 'let there be an Israel and to hell with the consequences'.[17]

The allies found themselves rivals for control of Middle East oil. During and after the Second World War, US and British oil firms competed for concessions in the Middle East. Various disputes pitted American firms against the British government, which frequently owned shares of British oil companies. Tension over oil questions briefly jeopardized the Anglo-American loan agreement of 1946, and in 1949 the State Department threatened to withhold aid allocated under the Marshall Plan unless Britain relented on the so-called sterling–dollar controversy involving American oil firms. As American officials consolidated their dominant position in Saudi Arabia after 1943, they jealously guarded their oil interests against perceived British competition. Between 1953 and 1956, a simmering dispute over Buraimi, an unpopulated oasis claimed by both British-backed Oman and US-backed Saudi Arabia, occasionally flared into crisis and even threatened a military conflict between British troops and US civilian employees of the Arabian-American Oil Company.[18]

Undeniably, the Anglo-American relationship in the Middle East hit its lowest point ever during the Suez imbroglio of 1956. American and British officials profoundly disagreed about the severity of Gamal Abdel Nasser's nationalization of the Suez Canal Company in July 1956. Eisenhower's refusal to endorse military operations against Egypt impelled Eden to hatch a complicated conspiracy, in which Britain, France and Israel conducted joint operations against Egypt while keeping secret their collusion. Feeling betrayed and calculating that the tripartite aggression would undermine Western security interests throughout the Third World, Eisenhower promptly used political and economic leverage to force the attackers to desist and to evacuate occupied territory. Eisenhower's actions deeply humiliated the British and French, briefly raising the spectre of a complete collapse in the special relationship.

Despite the anger and despair that characterized the Anglo-American disagreement at Suez – and it was severe – it was short-lived. Eisenhower's diplomacy proved to be the lone exception to the normal American practice of endorsing British policy in Egypt. There was no profound divergence of aims with regard to Egypt – both powers desired to see Nasser's power curtailed – but only a difference over tactics. Within a month of the showdown at Suez, British and American officials overcame the strain produced during the crisis and reaffirmed their partnership. Eisenhower, convinced that Britain had made 'a terrible mistake', considered the situation 'something of a sad blow, because, quite naturally, Britain has not only been, but must be, our best friend in the world'.[19]

Indeed, the Anglo-American relationship in global matters healed quickly and remained very close through the 1960s. 'The most urgent, and … the most delicate, task which confronted me upon becoming Prime Minister', Harold Macmillan later wrote, 'was to repair and eventually to restore our old relationships with Washington.' Eisenhower and Macmillan met at Bermuda in March 1957 in large part to repair the damage that Suez had inflicted to the relationship. The two leaders reaffirmed their personal friendship that dated to the years of the Second World War, and the mood during the meeting indicated that the tension of late 1956 had diminished substantially. Macmillan, who, like Churchill, had one American parent, made clear that he valued the special relationship, and Eisenhower, who had earned honorary British citizenship for his military command over combined Anglo-American armies in the war, reciprocated. 'Macmillan is, of course', Eisenhower wrote privately after the meeting, 'one of my intimate wartime friends so it is very easy to talk to him on a very frank, even blunt, basis'.[20]

At Bermuda, Eisenhower and Macmillan reached an agreement on nuclear weapons that consolidated their strategic partnership. The two leaders agreed jointly to deploy Thor missiles in Britain with a 'dual-key' provision, meaning that both powers would need to agree to their launching. Several months later, after the launch of the *Sputnik* spacecraft by the Soviet Union generated fears of a chink in the Western defence armour, the two powers negotiated a comprehensive atomic weapons agreement that remains in effect four decades later. The pact of 1957 restored the co-operation of the world war era and ended the restrictions mandated by the MacMahon Act by providing for the sharing of technology, nuclear fuels, and bombs and bomb components between the two sides.[21]

The nuclear partnership deepened and strengthened in the 1960s despite some tension over the Skybolt affair. In 1960, in the spirit of their partnership, Eisenhower and Macmillan agreed that in exchange for base rights for its nuclear submarines at Holy Loch, Scotland, the United States would provide Britain with Skybolt missiles, at the time still under development. Two years later, however, after Skybolt failed tests, Kennedy decided to scrap the weapon. Advisers who wished to elevate the stature of Germany within the Western alliance convinced him to deny Britain any replacement. Macmillan, under enormous political pressure in London, appealed with some desperation to Kennedy to make good the 1960 deal. In a meeting at Nassau in December 1962, Kennedy relented, agreeing to provide Britain submarine-based Polaris missiles on favourable terms.[22]

In a general sense, the nuclear partnership that emerged between the two states in the late 1950s reflected the larger Anglo-American alliance against the Soviet Union. To be sure, their leaders occasionally disagreed over the mechanics of policy toward the Soviets; in 1960, for instance, Macmillan regretted Eisenhower's refusal to apologize for sending U-2 spyplanes into Soviet airspace, a refusal that ended the East–West summit at Paris. On the other hand, Macmillan remained a close friend of Eisenhower and became a warm associate of Kennedy. He provided comforting reassurances after Kennedy's tough showdown with Nikita Khrushchev at the Vienna summit in June 1961, and his ambassador to Washington, David Ormsby-Gore, became a personal friend and member of the President's inner circle. It was no surprise that Macmillan defended American policy in the Cuban missile crisis.[23]

The recovery from the breach of Suez was also underscored by joint Anglo-American diplomatic initiatives in the Middle East, including coordinated military operations in Jordan and Lebanon in 1958. British and American officials reaffirmed their common desire to stabilize the Middle East against Soviet incursions and against revolutionary movements that might threaten their access to the natural and physical resources of the region. In the Eisenhower Doctrine of January 1957, the United States declared its determination to resist communist expansion through economic and military aid and military force if needed. British officials tacitly welcomed the doctrine as an instrument for upholding Western interests in the region in an era of declining British capabilities. British officials slowly realized – as Macmillan would broadcast in his 'winds of change' speech in 1960 – that the British had lost the ability to preserve their traditional imperial presence in much of the developing world.[24]

Combined military operations in the summer of 1958 clearly signalled a meeting of minds and a close working partnership. When rebels in Iraq overthrew its pro-Western government, apparently under Nasser's influence, Western officials feared that the deadly contagion of revolution might infect the friendly regimes in Beirut and Amman. Eisenhower and Macmillan urgently consulted and shaped a common reply. They considered but rejected the possibility of military intervention in Baghdad to reverse the revolution there, but agreed to co-ordinated military intervention in Lebanon and Jordan. US forces occupied Beirut to shore up the government, and British paratroopers – many ferried by US aircraft – occupied Amman. Officials in Washington and London carefully co-ordinated the military operations and consulted on tactical details. Britain and the United States could 'take complete satisfaction in the complete understanding and splendid co-operation which was evident between our two governments in these undertakings', Macmillan wrote to Eisenhower. If the two powers 'continue to act together in spirit and in deed ... I am sure we can deal successfully with any eventuality'.[25]

In marked contrast to Anglo-American closeness in the early Cold War, the relationship noticeably cooled as a result of security differences after 1964. The divergence stemmed from different diplomatic priorities. Lyndon Johnson concentrated on prosecuting the war in Vietnam while British leaders focused on European problems. Against a backdrop of Britain's declining status, American-British differences widened. Dimbleby and Reynolds characterize the relationship from 1963 to 1980 as one adrift, 'all at sea.[26]

Johnson's decision to Americanize the war in Vietnam after 1964 provoked Anglo-American tensions. British officials did not share Johnson's judgement that the survival of South Vietnam was essential to common Western interests, and they disapproved of the extensive US aerial bombardments of North Vietnam. Britain staked out for itself the role of peacemaker by occasionally proposing international ceasefire initiatives. Although British troops had fought in the Korean War, officials in London refused strong requests from Johnson to send military units to Vietnam. 'A platoon of bagpipers would be sufficient', Johnson told Prime Minister Harold Wilson in July 1966, 'it was the British flag that was wanted'.[27]

Meanwhile, Britain's eroding power lessened its ability to serve broad Western interests around the globe. Third largest in the world in 1954, the British army was smaller than West Germany's a decade later, and from 1953 to 1963, the British economy had fallen from third to fifth most productive in the world. In the mid and late 1960s, a series of runs on the British pound awakened British officials to their mounting financial limitations. In autumn 1967, a serious run compelled the Wilson government to devalue sterling and, to stem a budget crisis, to announce the withdrawal by 1971 of British forces from all posts east of Suez except Hong Kong.[28]

Britain's strategic retreat and fiscal woes confirmed in US eyes that Britain had fallen from great power status and thus contributed to a waning of the special relationship in the early 1970s. Prime Minister Edward Heath, Henry A. Kissinger later observed, attached 'new priority ... to European over Atlantic relations'. This conclusion contributed to President Richard Nixon's determination to devise security policy without consulting Britain as previous presidents had done. Nixon formulated *détente* towards China and the Soviet Union without considering the interests of Britain, which was left to shape for itself its most optimal position in Europe. Kissinger antagonized Britain by neglecting it, and Britain, although professing to welcome his declaration of 1973 as the Year of Europe, took little initiative to sell the plan to continental powers. The special relationship, forged as an anti-Communist partnership, waned as the United States learned to get along with Communists and as Britain lost power and stature relative to other European states. As the security partnership waned, traditional Anglo-American trade rivalries revived.[29]

In the late 1970s, Prime Minister Wilson tried with limited success to restore close Anglo-American relations. He reaffirmed the nuclear partnership and resumed the practice of close consultations on defence and security measures. On the other hand, President Jimmy Carter seemed indifferent to any need for close Anglo-American relations.[30]

In the Middle East, US and British policy also lost its sense of common purpose after 1965. As the British abandoned their imperial positions east of Suez, American officials felt a sense of freedom to make policy in the region unilaterally. United States officials neglected to consult London when responding to the Arab–Israeli War of 1967 and the subsequent War of Attrition. American and British interests actually clashed during the Yom Kippur War of 1973, when Nixon and Kissinger decided to airlift military hardware to Israel on an emergency basis to turn the tide of battle against Egypt and Syria. Citing their policy of impartiality in Arab–Israeli matters, but also worried about reprisals by Arab oil-producing states, officials in London denied the United States permission to use British air bases to shuttle the supplies to Israel. When the Soviets threatened to become involved in the Middle East war, Nixon and Kissinger issued a military alert without consulting the British, and Britain refrained from advocating America's position to the other European allies as Kissinger hoped.[31]

The decline in the Anglo-American relationship had important limits. There was no threat of a serious rupture on fundamental viewpoints towards the world, and interaction in the realms of culture, business, tourism and personal friendships promoted a sense of friendliness even when official relations cooled. Moreover, the sense of drift, as Dimbleby and Reynolds called it, proved to be temporary. Perhaps because President Carter and Prime Minister Margaret Thatcher shared a sense of peril regarding the Soviet invasion of Afghanistan, the traditional special closeness revived after 1980.[32]

The coincidence of the Thatcher government and the administration of President Ronald Reagan provided favourable conditions for renewed special relations. These conservative politicians shared a conviction that the Western powers must reinvigorate containment of Soviet communism and that a close Anglo-American partnership was an essential part of such a policy. Perhaps Thatcher also sensed the asymmetry in the Anglo-American relationship – Britain needed the United States more than the United States needed Britain – and shored up Anglo-American relations to advance her national interests. Thatcher and Reagan quickly updated and reaffirmed the nuclear partnership by agreeing in March 1982 to maintain jointly a Trident missile force in Britain. Thatcher offered support to Reagan's Strategic Defense Initiative proposal, which many European states were reluctant to approve. Reagan briefly questioned Thatcher's decision to engage in the Falklands War, and Thatcher tried to dissuade Reagan from occupying Grenada, but in both cases the dissenting leader rallied once troops were committed to battle.[33]

In the era of renewal, American and British officials also revived their earlier practice of co-ordinating policy on the Middle East. In 1986, when Reagan ordered US forces to bomb Libya, in revenge for alleged Libyan terrorism against US targets, Thatcher authorized those forces to use air bases in Britain. This show of support signalled a sharp departure from 1973, when Heath refused to embroil Britain in the US airlift to Israel. British officials also backed Reagan's ongoing initiatives to supply partisans resisting Soviet occupation of Afghanistan and Reagan's policy toward the Iran–Iraq war, even when the US Navy engaged in limited warfare against Iran. Even more important, Britain participated fully in the US-led war to liberate Kuwait from Iraqi control in 1990–91. British aircraft joined American ones in bombarding Iraqi targets and British units attacked occupied Kuwait in conjunction with US forces.[34]

This survey of the relationship between Britain and America during the Cold War suggests that the notion of a special relationship retains some validity. To be sure, the Anglo-American relationship was not uniformly and unfailingly close. There were moments when political and tactical differences generated friction that threatened to weaken or even to dissolve the partnership. The sense of Anglo-American specialness clearly diminished when security interests diverged. Differences in judgement about the danger of Asian communism, for instance, fostered a degree of tension between Washington and London in the Korean War era and even more so during the Vietnam War. The two powers experienced a serious breach over the most appropriate method for dealing with Nasser in Egypt. As Britain's strength declined and its attention centred on Western Europe in the 1960s, US officials decided important security matters with little regard for British interests.

On the other hand, such schisms in the special relationship proved temporary, and points of conflict between Britain and the United States paled in comparison to the underlying unity of purpose and direction shared by the two states. Since 1945, if not 1940, Britain and America nurtured a special relationship because their vital security concerns intersected. When the Soviet Union seemed most threatening to common interests – namely, the first two decades of Cold War and the 1980s – officials in London and Washington forged a close partnership to safeguard security. In implementing containment in Europe, erecting a joint nuclear shield and pursuing common interests in various regions of the Third World, the official relationship was marked by co-ordination, mutual reliance and unified purpose. The specialness survived temporary downturns and remained the defining feature of Anglo-American relations when the Cold War ended.

More difficult to address are the questions of whether the United States' rise to global dominance and the British decline from such stature were related causally or merely coincidental. To be sure, commercial competition, personality clashes, and tactical policy differences occasionally created the appearance that the United States deliberately sought to displace British influence and power, especially during the doldrums phase of the relationship. By contrast, however, evidence suggests that American officials perceived the value of having a strong ally to share responsibilities for defending common Western security interests during the Cold War. Feeling genuinely threatened by Soviet power, US officials naturally sought to preserve British stature and influence, notably in Europe and the Middle East.

The temporary downturn in the relationship might partially explain the interpretive differences among scholars of the Anglo-American relationship. The traditional emphasis on the special relationship that appeared in early scholarship coincided with the Anglo-American strategic consensus and was likely inspired by the desire on both sides of the Atlantic to prevail in the world war and the Cold War. Later revisionism reflected the actual contemporary decline in the feeling of specialness between the two countries. As the Cold War consensus collapsed in the late 1960s, revisionists stressed tension and discord in the relationship. The renewal of the special security partnership in the last decade of the Cold War inspired the post-revisionist view that the relationship had enduring special features after all.

Notes

1. For studies of British decline in the Middle East, see Anne Orde, *The Eclipse of Great Britain: The United States and British Imperial Decline, 1895–1956* (New York, 1996), pp. 129–92; Daniel Silverfarb, *The Twilight of British Ascendancy in the Middle East: A Case Study of Iraq, 1941–1950* (New York, 1994); Brian Lapping, *End of Empire* (New York, 1985); Elizabeth Monroe, *Britain's Moment in the Middle East*, 2nd edn (Baltimore, MD, 1981); Howard M. Sachar, *Europe Leaves the Middle East, 1936–1954* (New York, 1972).

2. Harry C. Allen, *Conflict and Concord: The Anglo-American Relationship Since 1783* (New York, 1959); David Reynolds, 'Roosevelt, Churchill, and the Wartime Anglo-American Alliance, 1939–1945: Towards a New Synthesis', in W. R. Louis and H. Bull (eds), *The 'Special Relationship': Anglo-American Relations since 1945* (Oxford, 1986), pp. 17–41; Fraser J. Harbutt, *The Iron Curtain: Churchill, America, and the Origins of the Cold War* (New York, 1986); Ritchie Ovendale, *The English-Speaking Alliance: Britain, the United States, the Dominions, and the Cold War, 1945–1951* (London, 1985); and Richard A. Best Jr *'Cooperation with Like-Minded Peoples': British Influences on American Security Policy, 1945–1949* (Westport, CT, 1986). Henry Butterfield Ryan examines the Greek and Polish crises to conclude that Britain deliberately forged an Anglo-American Cold War partnership to foster its own interests. Henry Butterfield Ryan, *The Vision of Anglo-America: The U.S.–United Kingdom Alliance and the Emerging Cold War* (Cambridge, 1987).

3. C. J. Bartlett, *'The Special Relationship': A Political History of Anglo-American Relations since 1945* (London, 1992), p. 179; David Dimbleby and David Reynolds, *An Ocean Apart: The Relationship Between Britain and America in the Twentieth Century* (New York, 1989), p. 355; Alan P. Dobson, *Anglo-American Relations in the Twentieth Century* (London, 1995), p. 168. See also Bradley F. Smith, *Ultra-Magic Deals: And the Most Secret Special Relationship, 1940–1946* (Novato, CA, 1993); John Baylis, *Anglo-American Defence Relations, 1919–1980: The Special Relationship* (New York, 1981); D. Cameron Watt, *Succeeding John Bull: America in Britain's Place, 1900–1975* (Cambridge, 1984); Richard H. Ullman, 'America, Britain, and the Soviet Threat in Historical and Present Perspective', in W. R. Louis and H. Bull (eds), *The 'Special Relationship': Anglo-American Relations since 1945* (Oxford, 1986), pp. 103–14; and

Geoffrey Warner, 'The Anglo-American Special Relationship', *Diplomatic History*, 13, 4 (Fall 1989), 479–99.

4. David Reynolds, *The Creation of the Anglo-American Alliance, 1937–1941: A Study in Competitive Cooperation* (Chapel Hill, NC, 1982); Christopher Thorne, *Allies of a Kind: The United States, Britain, and the War Against Japan* (New York, 1981); Wm. Roger Louis, *Imperialism at Bay: The United States and the Decolonization of the British Empire, 1941–1945* (London, 1984); Randall Bennett Woods, *A Changing of the Guard: Anglo-American Relations, 1941–1946* (Chapel Hill, NC, 1990); Herbert G. Nicholas, *Britain and the U.S.A.* (Baltimore, MD, 1963); Terry H. Anderson, *The United States, Great Britain, and the Cold War, 1944–1947* (Columbia, OH, 1981); Robert M. Hathaway, *Ambiguous Partnership: Britain and America, 1944–1947* (New York, 1981); Robin Edmonds, *Setting the Mould: The United States and Britain, 1945–1950* (New York, 1986); and Henry Pelling, *Britain and the Marshall Plan* (New York, 1988).

5. Richard E. Neustadt, *Alliance Politics* (New York, 1970); Rosemary Foot, 'Making Known the Unknown War: Policy Analysis of the Korean Conflict Since the Early 1980s', in M. J. Hogan (ed.), *America in the World: The Historiography of American Foreign Relations Since 1941* (New York, 1995), pp. 283–5; Roderick Macfarquhar, 'The China Problem in Anglo-American Relations', in W. R. Louis and H. Bull (eds), *The 'Special Relationship': Anglo-American Relations since 1945* (Oxford, 1986), pp. 311–19; Anita Inder Singh, *The Limits of British Influence: South Asia and the Anglo-American Relationship, 1947–1956* (New York. 1993); Nigel John Ashton, *Eisenhower, Macmillan, and the Problem of Nasser: Anglo-American Relations and Arab Nationalism, 1955–1959* (New York, 1996); William D. Rogers, 'The "Unspecial Relationship" in Latin America', in W. R. Louis and H. Bull (eds), *The 'Special Relationship': Anglo-American Relations since 1945* (Oxford, 1986), pp. 341–53.

6. Victor Rothwell, *Britain and the Cold War, 1941–1947* (London, 1982); Margaret Gowing, *Independence and Deterrence: Britain and Atomic Energy, 1939–1952*, 2 vols (New York, 1974); Timothy J. Botti, *The Long Wait: The Forging of the Anglo-American Nuclear Alliance, 1945–1958* (Westport, CT, 1987); Ian Clark, *Nuclear Diplomacy and the Special Relationship: Britain's Deterrent and America, 1957–1962* (Oxford, 1992); Jan Melisson, *The Struggle for Nuclear Partnership: Britain, the United States, and the Making of an Ambiguous Alliance, 1952–1959* (Groningen, 1993); Samuel F. Wells, 'The United States, Britain, and the Defence of Europe', in W. R. Louis and H. Bull (eds), *The 'Special Relationship': Anglo-American Relations since 1945* (Oxford, 1986), pp. 129–49; Dimbleby and Reynolds, *An Ocean Apart*.

7. Michael J. Hogan, *The Marshall Plan: America, Britain, and the Reconstruction of Western Europe, 1947–1952* (New York, 1987); Melvyn P. Leffler, *A Preponderance of Power: National Security, the Truman Administration, and the Cold War* (Stanford, CA, 1992); John Baylis, *The Diplomacy of Pragmatism: Britain and the Formation of NATO, 1942–1949* (Kent, OH, 1993); Dimbleby and Reynolds, *An Ocean Apart*, pp. 285–95.

8. Churchill quoted in Dimbledy and Reynolds, *An Ocean Apart*, p. 220;

Dwight D. Eisenhower, *The White House Years: Mandate for Change, 1953-1959* (New York, 1963), p. 249.

9. Dimbleby and Reynolds, *An Ocean Apart*, pp. 175-85, 221-22.
10. Eden quoted in Andrew J. Rotter, *The Path to Vietnam: Origins of the American Commitment to Southeast Asia* (Ithaca, NY, 1987), p. 216. See also Rosemary J. Foot, 'Anglo-American Relations in the Korean Crisis: The British Effort to Avert an Expanded War, December 1950-January 1951', *Diplomatic History*, 10, 1 (Winter 1986), 43-57; William Stueck, *The Korean War: An International History* (Princeton, NJ, 1995); Arthur Combs, 'The Path Not Taken: The British Alternative to U.S. Policy in Vietnam, 1954-1956', *Diplomatic History*, 19, 1 (Winter 1995), 33-57; Laura Belmonte, 'Anglo-American Relations and the Dismissal of MacArthur', *Diplomatic History*, 19, 4 (Fall 1995), 641-67; G. Wyn Rees, *Anglo-American Approaches to Alliance Security, 1955-60* (New York, 1996), pp. 106-34; Andrew J. Rotter, 'The Triangular Route to Vietnam: The United States, Great Britain, and Southeast Asia, 1945-1950', *International History Review*, 6 (August 1984), 404-23.
11. Peter L. Hahn, *The United States, Great Britain, and Egypt, 1945-1956: Strategy and Diplomacy in the Early Cold War* (Chapel Hill, NC, 1991), pp. 23-8, 49-56, 58-62; Michael J. Cohen, *Fighting World War III from the Middle East: Allied Contingency Plans, 1945-1954* (London, 1997).
12. Bruce R. Kuniholm, *The Origins of the Cold War in the Near East: Great Power Conflict and Diplomacy in Iran, Turkey, and Greece* (Princeton, NJ, 1980); and Silverfarb, *Twilight of British Ascendency in the Middle East.*
13. Hahn, *The United States, Great Britain, and Egypt.*
14. Magnus Persson, *Great Britain, the United States, and the Security of the Middle East: The Formation of the Baghdad Pact* (Lund, 1998); Hahn, *The United States, Great Britain, and Egypt*; Wm. Roger Louis, *The British Empire in the Middle East: Arab Nationalism, the United States, and Postwar Imperialism* (London, 1984), pp. 575-747. For works that emphasize that American and British officials, while in agreement on the fundamental need of a regional alliance against the Soviet Union, disagreed over the timing of the establishment of the pact and over certain of its terms, including US membership, see Rees, *Anglo-American Approaches to Alliance Security*, pp. 76-105; Steven Z. Freiberger, *Dawn Over Suez: The Rise of American Power in the Middle East, 1953-1957* (Chicago, 1992), pp. 83-106, and Elie Podeh, *The Quest for Hegemony in the Arab World: The Struggle over the Baghdad Pact* (Leiden, 1995).
15. Hahn, *The United States, Great Britain, and Egypt.*
16. Mary Ann Heiss, *Empire and Nationhood: The United States, Great Britain, and Iranian Oil, 1950-1954* (New York, 1997); James F. Goode, *The United States and Iran, 1946-1951: Diplomacy of Neglect* (New York, 1989); Richard W. Cottam, *Iran and the United States: A Cold War Case Study* (Pittsburgh, PA, 1988), pp. 95-114; Mark Hamilton Lytle, *The Origins of the Iranian-American Alliance, 1941-1953* (New York, 1987), pp. 192-212.
17. Wm. Roger Louis, 'British Imperialism and the End of the Palestine Mandate', in W. R. Louis and R. Stookey (eds), *The End of the Palestine Mandate* (Austin, TX, 1986), pp. 1-31 (quotations pp. 11, 27); Ilan

Pappe, *Britain and the Arab-Israeli Conflict, 1948–1951* (New York, 1988).

18. David S. Painter, *Oil and the American Century: The Political Economy of U.S. Foreign Oil Policy, 1941–1954* (Baltimore, MD, 1986), esp. pp. 59–74, 160–65; Aaron David Miller, *Search for Security: Saudi Arabian Oil and American Foreign Policy, 1939–1949* (Chapel Hill, NC, 1980); and Tore Tingvold Petersen, 'Anglo-American Rivalry in the Middle East: The Struggle for the Buraimi Oasis, 1952–1957', *International History Review*, 14 (February 1992), 71–91.

19. Eisenhower to Swede Hazlett, 2 November 1956, in Robert Griffith (ed.), *Ike's Letters to a Friend, 1941–1958* (Lawrence, KS, 1984), pp. 172–6. See also Hahn, *The United States, Great Britain, and Egypt*.

20. Harold Macmillan, *Riding the Storm, 1956–1959* (London, 1971), pp. 240–68 (quotation p. 240); Eisenhower to Swede Hazlett, 5 April 1957, in R. Griffith (ed.), *Ike's Letters to a Friend, 1941–1958* (Lawrence, KS, 1984), pp. 179–80.

21. Rees, *Anglo-American Approaches to Alliance Security*, pp. 138–46, Macmillan, *Riding the Storm*, pp. 313–41; Dimbleby and Reynolds, *An Ocean Apart*, pp. 238–40.

22. Harold Macmillan, *At the End of the Day, 1961–1963* (London, 1973), pp. 356–62; Dimbleby and Reynolds, *An Ocean Apart*, pp. 242–3, 252–7.

23. Macmillan, *At the End of the Day*, pp. 180–220; Dimbleby and Reynolds, *An Ocean Apart*, pp. 243–52.

24. C. J. Bartlett, *The 'Special Relationship'*, pp. 89–90; and Lapping, *End of Empire*.

25. Macmillan, *Riding the Storm*, pp. 502–37 (quotation p. 534); and Irene Gendzier, *Notes From the Minefield: United States Intervention in Lebanon and the Middle East, 1945–1958* (New York, 1997), pp. 296–363.

26. Dimbleby and Reynolds, *An Ocean Apart*, pp. 262–85, 307–22.

27. Dimbleby and Reynolds, *An Ocean Apart*, pp. 264–70 (quotation on p. 270); Lyndon Baines Johnson, *The Vantage Point: Perspectives on the Presidency, 1963–1969* (New York, 1971), pp. 253–55; R. B. Smith, *An International History of the Vietnam War* (London, 1991), vol. 3, pp. 108–13, 154–5, 365–6.

28. Johnson, *Vantage Point*, pp. 313–17; William Stivers, *America's Confrontation with Revolutionary Change in the Middle East, 1948–83* (New York, 1986), pp. 28–37; Charles H. Rieper, 'The Limits Reached: How International Monetary Policy, Domestic Policy, European Diplomacy, and the Vietnam War Converged in the 1960s', PhD dissertation, (Ohio State University, 1995).

29. Henry A. Kissinger, *Years of Upheaval* (Boston, MA, 1982), pp. 142–3 (quotation p. 163); Dimbleby and Reynolds, *An Ocean Apart*, pp. 275–85.

30. Dimbleby and Reynolds, *An Ocean Apart*, pp. 307–22.

31. Kissinger, *Years of Upheaval*, pp. 516–18, 707–22; Dimbleby and Reynolds, *An Ocean Apart*, pp. 282–4.

32. Minton F. Goldman, 'President Carter, Western Europe, and Afghanistan in 1980: Inter-Allied Differences over Policy toward the Soviet Invasion', in H. D. Rosenbaum and A. Ugrinsky (eds), *Jimmy Carter: Foreign Policy and Post-Presidential Years*, (Westport, CT, 1994), pp. 21–23; Dimbleby and Reynolds, *An Ocean Apart*, pp. 286–306.

33. Dimbleby and Reynolds, *An Ocean Apart*, pp. 330–38; Louise Richardson, *When Allies Differ: Anglo-American Relations during the Suez and Falklands Crises* (New York, 1996), pp. 212–15.
34. Dimbleby and Reynolds, *An Ocean Apart*, pp. 338–50; Dilip Hiro, *The Longest War: The Iran–Iraq Military Conflict* (New York, 1991), pp. 213–40; Michael A. Palmer, *Guardians of the Gulf: A History of America's Expanding Role in the Persian Gulf, 1833–1992* (New York, 1992).

Index

INDEX

Berman, Marshall 120
Best, Richard A. 289
Bevin, Ernest 158, 282
Bhabha, Homi K. 121
Bhagat, G. 67
Bhagwati, J. 160
Biagini, Eugenio F. 115, 122
Bigelow, John 145, 160, 161
Bird, Isabella L. 113, 121
Bishop, A. 274
Bjork, Gordon 66
Blaine, James G. 185
Blake, Robert 138
Blakely, R. 273
Blandy, G. 68
Blatch, Harriet Stanton 198, 205
Boer War 101
  and American finance 245–6
  financing of 244–5
Bolt, C. 208, 209, 211
Bolt, Robert 263, 273
Bolton, William 71
Bonar Law, Andrew 258
Bone, Muirhead 221
Boorstin, Daniel 227, 232–3, 234,
    235, 242
  *The Americans: The Colonial
    Experience* 237, 238
  The Democratic Experience 239
  *The Lost World of Thomas
    Jefferson* 236
  The Mysterious Science of the Law
    236
  The National Experience 239
Bordo, M. 165
Bosch, M. 210
Botti, Timothy J. 290
Bowater, Capt. John 36
Bowen, H. V. 21
Bowker, R. R. 147, 163
Bowring, J. 103
Boyd, Julian P. 66
Boyle, Daniel 188
Brace, C. L. 161
Bradbury, Malcolm 107, 120, 121
Breen, T. H. 34
Breitenbach, E. 209
Brennan, T. 273
Bretton Woods conference (1944)
    249
Brewer, J. 21

Bridge, Alan 265
Bridge, Charles 223
The Bridge on the River Kwai (film)
    262, 263
Bridges, Carl 37
Bright, John 94, 107, 111, 125, 138,
    145
Briley, J. 275
Brinkerhoff, General R. 147, 161
Brissot, Jacques-Pierre 89
Britain
  and American colonies
    foreign policy 9, 10
    imperial considerations 13–14
    trade 39–43
  army 285–6
  differences with America on
    foreign policy 279–80
  diplomatic relations with America
    103
  economy 286
  and the Falklands War 255–6
  and France, foreign policy 10
  and free trade 144–5, 158
  as a Great Power 244, 255
  image in America 212–23
  image in films 214, 261–6
  image in literature 214
  and India 15–16
  and Ireland 14–15
  and New York World's Fair (1939)
    213, 215–18
  post-War role 253–4
  and protectionism 154–5
  and 'special relationship' with
    America 276–9, 288–9
British Council, launch 212
British Guiana, dispute with
    Venezuela 100
British Library of Information, New
    York 212
British West Indies, and wine trade
    47, 48
Brittain, Vera, *Testament of Youth*
    269, 274
Brooke, John 138, 242
Brown, G. 274
Brown, Thomas N., *Irish-American
    Nationalism, 1870–90* 172, 173,
    174–5, 191, 192
Browne, Anthony Montague 141